10-MINUTE TECH

THE BOOK

MORE THAN 600 PRACTICAL AND MONEY-SAVING IDEAS FROM FELLOW RVERS

First Edition

TRAILER LIFE BOOKS

Editorial Director: Bob Livingston
Copy Editor: Jennie Keast
Editorial Assistant: Lynn Norquist
Production Director: Nan Caddel
Production Manager: Ann Forman
Interior Illustrations: Bill Tipton/CompArt Design
Cover Design: Mirante Almazan
Interior Design: Mirante Almazan

This book was set in Aachen BT, Berkeley Oldstyle ITCby BT, Bookman
ITCby BT and Futura BT and printed by Ripon Community Printers.

9 8 7 6 5 4 4 3 2 1

ISBN: 0-934798-59-1

CONTENTS

SAFETY

APPLIANCES

MAINTENANCE

AUTOMOTIVE

IN CAMP

SYSTEMS

STORAGE

TOWING

ACCESSORIES

SANITATION

DOORS, HATCHES, HANDLES

CLEANING, PROTECTING

TOOLS

LIVABILITY

SLAMMER JAMMER

My husband and I camp by the ocean all winter. The strong winds were continually making our RV door slam shut, and we were afraid that the door's glass would break. The factory door catch, consisting of a rod with a ball on the end that snaps into a rubber socket on the side wall, wasn't up to the task. Even when it was new, strong winds snapped it loose and slammed the door.

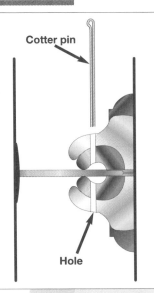

Cotter pin

Hole

Our solution cost only pennies. My husband drilled an ⅛-inch hole through the metal surround holding the rubber socket and also in the middle of the ball shaft. He next slid a cotter pin, anchored to the trailer body by a string, through the hole to lock the door in place. No more slamming door.
- ERIC AND V. MARIA MAYA, HUNTSVILLE, ONTARIO, CANADA

TIPSY TABLE

My trailer had a dinette table that wobbled. The following modification took care of the problem:

Using a screw-type jackstand usually used to stabilize an RV, cut off the top 2 inches. Slide the table post through the center of the jackstand, reinsert the post into the RV-floor receptacle, and drill and bolt the base of the stand to the floor.

If the jackstand opening is too big to hold the table post securely, make four cuts in the top of the stand, as shown in the illustration. Drill completely through the stand and table post twice, making sure one set of holes is separated vertically from the other by about a half inch or so.

Now insert two long bolts through these holes, install nuts and tighten securely—and your wobbly table is fixed for good.
- DOROTHY S. TOWSKY, CORAL SPRINGS, FLORIDA

CLOSEUPS • CLOSEUPS • CLOSEUPS

TINKERING WITH TILE

Unlined trailer shelves are a source of irritation to me. Contact paper doesn't stick well, and thumbtacks are not easily pushed into the bottom of the cabinet. Well, I found a solution that's easy, yet inexpensive.

The self-stick floor tiles sold at do-it-yourself or flooring stores are very easy to use. Economy tiles usually cost less than $1 per square foot and are frequently on sale for less than 50 cents.

These are easy to cut with a metal straight-edge and utility knife. When doing this, however, be sure to use a piece of scrap wood, or other disposable material, under the tile. Otherwise you may find yourself cutting into a table or countertop with equal ease.

Once the tiles are in place, you'll have attractively lined shelves that are washable and easy to keep clean.
- TIN GUTZKE, FRANKLIN, WISCONSIN

CLOSEUPS • CLOSEUPS • CLOSEUPS

THE KEY TO SUCCESS

If your RV is like mine, you have a ring full of keys for various compartments, hitches, bike racks, etc. It used to really frustrate me to have to sort through the entire selection until I found the one I needed.

Of course, trying to accomplish this task at night or in inclement weather was even more of a challenge. Much of the time I have dropped my flashlight while carrying out this ritual in the dark, and on more than one occasion I've been thoroughly soaked while grappling with keys during a rainstorm.

I overcame this problem by purchasing several colored plastic key circles from the locksmith. These fit over the heads of the keys. I then placed a dot of paint next to each lock, correspondent with the respective color-coded key. Now, the correct key can be identified with just a quick glance at the colored dot.
- EARLE G. THOMPSON, ROSEVILLE, MINNESOTA

AUXILIARY POWER FOR TRAVEL TRAILERS

Large motorhomes are designed to carry auxiliary generators as a source of 120-volt AC power. Travel trailers are not so equipped, usually because space and weight considerations preclude the installation of an auxiliary power plant.

I have a trailer but do not frequent full-hookup parks, and I had a definite need for auxiliary power to run things such as a vacuum cleaner, or to charge the batteries. So, I bought a 600-watt Honda portable generator.

I had ample storage space for the generator in one of the compartments in my trailer. However, in order to use it conveniently, I decided to create an access to the outside and have a special door and roll-out shelf fabricated. This addition allows easy access to the generator without restricting use of the remaining compartment area.

While the project of cutting a new opening in the side of the trailer and designing a new door and frame was not simple, patience and care resulted in a satisfactory installation. Total cost of the custom door was only $40.

The generator now sits on a special platform that slides in and out on heavy-duty drawer guides. Depressions in the feet of the generator fit over pegs installed in the slide. During travel, the slide can be locked with a steel pin, which passes through it and into the frame.

Because the Honda is not otherwise fastened to its platform, it can be readily lifted off for fueling and for use away from the trailer.

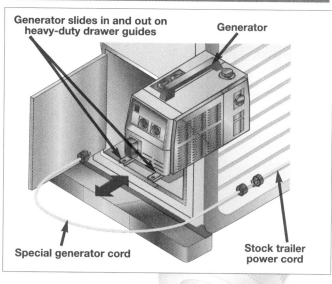

Generator slides in and out on heavy-duty drawer guides

Generator

Special generator cord

Stock trailer power cord

When in operation, the generator is outside its storage area. To protect it from exhaust heat, I installed an insulating baffle on the inside of the door near the muffler outlet.

I connect the unit to the trailer's electrical system through a standard three-wire power cord. It is routed from the generator compartment to the commercial power cord locker on the streetside of the trailer. This connector cord remains in place at all times.

I feel the arrangement is very safe. Whenever the commercial power cord is plugged into the generator line, there isn't any way to accidentally hook it up to an outside power source. Conversely, whenever external shore power is in use, generator output cannot be used.

My auxiliary generator now can be conveniently used to provide 120-volt AC power for light-duty use, provides a charging source for the trailer batteries and can be called into service should the tow-vehicle battery fail.

- WAYNE GUYMON, FULLERTON, CALIFORNIA

(**Editor's Note:** All after-market generator installations require special design care to assure that noxious exhaust fumes do not enter the RV through improperly sealed compartments, and that all combustible materials are properly isolated from oil/gas saturation and hot exhaust gases. Failure to adhere to appropriate construction and electrical codes could result in personal injury.)

ROLLIN' POLES

I have a screen add-a-room with attached privacy panels. Trying to roll them up can be quite a chore, if not impossible, for one person. I solved this problem by purchasing ¾-inch PVC plastic pipe, and cutting it to match the width of the panels. My panels have hook-and-loop tape on the bottom in three places, so I put hook-and-loop tape on the pipe to coincide with the tape on the panels. Now one person can easily roll the privacy panels up. If you don't have room to store pipe that long, you can cut them into shorter pieces and use a slip/slip coupling (without glue) to join them together when needed.

- RICHARD RICE, PORT HURON, MICHIGAN

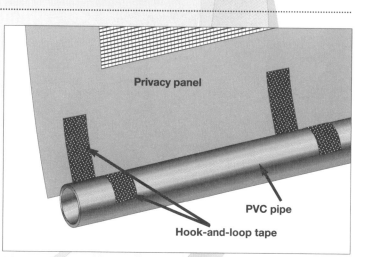

Privacy panel

PVC pipe

Hook-and-loop tape

DIRECT YOUR OWN VIDEO

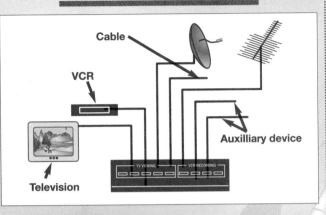

After relocating the television and video cassette recorder (VCR) to the rear of my fifth-wheel, I installed a new 75-ohm male video coax connector to attach the satellite coax cable. I also added an extra connector in case I want to use campground cable, when convenient. To use the original rooftop antenna, I ran the wiring from the manufacturer's location over and around my slide-out, to behind the new cabinets and connector box I bought to ease the complexity of having three possible outside video connections to attach to the back of my television. The connector box is from Radio Shack (5-input video selector, part no. 15-1266, $39.99). Everything connects through it. The "TV Viewing" group (five push-buttons that control incoming signals to the television) has hookups for shore cable, rooftop antenna, VCR input, plus aux 1 and aux 2. I put the satellite on aux 1. The "VCR Recording" group (four push-buttons that control incoming signals to the VCR) allows hookups for antenna, cable, and aux 1 and aux 2. Now I can switch between campground cable, satellite input or antenna-captured broadcasts from my viewing seat without having to manually swap the cables. Technology is tamed.
- *ALBERTA MORGAN, LIVINGSTON, TEXAS*

EPOXY CUPS

We all need to fix things while on the road (and at home), and quite often this includes needing to mix small amounts of epoxy or other two-part glues. To do this, we take home a few of the plastic one-service creamer cups that you get in a restaurant, wash them out, and save them until needed. They are just the right size for most jobs, and there's no clean-up afterward—just throw them away.
- *MIKE STEFFEN, LIVINGSTON, TEXAS*

CONTROLLING THE BED

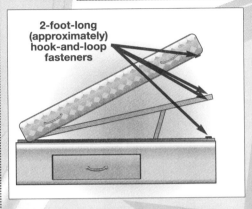

The full-size bed platform in our travel trailer is controlled by gas-pressure lift cylinders, which allow it to be raised for access to the large storage area. When arriving at our destination, we always find that the mattress has been bumped up and is resting on the extended lifts. Since we were concerned that this was hard on the lifts (to make matters worse, the mattress was probably bouncing up and down while traveling), we came up with a method for securing the platform.

We simply attached one side of a 2-foot length (approximately) of hook-and-loop fastener to the edge of the platform box at the foot of the bed. The other side was placed across the bottom surface of the platform itself.

Although we had doubts whether this would hold, we found our little project to work great. Now the bed stays put until we move it physically.
- *JAMES D. JORGENSON, BOX ELDER, SOUTH DAKOTA*

CLOSEUPS • CLOSEUPS • CLOSEUPS

DOUBLE-DUTY BREW FOR TWO

Never underestimate the multiple uses of the common stove-top coffee percolator when camping. Especially when you are cooking for just two people! It can be used for a lot more than just making coffee; it can also be used as a terrific mini double boiler. Just invert the basket over some water on the bottom and start boiling (you can even wrap the food in aluminum foil to keep the pot cleaner). The lid goes back on top, and before long the food is hot, juicy and delicious. It's also great for bringing leftover meals back for one more time, and corn on the cob can be boiled standing upright when the ears are broken in half. The fewer pots and pans you have to take along, the better, and I think the percolator is the perfect all-purpose pot.
- *JANET NEUMANN, ST. LOUIS, MISSOURI*

TAKING TEMPERATURES TIMES TWO

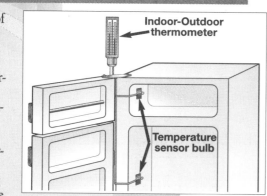

Most of us would like to know the temperature inside our refrigerator and its freezer portion without having to open the doors. Food that's not kept at proper temperature can spoil more rapidly, causing health problems. I have a simple and very inexpensive solution to monitoring temperatures. Buy two indoor-outdoor thermometers from your local Wal-Mart (or similar discount store) for around $7 each.

Carefully remove the staples holding the indoor glass tube in one thermometer housing and the outdoor glass tube in the other. Install the removed outdoor tube in the same housing, securing the other outdoor tube (the one left intact). Equalize the tubes so the temperatures read the same and then carefully bend the staples back into place. Locate the thermometer housing near the hinge side of the refrigerator and place one bulb on the freezer wall and one on the refrigerator wall. Use duct tape to secure the bulbs. Do not attempt to use screws or any other fasteners that put holes in the side walls of your refrigerator/freezer. Route the small capillary tubes through the door gaskets (they will not interfere with normal opening and closing).
- ART LONG, WEBSTER GROVES, MISSOURI

FREE WRAPPING

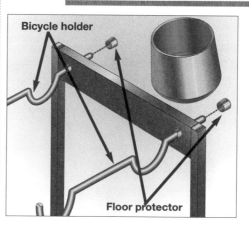

Want to add some protection from flying road debris and vibration chafing to those loose electrical wires that the RV manufacturer simply strung along the trailer frame? A simple, no-cost solution is to gather a bunch of plastic wiring sheath, designed for 120-volt AC wiring, that is discarded at every new-house construction site (after obtaining permission). The pieces measure from 1 to 2 feet and are slit lengthwise. That makes them easy to slip over exposed trailer wires. Since this material retains its original shape, it will remain tightly wrapped around your rig's wiring after installation, giving your rig's wiring system the appearance of a neat, factory-type "wiring loom." A wrap of electrical tape here and there along the now-protected wiring will finish the job.
- ROBERT D. ZOULEK, KINSTON, NORTH CAROLINA

PROTECTIVE PROPOSITION

RV owners frequently mount aftermarket hardware on the backs of their units. These have the potential of causing significant damage to the outer surface of the rig.

Such a condition, for instance, exists with the exposed nuts and/or bolts associated with bicycle holders.

Cheap protection is available, however. Just obtain the required number of floor protectors designed for use on bar stool legs. These come in several sizes; select the one that will just slide over the offending projection opposite the RV skin. Fill the protective cap about halfway with RTV silicone rubber, and press the piece into place over the protrusion in question. Once the adhesive has hardened, trim away the excess with a sharp knife.
- DENNIS R. BOWER, EDMONTON, ALBERTA, CANADA

NOISE MUFFLER

Is the blower fan on your RV exhaust vent noisy because of its high speed? If so, here's an inexpensive solution that will greatly reduce the noise, though not ventilation, for all but the most ambitious food preparation activities. The illustrated switch and the two 10-ohm resistors (Radio Shack part nos. 275-324 and 271-080) can be installed in the fan housing. The new switch should fit nicely right next to the existing fan/light control switch with the drilling of a small hole through the vent hood. Full blower speed is available whenever the new microswitch is in the "on" position.

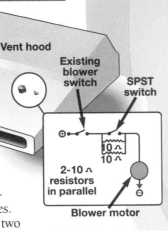

- *JOHN SAUNDERS, FALLBROOK, CALIFORNIA*

UNSTABLE TABLE

Here is a simple and inexpensive way to tighten up the wobbly dinette table that just won't quit bouncing around when your RV is on the move. All materials can be purchased from the local hardware store for under $8 and installed in less than 10 minutes. Just drill a pilot hole for the lag screw eyebolt into the RV floor and another hole through the table leg. The floor-mounted eyebolt should be positioned on the inside portion of the leg, so it is less visible when in use. Once the machine-screw-threaded eyebolt is in place through the table leg, and secured with a nut and washer, the turnbuckle can be installed and tightened. It takes less than a minute to remove the turnbuckle on those occasions when the table is lowered for conversion into a bed.

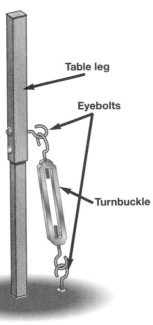

- *HARLAND E. MEGOW, POINT PLEASANT, NEW JERSEY*

WET WARFARE

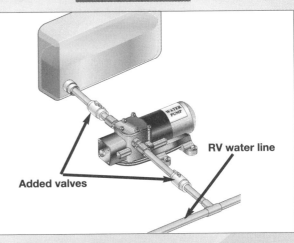

After filling my rig's freshwater tank in a campground, I connected to the park water system. The next day, I discovered the 12-volt DC water pump leaking badly—apparently due to a failed water regulator—and the carpet in my RV soaked.

First, I shut off the campground water supply. Then, unfortunately, I had to drain the just-filled freshwater tank in order to make the repairs. While fixing the problem, I decided to go one step further by installing a shut-off valve in the line between the tank and the pump, and another between the pump and the RV water lines. This allows me to remove the pump for service or repair without having to drain my freshwater tank or shut off the campground's water supply.

- *ROBERT BLUNK, GRAND JUNCTION, COLORADO*

WIRELESS WONDER

When an RV owner mounts a CB or amateur radio antenna, the project often entails cutting a hole through the RV's skin. This can have grave consequences, such as cutting into a steel framing member or electrical wiring. Also, there is always the leak potential.

Antennas that attach to the glass are now being marketed for cellular, CB and amateur 2-meter operations. I have all three and have had excellent results.

Such antennas mount easily on a vehicle's windshield with the supplied adhesive, and the tuning unit attaches similarly to the inside of the glass. With this done, the RF signal is transferred through the windshield to the externally mounted antenna.

Besides the convenience offered, other advantages include no holes to patch when it comes time to trade your rig, and the reusability of old antennas. I can simply remove them with a sharp putty knife.

Such products are available from J. C. Whitney at (312) 431-6102, and various electronics stores. They will couple through glass and fiberglass and require no ground plane. Cost is around $50.

- GLEN A. DEIBERT, FAYETTEVILLE, NORTH CAROLINA

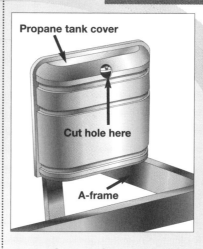

Antenna

Windshield glass

Tuning unit

VIEWABLE VALVE

Propane tank cover

Cut hole here

A-frame

Here's a suggestion for owners of travel trailers equipped with Cameo vinyl propane-tank covers. While this cover does dress up a rig, it makes it cumbersome to check propane-tank status. The only way to see if the automatic regulator has switched from an empty tank to a full one (and avoid running out of LP-gas late some night) is to remove the cover for a visual inspection. This may have to be done several times, depending on gas usage.

To alleviate this chore, I cut a 3-inch hole in the back of the Cameo cover. It is now easy to use a small hand mirror to view the regulator through this opening. I keep the mirror on the battery box for convenience when parked, and inside this box when traveling.

- LYNN NELSON, FRESNO, CALIFORNIA

MINI RAIN GUTTER

J-channel rain gutter   Roof of RV

I used so-called J-channel to create miniature rain gutters on the sides on my RV. This material, which is normally placed around residential windows during vinyl siding installation, can be obtained at large hardware stores.

To modify the J-channel, I used tin snips to remove the strip with nail holes. Next I removed the factory-installed flexible plastic trim that ran across the top edges of each side of my RV. With this done, I installed the trimmed J-channel and secured it with screws approximately every 6 inches.

I blocked off the opening of these channels at the front of the RV because I wanted the water to run off to the rear. This alteration works well, and has almost totally eliminated those ugly black streaks.

Editor's Note: To prevent possible water leaks into the roof structure of the RV, use silicone sealant (or equivalent) to seal all weather-exposed screw heads applicable to this project.

- CLYDE MACMASTER, RICHMOND, MAINE

◆ CLOSEUPS ◆ CLOSEUPS ◆ CLOSEUPS ◆

WELL-PLACED PLUG

*W*e have purchased several 12-volt DC items, such as a spotlight, an impact wrench, and a bilge pump. To use these items on the outside of the trailer, we found it necessary to install a cigarette-lighter socket (12-volt DC accessory outlet, Radio Shack part no. 270-1539, $6) with a rubber cap on the external battery cover. We drilled a hole in the cover of the battery box and installed the accessory outlet, held in place by one nut. Then we wired the outlet with 14-gauge wire, 1 foot of which goes to the positive (with in-line fuse) and negative sides of the battery.

- LINDA AND ROD GRAVES, ALLEN PARK, MICHIGAN

TANGLED WEBS

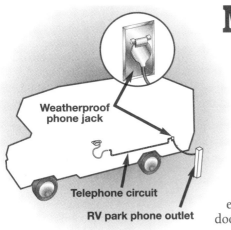

Weatherproof phone jack

Telephone circuit

RV park phone outlet

Most RVers who spend a month or longer in one location are having telephone service installed at their sites. In my travels, I have seen telephone wires entering through doors, windows, vents, and even electrical outlets. Not only are these approaches unsightly, it can be downright dangerous to route a phone line through a shore-power outlet.

I decided to install a permanent, weatherproof, modular telephone jack through an exterior wall of my RV. The jack assembly I used was intended to be used as an exterior phone outlet around the home. My installation, however, reverses its design by using the outlet jack to feed the telephone circuit to the interior of the RV. The opposing modular jack at the back of the jack box connects via modular cord to my own telephone.

I carry a 50-foot long modular cord, which I plug into the park telephone outlet after the phone company or park manager makes the connection on the other end.

Editor's Note: Use caution when cutting through exterior RV walls. Many sections contain hidden electrical circuits and plumbing that could be damaged.
- *FRED SPENCER, COLLINSVILLE, ILLINOIS*

SMALL, STABLE IRONING BOARD

Closed feet

Countertop

Partially open drawer

While traveling I carry a small ironing board with little legs that fold down. However, it was difficult to find a place to use this board that was comfortable. I found that if I tuck the ironing board under the countertop and support it by a partially-open drawer, I have a convenient surface on which to iron clothes.
- *RICHARD PREVALLET, MARBLE HILL, MISSOURI*

S H A R E W A R E

*A*re you a computer user? If so, there is a program now available to the RVer that will help with paperwork and planning.

The shareware program (not public domain) is called "The Motor Home Manager." Some of the titles on the menu are: Supplies, Campsites Index, Spare Parts Index, Trip Planning, Repairs and Projects, and Equipment Log. Shareware programs are available through on-line bulletin board services such as CompuServe and America Online, local user groups, CD-ROMs, and some mail-order disk vendors.
- *GEORGE TAYLOR, MUSCLE SHOALS, ALABAMA*

T H E   B E S T   O F B O T H   W O R L D S

*W*hen I bought my trailer, it came wired with two internal coax outlets for a rooftop antenna. However, there was no external hookup for cable television, which is often available at RV parks.

My son thought of an easy solution. We purchased a weatherproof coax-termination wall plate and the shortest length of premade coax cable we could find. From the outside of the RV, we drilled a hole through the wall, making sure it was close to the existing coax outlet.

(**Editor's Note:** Use caution when drilling through RV walls. Plumbing and electrical circuits may be present. Both shore and battery power should be disconnected while drilling is underway.)

After routing the short length of coax inside, we disconnected the rooftop antenna lead from one of the factory-installed coax outlets, and then reconnected the new cable feed line. Caulking was used to seal the edges of the outside coax receptacle before it was screwed firmly into place.

This fix now makes it easy to use campground cable when it's available. No longer do I have to go to the trouble of running a long wire through an open window to the outside cable stub. The second coax outlet remains connected to the rooftop antenna, allowing me to convert back to airwave reception when needed.
- *BILL VAN DER VORT, VANCOUVER, WASHINGTON*

LIFE'S MOST EMBARRASSING MOMENTS

We've all done it. With visiting guests aboard during a dry-camp outing, nearly every RVer has stepped into the bathroom without remembering to turn on the water pump. The dilemma: Shout to your spouse to correct your oversight, or return sheepishly to the switch location and activate it yourself.

To avoid such embarrassment, I added a second water-pump switch in the RV bathroom. It is wired parallel with the existing panel-mounted switch in the living area.

Installation is fairly straightforward, though methods will obviously vary from rig to rig. Run a new wire (at least 14-gauge stranded automotive wire) from the 12-volt DC fuse panel to one terminal of the new switch. If desired, you can tap into the hot wire running to the original pump switch.

Connect a wire to the other switch terminal, and route it to the pump (as illustrated). Either switch can now be used to activate the water pump, thereby eliminating the "wrong place, wrong time" syndrome. The only thing different that you'll have to remember is to turn off both switches.
- *CHARLES WEST, GRAND JUNCTION, COLORADO*

BATHING BEAUTY

If your RV is no longer under warranty, and big cracks begin appearing in the show walls of the rig, I have a cheap and effective fix.

First, remove the existing plastic wall from between the tub and ceiling. To replace it, obtain a good quality piece of flexible vinyl floor-covering, which is large enough to encircle the tub area. This can be purchased at most home-improvement centers, where you will likely find a wide selection of patterns and colors to suit your decorating tastes.

Cut this material to length, making certain that the tub-to-ceiling fit is reasonably tight. Using ceramic-tile adhesive, cover the shower stall walls using a spreading trowel with ¼-inch grooves.

Next, position the flooring material around the tub and press it firmly into place. If the corners do not curve properly, you may have to use a hair dryer or a commercial heat gun to warm the vinyl in these areas. The corners do not have to make a perfect 90-degree angle; they have a curvature of up to a ½-inch radius.

After the adhesive has had a chance to set for at least a day, use silicone caulking to fill in the seams around the top, bottom, and door/entry area. You don't want water getting into places where it shouldn't. Once this dries completely (allow another full day), the shower will be as good as new.
- *ROBERT C. WHITNEY, PENACOOK, NEW HAMPSHIRE*

ALWAYS READY

Two years ago I purchased an 8mm camcorder that I take along on all our RV outings. Because I used it a lot, it never seemed fully charged when I needed it most.

I took care of this problem by purchasing a portable voltage inverter that provides 120 volts AC from 12 volts DC. The unit is small and plugs into my RV's cigarette lighter. Now, whenever I use the camcorder at a sightseeing location, I just plug it into the inverter and charge the camera's battery as I drive. It's always ready to go.

Also, I found another advantage in having the inverter. My son can operate his laptop computer to his heart's content without running down the device's battery. I'm sure I'll find other uses for this nifty product as time goes by.
- *MIKE BARONDEAU, ROSCOE, SOUTH DAKOTA*

REGISTERING A COMPLAINT

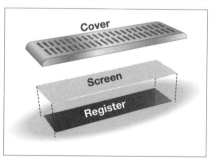

My family's new trailer has the heat registers located in the floor. When I saw this, I could just imagine a small object falling into one of these and rolling down one of the ducts out of reach. This probability was forestalled by removing the register covers and installing pieces of metal window screen to fit the openings. With these in place, the registers were replaced in their original positions. This little fix works great and, in addition to keeping debris out of the heating system, seems to stop lint from entering the ducts, as well.
- *MARJORIE A. TURRIFF, MONROE, MICHIGAN*

QUIET FAN

The bathroom fan in our fifth-wheel has a decibel rating just short of a jet engine at full blast. Ear plugs and cotton balls are a bit much to use while one uses the facilities, and the alternative—not to run the fan—is also unacceptable. I was browsing a flea market when I

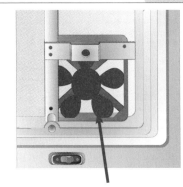

4-inch 12-volt DC "muffin" fan (used for computer cooling)

ran into a bunch of surplus 12-volt DC "muffin" fans normally used for computer cooling. A 4-inch fan was installed in place of the original in 15 minutes, and a switch was mounted where vertically challenged people can reach it easily. The new fan is so quiet that it's now necessary to lock the bathroom door to ensure privacy.
- *PAM STEFFEN, LIVINGSTON, TEXAS*

CHILLY THOUGHTS

I used to have a problem with the refrigerator in our travel trailer freezing up, especially on cool nights. In defense, I purchased an electric indoor/outdoor quartz thermometer. It has an adjustable alarm that warns me whenever the temperature is near freezing.

Installation was simple. I located the outdoor sensor of the unit on an interior wall of the refrigerator, between the shelves. Then I affixed the thermometer body to a convenient site near the refrigerator. Now, I can read both the interior temperature of the refrigerator compartment and the temperature within the trailer itself. It has been a blessing.

I tried a liquid thermometer first, but it burst one winter when the trailer was in storage. What a mess!

While I was at it, I also installed the same product in the cab of my truck—with the remote sensor located outside the cab. Here, the electronic thermometer alerts me to potential freezing road conditions, and has saved many mishaps. I purchased this product from J. C. Whitney of Chicago, Illinois; (312)431-6129.
- *EUGENE A. PRIMROSE, MANCELONA, MICHIGAN*

A STRETCH OF THE IMAGINATION

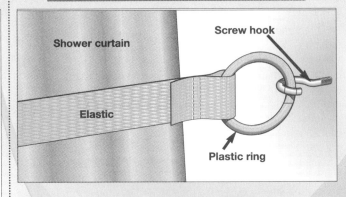

Here is an idea that makes it more convenient to use the shower/tub aboard my family's RV. We found that it was difficult to keep the shower curtain from sticking to us while showering in such a small space. I solved the problem by using two open-end screw hooks, a length of 1 × 36-inch elastic and two (2-inch-diameter) plastic rings.

The first step was to cut the elastic band to the same length as the tub. Then I threaded each end through a plastic ring and sewed it, a modification that shortened the elastic just enough so it would stretch taunt between the hooks I installed in the wall on each side of the tub.

While taking a shower now, we pull the elastic tight on the inside of the shower curtain to hold it away from us. This eliminates the sticking problem altogether.
- *NITA ROGERS, IRVING, TEXAS*

FOOD LIGHT

While restoring and upgrading an older fifth-wheel trailer, I faced the problem of a poorly lit area near the refrigerator. To correct this, I mounted a low-profile, 12-volt DC RV ceiling light with a sliding on/off switch about 6 inches above the fridge. The hot wire from the light was connected to an existing 12-volt DC fused circuit, and the ground wire routed to the unit's base behind the refrigerator frame.

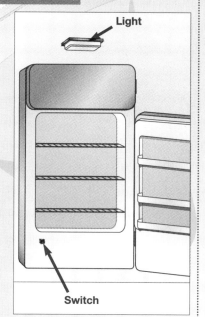

Next, I acquired a glove-compartment light switch from an auto-wrecking yard. After making a bracket to hold this spring-loaded switch, I installed the assembly inside the refrigerator, so it activates whenever the door is opened.

I grounded the switch to the refrigerator frame and attached the previously routed ground lead from the new ceiling-mounted light. The slide switch on the light is left on, so that the fixture illuminates automatically with the opening of the refrigerator door.

An additional grounded switch could be installed at a convenient location, so the new ceiling light could be used even with the fridge door closed.

- Robert L. Clark, Washington, Indiana

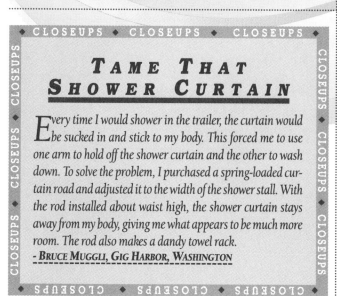

SWITCH CRAZY

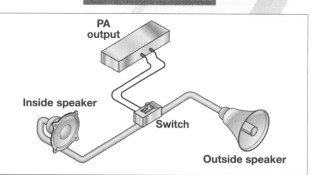

Here's another way of doing what someone suggested regarding the addition of an extra demand water-pump switch in the bathroom. My method requires replacement of the original switch and the addition of another, both single pole, double throw (SPDT).

By running one extra wire, it's possible to activate the pump from either switch location without having to verify that both are off during travel. On is on and off is off at either switch. Pilot lights, if desired, can be included, as shown in the wiring diagram.

- Paul Whiting, Walled Lake, Michigan

LOUD AND CLEAR

On most motorhomes, it's hard to get a message to anyone in the rear without pulling off the road, or yelling at the top of your lungs. However, in rigs that have CB radios, you can easily overcome this communication deficiency.

Most CBs have a public address (PA) circuit, so all you need to do is install a small extension speaker in the rear of your coach. With a flick of a switch on the CB, you'll be able to talk to anyone in the rear without diverting your attention from the road.

If you already have a PA speaker hooked up on the outside of your RV, and you want to retain it, simply install a double-pole, double-throw (DPDT) toggle switch in the speaker circuit. This allows you to easily choose either speaker.

- Bone Evers, Taylor, Arizona

CREAKY CRANK-DOWNS

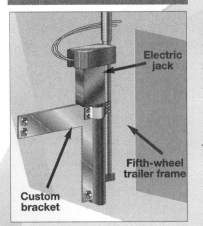

Electric jack

Fifth-wheel trailer frame

Custom bracket

With the onset of old age, my 1978 fifth-wheel trailer developed a problem with the manually cranked front jacks. Upon checking the price for new ones and considering a conversion to electric at the same time, I found myself facing the proverbial "sticker shock" head-on.

My solution was to purchase two electric jack posts intended for use on the ball-mount hitch of conventional travel trailers. This done, I then designed two custom brackets to secure these jacks in place with my rig's front storage compartments. I used 4 × ⅜-inch hot-rolled flat bar stock and seamless round tubing to clamp the commercial jacks in position. As in most jobs, the fabrication was easier than the designing. Once I had everything in place

to my satisfaction, I removed the factory rock-type switches from each jack head and reinstalled them in the same storage compartment used to access the original mechanical jacks. I ran heavy-gauge 12-volt DC wiring with appropriate fuses to complete the job.

Now I have independent front electric jacks at a cost considerably less than I would have otherwise paid. Moreover, I made the necessary repairs to the old mechanical jacks while involved with the installation of the electric models. This, and the fact that the new electric jacks can also be operated manually, gives me a double backup in case of electrical failure.

- PAUL O. SCRAGG, WINDSOR, ONTARIO, CANADA

◆ CLOSEUPS ◆ CLOSEUPS ◆ CLOSEUPS ◆ CLOSEUPS ◆ CLOSEUPS ◆ CLOSEUPS ◆

CHECKING IT TWICE

I've used these arriving and departing checklists for my rig, but they can be changed as required for anyone's use. I use them each time the motorhome is moved. I reduced them in size with a copying machine, then sealed them back to back in plastic. The check sheet is stored in the driver's door pocket. It has already saved my antenna!

Arriving Checklist
Inside
❏ 1. Set gearshift lever to "park," and set park brake.
❏ 2. Set generator as needed.
❏ 3. Set main breaker as needed.
❏ 4. Check range; be sure valves are off.
❏ 5. Lower the step.

Outside
❏ 1. If RV is positioned correctly, place wheel chock.
❏ 2. Connect power cable, turn breaker on.
❏ 3. Connect water hose/regulator; open valve.
❏ 4. Connect sewer hose.
❏ 5. Drain waste tank (left valve) and reclose valve.
❏ 6. Open gray tank (right valve) and leave open.
❏ 7. Install leveling jacks/blocks.
❏ 8. Open LP-gas tank valve; note quantity.
❏ 9. Light the water heater.
❏ 10. Lower the awning; lay the carpet.

Inside
❏ 1. Set the refrigerator power.
❏ 2. Set heat/air-conditioner as needed.
❏ 3. Set roof vents as needed.

❏ 4. Raise TV antenna; turn on booster.
❏ 5. Place/connect the TV set.

Departing Checklist
Outside
❏ 1. Check under the hood.
❏ 2. Check the tires.
❏ 3. Close the LP-gas tank valve.
❏ 4. Drain the waste tank; reclose the valve.
❏ 5. Flush and store sewer hose; close valve.
❏ 6. Disconnect/store sewer hose; install cap.
❏ 7. Close the water valve; disconnect hose/regulator.
❏ 8. Turn outside power breaker off; remove power cable.
❏ 9. Remove leveling jacks/blocks.
❏ 10. Raise the awning; store outdoor carpet.
❏ 11. Store all other items; close all of the compartments.
❏ 12. Remove wheel chock.

Inside
❏ 1. Raise the steps.
❏ 2. Set refrigerator power.
❏ 3. Set generator and main breaker as needed.
❏ 4. Be sure range valves are in "off" position.
❏ 5. Set heat/air-conditioning as needed.
❏ 6. Close roof vents.
❏ 7. Lower the TV antenna; turn booster off.
❏ 8. Secure TV set, etc.
❏ 9. Stop by dump station, if necessary.
❏ 10. Check out of campground, if required.

- GEORGE TAYLOR, MUSCLE SHOALS, ALABAMA

◆ CLOSEUPS ◆ CLOSEUPS ◆ CLOSEUPS ◆ CLOSEUPS ◆ CLOSEUPS ◆ CLOSEUPS ◆

RAPID RECYCLE

Our fifth-wheel trailer was delivered without a microwave oven, although it was prewired for one. When my husband installed a microwave, the project left us with an extra cabinet door, which we decided to put to use elsewhere. It was converted into an attractive magazine rack that now resides between two chairs in the trailer's living area.

My husband used ash wood for the sides of the rack, and stained it to match the oak finish that is on the door. For extra function, a small, removable tray was also built and finished using the same wood. To hold the tray in place, he added a thin piece of wood trim, which hooks over the top edge of the old door, as illustrated here.

It's really nice to be able to relax in our chairs and enjoy a hot cup of coffee as we take in the beautiful scenery.

- MRS. JIMMIE BUTLER, OOLOGAH, OKLAHOMA

TWIN TIPS

Here are two ideas that I use while RVing. Whenever I need to inflate my queen-size air mattress, I use my portable Dirt Devil electric vacuum cleaner. I remove the bag, but not the bag adapter. The mattress inflates in seconds, and it eliminates having to use a foot-powered air pump.

To keep my RV's shower and sink drains smelling fresh and clean, I use a soft, flexible bottle brush to reach down into the J-trap. A few strokes back and forth remove all the soap scum buildup and food residue.

- DANNY BURTON, HOPE HULL, ALABAMA

CLOSEUPS ◆ CLOSEUPS ◆ CLOSEUPS

NOW HEAR THIS!

It is often hard to carry on a conversation with a passenger seated in the back of the van or a motorhome while traveling. At least, that's what we discovered when our 6-year-old grandson started taking frequent trips with us. His voice is very soft and it was sometimes impossible for us to understand what he was saying from his seat in the back of our rig.

We solved the dilemma by installing an inexpensive, battery-powered intercom set. You can purchase a set at Radio Shack (part no. 43-222, $14.95). The palm-size master unit fits neatly in the center console of our vehicle. We control the volume, and in order to avoid distraction while driving in heavy traffic, we are able to turn the set off completely.

The connecting wiring between the two speakers/receivers was easily concealed beneath the carpet, giving the impression of a professional installation. High-tech wireless units are also available, if desired.

- VIVIAN FOX, CARTHAGE, TEXAS

OUT OF DARKNESS

I have a suggestion that I think will help others. As you know, it's always dark under the counter of an RV. To solve this problem, I mounted a small, 12-volt DC light bulb and microswitch near the door of each compartment. The switch must be mounted securely to the surrounding door frame, so it can't jiggle loose and turn the light on unexpectedly. Power can be tapped from any convenient circuit

- MANUEL MACHADO, GUSTINE, CALIFORNIA

DOWN SPOUT

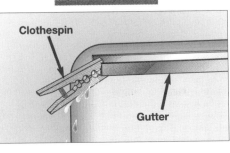

Roof downspouts always seem to leave black streaks along the trailer's side walls because the spouts are too short. After trying metal downspout extensions and small PVC tubing, which all eventually came off, I found the simplest and most effective solution: clip on a clothespin at each downspout. The water wets the wood and runs off at the end of the clothespin, well away from the side wall of the trailer. The clothespin trick works to control runoff from morning dew drips and major downpours. Remove the clothespins when traveling.
- TED BALESHTA,
SIDNEY, BRITISH COLUMBIA, CANADA

TRIPLE-DUTY TABLE

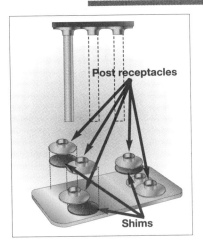

Being a person of small stature, I found my RV's dinette a design compromise that didn't work well for me. I often had to reach too far across it for comfort. This is how I solved the situation. I started by purchasing two pairs of RV table post receptacles (cost is about $8 per pair). I then installed these on the underside of the table next to the original receptacles, as illustrated. Because there was some overlap of the receptacles, I used a shim of Masonite under the new ones to assure a level installation. This easy modification lets me use the table either in the centered position as it was designed, or offset to either side for easier reaching. I really enjoy this setup for most situations. However, caution must be used when placing heavy objects, such as a sewing machine, on the table when it is positioned off-center.
- JEAN H. COOPER, ARLINGTON, TEXAS

ALMOST INSTANT HOT WATER

Want to do the morning dishes, but forgot to leave the water heater on overnight? Just put water into your coffeemaker. In a few minutes, you have 10 cups of hot water—and clean dishes.
- TONY DiMAGGIO, OAKDALE, CONNECTICUT

WIRELESS AND LOVING IT!

Having purchased a satellite DSS system for my RV, I was disappointed that I could not take advantage of the wonderful stereo sound while watching the television. Normally, this requires an additional stereo amplifier if the television isn't equipped with a suitable built-in sound system. Lacking space for an additional external amplifier and speaker system, I examined my RV's factory-installed AM/FM cassette stereo to see if I could somehow adapt it for use. Unfortunately, most automotive sound systems do not have hookups for input of external audio, but I did find a number of CD player-to-cassette player adapters available in automotive sound departments at major department stores. The cassette-like devise is inserted into the tape slot of the stereo and the wire would normally be plugged into the CD player. In my case, I plugged the wire into the audio outputs of my DSS receiver. This led to another problem: dangling wires hanging all over the place! I solved this dilemma by purchasing a wireless CD player adapter, instead. Actually, a mini-FM transmitter, unit (in my case, an Akron SoundFeeder, available at Target stores) is plugged into the audio outputs of my DSS system using a three-foot Y-adapter audio cable I purchased at Radio Shack (part no. 42-2475, $4.49). The FM transmitter (no insertable cassette or wires required) is powered by a single AA battery and broadcasts the audio signal from my video system to a clean FM frequency. Tune the radio to a blank area with no other transmissions, then dial the transmitter's broadcast frequency to the same frequency. Just match the signals and start enjoying true stereo sound with your video viewing. My total cost was less than $27, and I couldn't be more pleased.
- ALLARD COIR, PHOENIX, ARIZONA

ON THE ROLL

I use a plastic, 2-liter soft-drink bottle (cut as shown in the illustration) to hold both the paper towels and toilet paper in my rig on their respective rolls.

This method has often saved me from the hassle of rerolling countless spools of paper products that are unleashed by road vibration. The plastic shroud lasts forever and works on any size roll. If you shop around you can even have a choice of colors.

- M. C. Sidlo, Menahga, Minnesota

CLOCK WATCHERS

One of the first things we missed on our first outing with our new trailer was an illuminated digital clock like the one we have next to our bed at home. For a while, we kept a flashlight handy to check our watches.

Then, I realized that I could have an illuminated timepiece by installing an automobile clock module on the underside of a cabinet above the RV's bed. Such clocks are available from many auto-parts stores, costing between $15 and $25, depending upon the model selected. You can get either a light-emitting-diode (LED) style, or a vacuum fluorescent display. The latter has a brighter display during the day, but the LED is plenty bright for nighttime use.

Installation requires cutting a small rectangular hole in the underside of the selected cabinet, near an existing light fixture. Since 12-volt DC power is a necessity, its availability in your rig will dictate the clock's position. Wire according to the clock manufacturer's instructions, with one exception.

In automobile use, the clock display control wire would normally be hooked to the ignition switch, so the time could be read with the key on. While the current required to power the display is small (0.12 amp), it's enough to run down an RV's battery while the rig is in storage.

For this reason, you should install a display cut-off switch next to the clock, and use it whenever the RV is left unattended for long periods. The time-keeping function will continue, however, drawing only .003 amp during your absence. The switch I used costs less than $2.

- Jack Casson, Claremont, California

POOCH PALACE

Our new trailer has everything that we could want, except a place for Poco, our medium-size beagle. She prefers her own space whenever we travel, as do we.

At my wife's suggestion, I looked under the twin beds and found some extra space amid all the pipes, wires, wheel wells, etc. I cut an opening in the paneling under one bed, and walled in the space with ¾-inch pine framing and some leftover pre-finished paneling. I ended up with a space 25½ inches wide × 13½ inches high × 20 inches deep. I framed the opening, which is slightly smaller, with a prefinished outside corner molding.

Although we were concerned initially about whether Poco would like her new sleeping area, we observed that she had entered her new beagle bedroom—even before we had a chance to put on the finishing touches.

- Bob Combs, Dallas, Oregon

VENT FAN IMPROVEMENT

Hole cut to the diameter of the fan blades ← 13¼ inches → **Plexiglas** 13¼ inches

I have a roof-mounted vent fan in the bathroom of my rig, but it isn't very efficient at pulling air because of the open space around the fan blades. The extra space allows air to recirculate around the fan instead of being pulled through the vent. I solved the problem by cutting a panel of Plexiglas to fit into the vent opening. A hole was cut the diameter of the fan blades. I drilled holes to mate with the screws, which hold the vent screen in place, and installed the Plexiglas using the existing screws. Now the bath fan is more efficient at removing dampness and odors from the bathroom. The clear Plexiglas lets in plenty of light.

- Charles M. Finn, Belle, Missouri

TRICK TABLE TIP

Since most trailers do not come with end tables, I solved the problem of where to set snacks and drinks by adding a fold-down shelf on the panel at the end of the couch. In our particular case, I used the fold-down television shelf

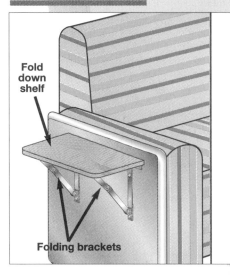

Fold down shelf

Folding brackets

from the bedroom, as we never use a television in there. However, the folding brackets and shelving can be easily obtained at any building supply store. If you want the wood grain and color to match perfectly, have your dealer order a spare television shelf from the factory. This has proven to work so well that I plan to install another one on the wall at the other end of the couch. Note: If you have a slide-out unit, pay very close attention to the clearance if you install it on or near the wall.
- DAVID SPARKE, CINCINNATI, OHIO

BYE-BYE BLACK STREAKS

For years I have been wondering what to do about the black streaks that come from the roof and small downspouts on the four corners of my RV. It's very hard to remove those ugly black streaks that show up after a good rain. To eliminate these streaks, I purchased four 2-inch

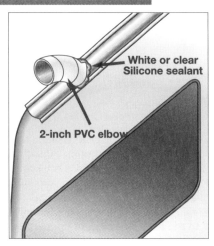

White or clear Silicone sealant

2-inch PVC elbow

PVC elbows for about 99 cents each at a local hardware store. The elbows were then notched so they fit flush with the ends of the drip railing. White or clear silicone sealant was used to hold the elbows in place. We said goodbye to black streaks.
- CHARLES P. ROELLE SR., VANLUE, OHIO

SOLID SUGGESTION

When we purchased our present travel trailer, I had BAL jacks installed instead of using portable, square-base screw jacks. However, with the BAL jacks mounted crosswise, the trailer exhibited a rocking motion whenever someone walked into it. I tried wheel chocks. They help, but I still wasn't satisfied.

I took the BAL jacks off the front of the trailer and remounted them lengthwise on each side. Now, with the jacks fairly tight, the rocking motion is completely gone.
- DONALD MANNING, CHARLES CITY, IOWA

CLOSEUPS • CLOSEUPS • CLOSEUPS

NEVER OUT OF TOUCH

Radio reception in mountainous area campgrounds is often very poor or altogether nonexistent. However, with a little bit of wire and two alligator clips, no one need be out of touch.

I used 70 feet of No. 16 automotive wire for my antenna design. This I wound into an 8-inch-diameter coil with about 30 wraps, secured in this configuration with electrical tape. About 3 inches of wire was left hanging loose outside the coil on each end to allow for easy installation of the alligator clips.

To use the antenna, I string approximately 70 feet of the same type of wire (with ends bared) from my camper to a nearby tree (be careful to avoid any power lines, and take it down if a thunderstorm approaches). One end is attached to an alligator clip on the wire coil inside my rig; the other end is routed through a window, draped over a branch and weighted with a steel bar to hold it taut. Setup is completed by attaching the other alligator clip on the wire coil to an interior metal object, such as a window frame.

This system will not bring in FM and TV signals because such reception requires a clear line of sight to the transmitter. However, placing the homemade antenna coil next to any AM and/or shortwave radio receiver makes it possible to literally tune into the world.
- KEITH LAMMLE, NELSON, BRITISH COLUMBIA, CANADA

TINT VS. SQUINT

The windows in my fifth-wheel trailer are very large, and the factory-installed shades do not keep the light out. To remedy this situation, I removed the shades from their brackets and unrolled them on a clean, flat surface. Next, I cut a piece of commercial vinyl window tint to match the dimensions of each shade. This I laid across the inside portion of the shade, and then stapled the top to the roller tube, so it would roll up and down with the

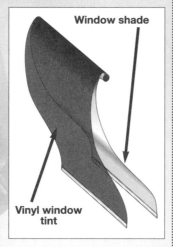

Window shade

Vinyl window tint

shade. This simple change keeps the sunlight out and helps control heat buildup. Also, the window tint has eliminated fabric fade inside the rig during extended storage.
- EILEEN JACOBSEN, ROCK LAKE, NORTH DAKOTA

HANG THOSE TOWELS AND CLOTHES

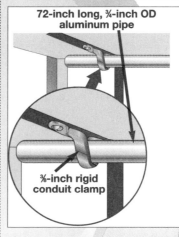

72-inch long, ¾-inch OD aluminum pipe

⅜-inch rigid conduit clamp

Living or traveling in an RV requires doing laundry, and some of those washed items must be hung up rather than placed in a dryer. Hanging clothing on cabinet door handles leaves much to be desired. Since our RV has twin beds with overhead cabinets on each side, we fabricated a simple pole to suspend our washing. We used a 72-inch-long, ¾-inch OD aluminum tube as our hang-up bar, and secured it between the two opposing (open) cabinets using ⅜-inch rigid conduit clamps and screws. The bar is high enough so that we can sleep under the hanging clothes and, when not in use, it stores neatly under the mattress.
- ELVIN SHAW, APACHE JUNCTION, ARIZONA

• CLOSEUPS • CLOSEUPS • CLOSEUPS •

RV ORGANIZER

Where did I put that metric socket set? Darned if I can find that water-pressure regulator! Now, I know I put that jack crank some place. Does this sound familiar? Well, here is a solution that will help you solve such problems.

Make an inventory of everything you put into the storage compartments of your RV. I use my computer to make a list of each item that I place in each area. If there are any changes to be made at a later date, using a computer makes it a lot easier. However, if you don't have access to a computer, the old pencil-and-paper method will work, as well.

After I make my inventory lists, I put them in zipper-type plastic bags and tape them inside each respective storage compartment. I also make a master list, which I keep inside the RV, so I immediately know which compartment to go to for a particular item. This is especially helpful if it is cold or raining outside.

This inventory procedure not only makes it a lot easier to find needed items, but also works as a checklist before each trip to assure that I have everything on board that I'll need. Of course, as we all know, Mr. Murphy can strike at any time. The thing you really need on a trip is usually the one item you left at home.
- ARNOLD "BEN" IRVINE, COOPERSBURG, PENNSYLVANIA

• CLOSEUPS • CLOSEUPS • CLOSEUPS •

INGENUITY ILLUSTRATED

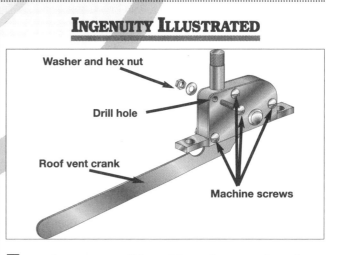

Washer and hex nut

Drill hole

Roof vent crank

Machine screws

In quick succession, all four of the roof-vent crank mechanisms on my 1986 mini-motorhome failed. This was caused by the worm-gear case halves separating at the pressed-on attachment points. At my RV dealer, I found that replacement units would cost me $8 each. After a little thought, I repaired the old ones for only 32 cents apiece.

I used a No. 30 bit to drill through the four pressed-together attachment points of the case. After this, I put a little dab of white grease on the internal worm gear and bolted the cases together with 6-32 by ¾-inch-long round-head machine screws, flat washers, and hex nuts. Now, the vent cranks work better than ever.
- WAYNE F. ROSTEK, CLAREMORE, OKLAHOMA

KEEPIN' IT ALL COOL

Our RV air conditioner did not cool the large kitchen/dining room in our 27-foot motorhome sufficiently, especially when we were cooking. The vents could not be angled enough to cool us off in the living areas where we spend most of our time. This is especially critical while cooking over a hot stove in the afternoon.

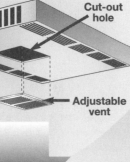

Cut-out hole

Adjustable vent

So, I cut an off-center opening (to align directly with the fan's airflow path) in the housing of the air conditioner unit. Then, I installed a standard heating/cooling vent by screwing it to the sheet-metal bracket inside the housing. After I painted the entire unit, it looked as if it had been factory installed.

Because the vent is adjustable, we can now easily aim the cool air where it is really needed, or close it off and use the regular vents at each end of the unit.

- DON J. MONTOVA, NEWARK, CALIFORNIA

SHRINK FIT

After a few years of camping in all kinds of weather, the vinyl side to my family's pop-up camper seemed to shrink. The hook-and-loop fasteners no longer aligned properly, making it

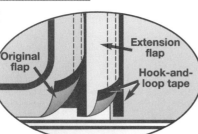

Original flap

Extension flap

Hook-and-loop tape

difficult to seal the rig against drafts and leaks. Surveying the situation, I could see where a small extension flap could be used to bring everything back into shape.

With this in mind, I purchased ¼ yard of outdoor vinyl in a color that matched the camper. Also, I bought approximately 4¾ yards of hook-and-loop material. I cut the vinyl into four 2¼ × 42-inch strips. These became my extensions. To each one, I sewed 42 inches of hook-and-loop fastener—making certain that the respective sides corresponded with that already in place on my camper.

Now, everything fits as it should. When it's time to pitch camp and set up the rig, I just attach the new extension pieces as illustrated. The procedure is quick and easy, and I can now seal the camper's vinyl enclosure without have to play tug-of-war.

- LOIS ROSSNAGEL, IRONWOOD, MICHIGAN

WHAT ABOUT BABY?

Hinges

Bunk beds

Child safety gate

We have a 26-foot 1993 travel trailer, which we love. However, with three children, we needed to make some adjustments. Our first concern was where to put the crib for our 1-year-old. After some thought, we came up with the idea of using the lower bunk-bed area to replace the crib altogether. We started with a wooden child-safety gate from Newline Juvenile Products in Suring, Wisconsin. This type has two spring-loaded clips that hold the gate shut.

Purchasing a couple of 2½-inch brass door hinges with removable pins and two small eye screws from the local hardware store, we installed the gate in the lower bunk opening (as illustrated). The eye screws were positioned so that the spring-loaded clips could engage them to hold the gate securely closed. Presto! we had a built-in baby crib and playpen that allowed us to leave our bulky portable crib at home.

- MIKE AND KATHY ZIEREIS, CLEVELAND, WISCONSIN

CLOSEUPS • CLOSEUPS • CLOSEUPS

FOIL THE HEAT

There is a great amount of heat that enters your RV via the various skylights during storage in the hot summer season. To cut down on this unwanted interior heat, I have come up with a simple solution: Foil the destructive rays with reflective aluminum foil! Measure a piece of large-size aluminum foil to fit the exterior surface of the plastic skylight with about a 1-inch double thickness border. Place a strip of hook-and-loop tape on the edge of the skylight and the other strip on the inside border of the aluminum foil. Press the sheet in place with the reflective side outward. This sheet can remain in place until fall, or be easily removed when the RV is in use. The strong rays of the sun will now be reflected away from the interior of the RV.

- MANUEL I. WEISMAN, AUGUSTA, GEORGIA

TIP AND TUMBLE

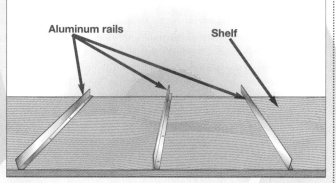

Aluminum rails   Shelf

Wall-mounted cupboards stretch for several feet across the front of our trailer. But, despite nonslip cushioned shelf liner, dishes and glasses still tumbled over while we were en route to our next RV destination. My wife and I knew we needed cupboard dividers, but didn't want anything that made it difficult to reach from one area to another.

So, we made a trip to the lumberyard and purchased an aluminum rail intended for holding dropped translucent ceiling panels, such as those found in household kitchens. After we measured the depth of our cupboards, the rail was cut into appropriate sections. Holes for retaining screws were then drilled about every 12 inches, and the sections were mounted on the shelves. The aluminum was spaced approximately 12 inches apart, as that best fit our arrangement of dishes. Other RVers who duplicate this project may need different spacing. Although these new partitions measure only 1¼ inches tall, they perform perfectly as stabilizing dividers.
- D. J. LANDPHAIR, HUMESTON, IOWA

A STRAPPING IDEA

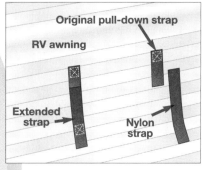

Original pull-down strap
RV awning
Extended strap
Nylon strap

Our problem was finding the pull-down strap that gets buried within a rolled-up RV awning, and once we found it, attempting to insert the pull rod into the flattened loop opening.

The solution: I added a length of nylon strap to the existing awning pull-down strap. I made this addition using nylon thread and 18 inches of nylon strap that I purchased from a local fabric store. Allowing a total of 6 inches for overlap when sewing the new pull loop, I made my strap extension 12 inches longer than the original.

The strap can be any length you desire, from just long enough to extend past the rolled-up awning, to a longer version that can be reached by hand. I chose the latter because I wanted to be able to open the strap's loop and insert the pull rod. Also, for strength and durability, a slightly larger strap is a better choice than a smaller one.
- LEON R. MILLER, MAPLE VALLEY, WASHINGTON

TABLE CACOPHONY

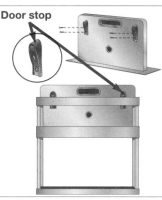

Door stop

After listening to the storable dining table in my RV announce every bump in the road, I decided to quiet my nerves by finding a way to immobilize this loose-fitting convenience. To do so, I bought two tapered rubber door stops, which I drilled and screwed to the bottom of the table at offending contact points near the top of the storage pocket.

Now, when the tabletop is lowered for storage, the door stops securely; however, you need to gently wedge the table into its compartment. After making this modification, I found that the door stops also hold the tabletop a fraction of an inch above the RV floor. This prevents contact and bounce while traveling—stifling noise in the process.

Perhaps the best part of this easy modification is that nothing shows when the table is set up for use, and the storage function works exactly as before. It's true, silence is golden.
- JAMES R. MILLER, PRESCOTT, ARIZONA

PEG-LEG HELPER

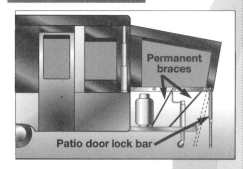

Permanent braces

Patio door lock bar

I use a telescoping patio door lock bar to assist me on those occasions when I have to unfold the family tent trailer alone. Because the lock bar is equipped with a twist-lock, its length is easily adjustable to temporarily support the slide-out bed extensions (instead of using my back) until I can install the permanent braces. A gentle kick to the base of the lock bar releases it, so I can repeat the process at the opposite end of the trailer. As I begin to fold the unit for travel, I use this device to once again support the beds.

Storage of the lock bar is easy. I just place it inside the trailer door for quick access. Telescoping, twist-lock patio door lock bars are available at most large hardware or home-supply stores for a nominal cost.
- *WILLIAM M. MARSHALL, GODFREY, ILLINOIS*

PLAIN JANE GAUGE

H ere's an easy way to make a freshwater level indicator for your RV. Purchase a couple of feet of clear plastic tubing and two pipe clamps from a local hardware store. Select tubing with a diameter that will fit snugly over the drain outlet of your freshwater tank.

To obtain a reading, open the drain valve and position the tubing as illustrated. It's that easy. However, to assure the water level is accurately depicted, don't plug the opposite end of the tube. Leave it open to the atmosphere.

After I've determined how much fresh water I have left, I close the drain valve and pull the tubing off the valve to empty it completely. This prevents dirt from entering the tank during the next check. With this accomplished, I reconnect the tubing and leave it in place, ready for use the next time I take the RV on the road.
- *CARL HEILBRUNN, ARROYO GRANDE, CALIFORNIA*

Water inlet

Plastic tubing

Water level

Drain valve

A 'BRIGHT' IDEA

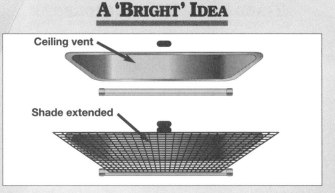

Ceiling vent

Shade extended

C eiling vents are great for letting air in and out of an RV. Unfortunately, when the sun streams through them in hot climates, a great deal of heat can build up inside the rig. In addition, strong sunlight has an adverse effect on upholstery fabrics and other interior furnishings.

I avoided these maladies by purchasing several roll-up-type car window shades from the automotive department of my local discount store. By loosening one side of my rig's ceiling vent frames, I was able to insert the shade mounting clips and retighten the frame screws to hold everything in place. This type of window shade comes with a piece of hook-and-loop material, which I attached to the other side of the vent frame.

To use it, all I do is pull the shade across the opening and secure it to the hook-and-loop retaining tab. In this position, the shade effectively eliminates intense sun rays while allowing proper ventilation. For those who are light sleepers, this type of shade also will soften bright moonlight filtering through the vent opening at night.
- *WILLIAM G. WOLTJEN, MURRELLS INLET, SOUTH CAROLINA*

◆ CLOSEUPS ◆ CLOSEUPS ◆ CLOSEUPS ◆

A SLIPPERY SITUATION

The shower floor in our new trailer became quite slippery once the soapy water hit it. To correct this—and possibly prevent some bruises or broken bones—we put a piece of the same material on the shower floor that we used to prevent our dishes from sliding around inside our RV cabinets when we travel. It works perfectly.

The brand we use is called Skoot-Guard, though there are others available. It is porous, dries quickly, does not mildew, comes in a variety of colors, will not clog the drain and, above all, is skidproof. Skoot-Guard comes in 12-inch widths, but if this isn't enough, two or more pieces can be used side by side.
- *M.S. "BUD" SILVERBLATT, CHULA VISTA, CALIFORNIA*

◆ CLOSEUPS ◆ CLOSEUPS ◆ CLOSEUPS ◆

STAND UP TO YOUR MOTORHOME

Is it hard for you to reach and clean the top of your motorhome's windshield? Do you have to search for a box or a stepladder to work on those windshield wipers? If so,

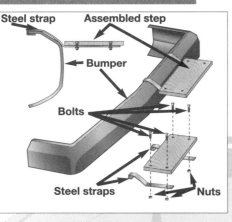

Steel strap • Assembled step
← Bumper
Bolts
Steel straps • Nuts

here's an easily constructed step that can be readily positioned at any spot on your motorhome's front bumper.

Materials needed:

2 pieces of 14 × ³⁄₁₆ × 1½-inch flat steel strap
1 piece of 6 × 14 × ¾-inch oak
4 (⅜ × 1½-inch) carriage bolts with nuts
Vinyl tape (or other suitable material) 1½ inches wide

Using a piece of stiff wire or an old coat hanger, shape a pattern for the two straps as shown in the illustration. (Note: The 90-degree downward bend of the straps where they pass over the front edge of the bumper is important. This will prevent the device from sliding rearward, and thereby becoming disconnected from the bumper when you step on it.)

If you don't have access to an acetylene welding outfit, have a local welding shop shape the two straps to match your wire pattern. Afterward, check the fit of the straps on the bumper, reshape as needed, and then trim the ends to equal length as required.

After you cut and finish the wood step, drill and attach the metal straps using the specified carriage bolts. Finish the project by lining the underside of the straps with vinyl tape to prevent scratching of the bumper.

- GLENN A. ROBERTS, BOULDER CITY, NEVADA

APPROPRIATE COUNTERMEASURES

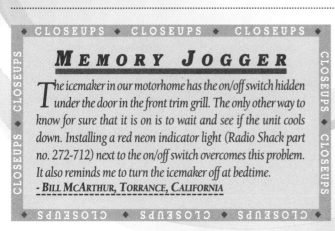

There never seems to be enough counter space in a recreational vehicle. This collapsible shelf design has really come in handy for me, and it can be dropped down for out-of-the-way storage when not needed. My shelf extends into the main doorway of the rig, but not enough to block a person's entry or exit.

To make your own version, first build a 1 × 3-inch framework in the necessary dimensions for your RV. This will add strength to the extension and create a suitable edge on which to glue a countertop laminate.

Next, cut a piece of plywood or chipboard to match the frame, and glue or screw the two together. Use contact cement to secure your selected laminate to the new counter extension.

Additional items needed include:
- a strip of piano hinge to attach shelf to existing counter;
- two metal U-brackets;
- a 2-foot hollow, metal 1-inch-diameter tube;
- a 1½-foot wooden dowel or broom handle (must fit inside tube);
- two bolts with locking nuts; and
- a bolt or pin to hold shelf in upright position

The exact length of the tube or dowel is not critical, but make sure that the wood dowel will fit all the way inside the tube when the shelf is down. Also, for adequate strength, be sure that there is a sufficient amount of dowel remaining in the tube when the shelf is up.

After attaching the shelf to the RV's counter with the piano hinge, install the U-brackets as shown in the diagram. Attach the wood dowel to the shelf U-bracket, and slip the metal tube over it before attaching the tube to the floor bracket.

Hold the shelf in the raised position and drill a hole through the metal tube and dowel. Install a locking pin and attach it with string to prevent loss. Finally, drop the shelf and drill a second hole through the dowel. When the locking pin is in place, the shelf will be securely held in the stowed position during travel.

- BARRY EMERY, ADAMS, MASSACHUSETTS

I'M BOARD

Bringing along a full-size ironing board on an RV trip can be a problem. The same is true of tabletop ironing boards. Many are too small to be efficient and are often unstable.

I made a custom RV ironing board, as shown in the illustration, out of ¾-inch plywood. A commercial board also could be modified to work in this fashion, just by removing its legs.

The ironing surface of my custom board is 12 × 40 inches. The top portion is attached to the 8 × 3-inch uprights with two 1-inch angle brackets to keep the ironing surface free of screw heads. The base is attached to the top board with a 1-inch overhang on the back side and a 3-inch overhang on the front side, which clears the edge of the dining table and leaves enough room so that the iron doesn't bump into the C-clamp used to secure the board.

An upright height of 3 inches is about the minimum clearance that will allow clothing to easily slide on and off the board's tapered end. The dimension can be increased as required to accommodate the user.

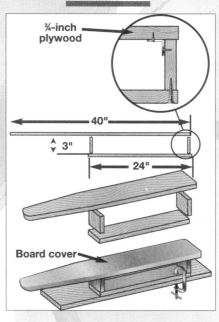

¾-inch plywood

40"

3"

24"

Board cover

Finish the project by attaching the 8 × 24-inch bottom plank to the uprights with 1½-inch screws. Countersink these screw heads because this surface will rest against the RV's tabletop.

If desired, the tapered end of the ironing board can be copied from a commercial cover and pad—both of which will be required. I decided to keep the taper to a minimum so as to retain maximum usable ironing surface. This was done by using a dinner plate for a marking template and sawing the ironing board to match.

Afterward, I placed the blunt end of the ironing cover and pad over the pointed end of the board and stapled it underneath. (The usual string ties cannot be used in this application.) Then I did the same thing with the opposite, tapered end of the cover/pad.

If desired, this portion of the cover could be cut off for a more finished appearance.

Once complete, your RV ironing board and C-clamp can be easily stored in a wardrobe, or under a sofa or bed.

- GORDON MUNRO, VICTORIA, BRITISH COLUMBIA, CANADA

STOPPING SHEET SHIFT

Here's an easy way to make up a bed in an RV, especially if it's equipped with a wall-to-wall mattress.

Slip a narrow metal rod (a curtain support or a dowel) through the hem of the bottom sheet and place it underneath the head of the mattress. Make certain that the rod is the same width as the bed. When done, tuck in the opposite end of the sheet.

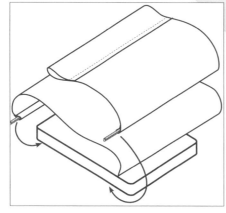

Now do the same with the top sheet, except insert the rod in the hem at the foot of the mattress. This trick keeps the sheets straight and smooth until you're ready to change them again.

- LILLIAN RUDD, DALLAS, TEXAS

No More Unrolling

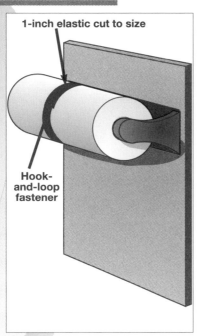

1-inch elastic cut to size

Hook-and-loop fastener

If you are having trouble keeping the paper towels from unrolling while on the road, strap the roll in place. Take a piece of 1-inch-wide elastic and cut a piece 14 inches long. Sew about a 1-inch piece of hook-and-loop fastener on one end and the opposing side to the other end of the elastic strap. Loop the elastic strap around the paper-towel roll— it will automatically adjust in diameter as the roll changes size.
- *BLAINE W. ATWOOD, HAMPDEN, MAINE*

CAN YOU HEAR ME?

Our television is located diagonally across the living area from where my husband likes to sit in our RV. Unfortunately, the television has a side speaker that faces toward the kitchen area. This forces us to turn the volume up more than is normally desirable, and I used to worry about disturbing the neighbors at RV parks.

Then, I remembered the existing speakers mounted just above the rig's couch. I decided to tap into these speakers by using the telephone's earphone attachment. This was easy, as all I had to do was cut the earplug off and then thread the wire up to the input jack of the radio/tape player directly above the television. It was the perfect solution to our predicament.

Now, I can adjust the balance through the radio so that it is louder on my husband's side. We can even cut the sound off completely in the bedroom if one of us is sleeping while the other wants to watch television up front. Most small televisions have an earphone jack, so others should have no trouble completing a similar modification in their own RV.
- *SHIRLEY KINGSLEY, MONTE VISTA, COLORADO*

FLOWER CHILDREN

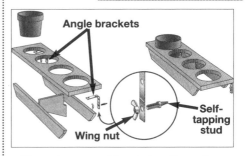

Angle brackets

Wing nut

Self-tapping stud

If you want to keep the "admiral" happy while traveling, consider bringing along a little greenery from home. Of course, this will require a portable window flower box.

All that's needed to construct a light-weight wooden tray are two 1 × 3-inch and one 1 × 8-inch pine boards. Also required are one 6 × 8-inch piece of ¼-inch plywood, two 3 × 3-inch steel angel brackets, two 8-32 bolts and two 10-32 self-tapping studs with wing nuts. Elmer's carpenter's glue helps hold all this together.

Prelocate and cut the flower-pot holes as illustrated. Glue and nail the 1 × 3s to the bottom edge of the 1 × 8. Position and mount the angle brackets so they match the existing attachment screws in one of your rig's windows. Finish by gluing the plywood piece to the middle of the potholder, so it will rest against the RV's side wall. Sand and remove all sharp corners before painting, and then install the two angle brackets.

Potholder attachment studs can be made by removing and replacing two external window-frame screws aboard the RV with 10-32, self-tapping studs. Alternatively, two new holes can be carefully drilled in the metal window frame to accept the studs. Hang the potholder on these studs, and retain the wing nuts. En route, the flower pots travel nicely in the shower stall, and the portable greenery holder fits well in the truck bed or in the underfloor storage area.
- *RUSS WALLWORK, SUMNER, WASHINGTON*

SHOES GALORE

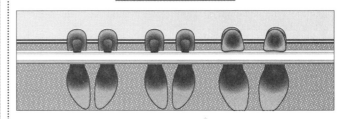

One of the storage problems in our fifth-wheel has always been where to put all the extra pairs of shoes we carry on trips. After some contemplation, we came up with an idea that solved our dilemma instantly. We attached curtain rods to the sides of our lift-up bed. Now, our shoes slip neatly behind the rods where they remain out of sight—covered during the daytime by the bedspread.
- *LEO AND OPAL GREEN, GROVE, OKLAHOMA*

PLATE STOP

Here is a simple way to keep dishes, bowls, and cups in place while traveling down the road. I use flexible doorstops and slip vinyl tubing over the springs for added stiffness, and to prevent marking the items that they secure.

Start by placing your RV dishes in their travel position. Make pilot holes in the appropriate cabinet locations with an ice pick. Then, screw in the doorstop and slip the vinyl cover into place.

Your dining service is now travel-proofed.
- *BOB TREMBLAY, FORT MYERS BEACH, FLORIDA*

MAP SAVER

Are your travel maps a mess from all those routes you've highlighted over the years? If so, here's a way to have the benefit of highlighting without the cluttered look. Fold your map so that your intended route is visible. Then, using household plastic wrap, encase the map tightly. Be sure to overlap the wrap, so it will remain tightly in place. Now you can set about the process of highlighting (with a permanent ink marker) the roads and attractions you intend to see. Wrapped this way, your maps will last longer and be easy to read for a long time to come.
- *M. L. KERCHNER, SAN JOSE, CALIFORNIA*

Plastic-covered map

GUEST RELATIONS

We RVers are an innovative type of people, and here's my way of solving the guest towel problem. A vertical paper towel holder next to the bathroom sink takes the place of cloth guest towels and keeps visitors from using ours. I quickly discovered that this works as well at home as it does in our trailer.
- *PHYLLIS WININGER, STANHOPE, IOWA*

STAIR STEPPIN'

By accident, I "tripped over" a solution for those times when you've finally leveled the coach only to find the step is nowhere near the ground anymore! My husband bought a "Stair-Stepper" to exercise on, which received little or no use. After dusting off the step for several months, I happened to measure the width, only to discover it was just as wide as our outside stairs and perfectly designed to be a portable step. Not only is the Stair-Stepper adjustable in 2-inch increments from 4 to 8 inches, but it is stable, easy to carry, lightweight, inexpensive, and can double as a small table or stool inside the coach, or even for exercising!
- *FLORENCE AND JOE YODER, TIGARD, OREGON*

BED MODS

My wife suffers from back problems and used to have a terrible time lifting the hydraulically assisted mattress platform in the back of our RV.

The first problem was that there wasn't anything for her to grab onto to raise the bed. I installed cabinet door handles to give her added leverage, but despite the twin-counterbalancing hydraulic cylinders, the setup was still too heavy.

I found the upper attachment brackets had three holes for adjustment. The cylinders were installed in the middle hole, so I moved the pivot point to the nearest holes. This increased the leverage a lot, but then the bed platform wouldn't go all the way down.

I drilled a "compromise" hole between the two that I had tried, and it worked perfectly. The bed now raises much easier.

While I was working under the bed, I noticed a considerable amount of oil on the shafts of the hydraulic cylinders. I figured that this could stain stored items that might come in contact with them. I solved this problem by cutting plastic tubes 1 inch longer than the shafts, and then slipping them over the shafts to serve as a guard.

Also, my wife was having difficulty seeing what she needed when the bed was raised, due to insufficient lighting. A couple of old backup lights and a push-button switch that turns the lights on when the bed is raised took care of this.
- *LYLE ALLEN, NEWPORT, OREGON*

VACUUM SUCKS VERMIN

Eureka! I have found it! No, not gold, but the best solution ever for getting rid of pesky insects inside of my RV. I was parked in a rural RV park in Texas near a horse stable. Bless 'em, we all love horses, but they are always accompanied by hordes of winged devils. I was out of insect spray, and had grown tired of smashing tiny bug bodies with my swatter, when my eyes fell upon my RV's central vacuum system. I plugged in the hose, cranked it up, and cornered a herd of blue tail flies in the window, followed by house flies in the john and some sort of flying fiends in the bedroom. In the flick of a mare's tail, all the bugs were gone—sucked into the depths of my trusty Eureka.
- Jay Walley, Lincoln, New Mexico

FORM VS. FUNCTION

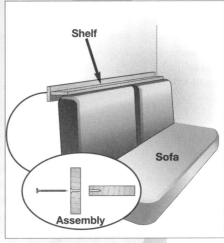

The convertible sofa in our fifth-wheel lacked any sort of convenient table or shelf for coffee, books, pencils, etc. There was also a troublesome 2-inch gap between the wall and sofa back; clearance was needed when the sofa was converted into a bed. Miscellaneous items placed on the sofa back would often disappear into the gap.

I solved both problems by making a simple, removable shelf to cover the gap and provide a resting place for loose items. This was constructed of two 1 × 4-inch boards (cut to sofa length), nailed and glued to form a tee. The piece was then sanded and finished with stain and varnish. I now have a drop-in shelf that fits solidly in the gap when needed and is removed quickly when the sofa bed is used.
- Dale Rockwell, San Jacinto, California

◆ CLOSEUPS ◆ CLOSEUPS ◆ CLOSEUPS ◆

THE NOSE KNOWS

There is a very easy, effective, and inexpensive way to remove offensive odors that accumulate inside an RV through normal usage. Purchase a box of scented fabric softener sheets made for use in a clothes dryer. When your RV is not in use for a few days, spread some of these sheets through the interior of your rig. Place one or two sheets on the sofa, the bed, chairs, and any other fabric covered area, including curtains. I use about six sheets in our 25-foot fifth-wheel trailer.

Leave the RV closed for at least a couple of days—longer if you want. When you are ready to use the vehicle, simply collect and discard the fabric-softener sheets. Then all you have to do is enjoy the fresh, clean scent left behind.

This idea works best in warm-to-hot weather, though it is worthwhile to spread the sheets around anytime that your RV is stored for more than just a couple of days. You can use the same method to freshen the interiors of cars and trucks.
- Robert E. Beaman, Round Rock, Texas

◆ CLOSEUPS ◆ CLOSEUPS ◆ CLOSEUPS ◆

SPACE SHIELDS

I have found that lightweight emergency blankets marketed under the brand name Polarshield work well for protecting RV interiors from solar rays and heat while the rig is in storage. The blankets are made from a thin polyester material that was originally designed for use in space exploration. The substance is about 90 percent reflective.

Cut the material to a size about four inches larger than the window you intend to cover. Use hook-and-loop strips about two inches long on each upper corner to hold the reflective sheeting in place. This method makes it easy to remove and replace the heat shields.

Polarshield emergency blankets are available at stores that sell self-camping equipment. The cost is around $3 for a packaged blanket that will fit in a shirt pocket, but unfolds to 54 × 84 inches.
- Stan Lewis, Fairfield, California

BABY'S BED

When we became new parents, we had no idea where we would put the baby to sleep in our 37-foot trailer. Playpens take up too much room, so my husband modified the closet in the bedroom area, turning it into a crib. This enables us to keep the baby close by and takes up no room at all in our RV. Once our son outgrows this area, we'll just convert it back to a functional closet.

- JANET KOWZIK, MIDDLEBORO, MASSACHUSETTS

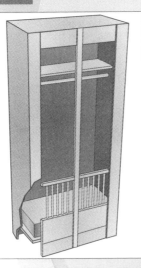

BETTER WATER-FILTER HOLDER

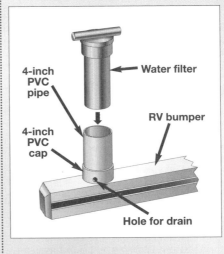

4-inch PVC pipe

Water filter

4-inch PVC cap

RV bumper

Hole for drain

Using a 10-inch piece of 4-inch PVC pipe and one 4-inch PVC cap, you can make a simple-to-use water-filter holder. Secure the cap to the rear bumper of your motorhome with two very short metal screws. Make sure that the screws are as close to the front and the rear walls of the bumper as possible, so they won't snap the sewer hose when it's being stored. Slip the piece of pipe into the cap (you needn't glue it, since it's a snug fit), and insert the filter into the pipe. You may want to drill a small hole in the cap to drain off rainwater. While on the road, simply store the pipe and filter together.

- JACK MEYERS, GEORGETOWN, ILLINOIS

CLOSEUPS ◆ CLOSEUPS ◆ CLOSEUPS

SPIFFY SPOTLIGHT

All you trailer and fifth-wheel owners have seen them atop motorhomes. You probably even felt just a twinge of jealousy at the time. I'm talking about those remote spotlights that are electrically controlled from the driver's position.

Think of the times when such a setup could have helped you find that seemingly hidden campsite late at night, read a dimly lit directional sign or keep you from turning down a dark, narrow, dead-end street.

Well, fret not. There's absolutely nothing to prevent trailer owners from installing a marine-style remote spotlight either on the roof of the tow vehicle or atop a camper shell.

Installation is not difficult, requiring more time than expertise to route the wiring harness from the tow-vehicle cab to the light. All electrical connectors fit together only one way, so about the only potential for heartburn is when you drill the mounting holes in the roof. Careful study beforehand will alleviate most of the stress.

Though I've seen only one such installation (mine), I'm betting that there are other people out there who are able to imagine what it would be like to have 50,000 remote-controlled candlepower at their fingertips. Trust me, it's a nice feeling to be able to look before you leap, especially when you've got yards of trailer in tow.

- RICHARD MATER, SANTA MARIA, CALIFORNIA

CLOSEUPS ◆ CLOSEUPS ◆ CLOSEUPS

SLEEPING SANDWICH

Since our couch doubles as the bed in our RV, we decided to simplify the nightly hassle of making up the bed with a mattress pad, sheets, a blanket, and a cover. We made a sheet and sleeping-bag sandwich.

Start with two sleeping bags that zip together into a double bag, then two full-size flat sheets (make sure they're of a size that will fit inside the bags), and sew the bottom hems to each other. Sew the side seams together about 15 inches to form a pocket. Zip just the bottoms of the bags together and lay them out flat.

The next part is optional, although it will allow you to sleep better. Position the sheet pocket on one sleeping bag and mark three or four spots to attach matching 1-inch hook-and-loop fasteners to the sheet pocket and the bag. This keeps the pocket from sliding out of position. Apply the hook-and-loop material, stick the pocket into position, zip up your bags—and you're ready for bed! Roll up the combination for daytime storage, and strip out the sheet pocket on laundry day.

- PAT STILES, ABILENE, TEXAS

Bed 'Room' Story

After the installation of a sleeper shell (1/4 shell) on my pick-up truck, it struck me just how little of the bed space remained accessible for storage. A

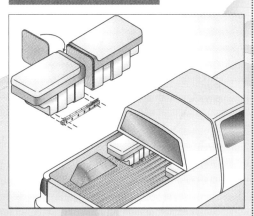

good portion of the available space was occupied by the fifth-wheel hitch.

Considering this shortcoming a challenge, I purchased a plastic crossbed toolbox originally manufactured for mini-trucks. I cut this in half and made two storage boxes by adding 1-inch soft-wood ends.

I installed these longitudinally under the sleeper shell and mounted them on industrial roller slides. The stationary part of the slides was secured with conventional fasteners to the bottom of the pickup bed. The result was two quick-access, lockable utility boxes that hide away under the shell when not needed.

To keep them from rolling fore and aft, I used industrial-duty bungee cords. The cords were attached between U-bolts installed in the sides of the toolboxes and bolts I inserted in the bottom of the truck bed. Any number of more elaborate restraints could be adapted to secure the boxes.

The storage boxes operate very smoothly with weights of up to 120 pounds each. Another bonus is that the space that re-mains between them—at least in a full-size pickup truck—is adequate to accommodate a portable AC generator nicely.

Add a pair of lights inside the boxes, wire them to the truck's cargo-light circuit, and you have convenient, around-the-clock access to your tools and toys.
- *Jim Alexander, Corona, California*

Sun Block

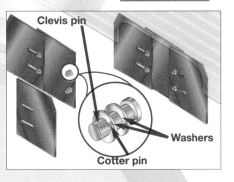

After recently spending more than $400 on a set of tires for my 25-foot travel trailer—having had to repace the old ones because of sun damage—I decided the new tires had to be protected. The old tires failed from severe drying and crack-ing. Well, a quick check at my local RV-supply house to price "store-bought" tire covers sent me away with sticker shock. I decided to make my own.

I first measured the wheel wells of my trailer to determine the critical dimensions. It turned out that a 57 × 28-inch cover would do nicely. I knew that a one-piece sheet of plywood would be difficult to install snugly, so I elected to make the cov-ers adjustable. The finished product readily expands to fit tight-ly within the well, and even remains secure in strong winds.

The accompanying picture illustrates how I approached the project. Including all hardware and paint, the cost was in-significant—under $20.

Though I used ⅜-inch outdoor-grade plywood, I think coat-ed Masonite would work just as well. Choose the kind that's treated on one side. The completed tire cover would already be waterproofed and attractively finished.
- *Philip A. Rowe Jr., Albuquerque, New Mexico*

Flying Glass

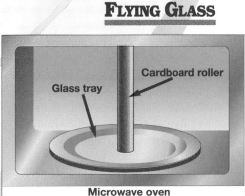

If you're tired of having to either store or heavily pad the re-volving glass tray in your RV's mi-crowave oven prior to travel, try this cheap and easy solution to "tray bounce." Just cut an empty paper-towel cardboard roller to a length that will fit snugly between the top of the microwave and the glass tray. This will wedge the tray safely in place, holding it there while you're en route.
- *Richard F. Legier, Highland, Illinois*

COOL WHEELS

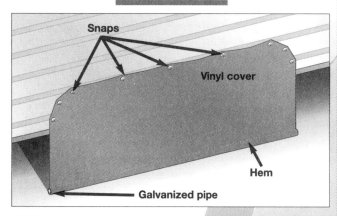

Snaps
Vinyl cover
Hem
Galvanized pipe

Here's my suggestion for an easy-to-make RV tire shade. I used standard upholstery vinyl (Naugahyde), which is available at most fabric stores. I even color-coordinated the material to match my rig. Then, using a household sewing machine, I created a hem at the bottom of each tire shade large enough to accept a length of ½-inch galvanized pipe, which I cut to the same width as the cover. The pipe provides sufficient weight to keep the covers from blowing away in strong winds.

My attachment method uses conventional snaps. The male portions of the snaps are installed around the perimeter of the wheel wells, and the female at matching locations on each cover. The shades are effective, as well as easy to use and store. When you are ready to move on, just unsnap the covers and roll them up on the pipe inserts. You can stow them in any convenient location aboard your rig.

- DEVERE HESS, PLYMOUTH, UTAH

HUMMING ALONG

My wife and I are on our sixth RV. We've found that the converters in all of our rigs have made a humming noise. However, the one in our present motorhome is excessively loud. I took it back to the dealer and complained, but was told that all converters are noisy.

I thought I could put some music with words next to the converter, so it wouldn't have to hum anymore. Realizing that wouldn't work, I tried another idea that did. I mounted the converter on rubber shock mounts, using rubber tubing in two sizes.

The larger-diameter tubing was sized so it would not slip into the mounting holes of the converter, but was long enough to hold the unit off the floor. I used the small tubing inside the larger to keep the mounting screws from touching the metal flange of the converter. The important thing is to prevent metal-to-metal contact that will transmit vibration noises to the RV's floor. I had to use a flat washer on top of the small tubing to prevent the screw head from slipping inside when I tightened it down.

One of my friends has done this to his converter, too. We are both happy with the results. The converters still hum, but they no longer transmit the vibration to the structure of the RV. In fact, my wife asked me if I was sure the converter was still working, since ours can no longer be heard unless we open the door to its compartment.

-CALVIN L. MILLER, CINCINNATI, OHIO

DECAL PRIDE

I read an article about a fellow RVer who did not see enough Good Sam decals displayed on the backs of RVs. I prefer not to stick decals on my rig, but I like to display them. I purchased a ⅛-inch thick piece of Plexiglas, the same width as my license plate and twice as high. I then drilled holes to match the mounting holes of the license plate. After bolting the Plexiglas to the top or bottom of your plate, you can apply your Good Sam and other decals to the Plexiglas. When you sell your RV, you can remove the Plexiglas and install it on the new rig. This leaves the old rig with no unwanted decals and you're ready to display your decals proudly on your new RV.

- ROGER BALDWIN, GREEN BAY, WISCONSIN

DOWN TO A TRICKLE

If you find that the water pressure inside your RV is inexplicably low when the rig is hooked up to city water, it may be that your water regulator is corroded.

Try soaking the device in a mixture of 1 cup of ammonia, ½ cup of white vinegar, ¼ cup of baking soda, and ½ gallon of warm water. Leave the regulator immersed for about an hour before removing it and rinsing it thoroughly.

This should dissolve the mineral buildup and allow the regulator to operate unobstructed once again.

- ROBERT BLUNK, GRAND JUNCTION, COLORADO

SHAKY MEALS

My family and I love our 22-foot travel trailer. However, it has a convertible dinette bunk that is formed by lowering the tabletop between the bench seats—an original design compromise that translated into a teetering dining table. Whenever anyone would lean on one side, the other would rise up unexpectedly.

The solution was both simple and attractive. The first step was to stabilize the fold-down leg where it contacted the floor. This leg had a tendency to wobble unpredictably. To solve this, I fashioned a square block of hardwood to act as a receptacle that holds the leg firmly in place.

Step two was to secure the end of the tabletop where it attached to the trailer wall. Using a ½-inch-wide strip of the same type hardwood, I drilled and countersunk four holes to accommodate the wood screws that now hold it in place. Using a small hand plane, I rounded the corner slightly for aesthetic purposes.

Before attaching either wood piece to the trailer, I sanded and stained both to match the existing woodwork in the rig. Several coats of polyurethane were also brushed on to provide finish protection. Prior to installing the hardwood strip on the wall, I applied strips of stick-on felt to its bottom surface to prevent marring the tabletop. Black-colored wood screws gave the project an attractive, finished look that closely matches the existing interior.

The result is that the tabletop is rock solid. I can now rest my elbows on the edge without fear of tossing something off the other end of the table.

- Luther McIntyre, Louisville, Kentucky

CLOSETS WITH CLASS

When it comes to clothes storage, nothing quite matches pleasingly aromatic cedar for insect protection. Begin by measuring the height and width of all surfaces you wish to cover. Though a fully lined closet might be nice, with cedar it's not necessary to cover every wall. In fact, at a much-reduced cost, the same protection and aroma will be present if you panel only one vertical surface.

You can purchase cedar boards that require planing, gluing, and clamping, or you can select either tongue-and-groove boards or 4 × 8-foot composite sheets made with cedar chips. The latter option only requires cutting the board to the sizes you need.

If you're gluing boards together, consider making them 4 to 6 inches wider than necessary. The resulting excess, after trimming, can be installed in the back of drawers.

Depending upon your RV, you may have to glue or screw ½ ×1-inch wood furring strips to selected closet walls. You attach the cedar panels to these strips using small nails or round-head brass screws. But before you do so, be sure to pre-drill holes in the cedar to prevent it from splitting.

Once in place, the only maintenance required of cedar is a light annual sanding to restore the aroma.

- Kenneth T. Deschler, St. Charles, Missouri

HELPFUL HOSE HANGER

It seems like about the only place that clothes can be hang-dried in an RV is in the shower. This is especially true with personal things such as stockings or hand-washed garments that call for drip-drying. The illustration shows how I tackled this need. The hanger can be constructed at a minimal expense and can be hung from the shower head or rail, allowing the water to drip into the shower basin. Of course, it can be hung outside, as well. We frequently hang ours on one of the rear-view mirror brackets.

- Ralph T. Welch, Roseburg, Oregon

Batter Up!

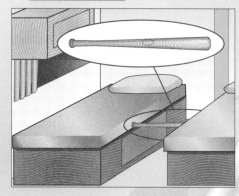

We used to experience trouble keeping the mattresses and bedding in place on the twin beds in our trailer while on the road. They tended to slide off en route.

To fix this, I considered hook-and-loop fasteners. Since we like to turn our mattresses occasionally, this would have created a problem. However, after some additional consideration, I finally hit upon a simple and inexpensive solution.

I measured the distance between the mattresses when they were all made up and ready for travel. Then, from a toy store, I selected a plastic baseball bat, which was just a bit longer than this dimension. Prior to travel, I force the bat between the beds, and they are both held firmly in place. When we stop, I simply toss the bat into the storage area under one of the beds.

- Bob Combs, Dallas, Oregon

Back-Wall Bolster

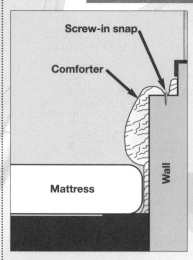

When camping in our older-model RV in areas where the weather is cold, we find that the back wall along the side of our bed is uncomfortably cold, even after my husband inserted some R-11 insulation behind the paneling. At first, we tried draping a blanket over the window sill and tucking it under the mattress. However, after tossing and turning during the night, the tangled blanket soon made us seek another solution. Coincidentally, at the same time we needed a new comforter.

After finding a bedspread that would complement the color scheme of the bedroom, I thought, why not buy another one to use as bunting for the wall? I cut the extra comforter to a length where it would roll over the window sill and extend down far enough to be tucked in under the mattress. We bought some screw-in snaps at an RV-supply store to fasten it in place on the ledge at the bottom of the window. The snaps made it easy to remove the bunting for washing.

From the living room, the bunting gives the appearance of a headboard and the illusion of an ultra-king-size bed, even though our bed actually stretches across the bedroom. The padded comforter bunting was the perfect solution to our problem, and my husband no longer suffers from the dreaded "camper's cold shoulder."

- Anne Rhodes, Woodland, Washington

CLOSEUPS • CLOSEUPS • CLOSEUPS

T U B I N G   I T

The plastic grocery bags you get in the supermarket are very useful in an RV. They're also cheap. Storing them, however, can be a problem.

An easy way to keep these bags handy is to squeeze the air out of them and stuff as many as eight in a cardboard paper-towel tube. I've used this idea for some time now, and have never run out of litter bags.

Another use for these cardboard tubes is for knife storage. Knives should not be put in a drawer with other utensils, as this will dull them quickly.

Flatten the tube first by rubbing it over the edge of a countertop. Small knives can be stored two at a time by folding the tube in half and taping it together.

I was in the sharpening business for 25 years and have used this method for keeping cutlery sharp during much of that time.

- D. A. Morton, Sedalia, Missouri

CLOSEUPS • CLOSEUPS • CLOSEUPS

P O W E R   S L I D E

Many RVs are built with very limited storage space for the electrical hookup cable. Storing the power line, especially on cold mornings, can be very frustrating. Skinned knuckles are common.

One way to minimize the problem is to first wipe the cable clean with a dry cloth and then spray it fairly liberally with silicone lubricant. This makes the cable rather slick so it can be folded away easily. One application of silicone should last as long as several months.

- Elwood A. Rose, Mineola, Texas

JUMPSUIT HANGER

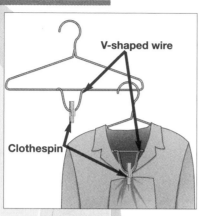

I wear jumpsuits but find them to be way too long to hang properly in my wardrobe closet. To accommodate my jumpsuits, I brazed on a V-shaped additional piece of hanger wire to the bottom center of another hanger. Before I completed the brazing, I threaded a pinch-type clothespin onto the V-shaped wire. The top part of the jumpsuit is draped over the hanger as usual, and the legs are folded up and held in place with the clothespin.

- *Charles B. Horton, Lander, Wyoming*

AND THE TIME IS

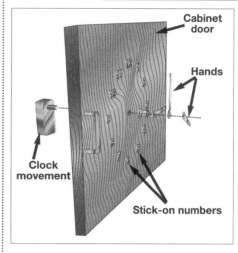

Need a clock? The one I installed in our kitchen looks like it was designed and installed by the factory, but it cost less than $6 and only took about an hour to complete. One of our kitchen cabinet doors is a solid wood panel.

After measuring the thickness of the door panel, I purchased a small, battery-operated clock movement, a package of clock hands styled and sized to match the existing decor, and some sticky-back numbers at the local crafts store. One caution: The threaded shaft on the movement should be about ¼-inch longer than the thickness of the door or panel on which the clock is being installed. This allows for a nut and washer on the front to secure the mechanism. Figure out where on the panel you want the clock, then use a compass to lightly draw a circle for number placement. Drill a hole the correct size to match the shaft on the clockworks. Mount the works on the door from behind, using the washer and nut included with the clock to secure it. Install the hour and minute hands, apply the sticky-back numbers on the line drawn with the compass, and pop in the AA battery that powers the timepiece, and you've got yourself a custom clock!

- *Les Baird, Anchorage, Alaska*

QUICK START

If you RV throughout the year and enjoy campfires, as we do, there likely will be times when you have to light your kindling in damp weather—with damp wood. Some of our fellow campers showed us what they did under these circumstances, and we liked the idea.

We now use a homemade fire-starter comprised of paraffin and sawdust chips. To make your own, put dry sawdust in a flat pan, and stir in some chopped-up paraffin. Using the lowest setting, heat this mixture slowly in the oven for about 30 minutes.

You will have to experiment with the amount of wax needed, as well as the time needed to completely melt it in the pan. We prefer that the sawdust emerge only slightly waxy, once the concoction is cooled. You may want to use more paraffin.

After breaking the large sheet of fire-starter into smaller pieces, we store it in an empty coffee can until needed. The mixture lights very easily and burns hot. This makes it perfect for use in damp conditions.

To purchase quantities of paraffin, check with stores that carry home-canning supplies (grocery, hardware, and hobby stores). A good source for sawdust chips is a pet store that sells bags of wood chips as nesting material for hamsters and other small animals.

- *P. R. McGowan, Redwood City, California*

MIXER FIXER

I was having a frustrating time of it with my battery-powered hand mixer. I've just got to have a yogurt shake in the morning, and when it was chilly my mixer barely spun and the batteries wouldn't stay charged. Just as I was about to throw the whole thing out, my husband, Paul, came up with a great idea. He took one of the beaters out of the mixer to see if it would fit in his portable drill. Not only did it fit, but it works perfectly. Although it only operates one beater, it does the job quickly, and it's very dependable.

- *Kay Shipley, Brandywine, Maryland*

UNDER THE TABLE

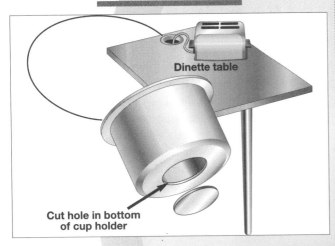

Dinette table

Cut hole in bottom of cup holder

Very often, the nearest 120-volt AC outlet to the dinette area in an RV is found under the table itself. To make it safer and easier to plug in a toaster, a coffeepot, etc., I cut a 3-inch hole in the tabletop to accept a commercially available beverage holder. Next, I drilled a 1½-inch hole in the bottom of the plastic drink receptacle.

This fix gives me a safe and attractive method of routing 120-volt AC portable appliance cords and, of course, doubles nicely as a cup holder. The cost of the project was 69 cents for the beverage receptacle, which I purchased from my local RV-supply shop.

- FRANK FITZGERALD, MIDDLETON, MASSACHUSETTS

GRIT GRABBER

Most of our RVing has been done in the Northwest, where it is not uncommon to encounter wet conditions. I have padlocks on my truck's spare tire and flow-through tailgate, and I often use locks on other accessories exposed to the weather. But the dirt and grime caused from driving in rainy areas used to leave these locks caked with crud, and they were very hard to open.

As an alternative to purchasing weatherproof locks, we now cover all outside padlocks with old tennis balls. I just cut a slit in the ball and slip it over the lock. If a more secure enclosure is desired, small notches can be cut in the ball where the hasp passes through the slit.

Besides keeping the padlock clean, a tennis ball also keeps it from rattling around, or from scratching whatever it rests against. Modified in this fashion, a tennis ball will fit most locks up to approximately 1½ inches in size.

- JERRY DANIELS, BREMERTON, WASHINGTON

◆ CLOSEUPS ◆ CLOSEUPS ◆ CLOSEUPS ◆

SCRATCHING THE SURFACE

*H*ere is an inexpensive method I use to keep my feline friend happy while RVing. Realizing that there is just no room in the family fifth-wheel for an expensive, sisal-wrapped cat scratching post, I decided on a different approach.

Eyeing the 25 × 2½-inch-diameter dinette-table post with that in mind, I purchased 20 yards of sisal rope from the local hardware store. This was wrapped tightly around the table post to form a built-in scratching post. The sisal rope encourages my cat to scratch it—not the RV furniture—a real relief.

This little addition should keep most traveling cats happy for the duration of an RV trip. If at first your cat isn't interested in the wrapped table post, try sprinkling a little powdered catnip on the sisal rope.

- DENISE J. O'GRADY, PRESCOTT, ARIZONA

◆ CLOSEUPS ◆ CLOSEUPS ◆ CLOSEUPS ◆

CLEAR-CUT VISION

*W*henever a new invention hits the market, many folks will ask themselves why they didn't think of it first. This was the reaction of members of our camping club upon seeing my husband's latest upgrade to our trailer. He reasoned that it would be much brighter inside the rig if he removed the factory-installed, opaque, front-window rock shield and replaced it with a piece of clear Plexiglas. This modification not only maintained the protective qualities of the original shield while letting in more light, it added another advantage that we hadn't considered. We now have the convenience of being able to see outside while parked for a few minutes at a highway rest stop.

- ALICE AND ROBERT DEACON, BURLINGTON, NEW JERSEY

SPOUTING OFF

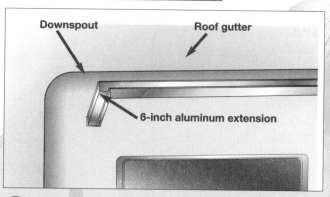

Downspout   Roof gutter

6-inch aluminum extension

Our fifth-wheel trailer has smooth white fiberglass side walls and a drip rail around the rig, close to the roof. It's easy to keep clean, with very few black streaks. The problem is at each end of the drip railing—the downspout only comes out from the side of the trailer about 2 inches. When parked in one place for an extended period, and perhaps when the rig is not perfectly level, rainwater dribbles off the short downspouts and leaves black streaks down the sides. I used aluminum roofing flashing to make a 6-inch extension for each of the four downspouts. They just clip on temporarily and can be removed while traveling. Now the rain from the roof clears the sides of the trailer, and there are fewer black streaks.
- L. PAUL WEBSTER, LYONS, MICHIGAN

CATCHY CATCH

Many RVs use nylon barrel catches to hold interior cabinet doors shut. The catches often break where they are fastened to the cabinet structure.

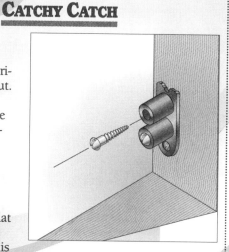

A permanent fix can be made by removing the broken barrel and drilling holes through the flat face. And, since the tubes are hollow, this can sometimes be done without completely removing the catch.

After drilling, use a No. 6 roundhead wood screw (plated or brass) that is ¼-inch longer than the barrel to resecure the catch. This will provide a secure anchor to the wooden cabinetry frame and prevent repeated failure. I have modified all of the catches in my travel trailer as a preventative fix.
- DON MOZYNSKI, REPUBLIC, OHIO

SAFETY

FISHING FOR FLATS

Old fishing rod

The problem: How to know when the vehicle you tow with your motorhome has developed a flat tire before it's too late and damage is done.

I solved this with an old fiberglass fly rod, retired from bass fishing and pressed into fishing for flats. Using plastic ties, I attached an 18-inch, hollow-brass curtain rod to the top holes in my towed car's front license-plate frame. Resting parallel to the bumper, this receptacle remains permanently in place.

Next, I sanded the large end of the fly rod just enough to achieve a snug fit inside the curtain rod, yet loose enough to allow each removal. I used a short bungee cord near the outer edge of the bumper to help hold the pole securely in place.

With the towed car hitched in place, the fishing pole should extend a few inches past the streetside of the motorhome, so the driver can see the tip in the outside rearview mirror.

As might be expected, the end of the fly rod will wiggle some, even when traveling on smooth roads. However, if the towed vehicle gets a flat, the tip will jiggle and jump as though you've just caught the biggest fish in the lake. Tie a bright ribbon to the end to help detect movement.

- EDGAR KINSEL, TOLEDO, OHIO

SHORT STEP

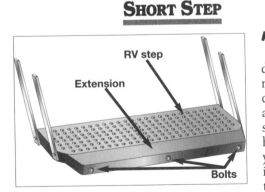

RV step

Extension

Bolts

The extendible door step on many RVs is quite shallow and can present a safety hazard when you're entering or exiting the rig. I overcame this problem and increased the step dimension by bolting a piece of 2 × 2-inch wood to the step flange with ¼-inch bolts. Also, I wanted to improve visibility, so I painted the extension bright yellow and the rest of the step light gray. Finally, I sprinkled some fine grain sand on the wet paint to improve skid resistance.

- ARDELL PETERSON, BELLINGHAM, WASHINGTON

SECURITY CONSCIOUS

Fifth-wheel hitch

After hearing about several trailers being stolen, I decided to make it a little more difficult to steal our fifth-wheel. I purchased one foot of ¼-inch steel chain and then padlocked it in place around the neck of our rig's kingpin. Two complete wraps can be made with the ¼-inch chain. The ⅜-inch chain also works, but only one wrap can be made with a foot of it.

I secured it with a good quality, hardened steel lock that does not have its keys duplicated every three or four locks. The cost of these runs between $5 and $15.

- G. R. WRIGHT, LARAMIE, WYOMING

CLOSEUPS • CLOSEUPS • CLOSEUPS
CLOSEUPS • CLOSEUPS • CLOSEUPS

WORKING IN THE WELL

Setting wooden leveling boards in place, changing an RV tire, checking air pressure, or putting on tire chains can be a real job. Trying to accomplish any of these tasks while juggling a flashlight in near-total darkness can lead to some unprintable language.

An easy solution is to add safe amber running lights in the wheel wells. Boat-trailer lights work well, because they're waterproof.

I installed a set of wheel well lights in my unit more than a year ago, wiring each fixture to a hot wire from the vehicle's parking light circuit. I grounded all of them through a common lead. Because we often leave for a weekend outing after work on Fridays, we usually set up and level after dark. These lights really help.

I've also gotten many compliments from fellow RVers on how nice our rig looks at night. Serendipitously, this modification has also enhanced the side lighting of our rig–making it more visible to other motorists after dark.

- BOB ZIMMER, SCHAUMBURG, ILLINOIS

CURRENT DIRECTIONS

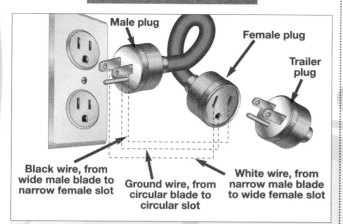

Male plug

Female plug

Trailer plug

Black wire, from wide male blade to narrow female slot

Ground wire, from circular blade to circular slot

White wire, from narrow male blade to wide female slot

I learned that not all campground receptacles are wired correctly, after getting a nasty shock from one of them several years ago. Since then, I have been checking receptacles. I have found 8 to 10 faulty outlets.

However, assuming that you're already parked in an otherwise ideal site, there is a way to safely connect your RV to some mis-wired outlets.

The most common hookup fault that I have found is reversed polarity. This occurs when someone has put the white wire where the black belongs, and vice versa.

When this is the case, I use a "polarity reverser" that I made from a 12-inch piece of three-conductor Romex wire. The wires between the power pins of the plugs on each end are reversed, thus producing the correct polarity inside my RV when needed.

A polarity reverser, such as that suggested, should be plainly marked to avoid inadvertent use under normal hookup conditions. Also, as an alternative to Romex, a weatherproof extension cord of suitable wire size should also work equally well for the purpose described.
- *THOMAS MOORE, ATLANTA, GEORGIA*

SAFE WIRING

The trailer plug that connects to the tow vehicle is very important. When the contacts become dirty, you can experience problems with lighting, battery charging, and brake function. To solve the problem while in camp or in storage, I cover the male connector with a condom (avoid the lubricated type, since the grease can attract dirt). You may substitute a balloon for the condom, although it will not work as well.
- *NANCY MCCORMICK, ATLANTA, GEORGIA*

OUT OF SIGHT, OUT OF MIND

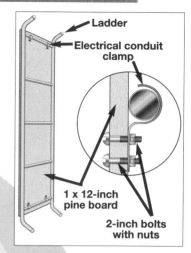

Ladder

Electrical conduit clamp

1 x 12-inch pine board

2-inch bolts with nuts

Many of us are forced to store our RVs under less-than-ideal security conditions. Under these circumstances, you may have found evidence suggesting that strangers have been walking on top of your rig. More often than not, the foreign footprints match children's shoe sizes.

Well, here's a low cost way of deterring unwanted guests from the roof of your RV. Most roof ladders are approximately a foot wide, so a piece of 1 × 12-inch pine is ideal for blocking access to the horizontal rungs.

Cut the wood to match the length of your rig's ladder, and secure it in place with four electrical conduit clamps. Place two clamps at the top and two at the bottom. Use 2-inch bolts with nuts to allow for each installation and removal. If necessary, the conduit clamps can be reshaped to conform to the ladder rung's shape.
- *JIM AND CHERYL ALEXANDER, CORONA, CALIFORNIA*

SPARE-TIRE LOCK-UP

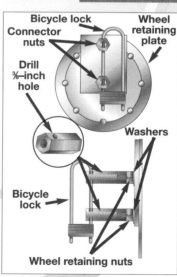

Bicycle lock

Wheel retaining plate

Connector nuts

Drill ⅜-inch hole

Washers

Bicycle lock

Wheel retaining nuts

Not wanting to become a victim of spare-tire theft, I decided to come up with a way to secure my tire without cutting or welding. Locate two connector nuts with the proper threads for the studs used on your mounting plate. Drill one ⅛-inch hole in the end of each connector nut and use them to secure the tire to the mounting plate. Make sure you tighten them with the tire in place before lining up and marking the hole locations. Once they are reinstalled and tight, just slip through and close a long-loop bicycle lock. Good quality locks are available at most hardware stores and especially at bicycle shops.
- *HUGH D. ROTHWEILER, GREAT FALLS, MONTANA*

KEYING THE JACKS

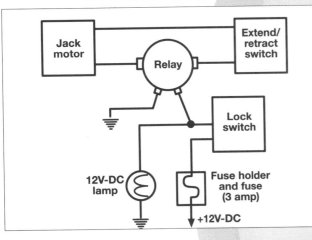

If you own a fifth-wheel, the thought of a mischievous kid playing yo-yo with the electric jack mechanism has probably crossed your mind. However, if this is a concern, the solution is simple. You need only install a key lock switch, relay, and wiring to achieve peace of mind.

The key switch should be conveniently located near the extend/retract toggle for the jacks. A good spot is next to the front access cover. I have included a red warning light to serve as a reminder to turn off the lock switch before retiring inside the rig.

The parts needed for this project are easily acquired from any Radio Shack or Napa auto-parts store. The straightforward placement in the jack circuit is depicted in the accompanying schematic diagram.

Once installed, it's pretty comforting to know that your jack system is safely protected from unpredictable pranksters.
- *Elwin Trump, Wymore, Nebraska*

SHOCK AVOIDANCE

In general, few RV owners think twice about hooking up to a campground's 120-volt AC electrical outlet. Perhaps that's the way it should be, but unfortunately not every campground outlet is wired properly or safely.

Ground and neutral lines may be reversed internally, as may neutral and hot circuits. Such combinations can pose a serious hazard to RV occupants.

But, with the help of an inexpensive plug-in circuit analyzer ($7 to $10 at RV-supply, hardware and electronic stores), it's easy to hook up with confidence. Just insert the device directly into any outlet you intend to use before you connect your RV.

Small neon lights will illuminate in various combinations on the face of the analyzer to identify circuit problems. Simple directions explain how to interpret the results. Be aware that most circuit testers will fit only 15-amp receptacles, so you'll need an adapter to check higher rated 30- and 50-amp sockets.

Though this procedure takes only seconds at each new stop, its value cannot be overemphasized. Initially, after your rig is connected to a (verified) good shore-power source, use the circuit tester inside to make sure all the outlets in the RV are wired correctly. Unless someone later works on the system, you need to perform this test only once.
- *(NO NAME)*

◆ CLOSEUPS ◆ CLOSEUPS ◆ CLOSEUPS ◆

BUBBLES COULD MEAN TROUBLE

I would like to share a technique that I have used for many years to keep tabs on my RV's LP-gas system.

I keep a wide-mouth bottle of children's bubble-blowing solution in my rig, along with a used toothbrush. I use this combination to check tank connections after refilling, and for routine surveys of all lines and connections.

This will detect small leaks better than anything I can mix. Most brands are nontoxic, and in my case, a 4-ounce bottle costing less than $1 lasts up to four years.
- *Wayne Desnoyer, Napa, California*

◆ CLOSEUPS ◆ CLOSEUPS ◆ CLOSEUPS ◆

FOR THE GIRLS

My girlfriends and I frequently camp in my travel trailer without our husbands. To relieve our fears of unwanted intrusion by humans or animals, my hubby devised a unique alarm system.

He installed twin Cadillac horns—purchased from a salvage yard—behind the outside access panel of our rig's refrigerator. He wired these to the 12-volt DC electrical system and a convenient switch inside the trailer.

My friends and I now feel safer, knowing we can alert someone should the need for help arise.
- *Jan Serwinski, Taylor, Pennsylvania*

SPIFFY SITE LIGHT

I was unhappy with the 12-volt DC porch light on my travel trailer. It was blindingly bright, was focused in only one direction, and was very attractive to insects—a circumstance that allowed the little pests to find their way into my rig every time the entry door was opened. Even with this outside light turned on, I would still trip on small stumps or other obstructions when walking around outside the rig at night.

I decided to use the trailer's clearance lights to increase nighttime visibility around camp as an alternative to the porch light, but I needed a simple method of powering these lights without hooking to the tow vehicle's light switch. Upon investigation, I found the positive feed line from the house battery to be readily available near the 12-volt DC fuse panel.

Starting at this point, I wired a 12-volt DC jumper line through an in-line fuse and an on/off toggle switch to the 12-volt DC clearance-light fuse in the panel. After this, I perma-

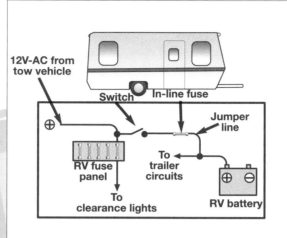

nently mounted the toggle switch and installed a fuse in the in-line holder that matched the rating of the one already in place at the fuse panel. Now, I can switch my trailer's clearance lights on from inside the trailer at any time.

These bulbs provide just enough warm glow light all around the rig to make them a practical alternative to add-on illumination. They also provide a convenient method of identifying the trailer when we return from taking after-dark walks around the campground.

There are some other advantages, as well. My tow vehicle no longer has to be hooked up in order for me to test all of the lights before the next state inspection time rolls around. Moreover, lighting the bulbs more frequently, as I now do, dries out the lens covers and bulb mounts, resulting in less corrosion and fewer lighting failures.
- J. FRED ETTLINE, CHARLESTON, SOUTH CAROLINA

STRING 'EM UP

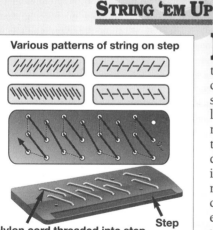

Various patterns of string on step

Nylon cord threaded into step
Step

Here's an idea for a decorative, non-slip, shoe-cleaning RV step surface that I learned from a fireman (he told me this is what the fire department uses on its ladders). Take nylon clothesline cord and sear one end so that it won't unravel. Tie a knot in the other end

and then sear it, too. Thread the cord up through an end hole in your RV step and pull tight. Feed the cord diagonally, no more than two holes at one time, back and forth across the step, pulling it tight as you go. Finish by tying a knot in the loose end, cutting, and searing the knot. A number of patterns can be used, depending on personal choice. You get the benefit of the non-slip surface and you can still close the step flat for travel. Total time for this project: 15 minutes.
- JOAN M. LOITZ, LIVINGSTON, TEXAS

ROVING RUGS

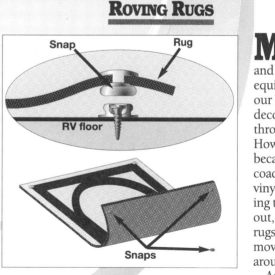

Snap   Rug
RV floor
Snaps

My husband and I have equipped our RV with decorative throw rugs. However, because the coach has vinyl flooring throughout, these rugs used to move around a lot.

As we were installing snaps to add window screening to our motorhome, it occurred to us that a solution to another problem was at hand. My husband added snaps at each corner of our throw rugs to keep them from shifting unpredictably around the rig. Now they stay put, and whenever the rugs need to be washed, they can be quickly unsnapped.
- CAROLYN PETERSON, SALT LAKE CITY, UTAH

PROPANE OVERFILL DANGER

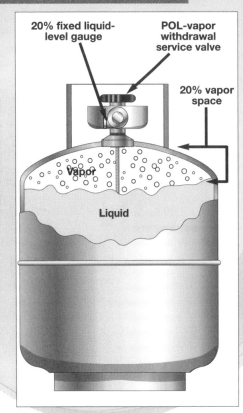

20% fixed liquid-level gauge

POL-vapor withdrawal service valve

20% vapor space

Vapor

Liquid

One of my propane cylinders "popped off" (released gas) one day while my trailer was parked in a campground, and it really got my attention. It seemed very dangerous, in view of all the nearby ignition sources such as the auto-matic-ignition water heater in my trailer and in other close-by RVs.

I didn't have to look far for information, because I had it right in my trailer. *The RV Handbook*, published by TL Enterprises, states that liquid propane expands when ambient temperature rises, and that cylinders and tanks always are designed with a 20 percent vapor space at the top to allow for the expansion.

Prior to the day when the gas release occurred, I had taken both my 7½-gallon cylinders to a local service station for refilling. I did not observe the refilling, but obviously the attendant must have overfilled the cylinders, not leaving enough space for expansion of the propane during the heat of the following day.

When the incident occurred, I heard a sharp sound and than a hissing noise. Apparently, it was gas coming out of the relief valve on one of the tanks. It lasted for only a few seconds. When I went outside, I could smell propane all around. I shut off both cylinder valves and put some distance between me and the rig, while the fumes dissipated.

Gas leakage doesn't automatically create the potential for an explosion, according to the book, which states that the right mixture of gas and air, 2.2 to 9.6 percent, must exist, along with an ignition source.

I don't believe I want to hazard a guess as to whether the mixture is right if I am ever involved in another gas release or leakage situation, and I plan to pay more attention from now on when my propane cylinders are refilled.
- *Raymond Stoddard, Memphis, Tennessee*

SLIDE-OUT STOPPER

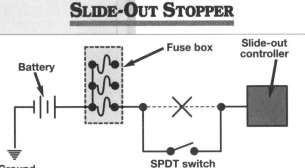

Battery

Fuse box

Slide-out controller

Ground

SPDT switch

Last winter, while staying in an RV park, I experienced a dangerous situation. I was sitting at the dinette table in the slide-out when shore-power flicked. When the power sta-bilized, the slide-out motor was activated and the slide-out was moving in! I jumped up and hit the switch to stop it and reversed it out to the extended position. Figuring the manu-facturer would have a retrofit kit to kill the controller while sit-ting, I called the manufacturer and was told I could pull the fuse if I thought it would happen again, as they had never heard of such a thing. I chose instead to fabricate a switching system. Since I had to make do, the single-pole, double-throw (SPDT) toggle switch is mounted to a piece of angle alu-minum and secured to the battery compartment. I moved the slide-out controller feed wire from the fuse block to one side of the switch, and added an 8 AWG jumper wire from the fuse block to the other side of the switch. That's it. Turn the switch to "On" when you have to move the slide-out, and leave it "Off" at all other times for absolute safety.

List of Materials:

3 inches of 1¼ x 1¼-inch light aluminum angle

1 single pole, double-throw toggle switch, rated at 50A 28 volts DC

1 push-on tab terminal

2 ring-tongue terminals

18 inches of 8 AWG wire

2 #8 × ¾-inch screws
- *Robert L. Chapdelaine, Oswego, New York*

PIPE LOVER

I am constantly finding new things to make out of PVC pipe. Soon after I bought my fifth-wheel trailer, I parked it in the driveway of my home. With concern, I quickly noticed that the hitch-pin box was right at the eye level of children. I also realized that anyone could acciden-

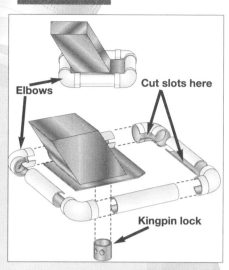

Elbows

Cut slots here

Kingpin lock

tally walk into the sharp-edged hitch and hurt himself, so I constructed a protective molding from 2-inch PVC pipe.

To do this, I used my table saw to cut the slots in the pipe and the adjoining elbows. Then, using PVC cement, I glued all but one end piece in place. This allows for each removal. I finished this piece by drilling holes in the bottom of the guard rails to allow rain and wash-water runoff to drain through.

Now I can slide this device on and off the pin box in an instant, and I feel more comfortable about children playing near the rig when it's parked. While I was at it, I made a kingpin lock out of 3-inch metal pipe with holes cut in it for a padlock.
- *KEN ISHOY, LILBURN, GEORGIA*

UNIVERSAL KEYS

*B*eware! Your rolling home-away-from-home may not be as safe as you think.

After we locked ourselves out of our Starcraft fifth-wheel, we tried frantically to regain entrance. Then, an RV neighbor offered his key.

Since it was getting dark, we gave it a try as a last resort before breaking in. To everyone's amazement, the door opened! We tried our key on another neighbor's trailer and found that it, too, opened.

Our advice is to add a sound dead-bolt to your RV entrance doors before it's too late. Don't take chances with your precious castle on wheels.
- *TRISH ROOS, LA MESA, CALIFORNIA*

HOLD ON

24-inch-long 1-inch steel square tubing

63-inch-long 1-inch steel square tubing

Chair leg protector

51-inch-long 1-inch steel square tubing

3½-inch-long 1-inch steel square tubing spacer

10-inch-long 1-inch steel square tubing

In order to provide a little more stability when entering and exiting my RV, I made a handrail using 1-inch steel tubing, which bolts to the steps. It took about 14 feet of tubing, and the sections were welded together (local shop) after I cut them to size with a hacksaw. The cost for scrap pieces totaled $8; new tubing should cost about $20. The pieces were cut as illustrated. Once the sections were in place, 3½-inch-long spacers (also made from 1-inch tubing) were welded to the handrail and a section of flat iron was welded to each spacer. The spacers provided the necessary clearance for the door to open and close. The handrail is bolted to the steps through the flat iron using two ¼ × 1-inch bolts in each section. A hole is drilled into the bottom class members, so that the handrail can be anchored into the ground (using a tent or awning stake when possible). A chair-leg protector is used in the end of the top railing so clothes or skin are not snagged. The handrail is well-supported by the ground and the bolts used to secure it to the steps.
- *HERB MCCAMISH, PLAINVIEW, TEXAS*

TWINKLE TIME

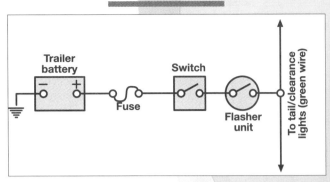

Here's my setup for an add-on electrical circuit that will flash an RV's clearance lights and taillights. This is useful for identifying the rig in an emergency, or just for decorative lighting.

- H. W. Lucy, Baltimore, Maryland

WELL-TREAD HITCH

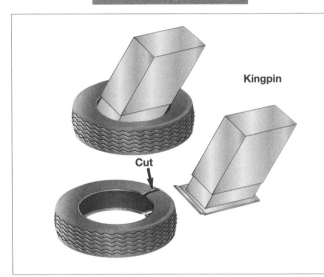

Fifth-wheel kingpins can present a real camping hazard, so I came up with a way to protect myself and others from accidental injury or grease smudges caused by running into the edge of the steel plate. After measuring the plate diagonally, I found a suitable used tire that could be hacksawed to fit as a protective device.

To install, I place the open ends of the tire to the rear of the kingpin plate, and the front of the plate under the front rim of the tire. To position the open ends of the tire on the rear portion of the plate, I only need to rotate the tire in opposite directions. I also installed a spring-type broom clip on the kingpin housing to hold the plug up and out of the weather.

- Keith Nieboer, Holland, Michigan

ONE IF BY LAND, TWO IF BY SEA

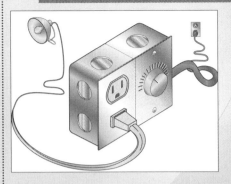

Having retired recently, my wife and I now have time for some cold-weather travel. Leaving our home in the care of a neighbor during freezing weather is simplified with an easy-to-make, and inexpensive, temperature-activated lamp switch. The device turns a light on if the heat fails. This eliminates the need for daily walk-in visits by the neighbors to verify that the furnace is working properly.

I attached a length of household electrical wiring with a plug to a thermostat from an electric baseboard heater. I then wired the output side of the thermostat to a standard outlet and, for safety and convenience, located both in an electrical utility box.

When we leave during the winter, we plug the assembly into a live house outlet and a bright lamp into a thermostat-activated receptacle. I use a clamp-on work lamp with a large metal reflector and face it towards a window easily observed by our neighbors.

With the thermostat-controller temperature set at 45 degrees F and the household thermostat left at 50 degrees F, my neighbors are warned if something has gone wrong with the heating system in our home. Hence, we have no worries about the inside pipes freezing during our winter travels.

The device is easily assembled at a cost of less than $20, and it's as safe as any appliance that operates by a flexible wire. I can say from personal experience that it works.

- Reginald A. Traband, Forest Hill, Maryland

◆ CLOSEUPS ◆ CLOSEUPS ◆ CLOSEUPS ◆

PERMANENT TAILGATE

To prevent the theft of your pickup tailgate, use a piece of perforated ¾-inch steel strapping (plumber's tape) cut to fit over the slot of the hinge-pin receptacle. Wrap the metal completely around the receptacle, so that two or three perforations line up on one side. Secure in place using a standard pop rivet. Most owners should be able to do this job in about a half-hour.

- Claude A. Pare, Umatilla, Florida

AUTO-MOTION

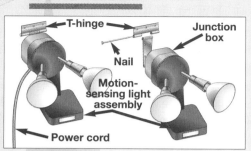

Many times, while parked in a dark campground, I've heard a noise outside my RV. By the time I could turn on a light, nothing was there.

I solved this worrisome problem with a motion-detector floodlight temporarily fastened to the side of my trailer. All I needed for this setup was an inexpensive motion-sensing light assembly (available at most hardware stores), a round plastic electrical junction box, a few feet of outdoor extension cord (12 feet in my case) and a metal T-hinge.

I sealed all the knock-out joints on the junction box except for the one on the bottom. This was used as an entry point for the extension cord. Next, I removed the factory-installed pin from the hinge to separate it into two pieces, and then I attached the long hinge to the back of the junction box (as depicted in the illustration). With this modification complete, I proceeded to wire and secure the light fixture to the junction box, according to the manufacturer's instructions. This project was completed by affixing the smaller hinge portion to a convenient mounting spot on the right side of my trailer.

When parked, I hold the light assembly in place and rejoin the hinge pieces with a nail. This allows me to quickly attach and detach my portable motion-sensing fixture. The extension cord plugs into an outlet in the side of the rig.

My wife and I have been awakened by cats, dogs, deer, raccoons, and people, but now we let them turn on the light so we can see what is causing the commotion.
- *ALLEN H. KOCH, RAPID CITY, SOUTH DAKOTA*

DOUBLE-DUTY STEP

My dog used to catch her claws in the perforated step of my trailer–often painfully. I put an end to the problem by covering the step with a carpeted piece of plywood. Another advantage to the carpeted step is that it helps trap debris from dirty shoes before it can be tracked into the rig.
- *M. R. PELLETIER, SINGLE SPRINGS, CALIFORNIA*

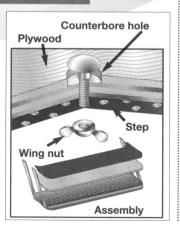

BATTERY COVERAGE

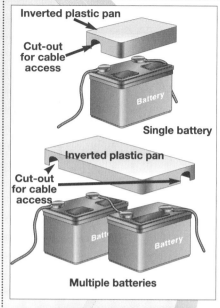

Batteries for motorhomes are mounted in a number of locations, depending on the manufacturer. Hopefully, they are protected from the elements. But when a friend bought a Class A motorhome recently, I was surprised that the batteries were placed between the front grille and radiator. Not wanting to find the terminals caked with ice or snow in the winter, or even saturated with rainwater and dirt while driving in the summer, he purchased two plastic baking pans of the right size to cover his batteries. He used tin snips to cut the needed clearance and access holes and secured them with nylon straps.
- *CLIFFORD LILLO, TORRANCE, CALIFORNIA*

◆ CLOSEUPS ◆ CLOSEUPS ◆ CLOSEUPS ◆

BRIGHTER PATH

During the years we have been RVing, we have worried if someone knocks on the entrance door when we are parked at night. With many rigs, it is virtually impossible to identify visitors just by turning on the outside entrance light. This can be a scary situation when you are stopped in a rest area or a parking lot after dark.

To solve this dilemma, some RVers have installed new light fixtures at great expense. However, we approached the issue by testing various 12-volt DC replacement bulbs. The bulb we found that gives off ample light, as well as fitting into the existing light socket, is a GE 1156 automotive backup light, the same bulb used on most late-model cars. It is readily available at auto-parts outlets for less than a dollar. Our replacement bulb makes it easy to see who's at the door, and it operates cool enough to prevent damaging the factory lens or light fixture.
- *DONALD TRACY, PLYMOUTH, MASSACHUSETTS*

NEVER AGAIN

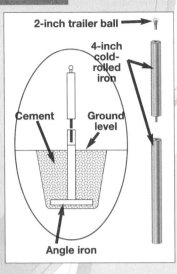

A fter my travel trailer was stolen out of my yard, I needed to make sure my new rig did not suffer the same fate. I began my quest by purchasing a 5-foot section of 4-inch-diameter cold-rolled iron. I took this to a machine shop and had it cut into two lengths, 2 feet and 3 feet. Both ends of each piece were drilled and tapped to accept a 1-inch bolt thread. Using the 2-foot length, I installed a 2-inch trailer ball on one end and a length of 2-inch all-thread in the other. The all-thread was spot-welded in place. Next, I bolted a 2-foot piece of angle iron to one end of the 3-foot section.

With this done, I dug a 2 ×2½-foot hole directly under where the coupler of my trailer is positioned when the rig is stored. I put the 3-foot section of cold-rolled iron into the hole with the angle iron first. Leaving a stub of cold-rolled iron exposed (as illustrated), I then filled the hole with cement.

Now, when I want to secure my new trailer in its parking spot, I screw the 3-foot section into place on the permanent anchor, lower the coupler onto the ball and, using a shielded-shackle lock pad, lock the coupler closed. To keep the 2-foot post from being unscrewed, I had a 3-inch-long piece of heavy-gauge metal welded in place. This will hit the trailer's A-frame, should anyone try to remove it. I know these measures sound a bit extreme, but my old trailer was never found, and my new one cost over $20,000. I don't think that an extra $75 to $100 is too much to spend in order to protect my investment.
- *Larry M. Porras, Los Angeles, California*

WHOSE FAULT IS IT?

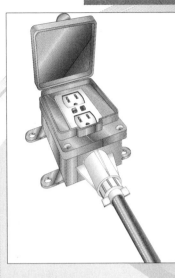

M y RV did not come equipped with a ground fault circuit interrupter (GFCI), and I have always been concerned about dangerous electrical shorts occurring when I am aboard the rig. Then, I hit upon the idea of making an inexpensive, portable GFCI outlet box. I reasoned that such a device would not only be usable with my RV, but also at home as a safe and reliable means of using power tools outdoors, or in basements not equipped with GFCIs.

My portable outlet is constructed of a plastic receptacle body, a plastic sealing cap and 6 feet of 14-gauge power cord with a 15-amp plug. This is a simple project that can be assembled in about an hour for approximately $22. Following are the materials needed:
- One ½-inch FSE plastic outlet box
- One single gang GFCI plastic receptacle cover
- One ¾-inch plastic female adapter (cemented into one end of the outlet box
- One ¾-inch metal stress-relief connector (installed in the female adapter)
- One 3-wire, 15-amp male plug
- One GFCI outlet
- 6 feet of three-conductor 14-gauge stranded wire
- Plastic PVC cement

These materials are readily available at most local hardware and home-center stores.
- *Richard Kendall, North Olmstead, Ohio*

EMERGENCY CONCERNS

D uring a medical emergency in a campground, everyone's RV looks alike to the response teams—especially during a large rally. One way to identify your location is to attach a security strobe light atop the rig's air-conditioner shroud. Once this is accomplished, the needed 12-volt DC wiring can be routed down the rooftop refrigerator vent and then to a lighted rocker switch conveniently located inside the vehicle.

The 100,000-candlepower Zenon strobe unit is available at Radio Shack for under $25 (catalog no. 49-527). When activated, the light will make a rig stand out from the rest. In addition to assisting medical crews, the strobe is also useful during mechanical breakdowns on the road (check local laws regarding legal roadway use of auxiliary lighting), and for security when parked.
- *D. J. Photopulos, Springfield, Missouri*

TWO FOR THE ROAD

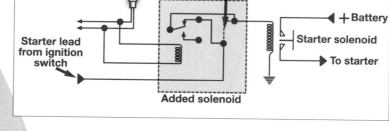

Here are two technical items that should be helpful to RV owners:

1. If the cruise control on your Ford-based motorhome sometimes disengages when you use the turn signals, the following may help. Before going to the expense of removing the steering column switch to look for bad wiring, check the stop/turn-signal bulbs at the rear of the vehicle.

A bad or intermittent bulb filament, poor contacts or a loose ground can cause the cruise control to act as though the brakes have been applied whenever the turn signals are used. To further pin down the source, take note if the problem occurs only when the left or right signal is activated. If in doubt, replace both bulbs, as difficult-to-diagnose, intermittent, internal shorts can occur.

2. If you have hydraulic levelers on your motorhome, you've probably experienced the fear of forgetting to retract them before driving away. Although many of these are supposed to be immune to damage, there is a simple and inexpensive way to ensure that you won't make this mistake.

Note that the hydraulic levelers may be retracted without the engine running, and that the "jacks down" indicator light on the instrument panel goes off when they come up into the travel position. It's a simple matter to connect the coil of a headlight relay (with normally closed contacts) in parallel with the indicator light. With this done, cut the wire to the engine starter solenoid, and connect it to the circuit contacts of the horn relay. (If a satisfactory headlight relay is not available, Radio Shack part no. 275-218 will work nicely.)

After these modifications, turning on the ignition while the jacks are down will energize the relay, open the internal contacts, and prevent the starter motor from cranking the engine.
- GEORGE J. LAURER, WENDELL, NORTH CAROLINA

ALARMING ADVICE

*T*alking with other RVers, I have found that many disable their rigs' smoke alarms because these devices often sound off during cooking. Some have even removed their smoke alarms altogether. This is a major safety concern.

I have found a simple and not very expensive solution (less than $10) to the problem. Just replace the alarm that was installed by the RV manufacturer with a kitchen alarm. This type of detector, which has a setback position that allows reduced sensitivity for a short period of time, is available at most hardware stores.

When the alarm sounds, or if you anticipate that it will, just press the test button and the unit will reduce its sensitivity to smoke and cooking odors. Full protection is automatically reset after a predetermined time period has elapsed.
- ED BURROWS, AGOURA HILLS, CALIFORNIA

HEAD BANGER FLAGS

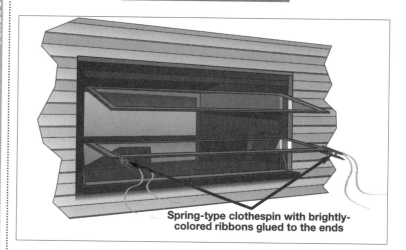

Spring-type clothespin with brightly-colored ribbons glued to the ends

Many shoulders have been gouged and foreheads gashed by unexpected contact with the sharp corners of open jalousie windows. When opened, these windows always seem to be at a lethal level along the sides of RVs. To call attention to these obstructions, I use spring-type clothespins with brightly-colored ribbons glued to the ends. The clothespins are clipped to the windows, calling obvious attention to them and reminding people to use caution when walking close to, or working around, the RV.
- HENRY A. STRONG, HOLYOKE, MASSACHUSETTS

INTRUDER INTERRUPTUS

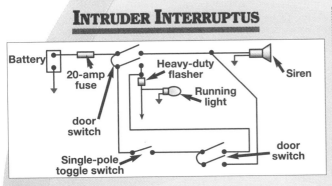

Battery
20-amp fuse
Heavy-duty flasher
Siren
Running light
door switch
Single-pole toggle switch
door switch

For about $20 you can put an alarm system on your rig that will send most would-be intruders scrambling. Mine is wired to work only while I'm inside my unit, but with an extra external switch hidden in an outside storage area or refrigerator compartment and two pushbutton door switches, it would work if your door was opened while you were away . If you sometimes camp in remote, isolated, or unfamiliar areas, the peace of mind is well worth the small cost, and if someone—or some furry thing—is fooling around outside while you're inside, a flip of the switch (best located beside your bed) activates a 120-dB siren and all of the outside running lights on the rig start flashing. The intruder is unlikely to hang around! I purchased my siren (Radio Shack part no. 49-488) for $23, and you can purchase a heavy-duty turn signal flasher, 20-amp in-line fuse, a double-pole, double-throw (DPDT) toggle switch, and wire at most any electronics store. Just follow the diagram and rest prepared. (Editor's note: Don't forget to disconnect the rig's power supply while working on any of the electrical connections.)
- *DALE WRIGHT, METROPOLIS, ILLINOIS*

CLOSEUPS ◆ CLOSEUPS ◆ CLOSEUPS

TOO HOT TO HANDLE

Under the best of circumstances, a hot curling iron with its awkward stand is difficult to rest on a countertop. In the RV bathroom, setting down a curling iron is all but impossible. Don't try, hang it instead.

Start by tying a loose knot in the power cord about 6 inches from the iron. (If your model has a coiled cord, skip this step.) Next, securely position a cup hook high on the wall. These inexpensive hooks are available at almost any variety or drugstore.

Now, plug in the iron and hang it on the loop of knotted cord. Use it as you normally would, but when you park it between curls, simply replace it on the hook. When finished, store the iron and hook together, ready for the next time.
- *RUTH READ CALHOUN, RUSTON, LOUISIANA*

PULLING THE PLUG

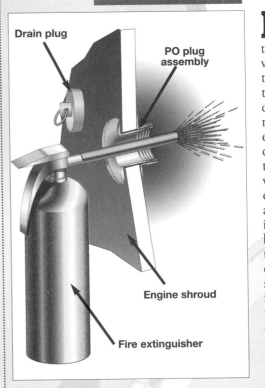

Drain plug
PO plug assembly
Engine shroud
Fire extinguisher

Most motorhome and van fires are traceable to the engine compartment. However, this is a difficult area to access with a fire extinguisher, and attempting to do so by opening the interior engine shroud during a fire risks both occupants and vehicle. Leaping flames and choking smoke can quickly drive you from the rig—a hazardous retreat that will likely result in a total RV loss.

Where fire is involved, no one can be absolutely certain of a favorable outcome. However, I decided to be better prepared for potential disasters by adding a fire-extinguisher port to the back of my motorhome's interior engine shroud. I reasoned that this would allow me to discharge, in relative safety, the contents of my two Halon fire extinguishers into the area where they would be needed most during an engine fire.

To adapt this idea to my motorhome, I first purchased a good quality 1¼-inch PO plug from my local hardware store. (A PO plug is the drain assembly used in the bottom of bathroom wash basins.) I bought a 1¼-inch hole saw at the same time.

To prevent the hole saw from catching and unraveling the carpet on the engine shroud, I heated the bottom end of the PO plug to a red-hot temperature and melted the carpet threads where the hole saw would make contact. With this done, I drilled the 1¼-inch hole through the engine cover and, after cutting off the excess drain pipe, installed the PO plug. The project was finished as I inserted the matching stopper into the "drain" opening on the back of the engine shroud.

Now, should an engine fire erupt, I can probably save the day by pulling the sink stopper from the extinguisher port and then directing flame-stopping Halon gas into the powerplant cavity.
- *GEORGE PONADER, SILVER SPRINGS, FLORIDA*

SOFT HEAD-BANGER

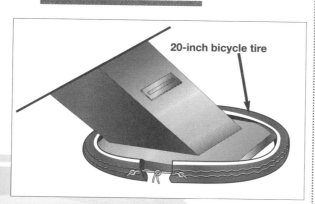

20-inch bicycle tire

After our first trip with our fifth wheel, I was concerned that someone, possibly myself, would be injured walking into the sharp corners of the hitch pin assembly. I discovered that a 20-inch bicycle tire is the perfect size for encircling the entire plate. It's light in weight and easy to handle and store. A new tire costs less than $5 if a discarded tire cannot be found. I cut the tire, drilled a hole near each side of the cut, and inserted a short piece of rope in each hole and tied the ends together to secure the tire to the pin assembly. I spin the tire so the rope is behind the pin assembly when parked. Using a piece of elastic rope would eliminate the need to retie the rope after each installation. Use a little caution when installing the tire; the edge of the tire bead can cut bare hands.

- FRED A. HIGGINS, ROYAL OAK, MICHIGAN

HELP FROM HISTORY

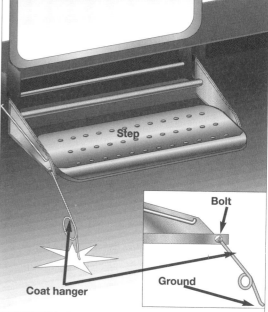

Step

Bolt

Ground

Coat hanger

Have you ever forgotten to retract your RV step before starting down the road? I did once, but fortunately didn't hit anything, or cause the expensive damage that I know is possible.

Using nothing more than a metal coat hanger, a bolt, a nut, and a washer, I came up with a simple and inexpensive way to prevent this potentially serious oversight. Do you remember the curb feelers that were introduced for use on automobiles in the 1950s? My little modification is a design variation of that idea.

Start by cutting and bending the hanger as needed to make sure that it reaches the ground whenever the step is down. Drill a ¼-inch hole in the outer corner of the step, bend a small loop on the end of the wire that will attach to the step, and maybe another in the middle to act as a spring. Secure the device in place using a ¼-inch bolt, nut and lockwasher. It's best to use a brass or stainless steel bolt that won't rust. Finish by making certain that the wire does not extend into foot-path traffic or touch the ground when the step is retracted.

Now, if you ever try to pull away without stowing the RV entry step, your new step feeler will save the day by dragging loudly and distinctly against the pavement to alert you.

If you want to get fancy, a chrome-plated hanger or a standard curb feeler can be used for a custom look.

- RICHARD A. RICHEY, CLINTON, OHIO

AN ALARMING LOOK

*E*njoy the benefits of a built-in alarm system aboard your rig without the cost. Simply construct a nonworking look-alike for less than $5 in parts, and the outside world will think you have an armed security system. This alone is often enough to ward off would-be burglars.

You can accomplish this by installing a flashing light-emitting diode (LED) on the rearview mirror support, dash, console, or other convenient place inside your vehicle. Another suitable location would be near the outside grab handle at the main entrance. Whatever location you pick, remember that visibility from the outside of the vehicle is the key to successful deterrence.

We use Radio Shack catalog nos. 276-036C (LED) and 276-080A (holder). After determining an installation location, we drilled the appropriate-size hole to retain the holder and installed the flashing red LED. Next, the short lead of the LED was connected to a ground circuit and the long lead to a 180-ohm resistor (Radio Shack part no. 271-014). Then, tapping into an always-hot 12-volt DC circuit, we installed a push on/off (SPST) switch (Radio Shack part no. 275-617A) and wired it to the resistor on the LED. Now, with the touch of a button, our RV looks like it is protected by an expensive system.

- JIM AND CHERYL ALEXANDER, CHINO VALLEY, ARIZONA

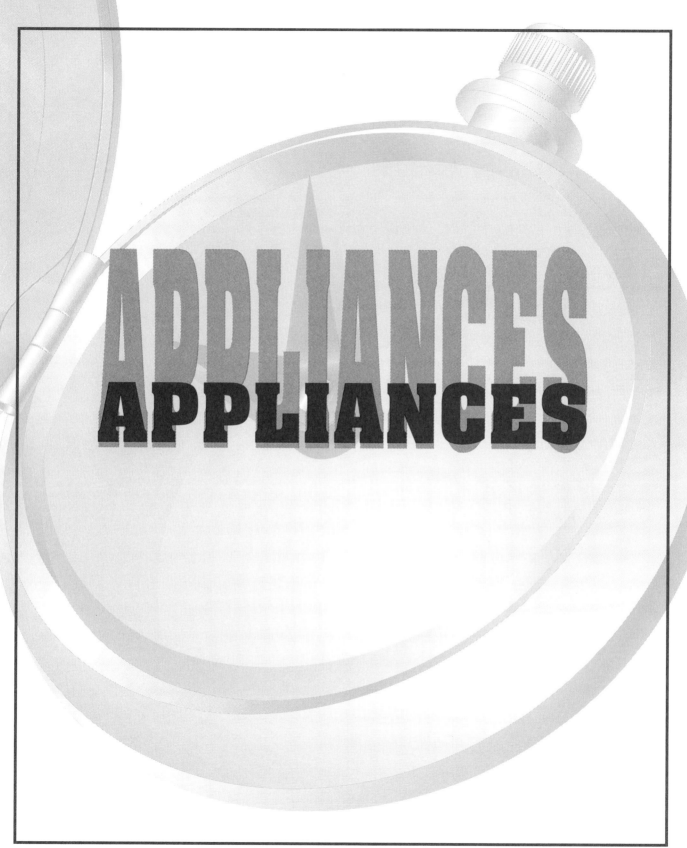

APPLIANCES

Havin' a Ball...Valve

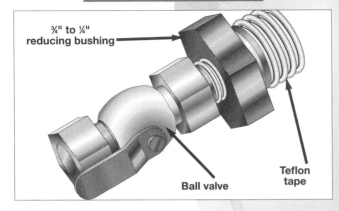

¾" to ¼"
reducing bushing

Ball valve

Teflon tape

Here is my solution to the problem of breaking off the plastic or nylon drain plugs that come in most RV hot-water heaters. I bought a ¾-inch to ¼-inch reducing bushing, a close ¼-inch pipe nipple and a stainless steel ¼-inch ball valve. I assembled them with Teflon tape, and threaded the assembly into the drain plug opening. Now, when I return from a trip, I open the ball valve and the tank drains. When it's empty, I close the ball valve. No more trying to fit an adjustable wrench into an impossible space to make ¼₄ of a turn to activate the old system. The original equipment may have been cheaper, but you only have to repair it a few times before the cost equals out.
- Don Cowles, Royal Oak, Michigan

Little Lock

My fifth-wheel trailer is equipped with a Norcold refrigerator that relies on a magnetic gasket to keep the doors shut. But having experienced an accidental opening during travel, I can say that finding food all over the floor is not a fun occasion. I started looking for a fix for this problem, and finally settled on using a Popular Mechanics-brand swing lock from Wal-Mart. Installing this on the refrigerator doorjamb, I found I could swing the lock closed to secure both doors at the same time. Of course, it unlatches with equal ease when access to the refrigerator is desired. The lock mechanism is brass-plated, looks good, costs less than $2 and took only about 10 minutes to install. Best of all, it works.
- A.O. Parker, Lakeport, California

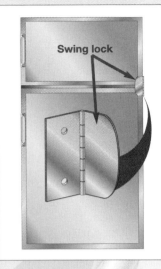

Swing lock

◆ CLOSEUPS ◆ CLOSEUPS ◆ CLOSEUPS ◆

Ready Rheostat

The noisy, high-speed exhaust fans used over RV stovetops can be slowed down and quieted with the installation of a rheostat control. This component, available at most auto-supply stores, may be best be identified to the counter person as the type used for heater switches in older cars.

To install, I cut into the "hot" wire leading to the on/off range-hood switch. At this point, I drilled a hole in the hood for the new rheostat and attached both ends of the cut wire to the switch terminals. If desired, the rheostat could be clamped in the vent hood. Most of these switches also come with clamp-on mounts.

With this modification complete, it's possible to run the kitchen exhaust fan at an infinite number of speeds. Operating it at a lower setting is much quieter and surprisingly, seems to vent the RV as effectively as full speed.
- R. Lyle Luttrell, Washburn, North Dakota

◆ CLOSEUPS ◆ CLOSEUPS ◆ CLOSEUPS ◆

Cooling Breeze

Adding a fan to blow cool air over the outside coils of your RV's refrigerator will help it cope with hot summer temperatures. A very good low-cost fan is sold by Radio Shack for $14.95 (part no. 273-243). This 12-volt DC fan draws about ¹⁄₁₀ the current of an RV light bulb.

Here's how to mount it.

Using small right-angle brackets, mount the fan under the bottom coil, with the airflow arrow pointing up. Be careful not to puncture the refrigerator's inner liner when drilling mounting holes. Connect the fan to a 12-volt DC source, being sure to include a switch for turning it on and off.

For people who mainly operate their automatic-ignition RV refrigerator on gas, the fan can be wired across the gas solenoid valve. This way, cooling air will flow only when the refrigerator needs it.

In both cases, it is very important to observe the correct voltage polarity when connecting the fan in the circuit. Use a voltmeter to determine this.
- Tom Kirkgaard, Pasadena, California

HOT-AIR DESPAIR

Because the performance of my RV's absorption refrigerator degraded in hot weather, I decided to add a forced-air ventilation system to assist in removing heat from the rear-mounted condenser cores. With my purpose clear, the search began for a suitable blower. Remembering a defective microwave oven that was lying around the house, I disassembled the unit and found a small, 120-volt AC, squirrel-cage blower assembly, which was perfect for the job. (Radio Shack has a 3-inch 12-volt DC fan capable of moving 32 cubic feet of air per minute, part no. 273-242, for $17.)

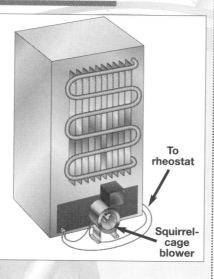

To rheostat

Squirrel-cage blower

This mechanism was installed through the refrigerator's outside access opening, directly beneath the condenser coils. A light-dimming rheostat designed for 120-volt AC use (available in most hardware/electrical stores), was added to control the motor speed because I assumed that a faster speed would be needed in hot weather. Experience, however, has proven that the slowest speed is sufficient to keep the refrigerator working efficiently in all temperature ranges.

In addition to a noticeable improvement in cooling, I anticipate the enhanced ventilation made possible by this system will greatly extend the life of my RV refrigerator.
- COY POSTON, VIVIAN, LOUISIANA

FRESH ICE...CUBED

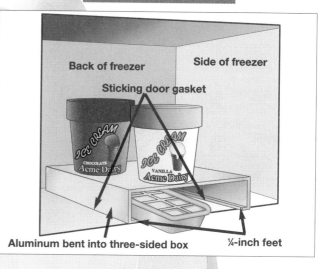

Back of freezer — Side of freezer — Sticking door gasket — Aluminum bent into three-sided box — ¼-inch feet

It seems like none of the trailers we've had offered any provision for making ice cubes. Sure they all had freezers, but there was never any special place set aside for the ice cube trays. If we had food in the freezer, there was never anyplace level for the trays to sit and you can't pile the food on top of them while they solidify.

So I made my own freezer shelf that fits on the bottom of the freezer, allowing enough room for two or three ice cube trays to be stored. This allows for food storage above the trays while giving us a flat area for the trays to freeze. In addition, the cubes freeze faster being at the bottom.

I use a piece of aluminum bent into a three-sided box with a ¼-inch lip folded flat for a reinforced footing. I used a sticking rubber door gasket under the feet and on the back of the shelf to hold the unit in place.
- KENNETH A. LLOYD, ELGIN, ILLINOIS

HEATING HOT WATER?

I've found that if you turn your water heater on only a few minutes before you need it, you won't waste a bunch of energy maintaining the temperature when you don't need it. Most water heaters will heat a tank of water in about 10 minutes, and even then, the tank will retain the heat. You'll still have hot water for a couple of hours, and look at the gas you'll save. That water heater running 24 hours a day is a huge waste.
- CHARLES MAY, DESOTO, TEXAS

FRIDGE ON THE FRITZ

My refrigerator seems to provide erratic service and at this time I would prefer not to invest any money in repairs or replacement. Therefore, I have come up with a method to help with the cooling. Since the freezer works fine and the lower part of the refrigerator does not cool adequately, I use two reusable ice packs (the blue ones commonly used in portable coolers). One is kept in the freezer where it becomes solid and the other one is kept in the refrigerator portion. Each morning, I swap the two.
- EUGENE COWART, LANCASTER, CALIFORNIA

Your RV is packed, and the family is ready to leave on a long-anticipated trip. Worse yet, you might be parked miles from anywhere when the dreaded red light on your automatic ignition refrigerator starts to flash, indicating a loss of power source. You contemplate canceling your RV outing. However, before you do, try this 10-minute remedy. Tools required: a screwdriver and a small brush.

Turn off the refrigerator. Remove the outside access panel and the plate that protects the burner assembly. Look closely to see if a "carbon bridge" has built up between the thermocouple and the electronic ignition tip. This is a common problem with propane-powered refrigerators.

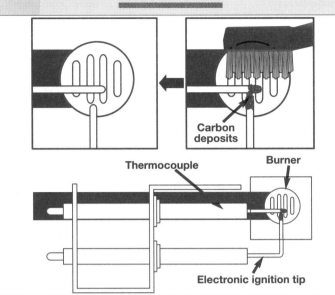

Carbon deposits

Thermocouple

Burner

Electronic ignition tip

If any carbon deposit is present, gently remove it. An old toothbrush is ideal for this purpose; so is a small wooden stick. Do not use any type of metal tool to remove the carbon. This could permanently damage the burner assembly.

After this maintenance has been performed, turn on the refrigerator. The green light on the status panel should illuminate. As a follow-up to this quick fix, have the distance between the thermocouple and igniter tip checked by a qualified technician the next time your rig is at an RV repair center. The spacing is critical, and not something you should try to adjust yourself.

- J.D. MEADE III, NAPA, CALIFORNIA

CLOSEUPS ◆ CLOSEUPS ◆ CLOSEUPS

YO-YO FURNACE

I would like to address a problem that often confronts people who camp in cold weather. The problem is the manner in which the furnace cycles on and off. When it first comes on, it heats the rig up, but usually hotter than desired, before it shuts off. Then the RV gets too cold before the heat cycle starts over again.

Fixing this condition is easy. Just snap off the thermostat cover and locate the anticipator adjustment. It will be either a slide or rotary device calibrated with numbers such as 1.0, .7, .5, .3, or .2. In most of the RVs I have owned, the heat anticipators were set on 1.0. This allows the widest temperature-cycle swing.

Through experimentation, I have found that a mid-range setting of .4 provides a much more comfortable living-area temperature. Once readjusted, the furnace will cycle on more often, but will run less each time.

- TOM BAKER, SYCAMORE, ILLINOIS

CLOSEUPS ◆ CLOSEUPS ◆ CLOSEUPS

CLOSEUPS ◆ CLOSEUPS ◆ CLOSEUPS

WHERE A NORTH WIND BLOWS

During warm weather, I found it difficult to maintain the proper temperature inside my RV refrigerator. The system operated acceptably, but the coils just couldn't dissipate the heat fast enough.

To overcome this problem, I connected a 7-inch portable fan (the kind with a large clothespin-style clip) to a bracket on the backside of the refrigerator. I adjusted it so the airflow was directed upward toward the coils of the fridge.

Whenever I set up in a campground, I turn on the fan and leave it running throughout my stay. Now, when the outside temperature is in the high 90s, the refrigerator stays cold. Even the ice cream in the freezer remains as hard as a brick.

I used a small 120-volt AC fan, which can be purchased at most hardware and discount stores. The fan on my rig is plugged into the same outlet as the refrigerator. A 12-volt DC fan could also be used, but wiring it may be more difficult if a receptacle is not available.

- ADOLPH CECULA, OAKTON, VIRGINIA

CLOSEUPS ◆ CLOSEUPS ◆ CLOSEUPS

SPLATTER SHIELD

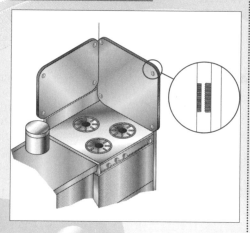

The paneling on two sides of our RV kitchen range was protected only by an ineffective, 3-inch splash back behind the stove. As it was, grease and other stains could easily spot the walls of our rig.

To overcome this, we purchased two sheets of clear acrylic, which we cut with a jigsaw to fit. We notched one piece, so it would fit around the existing splash back. Both sheets were then secured in place with four heavy-duty hook-and-loop fasteners purchased from a fabric store.

To avoid the possibility of mismatching the hook-and-loop fastener tabs, we peeled the paper backing off one side of each set and affixed them to the corners of the acrylic. Leaving the opposing pieces attached, we finished the project by peeling the paper backing and carefully placing our splash shield in position.

- D.J. LANPHAIR, HUMESTON, IOWA

COOKING REFLECTIONS

Chain

Mirror

Anyone using a microwave oven often likes to look through the glass door to check cooking progress or verify that the tray is revolving properly. However, due to the high mounting position of this appliance in my 1992 travel trailer, it is hard for anyone under 6 feet tall to see inside.

To resolve this difficulty, I mounted a small mirror on the ceiling of the trailer, directly above the microwave door. The mirror edge closest to the unit is mounted just above the oven frame, while the opposite edge is angled downward slightly. The lower portion of the mirror frame is supported by a short length of chain attached to hooks installed in both the ceiling and frame. Now, any person over 4 feet tall can clearly view the interior of the microwave to determine cooking status.

- DALE A. STONE, WAUKESHA, WISCONSIN

CLOSEUPS • CLOSEUPS • CLOSEUPS

REEFER QUICK-FIX

My 1987 travel trailer has a Dometic RM 2800 two-door refrigerator. The lower door has always opened and closed with some difficulty; however, it recently began dragging against the bottom of the refrigerator frame. This required lifting the door to open or close it.

I took the door off by removing the screws that secure the hinge stud located between the freezer and refrigerator compartment doors. The freezer door, by the way, will stay closed.

Purchasing a 1/8-inch-thick nylon washer at a hardware store, I installed this piece on the bottom hinge pin at the base of the refrigerator door. I set the door back in place and reinstalled the middle hinge assembly. My refrigerator now opens and closes more smoothly than ever.

- LLOYD NELSON, PORTLAND, OREGON

CLOSEUPS • CLOSEUPS • CLOSEUPS

KNOBBY SOLUTION

Does arthritis in your hands make the operation of your RV stove difficult? It did for my bride of over 30 years, and since I was reluctant to give up on her good cooking (especially the great pies and cookies), a solution just had to be found.

I simply replaced the original stovetop knobs with large, deep-grooved hot- and cold-water faucet knobs. My wife was once again able to obtain a firm grip on these controls.

Depending upon your rig's gas valve-stem configuration, using the knob set screw (perhaps combined with a wedge) will make the job easy. For the oven temperature dial, you can drill a 1-inch hole through the original knob, and epoxy the dial to the stem end of the new knob. Just be sure to line up the dial settings to the new knob position when off.

Now our stove has labels for HOT and COLD, instead of FRONT and REAR—but that just makes RV living more interesting and adventuresome.

- JOHN H. FREELS, COOLIDGE, ARIZONA

'CHANNELING' WITH ALUMINUM

Aluminum foil has many uses beyond the kitchen. For

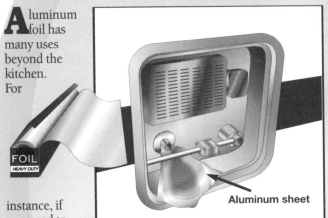

Aluminum sheet

instance, if you need to drain your RV water heater, make up a double layer of foil and tuck it around the outlet. After relieving pressure in the system by turning on a hot-water valve inside the RV, open the drain. The foil will divert escaping water away from the tank insulation, wiring and electronics, as well as the paper instruction sheet glued just inside the water-heater door.

If you think this works well, try using a similar approach the next time you have to change the engine oil and filter on your Ford-460 tow vehicle. First, form several layers of aluminum foil next to the engine block, and under and around the oil filter. Route the foil down and past the cross members of the frame to a drain pan. Punch a hole in the oil filter with a nail, and let it drain before attempting removal. Instead of dripping across the frame and onto the ground, the oil will obediently follow the aluminum channel you've made to the drain pan for recycling.

Another very nice aspect about using these temporary funnels is that cleanup is minimal, and the foil may be recycled with cans and other throwaway aluminum containers.
- *JIM AND RUTH VIREN, TACOMA, WASHINGTON*

BYPASS ACCESS

After adding a bypass kit on the back side of my hot-water tank, located under a side bed, I found it a nuisance to remove the mattress

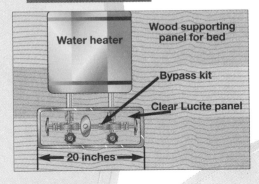

Water heater

Wood supporting panel for bed

Bypass kit

Clear Lucite panel

20 inches

and the supporting wood panel to change the position of the valves. I cut an 8 × 20-inch hole in the supporting wood panel directly over the bypass kit location. Using a router and rabiting bit, I put in a ¼-inch-thick Lucite panel. Now, I can just raise the mattress to check visually for leaks or lift out the Lucite panel to turn valves. This same access panel can be used in any location, especially where the supporting wood has been screwed in place.
- *OWEN C. SMITH JR., BALTIMORE, MARYLAND*

• CLOSEUPS • CLOSEUPS • CLOSEUPS •

SLIPPERY SLIDERS

To assure the smooth operation of our RV toilet's sliding valve, as well as the holding tank valves and connections, I spray each with WD-40 lubricant, working them a time or two while spraying. I've been doing this for years now, and have never replaced seals since I started the practice.
- *R.L. THOMPSON, CARTHAGE, MISSOURI*

• CLOSEUPS • CLOSEUPS • CLOSEUPS • CLOSEUPS • CLOSEUPS • CLOSEUPS •

KEEPING TABS ON FOOD TEMP

To monitor the temperature, so I can adjust the thermostat of the refrigerator when needed, I have installed a Radio Shack electronic thermometer with alarm. The device (part no. 63-1011) has a waterproof probe that is mounted inside the refrigerator. The read-out displays the current temperature as well as the highs and lows. In addition, an alarm will sound if the temperature goes above or below the set range. This is especially important if you have been away from your rig for a while and the refrigerator quit cooling for a period of time due to power problems. If you note that the temperature went too high at any time, you can discard food that may no longer be safe to eat. The unit uses a AA battery.
- *WALTER W. BREMER, SELDEN, NEW YORK*

SHELF DEFENSE

After two years of high-mileage RVing, I noticed corrosion on the steel shelves in my RV refrigerator. On closer inspection, I found that the shelf plating had worn through where it was contacted by glass and metal containers. Additionally, black marks had developed under the aluminum beverage cans typically stored on the door insets. This required constant cleaning.

To remedy this irritation, I first cleaned the corrosion from the steel shelves, and then applied a fast-drying nontoxic protective coating to stop any further rusting. I then obtained a sheet of No. 5 (⅛-inch) mesh perforated plastic canvas (used for needlepoint and cross-stitch) from my local fabric and craft store. This material is available in 13-¼ × 22-inch sheets that sell for approximately $1 each. The material, which is easily cut with a pair of scissors to fit the refrigerator's individual steel and door shelves, protects these surfaces from contact-induced wear. The shelves are easily removed for cleaning when necessary.

I have used this plastic liner in my Dometic refrigerator for over two years, and can report that shelf wear has been eliminated. The interior also stays much cleaner. I have not detected any decrease in the refrigerator's ability to cool, nor have any of my friends who have also incorporated this fix into their respective RVs.

- ROBERT L. SOLVASON, SILVERTON, OREGON

HOT STUFF

Since we winter in Ohio, we subject our 40-foot fifth-wheel trailer to some real climatic tests. I recently discovered that the flexible heat duct that's connected to the furnace had been damaged by the super-heated air produced by this appliance.

Attachment of the duct to the furnace plenum had been accomplished by using a plastic wrap tie. It had shrunk from exposure to heat and slipped off, taking the duct with it. This allowed a considerable amount of hot air to recirculate through the furnace, causing the high-temperature limit switch to cycle on and off.

To resolve this problem, I installed three 90-degree aluminum elbows that are commonly used for dryer vents. I used a small sheet-metal screw to secure the 4-inch tube to the furnace plenum outlet. (Some modification to the aluminum ducting may be necessary, so be prepared to trim as required.)

I believe the increased inside dimension of the metal elbow, along with its smooth finish, has significantly increased heated airflow to the remote vents located throughout the trailer. It will also prevent a reoccurrence of the ducting failure I originally experienced. Total cost in my case was less than $10.

- JERRY WEYGANDT, WADSWORTH, OHIO

MAINTENANCE

MAINTENANCE

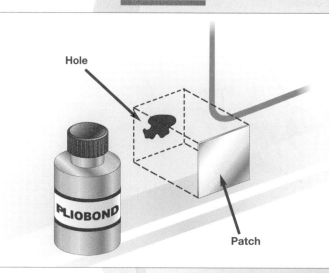

Hole

PLIOBOND

Patch

Minor accidents in which the skin of a trailer is dented or punctured can happen to even the most careful RV owner. However, this type of damage can often be repaired successfully by an owner—foregoing expensive professional mending. Unfortunately, many RVers are deterred from attempting such repairs, either because of inexperience or lack of proper tools. It comes as a surprise to many that neither of these perceived necessities is required in most cases. However, I must point out that my exterior-skin-repair suggestion lends itself only to rigs that have smooth outer walls. It will not work on models finished with corrugated or textured surfaces.

Improvements in adhesives over the past 20 years have made it possibly to stick virtually anything to anything. Taking advantage of these advances can help even the least handy RVer patch a damaged coach. All that is needed is a stout pair of scissors, a roll of aluminum flashing from the local hardware store, and a small container of Pliobond contact adhesive.

Initiate the skin repair by verifying that damage is truly only skin-deep, not structural. Then remove loose or distorted skin to make way for a smooth overlay of aluminum. Cut the flashing to cover the surface damage, allowing sufficient overlap for secure bonding. Next, apply the patch to the intended repair area and mark its final position with a pencil. This will allow you to properly index the piece after the adhesive has been applied.

Follow the instructions on the Pliobond container, taking special care to clean the patch and the adjoining area to be overlaid with a good degreasing solvent. Dirt and grease will prevent reliable adhesion. Once the glue has set both on the patch and around the damaged area (about 15 minutes), carefully position the patch into place, using the pencil outline as a guide. Let only one end touch at first, slowly pressing the rest of the aluminum into position. Take your time. You only get one chance. Burnish rough edges as required.

If you haven't previously used contact cements, I suggest you practice with a couple of scrap aluminum pieces before proceeding with the final repair of your RV. Once the actual patch is in place, it will take several hours before the Pliobond sets up to full strength. However, good adhesion will be in evidence within one or two hours. Let it stand overnight before attempting to spray-paint the patch to match the rest of your rig. Use several light coats sprayed 5 or 10 minutes apart instead of relying on one heavy application of paint. This will prevent, or at least minimize, unsightly runs.

By the way, proper colors can often be purchased from the respective RV manufacturer or dealer. But, failing this, many hardware stores can now match RV colors, using a computer identification process. You'll need to take in a matching piece, such as a storage compartment door, to help them get it right.
- *FREDERICK G. YOUNG, P. E. MISHICOT, WISCONSIN*

WILD COMPASS NEEDLE

Ever wonder if all your trailer brake magnets are working? You can move the vehicle forward slowly and activate the brake controller, but it's still possible that all the magnets may not be working. A simple method for checking magnet function is to use a common magnetic compass and solicit the help of a second person. While your helper holds the compass about 3 inches below the wheel hub—close enough to the rim without touching it—activate the brake controller. If the compass needle dances wildly, then the magnet is working. Proceed to the next wheel. Make sure the compass needle has settled down before making the test. If any magnet fails to move the needle, have the brakes checked by a qualified RV technician. It's still necessary to have your brakes checked once a year or every 12,000 miles. The magnets may be working, but the other components may be worn or defective.
- *DEUEL C. MCELREATH JR., THOMASVILLE, GEORGIA*

CHEAP FIX

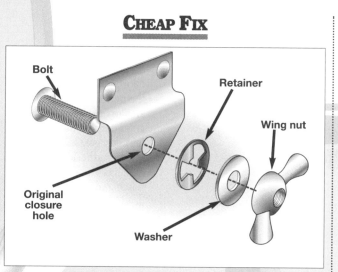

Bolt

Retainer

Wing nut

Original closure hole

Washer

Recently the closure on the door of my RV's water heater broke off in my hand. There was no way to keep the door closed once this happened, so I put my ingenuity to work and fixed it. I slid a ³⁄₁₈ × ³⁄₄-inch bolt through the old closure hole and held it in place with a ³⁄₁₆-inch push-on retainer.

Closing the heater door, I then slipped a ³⁄₁₆-inch flat washer over the bolt and installed a ³⁄₁₆-inch wing nut to hold the door shut. I had to enlarge the existing hold to accommodate the bolt with a few strokes of a small round file—but only very slightly. The fix is simple, effective and economical; total cost was a mere $1.06.

- FRED L. TIMM, MILWAUKEE, WISCONSIN

ONCE AND FOR ALL

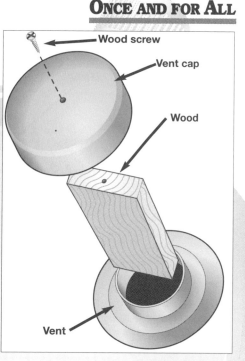

Wood screw

Vent cap

Wood

Vent

I grew tired of replacing the plastic caps that cover the vent exits on the roof of my RV. These are easily brushed off by low-hanging tree branches. To permanently secure these caps, I snapped them off their vent tubes and inserted a length of wood into the opening.

I took care to make sure that the selected piece was not so large that it blocked venting action of the tubes.

The wood should be inserted about 8 to 10 inches into each outlet and must produce a snug fit. Drill a small hole in the center of each vent cap, and secure to the wood inserts with a brass screw. No more lost vent caps!

- HENRY J. CORMIER, CLAREMONT, NEW HAMPSHIRE

A SLIGHT FLAW

*H*aving recently bought a nice used travel trailer, I found only one significant flaw—a tear through the skin on the rig's entry door. The damage was superficial and did not require complete replacement of the door or hardware. After considerable effort, I still had not found a source for the new skin.

Then I came up with an idea that turned out to be ideal. I bought a piece of aluminum from a patio enclosure dealer. It had a nice grain that closely matched the original door skin and was easy to install.

For the reasonable cost of $30, I now have a door that looks brand-new. If others have similar damage on their aluminum-skinned RVs, I suggest a visit to the local patio-supply dealer. They are located virtually everywhere.

- RICHARD G. WALKER, RAVENNA TOWNSHIP, OHIO

LUGGING DRAIN PLUG

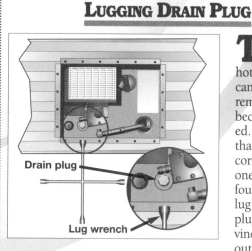

Drain plug

Lug wrench

The drain plug in a hot-water tank can be difficult to remove if it has become corroded. I discovered that, by using the correct size of one end of my four-star wheel lug wrench, the plug can be convinced to come out with moderate effort. The wrench makes the plug easy to reach and provides plenty of leverage. And the best part: the wrench is always with the RV.

- NOEL RALSTON, CLEAR SPRING, MARYLAND

WEAR REPAIR

My wife and I have been full-timing for over two years in a fifth-wheel trailer. Obviously the entry door gets a lot of use. This caused the screen door to wear and begin dragging on the bottom of the door frame.

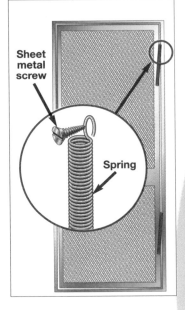

Upon inspection, I discovered that the hinge had worn badly, allowing the door to drop from its original position. After considering several possible repairs, I purchased two springs that are approximately 7 inches long by ¼ inch in diameter. These springs can be obtained at most hardware stores at minimal cost.

Then, using ½-inch-long No. 8 sheet-metal screws, I attached the end of one spring to the door frame about 24 inches down from the top. I installed the other spring similarly, but 24 inches up from the bottom. I stretched the springs about 2 inches, and then screwed them to the screen-door frame (as illustrated).

In the process of making this repair, I found it necessary to be certain that the spring-retaining screws did not inhibit the normal closing of the main and screen doors. The screws must be spaced so that there is no interference.

These new springs have relieved all the downward pressure on the screen door, so it now opens and closes quite freely. A side benefit of this modification is that it will prevent further wear on the hinge.

- WILLIAM WOODARD, SAN ANGELO, TEXAS

PART-TIME LIGHT

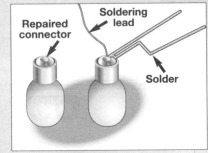

Do your RV's 12-volt DC bulbs flicker and fail from time to time? Do you have to hit your flashlight once in a while to get it to illuminate? I had just such problems with the lights in my 31-foot trailer. Upon investigation, I determined that the soft lead center tip connection of these bulbs flattened under the pressure from the socket contact spring. Unreliable lighting is the result when this occurs. When I encounter the situation, I correct it by removing the offending bulb and placing it into a suitable holder with the terminal facing upward.

Using a low-wattage soldering iron (with the tip properly tinned), I heat the flattened connector sufficiently to flow on a little rosin-core solder. (Suggestion: Verify that the light tests good before going to all this trouble.) Be careful not to overheat the terminal during this procedure or to let the new solder form a bridge between the center connection and the bulb case. Once this is done, I use a fine-toothed file to round the built-up terminal to a profile near that of a new bulb. This fix works on virtually all 12-volt DC and flashlight bulbs.

- HOMER E. PARKER, BIRMINGHAM, ALABAMA

◆ CLOSEUPS ◆ CLOSEUPS ◆ CLOSEUPS ◆

TRICKY TROU-BLESHOOTING

Many times, the 120-volt AC GFCI (Ground Fault Circuit Interrupter) receptacle found in newer RVs will trip for unexplained reasons.

Though hard to find, one of the most common causes is moisture buildup within exterior-mounted electrical receptacles. A second contributor to circuit malfunctions can be excessive moisture in the rig's bathroom—a condition that can adversely affect the GFCI outlet in this area.

Caution: Disconnect AC electrical power from the RV prior to performing this maintenance.

The solution to both problems is to spray the receptacles with an ignition-wire-drying spray. There are several such moisture inhibitors on the market, available at auto-supply stores. When using, be sure to direct the spray so that all of the receptacles' interior parts are coated.

- VINCENT G. KOROLL, WINSTON-SALEM, NORTH CAROLINA

◆ CLOSEUPS ◆ CLOSEUPS ◆ CLOSEUPS ◆

SMOOTHING STICKY STEPS

A small build up of rust and road debris is all that is needed to make the entry step sticky and difficult to open and retract. A simple way to clean them is to use a wire brush (a hand brush or more that attaches to a drill motor) and clean the truck and pin. Wax the track with a bar of paraffin wax. Dirt won't stick to the wax and it works like grease. A candle can also be used if you have trouble locating paraffin wax.

- NORBERT A. GALECKE, ANTIGO, WISCONSIN

BEAUTY ON A BUDGET

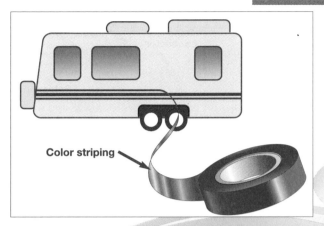

Color striping

On a recent tour with our new 25-foot travel trailer, my family decided that our truck and trailer should have cosmetically matching colors. A visit to an auto paint shop proved that this route was too costly. I then visited an auto-paint-supply house and discovered an economical method of matching up the two vehicles.

For $33, I bought 150 feet of 1-inch, solid-metallic burgundy striping that matches the color of our truck. This is the same striping that car and van customizers use to dress up their special paint jobs. It comes in a vast array of colors and widths.

To successfully apply this material, the surface of the tow vehicle and the trailer must be cleaned of all dirt and wax. I used the recommended cleaner to assure that no residue remained. Next, I lightly marked the length of the trailer with a pencil, so the finished trim line would be level.

Installation is simplified by the easy-peel paper backing that protects the adhesive from contamination until final application. I carefully installed the accenting tape both above and below the waist-high color band that already encircled the rig. The finished job looks great.

As of this writing, the tape is holding as advertised, and the color match is close enough to look like it's a custom paint scheme. This was a cost-effective solution that required little time and effort.
- *MORRIS J. FRUITMAN, VACAVILLE, CALIFORNIA*

BUILDING A NEW DOOR

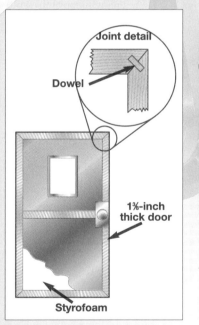

Joint detail

Dowel

1⅜-inch thick door

Styrofoam

A few months after purchasing a used trailer, I discovered the inside of the entrance door was full of dry-rot. Apparently, water had been seeping into the door from around the glass pane mounted in the top section. After receiving estimates ranging from $250 for repairing my door to more than $450 to replace it, I decided to take it apart and repair it myself.

The door was constructed of a 1⅜-inch-thick wooden frame and paper honeycomb sandwiched between two thin aluminum sheets. Dry-rot affected the lower part of the frame and most of the honeycomb material. I had a local woodworker rip and plane a piece of dry 2 × 4-inch wood to 1⅜ inches, and built a new frame using dowels and glue. Finding 1⅜-inch-thick honeycomb material was impossible, so I purchased a sheet of 1½-inch-thick Styrofoam at a home center, laid it on the ground and positioned a sheet of plywood on top of it. I walked heavily on the plywood, compressing the foam to the required thickness. I then cut the foam as required and secured it in place with water-resistant spray glue. The whole assembly was bolted back together and reinstalled on the trailer. The glass pane was carefully caulked with silicone sealer. My total cost was approximately $20, and now I have a door that is more rigid and better insulated.
- *RAUL M. BIASCOECHEA, LONG BEACH, CALIFORNIA*

DRAWING A BEAD

*O*ur travel trailer is 11 years old, and we've used it extensively in all kinds of weather. We have awnings all around and use them frequently, but over the years our awnings have gotten a few small tears and holes due to chafing, and the typical raw-edge bindings that have broken or come loose. My wife suggested I use her hot glue gun from her hobby supplies kit to see if it would mend the awning material, and it works just fine! Now, if I see any holes, small tears, or binding problems starting, I just get out the glue gun. A small bit of glue usually fixes the problem before it becomes a major repair. Care should be taken to keep the hot tip of the glue gun from actually touching the vinyl awning, as it may melt some materials on contact.
- *BILL SHULTS, DENTON, TEXAS*

SAGGING CEILING

If you own an older RV with a roof-mounted air conditioner (AC), your vehicle is probably experiencing some roof sag, caused by the weight of the AC unit. This situation allows rainwater to collect and stand around the base of the unit. In my case, water would leak into the trailer after it was taken off the leveling jacks and moved. Because this also happened during periods of extended storage, the trapped water eventually rusted holes in the roof and resulted in an expensive repair bill.

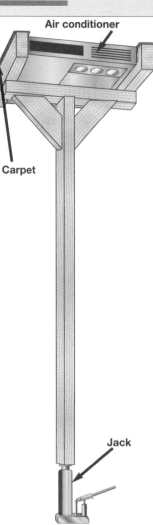

Air conditioner

Carpet

Jack

I reasoned that this could be avoided in the future by building a roof support to be used while the RV was in storage. This device, which cost less than $5 to build, can be installed or removed in about a minute. Interestingly, after 10 months of using this support, I have found that the RV's roof structure has almost returned to normal and now allows normal drainage when I'm using the rig.

To build the AC support, I used two 8-foot pieces of 2 × 4-inch housing stud, a 12 × 24-inch piece of carpet, and an old automobile jack purchased from the junkyard. I cut one stud into three 2-foot lengths and two 1-foot lengths. Next, I shortened the second stud to 62 inches for use as the vertical upright portion of the support. The three 2-foot pieces should be fabricated to fit around your particular AC, and then nailed to the vertical post. The carpet should be nailed or glued to this part of the project, and the remaining 1-foot stud sections used to brace the vertical/horizontal connection. These may be tapered at 45 degrees for better support.

When installing this device, I place it under the two ceiling joists that the AC is resting upon, position the jack, and crank it up until I feel the roof is fully supported. This is a simple project that will add years to the life of your RV.
- Daniel Verzqyvelt, Gulfport, Mississippi

MUSTY MANOR

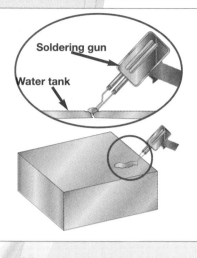

Soldering gun

Water tank

My wife and I own a 1989 Bounder 27D, which we use every weekend. It is our mobile motel, and we depend completely on the rig's standalone capability.

Several months ago, our freshwater tank developed a leak. The problem turned out to be a crack in the forward area of the tank. I tried several conventional patch kits, but each time the material would not adhere to the plastic walls, and the leak would start up again.

In frustration, I finally removed the tank completely for a more permanent fix. I found the tank to be so flexible that, regardless of patching material, the displacement caused by filling the tank would just lift off the repair.

I decided the solution was plastic welding. By running a soldering gun with a smoothing tip (Weller Universal with 6160 tip), I was able to melt plastic tank material from both sides of the crack into the defective area—eventually closing the seam completely. Once the tank was removed, the entire repair took about 10 minutes.
- Donald P. Benford, Pensacola, Florida

◆ CLOSEUPS ◆ CLOSEUPS ◆ CLOSEUPS ◆

A STONE'S SCRUB

*H*aving trouble keeping the raised white letters on your tires clean and new-looking? Here's a simple solution: The next time you are out camping and you are near a stream, pick up a palm-size smooth rock (the smoother the better). When you wash the rig, soap up the tire sidewalls and rub down the white letters (or stripes) with the smooth rock. Rinse when you are finished. The tires will be as clean as brand new. If you need a little stronger cleaner—as I do—squirt the sidewalls with Simple Green or a similar product and use a stiff brush before using the rock. The better the rock fits in your hand, the easier the job.
- Fred Dawn, Kent, Washington

◆ CLOSEUPS ◆ CLOSEUPS ◆ CLOSEUPS ◆

TRUSTING THE FLAKES

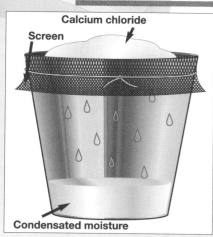

Calcium chloride

Screen

Condensated moisture

Interior moisture buildup can be a problem whenever an RV is in extended storage—summer or winter. Here is an idea that I have used successfully for many years. It does a very good job of removing moisture, and keeps a rig from smelling musty.

I use one ½-gallon and two 1-gallon plastic pails to set up my moisture trap. Next, I use plastic window screens to cover the tops of these buckets, leaving enough material hanging over the top to fold down and secure with either wire or string.

With this done, I pile calcium chloride flakes (available at farm, feed, or garden stores) on top of the screens of each bucket. Then I put the two 1-gallon pails inside my trailer and the ½-gallon one in the large storage compartment.

Used in this manner, the calcium chloride flakes absorb moisture from the surrounding air, and deposit it as liquid into the pails. When the flakes are gone, I just dump out the liquid and deposit more flakes atop the bucket screens.
- DWIGHT BEACHLER, MEDINA, OHIO

REALLY BUGGED

When I broke my travel trailer out of storage last spring, I was chagrined to find that the manual water-heater pilot would not light. Somewhat inconveniently, my family and I spent an entire week heating water on the stove. Upon investigating the malady after returning home, I found the pilot-light orifice plugged by insects. When relating this annoying experience to a casual acquaintance, I was advised he has an inexpensive, foolproof way of keeping nesting bugs and spiders from inhabiting his RV. A couple times a year, and especially before battening down for the winter, he purchases a box of pest strips and cuts each into smaller segments. These pieces, he says, were distributed in storage compartments, under couches, and other areas where critters might crawl in for the duration.

Having tried this simple procedure, I'm pleased to report that it works. I've had no more problems with our insect brethren. Of course, to ensure safe use of this product, be sure to read the precautionary statement on the back of the package beforehand. Effective life of the strips is reported to be approximately four months.
- CHUCK CAMPBELL, THOUSAND OAKS, CALIFORNIA

QUICK (AND CHEAP) SCREEN REPAIR

Small tears or holes in a window screen will certainly become large holes in short order. A simple way to "patch" a hole or tear is to call that old standby, hook-and-loop tape, into service. Cut a piece of ¾- or 1-inch hook-and-loop tape the length of the tear or the size of the hole. Use the sew-on hook-and-loop material—the stuff without the adhesive on the back. Hold the loop side against the screen and push the hook side into it. The two sides will attach to each other, forming a strong cover for the damaged portion of screen. A 36-inch strip of the hook-and-loop material costs around $1 and is available at most sewing centers.
- FRED E. ALTRIETH JR., ROCHESTER, NEW YORK

T-HANDLE JAM

While emptying the holding tanks on my newly purchased 5-year-old RV, I had to exert considerable force on the slide valve T-handles. I dreaded the thought of pulling the shaft out of the slide, which would necessitate a major repair. Fortunately, no damage ensued. However, I decided that something had to be done to prevent a problem in the near future.

I began by flushing the holding tanks and then allowing plenty of time for the open slide valves to dry. At this point, I applied silicone spray lubricant to the valve's moving surfaces. This greatly reduced the opening and closing effort required, and in the process, alleviated my fear of a broken slide T-handle.

I now make it a point to apply the silicone spray whenever I detect a slight increase in slide friction. This minor preventive maintenance should keep holding-tank service from turning into a major repair.
- JOHN M. ANTOLICK, VERONA, NEW JERSEY

MAINTENANCE ANXIETY

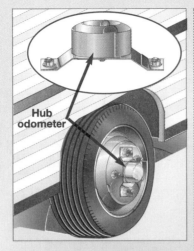

Hub odometer

After pulling a fifth-wheel trailer for several years, and trying to keep track of its accumulated mileage for service purposes, I struck upon the idea of installing a hub odometer like the truckers use. I checked with a truck-parts store, and found they needed specific information prior to special-ordering such a product for me.

Because a hub odometer records mileage based on wheel revolutions, it is first necessary to determine tire circumference of the vehicle to be equipped. My rig has LT 245/75R-16 tires with 93-inch circumferences. After discerning this figure, I multiplied the number of feet in a statute mile (5,280) by 12. This told me that there are 63,360 inches per mile. I divided this number by 93 inches to arrive at 681.3 tire revolutions per mile.

Then I ordered an Accu-Trak hub odometer (model no. AT-31), which is designed for 680 tire revolutions per mile, from a truck-equipment dealer. I can now check the hub odometer to find the actual accumulated trailer mileage. This tells me when I need to have the brakes adjusted, the wheel bearings repacked, and the tires rotated.

It is a simple and inexpensive job to install a hub odometer. The model I purchased came with a mounting bracket that fits over two wheel studs; cost was $38.90. Also, as was the case with my fifth-wheel, the odometer can be used with wheel covers by drilling a hole in the center of the cover. I think every new trailer should come with a hub odometer already installed.
- *Melvin Perkins, Missoula, Montana*

HIDE THAT HOLE

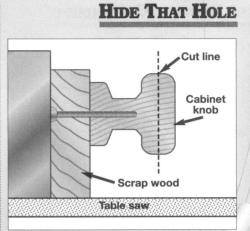

Cut line

Cabinet knob

Scrap wood

Table saw

After rerouting a propane line in my Scamp fifth-wheel, I was left with an ugly ½-inch hole in the front shell of the trailer behind the propane bottles. However, I found a perfect solution to my problem (or for that matter, any small punctures or holes in the RV skin) for slightly over $2. At a local hardware store, I located a plain white plastic cabinet knob whose color matched the trailer shell perfectly. I attached the knob to a piece of scrap wood so that I had a flat reference surface, and then used my bandsaw to carefully cut off the top of the knob, as shown in the diagram.

(Make sure that the screw is short enough or the wood scrap thick enough so that the saw blade will not hit the screw.) If you do not have access to a bandsaw, clamp the wood in a vise and cut the knob with a hacksaw. The top of the knob became my custom hole patch. I coated the back of the patch evenly with white RTV silicone adhesive, and pressed the patch into place over the hole. I used a wet finger to remove excess silicone and smooth the joint around the edges of the patch. There were other knobs available at a slightly higher cost that featured pretty floral designs. If the hole was in a more obvious place, using one of these knobs could turn an unsightly blemish into a very attractive ornament.
- *John W. Irwin, Austin, Texas*

◆ CLOSEUPS ◆ CLOSEUPS ◆ CLOSEUPS ◆

EASY VENT CLEANING

*I*f you have a problem with leaves and debris getting onto the screens in your roof vents, use your wife's hair dryer—set on cool—to blow through the screens. The "forced" air will blow away the debris. No ladders, no climbing, and it works like a charm.
- *Hal Cubberley, Live Oak, Florida*

◆ CLOSEUPS ◆ CLOSEUPS ◆ CLOSEUPS ◆

THE ANTS STOPPED MARCHING

*T*o eliminate ants from entering my RV by marching up the water hose and power cord while hooked up to campground facilities, I use a small amount of petroleum jelly or lubricating grease. I coat a 2-inch section of the water hose and power cord about the entire surface. This stops these pesky insects in their tracks. Clean-up for travel only takes a few moments using a paper towel.
- *Bob Jackson, Merritt Island, Florida*

WATER SYSTEM WINTERIZING

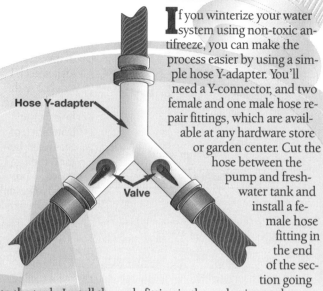

Hose Y-adapter

Valve

If you winterize your water system using non-toxic antifreeze, you can make the process easier by using a simple hose Y-adapter. You'll need a Y-connector, and two female and one male hose repair fittings, which are available at any hardware store or garden center. Cut the hose between the pump and freshwater tank and install a female hose fitting in the end of the section going to the tank. Install the male fitting in the end going to the pump. Attach these two ends to the Y-connector (the main fitting and one left of the Y). Obtain another 3-foot section of hose (or the length needed to provide each access to the free end), and install the other female fitting in one end. Connect it to the other leg of the Y.

In use, you simply drain the freshwater tank and the hot water tank. Close the hot-water tank bypass valves (install the valves if you don't already have a system), and the valve in the Y-leg going to the water tank. Open the valve on the Y-leg going to the new hose. Insert the other end of the new hose into the bottle of antifreeze and turn on the pump. Open each faucet (including the shower and toilet) until antifreeze flows smoothly.

Put a cork in the hose end when done.
- *Ernest E. Rink, Nebraska City, Nebraska*

DYED IN THE WOOL

Red Food Color

I had a pinhole leak around a window in my motorhome that defied all attempts to locate and repair. In spite of careful applications of RTV silicone, water would still seep through.

In desperation, I raided my wife's spice shelf and found a bottle of red food coloring. I mixed this to a ratio of about 50 percent dye to 50 percent water. Then, while my wife observed from inside the rig, I slowly applied this colored liquid to the edges of the offending window with an eye-dropper. I started at the bottom and worked my way up around to the top until she saw red. I knew then we had found the leak. Because food coloring is water soluble, the resultant stains wiped off with a damp rag.

I fixed the leak using another item from the kitchen: a huge, cook's, plastic-bulb turkey baster of the variety used for shooting cooking juice and spices into meat. I filled this device with marine-grade RTV silicone, and slipping the slender needle under the window trim and molding, injected the sealant directly into the trouble spot. This method eliminated those ugly gobs of silicone sealant often seen on do-it-yourself repair jobs.

The window doesn't leak anymore, but my wife is still "seeing red" over the sacrifice of one of her cooking utensils. To keep the peace, the next time we are bothered by a difficult water leak in our RV, I think I'll obtain one of those huge horse syringes from the local veterinarian.
- *Jay Walley, Sparks, Nevada*

◆ CLOSEUPS ◆ CLOSEUPS ◆ CLOSEUPS ◆ CLOSEUPS ◆ CLOSEUPS ◆ CLOSEUPS ◆

OBSOLESCENCE WOES

We recently discovered that the rubber grommet used on our older-model Avion trailer to hold the entry door open is no longer available. This frustrated our efforts to keep the door from slamming shut in all but the lightest breezes.

We found an unlikely solution, however, in the form of an automotive PCV-valve grommet. Marketed under the Help brand name, part no. 42065 does the job nicely. This company's displays are common at most auto-parts stores.

The grommet, which has a ½-inch internal diameter, is also useful for protecting electrical wires or plumbing lines where they pass through bulkheads. The grommet may work on other trailers as well.

For $1.60, we were able to solve our obsolescence dilemma without altering the original door-stop design of our 1977 Avion. The door now stays open, completely unaffected by gusty winds.
- *Ronald Carlson, San Diego, California*

◆ CLOSEUPS ◆ CLOSEUPS ◆ CLOSEUPS ◆ CLOSEUPS ◆ CLOSEUPS ◆ CLOSEUPS ◆

LIGHT UP YOUR LIFE

Your RV's headlights may leave a lot to be desired. If so, a visit to your local auto-parts outlet may solve this deficiency. If the rig is not already so equipped, consider quartz-halogen replacement. These beams are available in a wide variety of sizes to fit most RVs, and cost less ($40 to $50) than after-market driving lights.

The words "quartz halogen" or "halogen" will be found on the headlight's lens if it is of the newer variety that emits a brighter illumination pattern than older types.

If you already have quartz lights and you don't believe they're lighting up the road as far ahead as you think they should at night, the beams may be misadjusted. Have them checked by a qualified mechanic when the RV is loaded as it would be for a trip. Headlights should always be realigned after a bulb replacement. Doing this will not only confirm proper aim, but it's a nice courtesy to those who must face your vehicle after dark.

- RICHARD MATER, SANTA MARIA, CALIFORNIA

QUICK CLEAN

As the owner of a power slide-out-equipped trailer, I found myself trying to figure a way to clean off the slide roof before stowing it after each stopover. First I used a ladder and broom, but that proved to be a big hassle. I now use a Toro 850 Super Blower/Vac, though any brand would likely work. The power head and three small plastic nozzle extensions are lightweight, and only take about one cubic foot of storage space. I have used this tool not only to clear leaves and debris from atop the slide-out, but to dry it off after a rain.

- CLEVE HARGIS, CAMDEN POINT, MISSOURI

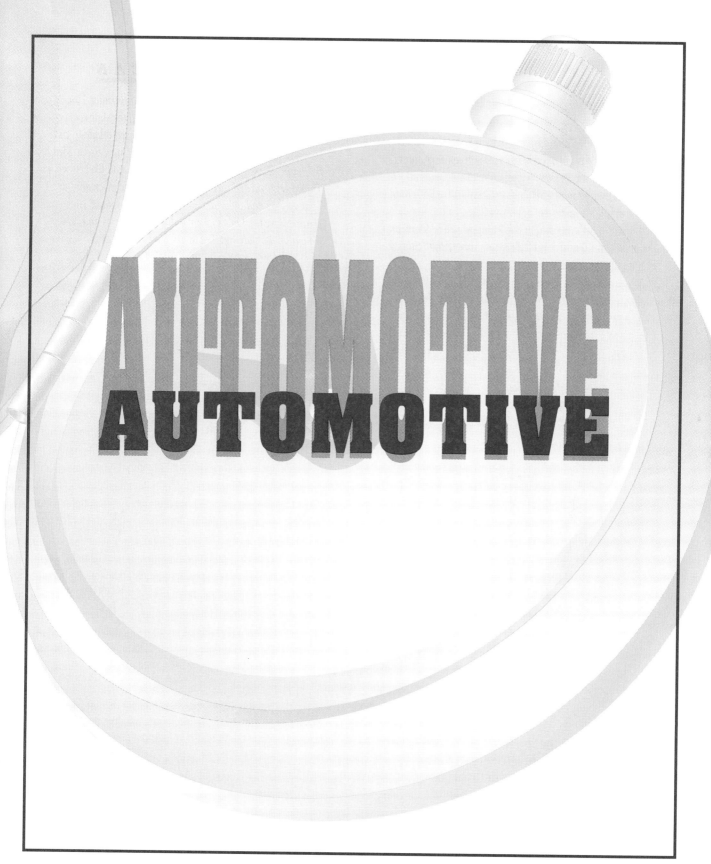

AUTOMOTIVE

SLIP-SLIDIN' ALONG

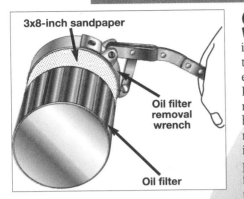

3x8-inch sandpaper

Oil filter removal wrench

Oil filter

Some spin-on oil filters are installed in locations that could even stump Houdini, and the removal process becomes even more aggravating if some gorilla put the last oil filter on so tight that the standard filter wrench won't budge it. The tool just slips.

Try folding a piece of 3×8-inch sandpaper lengthwise over the filter wrench hoop. Any grit number will do. Once in place, the sandpaper roughness imparts a nonslip surface to the wrench, so it can get a grip on the oily filter housing.
- (NO NAME)

COOL ADVICE

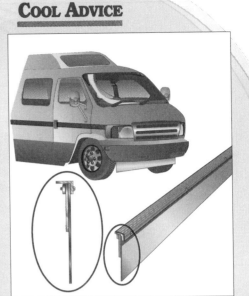

I encountered marginal overheating whenever towing a 34-foot travel trailer with my 351 V-8-equipped Ford van. This occurred even in mild temperatures.

After checking the belts and radiator, and then replacing the fan clutch to no avail, I decided to try a front-air dam. I heard that such dams create a low-pressure area below the engine compartment, thereby moving more air through the radiator and improving cooling.

However, since I had more time than money, and with prices for commercial air dams running approximately $100, it seemed time to be innovative.

I decided to make an air dam with basic construction materials. This required about 6 feet of ¾-inch angle iron, a ¾ × ⅛-inch iron strap, and a 12×.060-inch fiberglass sheet. I cut the fiberglass lengthwise to form two pieces, one 8 inches wide, the other 4 inches.

The metal strap and angle were used to sandwich the fiberglass pieces, whereupon I drilled the assembly to accept 1-inch-long No. 10 screws on 9-inch centers. I used lock washers and nuts to retain everything in place, and the finished dam was painted to match my rig.

On Ford vans, the dam will mount on the frame extensions that hold the front bumper using 1 × ¼-inch Grade 8 bolts and lock washers. Of course, other vehicles may require that the individual pieces be cut in a different manner.

Dimensions are not critical, but my selected bolt sizes and material specifications have given proven service. You'll have to adjust the length of the dam to match the width of your rig, and remember, allow for sufficient road clearance.

The results of my experiment proved to be worth the effort. My van no longer overheats, even in severe temperatures.
- E. K. WOOLLEY, SHAWNEE, OKLAHOMA

CLOSEUPS ◆ CLOSEUPS ◆ CLOSEUPS ◆ CLOSEUPS

EXAM TIME

I hate the mess associated with disassembling, cleaning, and repacking wheel bearings. Grease and dirt get everywhere, especially under my fingernails.

Though I often put the project off for as long as possible, I eventually capitulate. Having witnessed the expensive and catastrophic havoc that dry bearings can wreak, I fully understand the importance of periodic wheel-bearing service.

Nowadays, I attack the project differently. I keep an inexpensive box of medical gloves handy, so I can slip into an artificial latex skin whenever it's time to pack bearings. It's great to be able to slip and slide through the project, knowing that my hands will be unstained once it's complete.

Most such gloves do not fare well against harsh solvents or gasoline. Quick deterioration under these conditions makes them unsuitable for such duty. However, oils and greases do not seem to affect them.

A box of 100 gloves sells for about $5 at discount and warehouse outlets. Once aboard your rig, you will likely find many other worthwhile uses such as tire changing, genset servicing, engine maintenance, and general hookup chores.

Of course, I realize that the soiled gloves, particularly when used with the frequency I suggest here, will contribute to the landfill problem now facing us. For this reason, I often wash them before removal. This allows me to reuse a pair of gloves two or three times before discarding.
- RICHARD MATER, SANTA MARIA, CALIFORNIA

CLOSEUPS ◆ CLOSEUPS ◆ CLOSEUPS ◆ CLOSEUPS

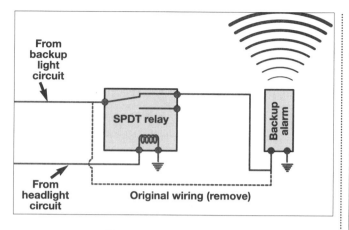

SILENCE, PLEASE

Backup alarms are great for catching the attention of those walking behind large vehicles when the driver doesn't have a clear view of the rear. These alarms are normally wired into the backup-light circuit, so they operate whenever the vehicle is put in reverse.

However, the high-pitched beeping of such devices can get very annoying if an RV so equipped must be maneuvered into a space late at night. An inexpensive relay in the alarm circuit gives the driver an effective way to mute the beeper whenever the driver feels it is safe to do so.

Since the rig's headlights are not usually needed during backing, I decided to wire the relay coil directly into this circuit. Next, I connected the backup alarm across the normally closed relay points. Now, the beeper remains silent whenever the headlights are turned on.

This cuts down on unnecessary noise pollution and contributes to good neighborly relations. It also prevents drawing unwanted attention to yourself on those occasions when you are having an unusually difficult time maneuvering into position.
- Bob Martin, Surrey, British Columbia, Canada

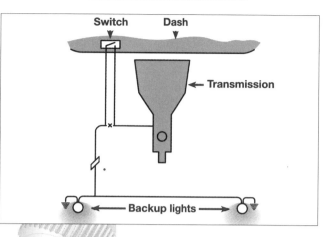

When arriving at a campsite at night, the task of backing into an unknown spot is made more difficult by the reflection of your tow vehicle's backup lights off the front of the trailer. The offending lights can be extinguished during these times with the installation of a switch in the backup-light circuit of the tow rig.

The switch can be purchased at any auto-parts store. The type you select depends only on your personal preferences. There are SPST toggle and rocker versions that work equally well.

The wire leading to the backup lights is usually attached to the reverse switch near the base of the steering column under the dash or on the transmission under the vehicle. Find this wire, and verify it with a test light by operating the backup lights. Then cut the wire, and splice the wires running from the new switch into the circuit at this location.

I put my backup-light kill switch beside the electric brake controller, which I have mounted under the dash. It could, however, be located in any convenient spot near the driver.
- Andy L. Hughes, Rustin, Louisiana

GOING UP

Finding space to mount the various gadgets we want in the tow vehicle's cab always taxes my ingenuity. Such was the case when I decided I needed an altimeter aboard. My wife takes medication that makes her hypersensitive to altitude. Monitoring our elevation is, therefore, critical.

After some thought, I decided to put the unused cigarette-lighter receptacle aboard our Dodge Dakota to work. I removed the lighter's knob and replaced it with an ⅛-inch-thick plastic scrap, cut to match the altimeter's mounting base. This is a modification that can be quickly undone when need be. Best of all, it leaves no unsightly holes or sticky tape residue.
- J. Roger Ridgway, Big Spring, Texas

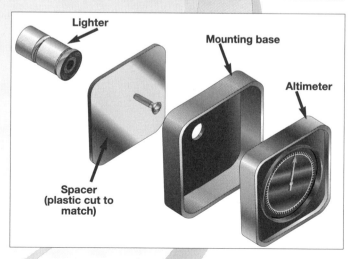

SOLUTION FOR SPOOKY SHIFTING

The Ford C-5 and C-6 automatic transmissions occasionally develop a shifting problem that you may be able to diagnose and repair yourself. The scenario goes something like this: Shifting becomes harsh, abrupt and erratic. You may also notice blue smoke coming from the vehicle's exhaust pipes. This might give you visions of your rig being taken down the street behind a tow truck on its way to the fix-it shop.

But, before you jump to such conclusions, first crawl under your rig and look for the modulator on the transmission. It resembles a small, in-line gasoline filter with only one hose. This goes to either the engine's intake manifold (gas models) or the vacuum regulator valve (diesels).

If the hose has fallen off the modulator, you have found the source of your shifting problem. Simply reinstall the hose if it looks OK. If not, replace it with a new one.

But what if everything looks like it's properly attached? Don't give up yet. Pull the hose off the modulator and see if there is oil in it. Oil indicates a failed modulator diaphragm, and means it's replacement time.

This type of failure also accounts for the presence of blue exhaust smoke on some engines. It's caused by transmission fluid being sucked into the intake manifold and burning in the combustion chambers (good valve stem lubrication!). Modulators are available from Ford for about $40, and are preset for your particular transmission.

Installation of either version can be accomplished by pulling the hose off the old modulator, removing the retained bold and bracket, and then the modulator itself. While you're at it, take the control rod out of the transmission case, and check it for dirt, varnish, or damage.

Place the cleaned control rod inside the new modulator, and install the assembly back in its receptacle in the transmission case. Reinstall the retaining bracket and bolt, and tighten to 35 ft-lbs on the C-5, and 15 ft-lbs on the C-6. Don't forget to reattach the vacuum hose.

- LEE WEINMANN, ST. AUGUSTINE, FLORIDA

THUMP JUMPER

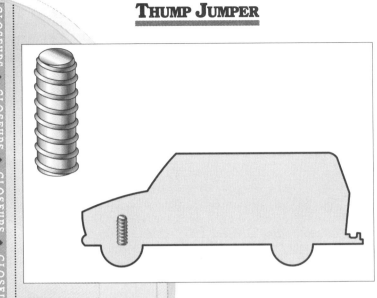

We pull our travel trailer with an older Chevrolet pickup truck, and have been using Air-Lift bags in the rear coil springs since we began towing. As the truck started to age, it became apparent that the front coil springs were sagging and in need of some help.

Being already familiar with the Air-Lift product, I felt that adding them to the front springs was worth a try. I purchased and installed a set.

After experimenting with different air pressures, I found that they not only returned the truck to its stock height, but also eliminated most of the irritating "thump-thump" caused by freeway expansion joints. The truck also rides and handles much better.

- JACK EWALD, WEST UNION, OHIO

VISUAL CLUES

If you're over 45 years old, like me, it may be hard to see those faint little "full" and "add" marks on your rig's engine-oil dipstick. You can't get younger eyes, but you can fix the dipstick.

All that's needed is a metal file. Pull out the dipstick and place it in a vise. Next, file two ⅛-inch V-shape notches into the edge—one at the full mark, another at the add mark. Carefully clean the dipstick and then slide it back into the engine.

When you pull the stick out, those notches stick out like sore thumbs because the oil clings to them. This makes it a lot easier to check your own oil without putting on the cheaters. Best of all, the fix is free.

- JOE ANDRUCYK, GAMBRILLS, MARYLAND

Notches

BREAKAWAY BEEPER

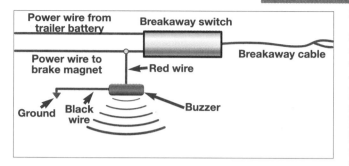

Power wire from trailer battery

Breakaway switch

Breakaway cable

Power wire to brake magnet

Red wire

Ground **Black wire**

Buzzer

Recently, while my travel trailer was parked and unattached to a tow vehicle, the breakaway cable was accidentally and unknowingly pulled out of its socket, thus activating the brake magnets. The trailer was hooked up to a 120-volt AC power supply, and the activation was for several hours. Such a situation can be damaging to the brake magnets, and if the trailer is on battery power alone, it can run the battery down. To prevent this from happening again, I have installed a warning buzzer in a protected spot on the trailer tongue. To do this, I tapped into the normally uncharged wire from the breakaway switch to the brake magnets, and ran a lead to the red lead of a piezo buzzer (RadioShack part no. 273-060, suggested retail price $3.29). Then, I took the other lead (black) from the buzzer to a ground on the A-frame. This is a simple electrical hookup, but one does have to remember that piezo buzzers have polarity, and that the black lead from the buzzer must go to ground. Now, if the breakaway brake switch cable is accidentally pulled and activated, there will be a warning signal, which I hope will alert me before real trouble develops. The buzzer does beep when the tow vehicle brakes are applied, but not loudly enough (buzzer is rated at 85 db maximum) to be heard in the tow vehicle.
- ROBERT A. LOWRY, BOULDER, COLORADO

FAIR WARNING

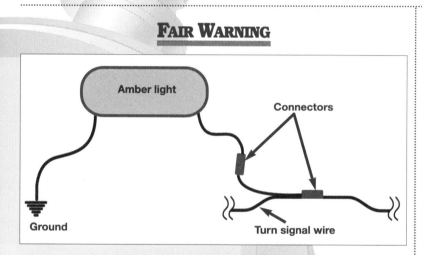

Amber light

Connectors

Ground

Turn signal wire

I have a 35-foot travel trailer that I tow with a full-size van. However, the van has no side turn signals from which an adjacent driver might be able to learn of my desire to change lanes. I have found that most drivers are courteous and will help you if they know your intentions.

A simple fix cost me just $9.50. It required only two flat, oval amber clearance lights (Blazer C84WIA), four wire connectors, about 4 feet of automotive wire, and two extra-bright replacement bulbs (Victor 906 or 921), which I installed for better signal visibility. If you mount your lifts on a surface other than sheet metal, Molly bolts or their equivalent may be required. Regardless of the mounting method, a good electrical ground must be provided.

The locations I chose for mounting these new lights were on the side of the van's nose (at eye level for automobiles). In the case of my Ford, just below the side running light proved to be the best location. I was able to route the necessary wiring through the running-light opening and connect as illustrated.
- E. K. WOOLLEY, SHAWNEE, OKLAHOMA

WHERE THE COOL WINDS BLOW

Cold-air vents to dashboard

AC plenum

Fresh air vent

Firewall

2-inch opening

Trailer hitch receiver plug

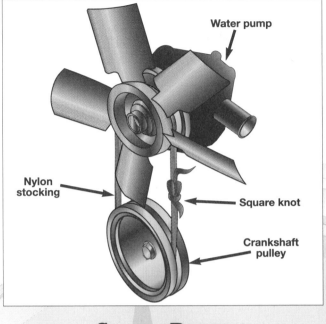

Water pump

Nylon stocking

Square knot

Crankshaft pulley

GETTING BELTED

The dash air-conditioner plenum chamber in motorhomes and tow vehicles can periodically become clogged from leaves and other debris that have entered through the fresh-air intake grill. This decreases the cooling efficiency greatly, because the airflow through the evaporator core is restricted.

Ask a dealer, and you'll be told that the entire housing must be removed for cleaning—at a cost of several hundred dollars. The refrigerant gas must first be discharged and lines disconnected, after which the housing can be removed and the debris cleared.

You can solve this dilemma in 10 minutes by doing some engineering that Detroit forgot to do. Just make an access hole in the evaporator housing so the chamber can be vacuumed.

To begin with, you will need to purchase a square, black, molded plug, the type used to cover the 2-inch trailer-hitch-receiver opening. After this, find the large plastic housing located against the firewall under the vehicle's dashboard. This item is typically installed on the passenger side.

Determine the location of the evaporator and heater core inside this housing by referring to a factory service manual. When a suitable area for cutting has been located, place the square plug in position and scribe around it.

With great caution to avoid damaging the evaporator, use a wallboard knife to carefully cut a square hole in the ⅛-inch plastic plenum chamber. Wear goggles, just in case you miscalculate and strike the pressurized refrigerant gas. Remember to keep the hole slightly undersize. You want the receiver plug to fit securely when used to close off this access port.

When finished, you'll have an opening in the evaporator housing that can be used as needed to vacuum debris from around the evaporator.

- Roger F. George, Altamonte Springs, Florida

Thaaawunk! You hear a strange, muffled sound from somewhere near the engine. It only lasts a second or two. Only slightly startled, you continue on your way. Then, you notice the glare of the little red alternator light on the dash. Then, the engine overheat bulb snaps to life. Bad news: One or more of the engine's drive belts is going AWOL.

It's possible to travel some distance during daylight hours without a functioning alternator. Just turn off all electrical equipment and drive to the next repair facility. Not so without the water pump.

However, there is a chance you can extricate yourself from this dilemma with a single pair of women's nylon hose (not panty hose). Start by gaining access to the front of the RV's engine. Clear any belt debris from the pulley track. This done, wrap one leg of the hosiery around the crankshaft pulley (bottom-most pulley), and stretch it tightly around the corresponding water-pump pulley (the one attached to the fan). Tie off your handiwork with a tight square knot made as small as possible.

Don't try to get fancy and drive accessories other than the water pump with this makeshift setup. The nylons will fail quickly, if you do.

Also, if the only product your donor has to sacrifice is panty hose, make sure you first cut off the panty portion before attempting this fix. You won't get far if you try wrapping a complete, uncut pair around the engine pulleys. If you have a choice, support hose are even better than regular.

While the finished repair won't look pretty, by driving slowly you can probably keep the water pump churning long enough to reach help (watch the temperature gauge). The lesson here is to carry spare belts on your next trip.

- (no name)

OIL TOIL

I read with interest a "10-Minute Tech" tip on changing transmission fluid by using a hand-held pump to remove fluid from the pan.

Some time back, I took issue with the fact that when you change only pan fluid, you are actually only replenishing about 4 quarts of the 12 or more quarts held in the transmission. The following simple steps will allow complete fluid change:

1. After removing and draining the transmission oil pan, and changing the filter and gasket, reinstall the pan and fill with new fluid of the type specified by the vehicle manufacturer. This should amount to about 4 quarts.

2. Now, locate and disconnect the discharge tube from the transmission at the vehicle's radiator. Attach and clamp a rubber hose to the tube, and route it into an adequate drain basin.

3. After you start the engine, the transmission oil pump will pick up new oil from the pan and discharge old fluid from the open tubing.

4. The engine should be turned off, and the transmission pan refilled as bubbles start to appear in the discharged fluid. Depending on the total capacity of the transmission being serviced, this cycle may have to be repeated several times before fresh fluid is observed at the discharge tubing. A distinct color change will be seen.

5. Reconnect the discharge tube at the radiator, adjust transmission fluid level as needed, and start the engine to check for leaks.

This additional fluid change takes less time than the initial changing of the fluid contained in the pan. I believe that the advantages of a total oil change far outweigh mere replenishment.
- JIMMY NEWTON, VIDALIA, GEORGIA

THERMOSTAT APPRECIATION

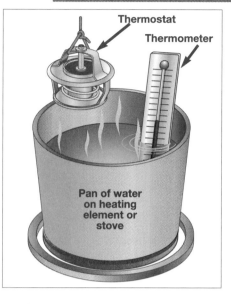

Thermostat

Thermometer

Pan of water on heating element or stove

Engine thermostats are hardy little devices that seldom give trouble. However, when they do fail, engine problems can abound. If stuck closed, a faulty thermostat can cause severe overheating and pinging. Those that give up the ghost in the open position prevent an engine from reaching normal operating temperatures—which can cause many difficulties.

Should you suspect a faulty thermostat, follow the upper radiator hose to where it meets the engine intake manifold. The thermostat is behind the housing bolted to the intake manifold, and with the engine cool, it can be accessed quickly by removing two bolts.

Once you have the thermostat in hand, determine its initial opening temperature from the number stamped somewhere on the device. Next, prepare a pan of water in which you can submerge the unit. Support the thermostat so that it is not lying directly on the bottom of the pan, insert a suitable kitchen cooking thermometer, and begin heating the water on a stove-top burner.

If you have a 190-degree F thermostat, it should begin to open around 190 degrees F, and be fully open by about 195 degrees F. If it does not perform properly, replace it with a new unit of the same temperature rating.
- (NO NAME)

HOT FLOORS

Exhaust systems on motorhomes and tow vehicles can generate a lot of heat, especially on long and slow uphill grades. The air isn't rushing under the vehicle fast enough during these times to properly dissipate the heat. The high temperatures can damage nearby components, or make some areas of the vehicle floor uncomfortably warm.

However, simple heat shields can alleviate these problems. You can make custom shields from sheet metal and secure them in place with muffler clamps. These components will form an effective heat barrier between floorboards and critical underbody components.
- JOE MARKSTEINGER, ALBUQUERQUE, NEW MEXICO

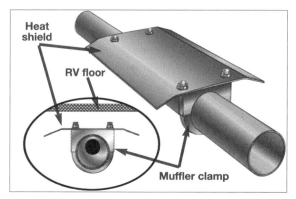

Heat shield

RV floor

Muffler clamp

RUST REMEDY

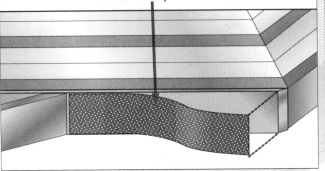

4-inch nonslip stair tread

A common problem with travel trailers is that, soon after delivery, the forward frame member gets nicked and chipped by road debris. This allows the exposed steel to rust. Priming and painting is not the solution, since the new finish will also become damaged in short order.

As a cure, I purchased a 3-foot length of nonslip stair tread from a hardware store. The material comes in a 4-inch width that is ideal for covering and protecting the frame members from rocks. Installation is simple because of the self-adhesive backing. The gray color even matched my trailer's frame.

I've now logged 6,000 miles on the rig since applying the stair tread, and no longer have the problems of a rusting trailer frame.

This fix only cost me about $4.
- *JACK JOYNT, FARMINGTON HILLS, MICHIGAN*

◆ CLOSEUPS ◆ CLOSEUPS ◆ CLOSEUPS ◆

RUST BUCKET

Many RV battery trays develop corrosion unless the owner constantly monitors the problem. Here is a way to treat, or at least slow down, the corrosion. First, remove the batteries. Next, bathe the tray and hardware with a solution of water and baking soda to neutralize any acid. Rinse with water and allow to dry completely. If rust is present, scrape off as much as possible and treat with an antirust treatment like Duro Extend or its equivalent (available at auto and hardware stores) according to instructions.

Spray the entire tray and hardware (except bolt threads and nuts) with rubberized undercoating.

Note: wear eye protection and rubber gloves while accomplishing this project.
- *PAUL L. LINDSTROM, WOODLAND PARK, COLORADO*

◆ CLOSEUPS ◆ CLOSEUPS ◆ CLOSEUPS ◆

PESKY PCVs

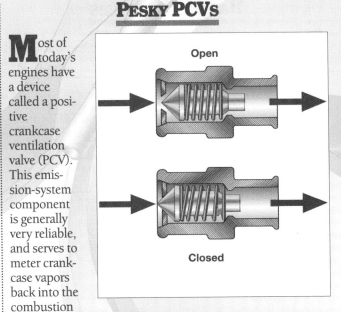

Open

Closed

Most of today's engines have a device called a positive crankcase ventilation valve (PCV). This emission-system component is generally very reliable, and serves to meter crankcase vapors back into the combustion chambers for burning. The PCV is a simple device—a plastic or metal housing in which a spring-loaded check valve is contained. Often found in a rubber grommet on the engine's valve cover, the interval valve is held off its seat by a wimpy little spring, which allows the valve to close easily under high manifold vacuum.

If a PCV sticks open, or if its associated hoses develop a significant leak, problems such as rough idling and stalling can develop. Should your engine develop such symptoms, one of your first checks should be to look for a failed component within the PCV circuit. Sometimes nasty idling habits can be corrected by merely reconnecting or replacing a vacuum hose.

The internal valve should rattle when the PCV is removed from the engine and shaken vigorously. While these devices can be cleaned and reused in a pinch, it's best to replace them periodically. If you do clean a PCV, wash it only in diesel fuel, mineral spirits, or a strong dishwashing detergent. Don't use lacquer thinner or acetone to clean a plastic-housing PCV. I know a fellow who soaked one in lacquer thinner for about 10 minutes, and when he looked in the coffee can, he found a black blob wrapped around a spring and valve.

After rinsing, blow through the engine end of the valve to make sure it seats firmly and does not allow air to pass.

If a PCV cannot be repaired in the field, and uncontrollable engine stalling results, you may have to temporarily plug off the hose leading to the intake manifold until a replacement can be obtained. Just be sure to replace the PCV, and remove the blockage as soon as possible.

Replacing the various PCV hoses every few years is good preventive maintenance. They can become brittle or swollen, and fail. The valve itself is relatively inexpensive, at least for gasoline engines, so most folks just replace them on a regular basis.
- *LEE WEINMANN, ST. AUGUSTINE, FLORIDA*

BACKUP BLINDNESS

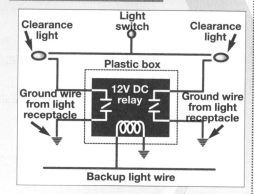

Sooner or later, those of us using dually pickups as tow vehicles have to back up our truck-and-trailer combinations at night. However, the minute you look in the rearview mirror to begin this process, you find yourself blinded by the amber clearance lights installed on the front sides of the rear fender extensions.

My brother and I decided to eliminate this occasional annoyance with a simple electrical circuit. We purchased a 12-volt DC relay (normally closed) and a plastic project box, into which we built the circuit shown here. The relay was installed in a manner that electrically interrupts the wiring to each rear fender light whenever the truck is shifted into reverse. This extinguishes the lights, dramatically improving rearward visibility during nighttime backing operations.
- *J. Ed Harnist, Bowling Green, Kentucky*

QUICK WAY OUT

My motorhome, like many, has the spare tire lying on its side in an outside storage compartment. This space has a limited height, which makes accessing the tire quite awkward. In my case, it must first be retrieved by pulling on an attached strap and then tilted just right so it can be removed.

The spare is heavy, and is particularly difficult to move across the carpeted storage-compartment floor. To make matters worse, the tire must slide over the lip of the aluminum door frame before it can be removed. This creates so much restriction that it takes two people to finally get the tire out.

But, this is no longer a problem in my rig. I decided to insert one of those heavy plastic sheets that children use for snow sledding under the spare. This allows me to grasp the handle on the plastic sheet and easily slip the spare out of its compartment. The plastic device that is used to hold lawn and garden bags open also works nicely for this purpose.
- *Earle G. Thompson, Roseville, Minnesota*

BETTER COOLING

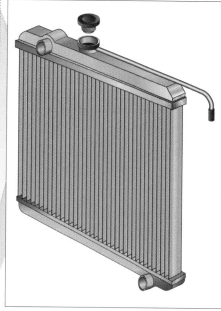

My rig, a 1977 Dodge motorhome with a 440 V-8 engine, has always run hot. I have had the radiator rodded a couple of times, but recently I took it to a radiator shop that performed a change that I wish I could have had years ago.

The shop manager pointed out that on some motorhomes, like mine, the inlet and outlet of the radiator are on the same side. He said this uses only a fraction of the radiator's potential because the hot water entering the radiator at the top has only to flow through the tubes downward to the outlet tube directly below. Moving the outlet to the other side apparently causes a more uniform flow through all the tubes.

I have not had any heating problems since this was done.
- *Bones Evers, Taylor, Arizona*

FUMBLE FINGERS

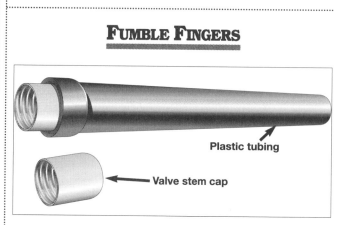

Plastic tubing

Valve stem cap

A short length of rubber or plastic tubing, which produces a snug fit over tire valve-stem caps, can save much frustration and prevent skinned fingers when servicing inside dual tires. Just slide the tubing over the valve cap to remove or replace with ease. The "tool" is simple and inexpensive, and doesn't take up much room in a toolbox.
- *Bill McArthur, Torrance, California*

THE DIESEL TRAP

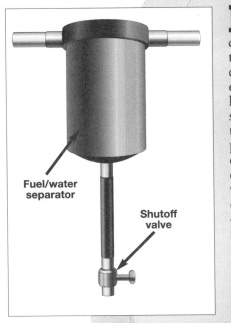

Fuel/water separator

Shutoff valve

Many RVers are using diesel-powered tow vehicles these days. Some also encounter problems with slow starting. While there are several possibilities that can cause such a condition, one which is often overlooked is a drain leak in the fuel/water separator housing.

When the vehicle is parked, fuel can drip out of a defective drain valve, lowering the fuel level inside the separator. When this happens, the engine must be cranked longer to refill this container, which could burn out the starter. Replacement of a factory fuel-water separator assembly can be expensive. However, this isn't necessary. For about $2, a simple ¼- or ⅜-inch shutoff valve can be installed in the existing drain line using a ½-inch hose clamp. This will stop the unwanted fuel leak.

Also, you can avoid prolonged starter use when it is necessary to drain contaminated fuel from the separator. Just unscrew the water sensor, and fill the reservoir to the top with clean diesel fuel. The engine should start quickly. Do the same after replacing the fuel filter.
- JOHN G. WARLICK, RICHMOND, VIRGINIA

KEEP TRACK OF YOUR CAP

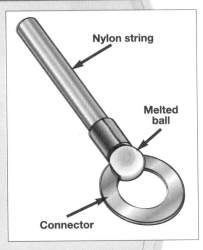

Nylon string

Melted ball

Connector

Here's a tip for RVers who own rigs without gasoline cap tethers. I modified mine in about 10 minutes using two "ring tongue" electrical connectors (Radio Shack part no. 64-3030) and a 6-inch piece of nylon string. Thread the nylon string through the wire end of the electrical connectors, and melt the string ends so a small ball prevents the string from pulling back through. Using a ⅛-inch sheet-metal screw, I attached one end of my homemade tether to the center outside of my gas cap. The other end of the tether is attached to the motorhome. No more lost gas caps.
- RONALD CURTIS, READING, MICHIGAN

TAILGATE THIEVES MAY THINK TWICE

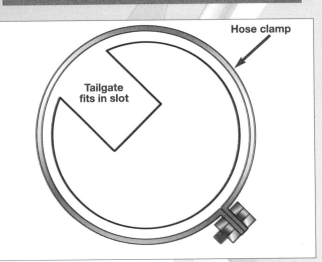

Hose clamp

Tailgate fits in slot

To slow down small-time thieves from stealing my pickup's tailgate, I bought some heavy galvanized pipe hanger strap, a 1½ × ¼-inch bolt, and a ¼-inch locknut (all available in any good hardware store). I bent the pipe strap to fit the slotted end of the tailgate hinge, stuck the bolt through the strap holes and tightened the nut. (It's easier to snug down if you use a socket wrench.) It won't stop professionals, but it makes the tailgate much more difficult to remove—and steal.
- DE VERN BATEMAN, MANCHESTER, MICHIGAN

TRASH STASH

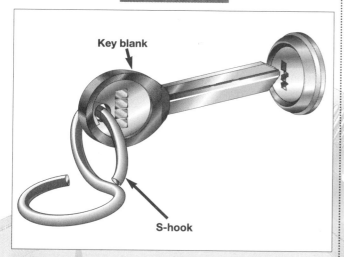

Key blank

S-hook

My new tow vehicle has no facilities from which to hang a trash container. There are no knobs or protruding metal parts to which a magnetic hanger can be secured. Giving this matter some thought, I purchased a key blank that fits into the glove compartment's door lock. To this I attached a large stainless-steel S-hook, which I had bent about 90 degrees to prevent it from rubbing against the glove compartment door. The final step, of course, is to hang a suitable-size trash bag from the hook. This little modification works great, and the inside of my tow rig is always free of litter.
- BILL STEIN, FREEPORT, TEXAS

ROADSIDE FLASHER

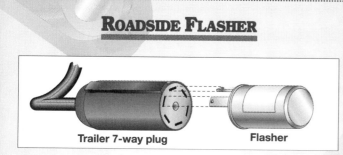

Trailer 7-way plug **Flasher**

If you ever have to leave your trailer on the side of the road, it's a good idea to have your running lights flashing to warn surrounding traffic.

This can be done by plugging a two-prong flasher (available at any auto-parts store) into the power and running-lights circuits of the trailer connector. The location of these circuits may vary from connector to connector, but on our Bargman-equipped rig, we are able to insert the flasher directly into the receptacle without wiring adapters (see illustration).

When camped in a large RV park, we often use our flashing running lights to help visiting friends find our rig at night.
- FRED SHAPIRO, PALM DESERT, CALIFORNIA

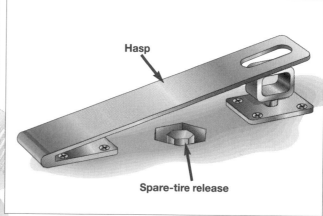

Hasp

Spare-tire release

SHREWD SAFEGUARD

My husband and I recently purchased a 1995 ¾-ton pick-up to tow our fifth-wheel trailer. We were very happy with the convenient method provided to remove the spare tire from under the truck, but were worried that the simplicity might also make the tire easy to steal. We devised the following safeguard.

There is a receptacle at the bottom of the tailgate that accepts the male-end socket wrench needed to lower the tire. We simply used a metal locking hasp to cover this hole and block removal of the spare. The locking portion was installed on one side of the hole, the hasp on the other.

Unfortunately, the plate wasn't quite long enough to reach across the opening, so we cut and welded in another piece of metal to increase the length. Hasps with a longer dimension may be available in your area, though we were not able to locate any.
- V. MARIE AND ERIC MAYA, HUNTSVILLE, ONTARIO, CANADA

◆ CLOSEUPS ◆ CLOSEUPS ◆ CLOSEUPS ◆

SIMPLE FIX

I lost several expensive motorhome wheel covers when going over cattle guards and railroad tracks, until my wife came up with a suggestion that solved the problem. I positioned one side of a hook-and-loop fastener strip between the locking fingers of the wheel covers, and the other side directly opposite on the rim of the motorhome's wheels. To assure good glue adhesion, I sanded both the rim and the inside of each wheel cover before installation of the fastener strips. This idea has worked very well; all my rig's wheel covers are still in place after several long trips.
- DONALD F. HAGQUIST, CRESCENT CITY, CALIFORNIA

◆ CLOSEUPS ◆ CLOSEUPS ◆ CLOSEUPS ◆

FEET FOR SAFETY

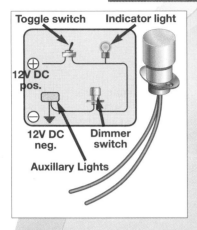

Toggle switch   Indicator light

12V DC pos.

12V DC neg.   Dimmer switch

Auxillary Lights

When out in the boondocks on those black-as-pitch nights, two-laning it to the next campsite, how many times have we had our legal auxiliary lights on, only to come face to face with an oncoming driver? Reducing our light output means removing a hand from the wheel and groping around in the darkness for the off switch.

Keep your hands on the wheel and use your foot, instead. Simple to install (at a cost of less than $10 at most auto-parts outlets), an extra floor-mounted dimmer switch will do the trick. Use the flat-bottomed style with screw ears on opposite sides, and wire it into your auxiliary light circuit in place of the toggle or rocker switch indicated in the directions. Or, use the floor switch as an "interrupter" and use both switches to control the lights. If the dash-mounted switch does not have a "pilot" light to inform you when the auxiliaries are on, or if you're using just the dimmer switch, you may want to install an indicator light where it's easily visible.

Since most dimmer switches have three terminals and no connection diagram, use a voltmeter or the old trial-and-error method to determine which two of the three terminals to use.

- Bob Zimmer, Schaumburg, Illinois

AIRLESS OUTING

My suggestion for changing flats or blowouts on tandem-wheeled travel trailers may help some readers. The procedure will save a lot of time should the need arise to change a tire in a remote location.

1. Slightly loosen lug nuts on the wheel to be removed.

2. Using the same technique as when leveling the rig, place several 2 × 4-inch boards in front of the good tire adjacent to the flat. Pull the trailer up on these boards. This action will allow the flat tire to swing free. (After you have done this once, you will know how many boards to use in the future).

3. Carefully chock and block the opposite trailer wheels, and set the tow vehicle's parking brake.

4. Remove the lug nuts and replace the flat tire with the spare. Be sure to snug up the lug nuts, so that the replacement wheel seats fully against the brake drum.

5. Remove the chocks and drive off the blocks. Complete the repair by properly tightening the lug nuts. Get the flat tire fixed or replaced as soon as possible. You could need another spare at any time.

- William A. Potts, Lexington, South Carolina

SHIPSHAPE SHAFT

The ignition distributor in the GM 454 V-8 has a two-piece shaft that is part of the mechanical spark-advance system. If these two parts are not free to rotate several degrees, one within the other, the ignition timing will not be correct.

The problem should be corrected quickly, because it can affect starting, as well as contribute to pinging, reduced fuel economy, and poor overall engine performance.

The distributor cap must be removed to check for relative freedom of movement between the two shafts. Grip the rotor and try to rotate the top shaft against the pull of the centrifugal advance springs.

If movement is evident, remove the rotor and sparingly lubricate the mechanical linkage with 30-weight motor oil. Don't forget the felt wiper, if your distributor has one. Reinstall the rotor and cap, making sure that both are squarely and firmly seated.

If you can't induce movement, or if the rotor will not return to its normal position, remove the rotor and spray the center shaft with WD-40 while working it back and forth. If this loosens the advance mechanism, wipe off the excess spray lube, then oil it, as described earlier. Replace the rotor and cap, and check the initial ignition timing with a timing light.

Sometimes, however, the two shafts cannot be freed in this manner. If this is the case, have the distributor removed and repaired by a qualified mechanic.

- George Taylor, Muscle Shoals, Alabama

POWER TO THE PREPARED

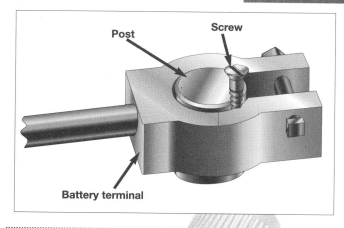

Post Screw

Battery terminal

Finding myself stalled on a cold, rainy afternoon with my tow vehicle, it didn't take me long to determine that the problem was a loose battery terminal. Of course, all my tools were back at the campsite—except the Swiss army knife that I always carry.

Using the screwdriver blade in the knife, I removed a nonessential sheet-metal screw from the engine compartment and installed it between the battery post and the terminal. (Note: Care is required when doing this to prevent going too deep and cracking the battery case.) Installing the screw in this manner will cut into both the terminal and the post sufficiently to make a good connection. Once power is restored, you are on your way to a place where proper repairs can be made.
-*Wayne E. Smith, Berwick, Pennsylvania*

TROUBLES IN ISOLATION

The battery isolator on your rig allows the starting and auxiliary batteries to be charged by the alternator when the engine is running, and discharged separately when parked. (An isolator uses high-current diodes connected anode-to-anode to prevent one battery from discharging others in the system.)

If you suspect your RV's isolator is not doing the job, use the following test to verify its function. While there are several ways to check these devices, my method does not require any test equipment other than a 12-volt DC bulb, a socket with wires, and appropriate connectors.

1. Remove the isolator from the RV by disconnecting the wires from its terminals. Be sure to tag everything for accurate reconnection later, and do not allow any of the wires to become grounded. Also, do not attempt to start the engine while you have the isolator removed from the vehicle.

2. With the device on your workbench, clean and visually inspect it for signs of damage, overheating, etc.

Test one Test two

3. If everything appears OK, connect the positive terminal of a 12-volt DC battery to the input terminal on the isolator. This is usually the center connection.

4. Using a 12-volt DC light and socket, connect one lead to the negative post of the battery.

5. Test One will determine the conductivity of the internal diodes.

Test One: Touch the second wire from your test bulb to the isolator's output terminals, one at a time. The bulb should light each time. If it doesn't, that side of the unit is defective.

6. Test Two will determine the blocking action of the internal diodes. In preparation, disconnect the wires from the battery and reconnect them in reverse of the order described above.

Test Two: With battery polarity now reversed, repeat the instructions in Test One. This time, the bulb should not light; if it does, then you know an internal diode has failed.

If the isolator does not pass both of these tests, it should be replaced with a new model having the same, or greater, current-handling capacity. During reinstallation, put a dab of silicone dielectric grease, if available, on each terminal screw and on the mounting surfaces to help the isolator dissipate heat.

At this point, you should also check any circuit breakers that are to be reconnected to the isolator's output terminals.

A simple test is to connect the breaker and your test bulb in series with the 12-volt DC battery (polarity doesn't matter). The bulb should light if the circuit breaker is functional. If it doesn't, replace the breaker with one of the same current rating.
- *George Taylor, Muscle Shoals, Alabama*

JUST LIKE NEW

New taillights

Wires

GO RV GO

For some time now, I have admired the stop- and turn-lights mounted high on the rear corner of many new vans. I decided to duplicate this modification on the rear of my fifth-wheel trailer.

After removing the factory-installed light assemblies, I used a round file to notch the lower edges of the fixtures. Through these new openings, I routed a three-wire, exterior-rated conductor to the vertical trim strip on both outboard sides of my fifth-wheel. Four clips on each side hold the wires in place for a very neat and clean look.

The new taillights were installed at the 6-foot level and then connected to the add-on circuits. They give me the extra margin of safety usually found only on late-model RVs.

- LANE WELLS, THREE RIVERS, MICHIGAN

INSTALLING SNOW CHAINS MADE EASY

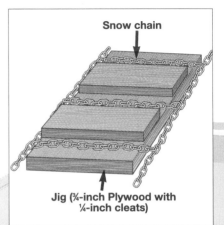

Snow chain

Jig (¾-inch Plywood with ¼-inch cleats)

When installing snow chains, the common procedure is to lay them on the ground and drive over them. But they often get bunched together under the tire, making it almost impossible to hook the ends together. An easy-to-make jig allows the chain to remain fully adjustable while under the tire. The jig is simply a piece of ¾-inch plywood, with ¼-inch cleats, sized to fit between the cross chains, attached about 1 inch apart.

To use, lay the jig in front of the tire, lay the chain over the jig with the cross chains in the slots and the long side chains lying on the ground. Drive onto the jig and the cleats will hold the tire off the cross chains so they can be moved, thus allowing the long side chains to be fully extended and hooked up.

- MICHAEL F. WILSON, SAN DIEGO, CALIFORNIA

WHAT ARE YOUR COLORS?

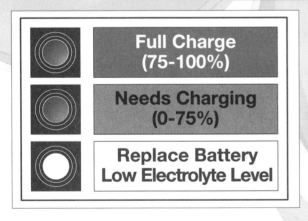

Full Charge
(75-100%)

Needs Charging
(0-75%)

Replace Battery
Low Electrolyte Level

You turn the key and all you hear is *click, click, click*. Ah, you think, it must be a dead battery. You pop the hood and look at the "magic eye" on the rig's maintenance-free battery. That's funny; normally the color is green, not light yellow.

You ask your neighbor for his opinion, and all he says is, "Hey man, I don't know what it means. Let's just jump-start it and get you going!" Whoa, it's time for a break. A dead battery must be capable of accepting a charge or a jump-start, and that may not be the case here.

As you look down on the mini-hydrometer that's found in some maintenance-free batteries, you generally will see only one of three colors. Green is normal, indicating a charge level between 75 and 100 percent. Black means that the battery is deeply discharged-below 75 percent. A bright, semi-yellow charge indicator, however, tells you that the electrolyte level has dropped below the recommended level. A wise RVer will know these colors and heed their meanings.

Attempting to jump-start a battery that is too low on electrolyte can be dangerous. Unfortunately, such a scenario usually calls for a replacement battery. This is because most maintenance-free styles are sealed and cannot be served with distilled water. Once the electrolyte drops below the charge indicator, the battery's fate is also sealed.

If the failed battery is relatively new, be sure to have your RV's charging voltage checked. If it's too high, a battery's electrolyte will boil away in a hurry.

- EUGENE STAGNER, ANAHEIM, CALIFORNIA

MIRROR WITH A VIEW

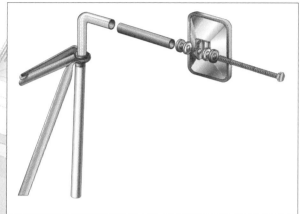

Foresight is usually better than hindsight, at least when it comes to trailers. The standard Ford mirrors on my Class C motorhome left something to be desired when it came to providing a good curbside view to the rear. I was seeing more of my rig's awning support arms than anything else.

There are, perhaps, more sophisticated remedies on the market, but a very effective, inexpensive, quick fix is also available. All that's required is one 8 × ⅜-inch bolt and a 7 × ⅜-inch length of galvanized pipe.

Remove the original bolt that secures the curbside mirror, being certain to save all existing washers. Reinstall the washers on the new bolt, insert it through the mirror bracket and the new lengths of pipe, and thread it into the mirror mount. Leave the bolt loose enough to allow for later adjustment.

Because of the added wind-generated leverage caused by this modification, I had to remove the nylon washers at the pivot end of the mirror supplement arms. This was done to ensure the mirror adjustment would hold during travel, and whenever the door was opened and closed.

Finishing of the mirror extension can be done with color-matched paint or decorative tape. If painting, it's probably best to do so in advance of final installation. Taping can be done easily after the mounting bolts have been properly secured.

The completed project has greatly improved my rear view during passing and other maneuvers.
- *R. A. Laukhart, Warren, Ohio*

ECONOMY BEGETS ECONOMY

Because my gas mileage was lower than expected in my Chevy Suburban, I began looking for ways to improve it. After reading about wind deflectors

Plywood covered with rooftop flashing

Angle iron

Roof rack

that claim large increases in mileage, I decided to try this approach. However, commercially produced deflectors cost as much as $350, so I started thinking about building my own.

Looking at my Suburban's roof rack, I noticed full-length grooves on both sides, allowing the factory Z-rail to slide back and forth. I reasoned that this could also be used to support a deflector of my own design.

I selected angle iron and ¾-inch plywood for this project. After cutting the plywood to size, I covered it with metal rooftop flashing for weather protection. The angle-iron support is attached to grooves in the roof rack. This allows the deflector to fold when not needed. My total investment for the project was approximately $26.

As originally hoped, I have experienced a significant gain in gas mileage since installing the deflector.
- *Denny Spell, Terry, Mississippi*

STUBBORN FILTER

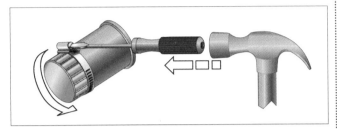

There are many ways to free a spin-on engine oil filter that has been aggressively installed. Here's another method to consider.

Obtain a large worm gear clamp and place it around the circumference of the offending oil filter (two smaller ones joined together will also work). Tighten securely in place and then, using a soft mallet, tap the clamp until the filter assembly begins to loosen. Finish removing by hand.

To avoid this problem in the future, remember to always apply a thin coat of oil to the sealing gasket before spinning a new filter into place. Once it is finger-tight, rotate the filter no more than an additional ½ to ⅔ of a turn.

- TL

BRISTLING WITH ADVICE

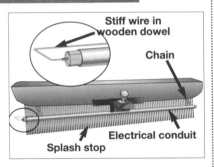

I purchased a splash stop from Camping World to help keep road debris from slinging all over my towed vehicle. Friends, however, told me that the wind would lift the shield bristles and still allow rocks and grime to reach my car. Taking these comments to heart, I set about finding a way to keep the splash stop brush from blowing uselessly behind my motorhome.

I acquired a length of ½-inch electrical conduit and cut it to match the width of the bristle skirt. Then, I attached two sections of small-link chain to the conduit and made both long enough to position the pipe about halfway down the debris shield.

I finished my project by inserting a short section of ½-inch wooden dowel into each end of the conduit, drilling a small hole in the end of each insert, and positioning a stiff wire in both dowels. I bent these wires around the outer splash stop bristles to help keep my conduit modification in place. The whole setup works great and protects the finish of my towed car very well.

- E. A. DICKSON, SAN DIEGO, CALIFORNIA

BLINDING LIGHT

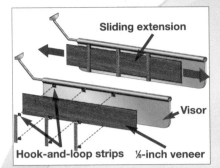

The fixed lateral position of sun visors on many motorhomes makes it nearly impossible to cover all areas of their massive windshields. More often than not, the sun shines through an area where the visor cannot reach.

I solved this problem by making a sliding extension for the visor. I fabricated it from ⅛-inch veneer (mahogany in my case), which I trimmed slightly shorter and 3 inches narrower than the existing visor. From the same veneer stock, I cut three pieces—each ¾ inch wide and 1½ inches longer than the width of the extension panel.

To apply end of these "brackets," I applied ¾-inch squares of hook-and-loop tape. This secures the brackets to the back of the motorhome's visor. The extension is firmly held in place, but will still slide in either direction to block out offending sunlight.

- DICK CHAPIN, BELMONT, CALIFORNIA

DOUBLE-DUTY GAUGE

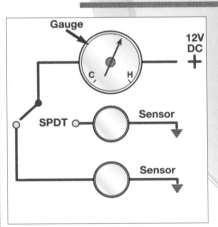

Here's a way to monitor the temperature of your engine oil and automatic transmission fluid with the use of just one gauge.

Purchase an instrument with a 100- to 350-degree F temperature calibration, and install it in a convenient location on the dash of your rig. At the time of purchase, order a second sending unit. Follow the directions for placing the sensor in the engine oil pan. The transmission pan can be modified with a brazed fitting capable of accepting the second sensor; drain-plug adapters are also available for some models. Be sure to allow clearance for the sensor to extend into the pan.

Use a single-pole, double-throw (SPDT) toggle switch to wire both sending units to the single gauge. This will save the expense and clutter of a second instrument.

- GEORGE KENNEDY, ORANGE, TEXAS

PULL TOP CAP A SNAP

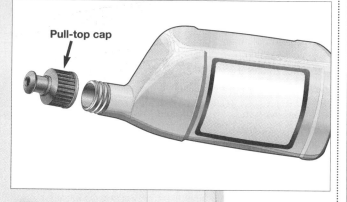

Pull-top cap

The pull-top caps found on drinking water and syrup bottles fit nicely on one-quart plastic motor oil, power steering, and transmission fluid containers. The pull-cap permits maneuvering the bottles into hard-to-reach places without spilling and frequently eliminates the need for a funnel.
- Ron Uhle, Tucson, Arizona

DRY AS A BONE

If you personally change the motor oil in your tow vehicle or motorhome, you are well acquainted with the confident feeling that the job was done right. The one cautionary step overlooked by nearly everyone doing his own oil change is prefilling the new oil filter prior to installation. Not even all the pros do it.

A dry filter means that the engine's oil pump cannot pressurize internal oil galleys until this 1- to 2-quart void is filled. Simply put, by failing to perform this important oil-change step, you can force your vehicle's engine to run for up to 30 oil-starved seconds *before* wear-preventing lubricant can reach vital parts.

Thankfully, it's a simple matter to avoid this unnecessary period of accelerated engine wear. All you have to do is top off the filter with oil before you spin it into place. (A word of caution: Be certain to deduct the amount of oil used for this purpose from the total engine-fill specifications. If you don't, an overfilled crankcase will result.)

As might be imagined, this job is easily accomplished if the filter mounts vertically on the engine. However, it is slightly more time-consuming and tricky if your power plant has its filter canister placed in a near-horizontal plane.

When filling these filters, pour the oil in a little at a time, turning the container on its side and rotating so the dry element material can absorb as much of the lubricant as possible. Continue pouring only until the oil level reaches the bottom of the threaded opening as the filter is held in the horizontal plane. Be careful not to overfill, or you'll experience spillage during filter installation.

Adopting this prefill precaution requires only a small extra effort. The reward for your thoroughness is near-instant lubrication at engine start-up, and a power plant undamaged by owner-induced oil starvation.
- Richard Mater, Santa Maria, California

• CLOSEUPS • CLOSEUPS • CLOSEUPS

CHAINING UP

*A*s the superintendent of a large postal fleet, I have considerable experience at using snow chains on dual rear tires. I take issue with the way some RVers install tire chains.

Often, only one chain is installed on the outer dual. This will wipe the snow and ice from under that tire, and leave the unchained tire spinning high and dry. When this happens, you can't move the rig.

My recommendation is to buy a full dual set of chains; they are worth the extra cost if you ever need them. For only occasional use, you don't have to buy the more expensive versions with center ties. Serious winter driving, though, justifies the higher cost of these models.

For the record, chain tighteners are usually a joke. They may look good while parked, but at 25 mph, centrifugal force stretches the rubber tensioners and will accomplish nothing. Your best bet is to tighten your tire chains with side tie links.

A tight chain set lasts four times longer than those allowed to slap loosely on the pavement. Poorly secured chains also chew up the tire sidewalls.

I have found the best way to install snow chains is to raise the vehicle with a floor jack.
- Elmer Pinkerton, Elmwood, Nebraska

• CLOSEUPS • CLOSEUPS • CLOSEUPS

BOILED IN OIL

Oil filter

Punch a hole at lowest part of oil filter

Strike here with hammer

We've all done it at one time or another—unscrewed that spin-off oil filter while performing an oil change and suddenly had hot motor oil running over our hands, streaming down our arms, splashing all over the engine compartment, and finally making a big mess on the ground.

You can avoid this decidedly unpleasant oil bath by first punching a small hole in the filter case at its lowest point. Depending upon the mounting angle of the filter case, this could be either on the side or at the bottom of the filter.

Let the oil drain directly into your drain pan. When the oil flow dribbles to a stop, unscrew the filter. No muss, no fuss, no burns.

- (NO NAME)

A STRAPPING IDEA

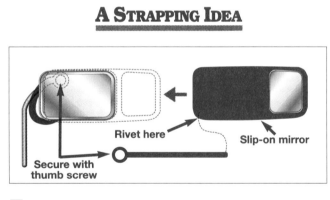

Rivet here

Slip-on mirror

Secure with thumb screw

I pull a fifth-wheel trailer and own a set of custom CIPA towing mirrors that conveniently slide over the factory mirrors of my tow vehicle. They are designed to be held in place by a thumb-screw and plastic wedge arrangement. However, as my wife and I were returning from a trip to the lake with our rig, the passenger-side mirror extension loosened and fell off at 55 mph. Needless to say, I had to order a replacement. This time, though, I devised a safety feature that really works.

I modified a heavy black rubber bungee strap to retain the mirror extension firmly in place. One end of the strap is pop-riveted to the slip-on mirror. The other end fits around the existing truck mirror and is secured by the screw knob of the slip-on mirror. This procedure requires removal and replacement of the knob. My simple addition has kept my CIPA mirrors firmly in place with no further losses.

- BILLY BULLINGTON, NEWARK, ARKANSAS

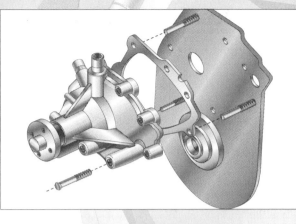

GASKET FINESSE

For those of us who tackle engine water-pump replacement on our tow vehicles, motorhomes, or cars, here is a helpful hint for installation.

One of the toughest tasks when installing a new pump is maneuvering it into place without disturbing the gasket, and holding it there long enough to start the mounting bolts into their holes. Despite being glued into position, the gasket can become misaligned as the pump is jockeyed around.

To make this task easy, acquire two or three bolts of the same thread size and pitch as the pump bolts, only ½- to ¾-inch longer. Cut off the heads, and lightly thread the topless bolts into any of the water-pump mounting holes in the engine block.

This method provides perfect alignment for the pump as you slip it into place, and at the same time, assures that the gasket will stay put without becoming cut or twisted. Finish the project by installing the original mounting bolts and removing the guide bolts.

- RICHARD BATTENBERGER, MOUNT HOLLY, NEW JERSEY

◆ CLOSEUPS ◆ CLOSEUPS ◆ CLOSEUPS ◆

USING YOUR NOODLE

I found a good way to protect the roof of your tow vehicle or trailer when carrying a temporary load on it. I purchased a couple of "swim noodles" from the toy store (a long tube of solid foam-plastic) for about $3.50 each, and they work perfectly as a make-do rack for transporting canoes and such. Of course, you still have to tie down your load securely to prevent it from shifting. But this kid's toy really makes an inexpensive, yet reliable, way to protect your vehicle's finish.

- GEORGE FIPP, JACKSONVILLE, FLORIDA

MIGHTY MUD FLAPS

Here's an idea I came up with for removable, extra-wide, trailer-protecting mud flaps for my tow vehicle. The project requires two 30-inch pieces of light-gauge, 2-inch-square tubing. Bolt the mud flaps to the tubing as illustrated.

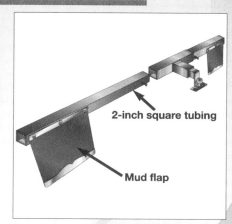

2-inch square tubing

Mud flap

The height and width can be varied to suit individual applications. With this done, it is a simple matter to slide the square tubing into the side openings of the hitch receiver.

However, some type of stop—either a bolt or maybe a nut welded on the 2-inch square tubing at the proper location—is needed to keep the mud-flap assemblies correctly positioned. After installation, a bungee cord can be used to hold everything in place.

This setup eliminates the need to drill holes in the receiver for retaining pins, an action that might weaken the hitch platform. If finding the proper-size mud flaps is a problem, I suggest trying a large truck stop where it might even be possible to acquire cheaper, used versions. I've used my set on two different trailers, and they've done a fine job of protecting these rigs.
- *Bill Webber, Shullsburg, Wisconsin*

SEAT-BELT SALVATION

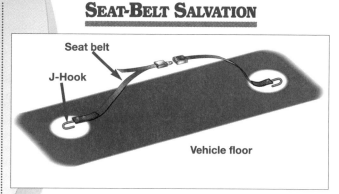

Seat belt

J-Hook

Vehicle floor

The GM Suburban has a cavernous interior that can accommodate considerable camping gear when the third seat is removed. The problem is that there are no tie-down hooks to secure loose items. Not wanting to mar my Suburban's interior with permanent tie-downs, I came up with another method.

I noticed that, with the rear seat removed, the outboard female seat-belt buckles remained attached to the wheel wells of the vehicle. At an auto junkyard, I looked for a GM vehicle having seat belts that matched the interior color of my Suburban. I purchased two 2-foot sections with male ends and bolt-down floor mounts. Auxiliary belts such as these can also be purchased at most auto-parts stores.

At the local hardware store, I purchased a couple of J-hooks, 3¼-inches long, that are made from ⅜-inch round stock, flattened and drilled on one end for bolts. I installed these hooks by securely bolting them onto the metal mounting plates with Grade 5 bolts and equivalent washers.

To use these belts as tie-downs, I installed the hooks into the floor brackets that are normally used for mounting the third seat, wrapped the belts around the storage items, and snapped the buckles into place at the existing belt locations. A simple tug on the seat-belt-adjusting strap tightens everything down nicely.

These tie-downs are quick and easy to make, as well as inexpensive. When not needed, they store out of the way, under the center seat.
- *Harold Prather, Georgetown, Kentucky*

WIPER GARAGES

During periods of extended storage, the windshield-wiper blades on your motorhome can be protected from the effects of sun, ozone and pollution by using short pieces of extruded black-foam pipe insulation. Hardware stores sell this material in 8-foot lengths, with inside diameters of ½, ¾, and 1 inch.

Choose the diameter that will give a loose fit around the wiper blades of your rig. Cut the foam insulation into sections that are an inch or two longer than the blade to be protected. Split these lengthwise, and install them over the blades. Finish by cutting out a small area to clear the blade attachment points.

Now, your wipers will be protected from the elements.
- *Jim Rodgers, Black Forest, Colorado*

QUICK DRY

Whenever I wash my van, RV, or car, I use my power leaf-blower to quickly remove the excess water from hard-to-reach places around body trim, door hinges, windshield wipers, etc. This method makes fast work of getting any vehicle dry.
- *Bill Fleckles, Elmhurst, Illinois*

DISGUISED DRIP

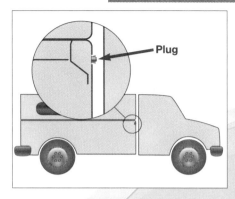

Plug

I had a leak problem with my 1993 Dodge pickup, and at first I thought it was because the shell was not properly installed. Some of the stake holes were not adequately covered by the shell-mounting gasket. Stopping these leaks required only a slight realignment of the shell. Despite this correction, I still was finding water in the truck bed during rainstorms.

Upon investigating further, I noticed the probable culprit. The top, front edge of the pickup box is formed by bending the sheet metal back and down before welding it to the box. This loop is open at both ends, which isn't a problem, since it is wholly contained inside the bed. Surprisingly, however, there is a 1-inch hole in the forward-bed bulkhead that can allow water to enter and drip into the storage area.

Sealing this hole was easier than I initially thought. I purchased a 1-inch-diameter rubber expansion plug (the type used to seal engine-block "freeze" plug holes), inserted it into the leaking opening, and tightened it down. This did the trick—no more leaks. My cost was $1.99 plus tax.

- *Richard M. Clark, Long Beach, California*

FAIR WARNING

I had to rebuild the floor in the rear of my trailer after it became wet, and over a period of time, rotted away. Even the 2 × 4-inch floor joists had to be replaced. This was time-consuming, indeed, and I was naturally interested in what had caused the problem in the first place. What I found was that undetected moisture had leaked past the gasket surfaces of my rig's exterior storage cabinets as I drove on wet, rain-swept roads.

I knew that the weatherstripping was getting thin, but because there was a drip molding over the doors, I didn't worry about water leaks. However, when looking in my mirrors while driving in rain, I could see the tremendous amount of water being sprayed against the RV. This can force water past all but the best-sealing surfaces.

Take heed: That weatherstrip gasket around those outside doors isn't just to keep out dust and bugs. Its primary job is to lock out moisture. For this reason, I suggest that others check the gasket condition on their rigs, and if replacement is needed, do it immediately. Make sure you get the right width and thickness of weather-stripping from your RV dealer, and replace those gaskets every three or four years to keep your rig in tip-top shape.

- Tom Gutzke, Franklin, Wisconsin

PEG-LEG RV

Here is my suggestion for a travel trailer axle skid, which prevents a flat tire from being cut by the wheel. Because the skid creates considerable noise when it touches the ground, the tow-vehicle driver is quickly alerted to a tire problem on the trailer. Additionally the device also helps avoid a catastrophic tire fire, which could be caused by the heat generated from a rolling flat tire.

The skid can be built from 6-inch-diameter well casing and steel bar stock. Both are ¼-inch thick by 2 inches wide. Two thicknesses of well casing, welded together, are required to complete each wheel skid, and the finished piece should include an internal reinforcing plate, as indicated in the diagram. If you do not have fabrication and welding experience, be sure to consult a qualified shop to have this item manufactured.

During installation, make sure that there are at least 1½ inches of clearance between the skid and the roadway when the trailer is sitting on level, hard pavement with properly inflated tires. At the same time, confirm that the tire cannot rub on the skid during rotation.

- *Al Fuller, Hudson, Florida*

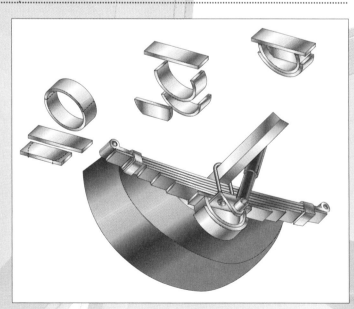

CUSTOM BED

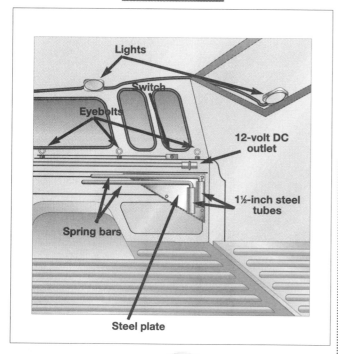

Lights

Switch

Eyebolts

12-volt DC outlet

1½-inch steel tubes

Spring bars

Steel plate

I use a full-size pickup as a tow vehicle, and I have made a few simple modifications that have really improved it. For instance, the camper shell that covers the bed area was mounted with three ¼-inch bolts on each side. I removed these and replaced them with ¼ × 1-inch eyebolts. After this, I added several more eyebolts to each side of the pickup bed. I have found these very handy for securing camping and scuba gear in position.

Next, I ran a wire from the 12-volt DC power line in the tow-package wiring harness to a standard cigarette-lighter outlet, which I installed in the truck bed. I also installed a switch and several 12-volt DC lights inside the shell that feed off this line. A 10-amp fuse was used to protect the circuit.

The lights are handy during hitching operations at night, and the lighter receptacle works well for powering 12-volt DC accessories, such as a small air compressor, a vacuum, or a handheld spotlight. The items needed to duplicate this project are available at any major auto-parts store.

Finally, I came up with a simple bracket to secure the equalizer spring bars safely inside the shell after unhitching my trailer. Selecting a triangular 10 × 10-inch piece of ⅛-inch steel, I welded two 4-inch pieces of 1½-inch steel tube to it. This mounting plate I then fastened to the right-rear corner of the pickup bed with several large sheet-metal screws. Whenever I store the spring bars in the metal bracket tubes, I attach a bungee cord to the pull-up chains, then stretch it and hook the other end to one of the eyebolts in the bed. This keeps the bars tightly in place and prevents the chains from rattling.
- *GREG ANDERSON, MOORHEAD, MINNESOTA*

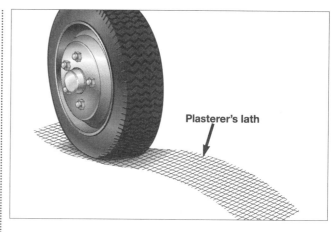

Plasterer's lath

TRUE TRACTION

Sometimes, a vehicle stuck in mud or sand only needs to move a few inches in order to regain traction. In such situations, I have successfully used two pieces of metal-mesh plasterer's lath to extract my vehicle. By placing the lath sections either in front of or behind the drive axle wheels (depending on the best escape route), both tires will grip and allow enough movement to get the vehicle back onto a solid footing. Not only will the lath help extract your vehicle from a frustrating, sometimes dangerous predicament, it also will save a great deal of wear and tear on your vehicle's driveline and tires. Of course, if a tow truck is not needed, you also will benefit financially.

The amount of lath material required is approximately 10 × 30 inches, depending primarily on tire size. The metal mesh is available at building-supply stores and is normally paint-primed or galvanized. It doesn't seem to rust, is easily stored flat just about anywhere aboard an RV, and can be used over and over. This method works on ice, snow, mud, and sand.
- *LLOYD SCHICK, SURREY, BRITISH COLUMBIA, CANADA*

CLOSEUPS • CLOSEUPS • CLOSEUPS

DIRTY CONTACTS

To clean those dirty contacts on markers, stop- and tail-lights, the turn signals, and trailer connector/receptacle, I use approximately 1 ounce of cider vinegar and add a little table salt. I apply the "cleaner" with an acid brush or similar applicator, and when the contacts are clean, rinse them with water from a spray bottle. I then dry the contacts with a hair dryer (you can also use compressed air). Works great here in rainy country.
- *CHAS H. WEBB, GRESHAM, OREGON*

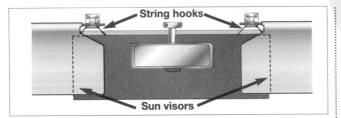

String hooks

Sun visors

SUN VISOR EXTENSION

If you're plagued by glaring sun that comes through the part of the windshield that is not covered by the sun visors, you can block it out for less than a dollar's worth of materials and a little time. Measure between the two inside hooks that hold the sun visors in place. Cut material dense enough to block out the sun's rays and long enough to overlap both hooks (match the color to the interior of the vehicle). The width should be approximately that of the sun visors. Using string "hooks," the new center visor can be hung in place after removing the vehicle's visors from their hooks; the visors can then be rehooked, leaving the material in place. When not in use, you can roll it up and secure it with a piece of hook-and-loop material, or remove it and store in the glove box.

- *RICHARD PEARCE, SALT LAKE CITY, UTAH*

ALASKA ROCK PROTECTION

¾-inch PVC pipes

Ties made from electrical (insulated) wires and wrap ties

¼-inch hardware cloth

While traveling in Alaska, I noticed a number of RVs with rock guards protecting headlights and windshields. I built my own by using ¾-inch PVC pipe for the frame, with a horizontal support in the center. The project required the use of three long, equal-length pieces, four short, equal-length pieces, four angle connectors, and two T-fittings. I covered the frame with ¼-inch hardware cloth, held in place with ties made from electrical (insulated) wire and wrap ties. Pads—attached with bungee cords—were used on those portions of the frame that came into contact with the vehicle. (Always use caution when using bungee cords; never pull them too tight.) Since the frame was not glued together, it could be taken apart and stored for a later Alaskan adventure or during another trip where gravel roads presented a hazard.

- *BOB BOYDSTON, LINDSAY, OKLAHOMA*

OUT OF SIGHT, OUT OF (CROOKS') MINDS

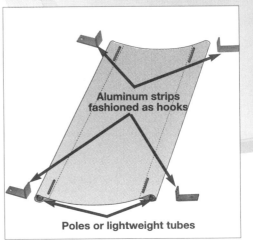

Aluminum strips fashioned as hooks

Poles or lightweight tubes

Adding a shell atop a pickup bed provides a generous storage area that is out of the weather. The only drawback is that sticky-fingered types (crooks) can look through the windows and be tempted to break in and relieve you of your "stuff." On the premise that "out of sight is out of mind," a tarp, bedsheet, or other cover can be used to conceal the cargo. The use of a cover can be made much more convenient if it's cut to size and pockets are sewn in along both long sides. Poles or lightweight tubes can be inserted into these pockets, providing an easy way to maneuver the cover without climbing into the bed. Hooks can be fashioned using a strip of aluminum and fastened to the sides of the bed to support the poles.

- *HERBERT A. SUTTON, TREASURE ISLAND, FLORIDA*

CLOSEUPS • CLOSEUPS • CLOSEUPS •

FIRST-CLASS JUMPERS

Murphy's Law seems to come into play any time someone needs a jump-start. The moment of necessity usually occurs when it's raining or snowing. With this in mind—and to make battery jump-starts easier, faster, and safer—I installed a pair of remote battery terminals on my rig. These are available from many automotive parts stores or mail-order performance equipment catalogs.

The terminals are insulated and can be installed through sheet metal. I mounted them in my rig's fiberglass front spoiler; in any case, mount them where there's no chance of a short circuit. The terminals come with black and red rubber caps for ease of identification and protection from the elements. They're convenient and functional.

- *BILL SODERLIN, DEERFIELD BEACH, FLORIDA*

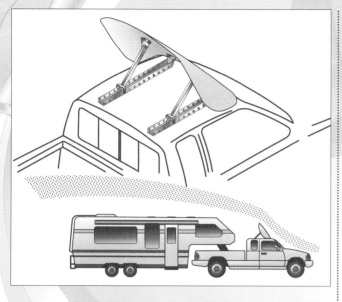

INTO THE WIND

Having traveled many miles pulling a fifth-wheel, I know what it's like to be severely buffeted by large trucks, and to watch the gas gauge fall in a West Texas headwind. I decided to take action to improve these conditions.

I elected to save some money by building my own pickup-mounted wind deflector. Taking a hint directly from the 18-wheelers, I visited a big-rig wrecking yard. There, I was able to purchase a used fiberglass deflector for ⅓ less than the price of commercially produced RV versions.

With a little thought and elbow grease, I now have a wind deflector that is totally adjustable through a 90-degree range. My daughter helped with the painting to produce a professional-looking finished product that almost covers the front of my fifth-wheel.

So, for anyone towing tall fivers that never seem to find a tail wind, here's an economical way out.
- *RODNEY HUFFMAN, LONGVIEW, TEXAS*

IMPRESSIVE ILLUMINATION

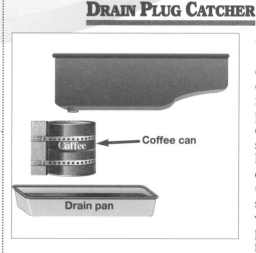

RV ceiling lights

After finding it impossible to read a road map by the factory dome light in my last two trucks, I decided to replace this dim fixture in my current truck with a pair of ceiling lights like those found in many RVs. To accomplish this modification, I wired one of the lights to the door switches, so that it would always come on when people enter the truck. The second light was connected to a convenient 12-volt DC source, which allows it to be activated manually. In trying to match the curvature of the truck's roofline, I found it easier to install two single fixtures, as illustrated, rather than one containing double lights. Once in place, these fixtures provide an impressive amount of light.

(*Editor's note*: During installation, either select or install a new circuit that includes a fuse appropriate to the fixture being installed. Use caution when mounting lights to avoid creating an impact hazard to passengers in a vehicle crash.)
- *LANE WELLS, THREE RIVERS, MICHIGAN*

DRAIN PLUG CATCHER

Coffee can

Drain pan

To keep from dropping the oil pan plug into a drain pan full of hot engine oil, I solicited the help of a small coffee can (13-ounce size). I wrapped two pieces of perforated pipe strap around the top and bottom of the can to hold a 1 × 3-inch wood "handle" in place (using ¼-inch screws). I then punched numerous holes in the bottom of the can using a large nail. When I change the oil, I hold the can below the drain plug while I remove it. The oil filters through to the drain pan, and the plug is caught by the can.
- *ARTHUR W. WAGNER, KERRVILLE, TEXAS*

NOVEL BATTERY-WATER FILLER

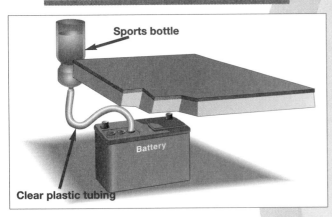

Sports bottle

Battery

Clear plastic tubing

I have a fifth-wheel trailer equipped with an alarm system; the horn is mounted in the battery compartment, above the three batteries. This arrangement makes it impossible to use the automatic-stop battery filler used by most service stations. It's also impossible to use a glass or funnel. While my situation is somewhat unique, I know of other RVers who complain that access to their batteries is difficult; it's a real pain in the neck to disconnect and remove the batteries every time they need water. I solved the problem with a squeezable sports bottle. I fill the bottle with distilled water, and hang it from the awning arm, and the hose can be used easily inside the compartment for filling the batteries. I use a compact mirror so I can see clearly and can fill each cell properly.

- TOM MCELHINNEY, HOUSTON, TEXAS

THE BEST OF BOTH WORLDS

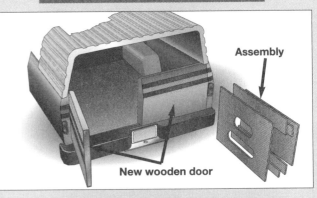

Assembly

New wooden door

For many years, I pulled a trailer with a van that had two rear doors, which permitted access with the trailer still attached. When a used Ford pickup became available, I decided to make the change for a number of reasons. But, I had been spoiled by the configuration of the van, plus I found it difficult to climb over the tailgate, whether it was up or down. Achieving unrestricted access to the shell-covered truck bed required unhitching the trailer. Something had to be done.

After some careful thought, I designed and built two doors to replace the pickup's tailgate. They were constructed of plywood, then painted and installed on their own hinges. I even adapted the original aluminum trim and logo. When the doors are closed, most people don't realize that it's not the original tailgate.

- EDWIN BUCK, HOMELAND, CALIFORNIA

CLEARED FOR LANDING

Because my wife and I work, most of our camping is done on the weekends. This means that we usually arrive at a campground on Friday evening after it is dark. In fact, this happens often enough that I have installed two special backup lights. These allow us to use the mirrors on our 31-foot motorhome to position the vehicle in its assigned site, avoid obstacles, and do hookup work using a low-level light system that doesn't disturb our neighboring campers.

The lights are mounted to the side skirts, just behind and to the outside of the front wheels. They are 12-volt DC tractor work lights, 4 inches in diameter, purchased from an auto-parts store for about $15 each. With the beams of these lights shining back, parallel to the ground, it's easy to see hookups, trees, and any obstacles from the driver's seat.

To determine how to hook up the lights, be sure that the vehicle is on level ground and that the rear wheels are chocked, both front and back. Set the parking brake securely. Turn the ignition key to the "on" position, and with the engine turned off, place the shift lever in reverse. Use a test light to find the hot backup-light circuit. Once the right wire is found, a splice can be made, and a 14-gauge wire run to each new light. Run a ground wire of the same gauge from each new light, and secure to a suitable place on the rig's frame.

I found that the fuse already in my system was capable of carrying the extra two lights with no problem. If that is not your situation, a relay can be used to provide power from the battery (fused), and the back-up light circuit can trigger the relay. By positioning the lights outside the tires, you prevent damage from stones.

- PETER C. SIGNOROTTI, MIAMI, FLORIDA

SHINY LUG NUTS

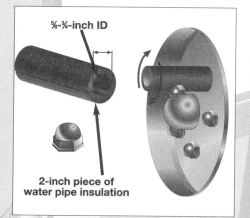

⅝-¾-inch ID

2-inch piece of
water pipe insulation

Cleaning the chrome lug nut covers on stainless-steel wheel covers or wheel liners can be time consuming, and is definitely not fun. Here's an easy way to accomplish the job: Purchase a 4-inch length of ⅜- to ¾-inch ID foam rubber water pipe insulation, available at most hardware stores. Cut off a 2-inch-long piece. Dip this short piece of insulation in soapy water, push it over the lug nut cover, and rotate it a few times. All the mud and dirt will be removed from the lug nut covers, and you will have enough of the insulation left over so that you can share the material with your neighbors.
- *Glen A. Diebert, Fayetteville, North Carolina*

ONE WHEEL IS BETTER THAN TWO

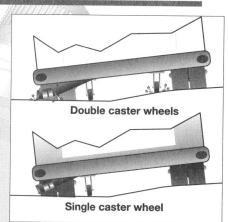

Double caster wheels

Single caster wheel

After losing the sewer valve assembly that's on the left rear of our RV while coming out a steep gas station ramp, I decided to mount a couple of caster wheels to protect the new parts. While departing a particularly steep ramp, I lost the valve assembly again. I finally figured out that the opposite caster wheel, which had nothing to protect, was causing the problem. I removed it, leaving only the wheel on the left side, and have not had any more problems.
- *Bud Rinker, Santa Barbara, California*

CAMOUFLAGED CAP

My motorhome is built on a Chevrolet chassis. The radiator cap is located almost 2 feet behind the front grille. In this location, it was difficult to remove the cap to add coolant. I discovered, however, that this opening was connected to the radiator through a very short section of straight radiator hose.

I reasoned that I could relocate the radiator cap and cooling-system opening by installing a longer piece of hose. I did so by using an 18-inch length of straight hose. Now the cap is located only 1 inch beneath the hood, where it is easily accessible for the addition of coolant when needed.

After this modification was done, I found that the old mounting bracket was useless. So, I fastened the entire assembly to a sheet-metal baffle between the radiator and the front grille using two muffler clamps.

Be sure the engine is cold before removing the radiator cap, and check for leaks when done. Please note that it's important to ensure that the new hose doesn't slope downward—away from the radiator. Coolant capacity could be reduced if it does.
- *Adolph Cecula, Oakton, Virginia*

CAMPER DIRT BLOCKER

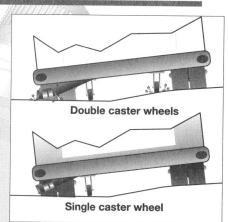

Wood screws

Tube-like
flotation
device

Blocks of wood to fit
into the stake pockets

The small gaps between the bottom of our truck camper and the top of the truck bed rails allowed rain and dirt to infiltrate the storage areas of our camper. I purchased three of the solid-foam tube-like flotation devices known as Funoodles or Swim Noodles, and adapted them to fill the voids. First, I cut small blocks of wood and fit them into the stake pockets in the truck bed. I then laid the foam onto the bed rails and secured them by nailing into the blocks of wood. When the camper was lowered onto the bed of the truck, a seal was created.

Although the weight of the camper presses the foam firmly into place, the nailed sections ensure that the foam does not blow loose while driving at highway speeds. We used about $6 worth of foam, which comes in many colors for those who wish to match the paint on the camper.
- *Daniel Gray, Frankfort, Kentucky*

QUICK DIP

I have a Win-
nebago
Class A mo-
torhome with a
heavy engine
cover that used
to frustrate my
attempts to
check the
transmission-
fluid level.

In order to
make the job
easier, I cut a 4-inch hole in the cover directly over the dipstick. I installed a couple of hinges, a latch, and a knob, and I
used the cut piece to make an access cover.

All I have to do now to check the transmission-oil level is
flip open the access cover.

- LEONARD M. WIMMER, SOUTH SAN GABRIEL, CALIFORNIA

BE A FLASHER

Glare and bright sunlight can
often obscure an RV's flashing turn signals from other drivers.
Those vehicles traveling alongside
a large rig may not have any warning at all that you're planning a
lane change.

Adding auxiliary signal lights to
the outside mirror brackets can help
overcome such deficiencies. Toward
this end, the mirror-mounted turn
signal lights used on large semitrac-
tors are readily available, but are
probably a bit bulky for most motorhomes and tow vehicles. Fabricating your own light kit is simple.

Smaller lights that are more in
proportion to your rig can be cho-
sen from the array of RV marker lights sold by RV and automotive-supply stores. You'll need four: two red and two amber.

Next you'll need to obtain two $6 \times 1 \times \frac{1}{16}$-inch aluminum
strips. These will be formed into brackets to hold the marker
lights. Several feet of 16-gauge automotive wire, electrical
tape, rubber grommets, and six machine screws with nuts
(sizes 6-32) will also be needed to complete the project. Some
vehicles may also need a heavy-duty turn signal flasher.

Form the aluminum strips around each mirror bracket, and
drill for one machine screw (Figure 1). Drill the opposite end
to match the mounting holes in the marker lights you've selected, and assemble the lights with the red lens facing to the

rear of the RV. Certain marker
lights may require minor modifications to make them fit flush on the
aluminum bracket.

Make the bracket holes slightly
smaller than the attaching screw
since the lights will need good
metal-to-metal contact at this
point to be properly grounded.

With this complete, you can now
decide whether to run the power
wire outside the RV's mirror bracket
tube, or drill the ends of the bracket
and route the wire internally.

Regardless of the method you
choose, the next step requires
drilling the vehicle door and side
wall to provide a path for the
power wire to reach the vehicle's turn-signal circuit. Be sure to
install rubber grommets at all locations where the wire passes
through bare metal. Depending upon which is easiest, you
can tap into the RV's sidelight marker (if it flashes during
turns) or the front signal.

Solder and tape all electrical connections. Use a small bead
of silicone sealer to weatherproof the seam between the two
marker lights, and you're done.

Your next trip should prove the value of your mirror-mounted flashers, because more drivers will see and react to your
signaled intentions.

- LEON BOECK, EASTON, MINNESOTA

Convenient Canteen

Since my family does a considerable amount of primitive camping in the desert and Baja, California, an adequate water supply for our RV was a problem, especially when we traveled with our two frequently thirsty dogs.

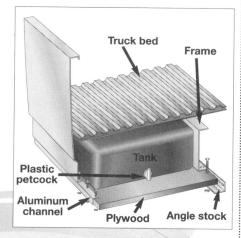

Carrying portable plastic jugs was one solution, but they take up valuable storage space and are a pain to handle. I wanted something convenient and reliable.

I found a space under the truck bed that was sufficient to house one or two standard 12-gallon ABS Rocket brand (or equivalent) tanks. These are sold at most RV-supply stores. While my project was tailored specifically to a 1990 Ford F-250 pickup, the basic idea should be adaptable to other makes and models.

A base of painted exterior-grade plywood is used to support the weight of the loaded tank (approximately 100 pounds). This plywood is held on one side with predrilled angle stock and on the other side with a length of ½-inch I.D. aluminum channel. On the Ford, I was able to use existing holes in the frame, through which I could install long bolts to hold the angle and plywood. (*Editor's note: Most manufacturers do not recommend drilling holes in frames.*) The channel side is fastened to the truck body with screws placed every 6 to 8 inches. All fasteners were "potted" with RTV silicone sealer to prevent rust and allow for easy removal in the future. I used standard strips of camper shell "cap tape" for cushioning and damping on all sides of the tank where it contacts the mounting structure.

Tank preparation was begun by installing a plastic petcock in the predrilled bottom-center hole. A hole saw was used to cut the fill hole at the top center of the tank, and ABS cement applied to bond a collar into place. The filler hole was attached and clamped onto this opening prior to tank installation. Using wood blocks, I raised the tank up into the recessed underbed mounting location, and secured it with bolts and nuts. Next, I cut a hole in the fender well shield of the truck, and passed the filler hose through to an accessible location. The project was completed by attaching a hose clamp to the end of the hose, so it can't slip off, and then installing a standard PVC cap to close the opening. This allows the tank to be easily filled with a garden hose.
- *Bob Howe, San Diego, California*

Silicone Brake Enhancement

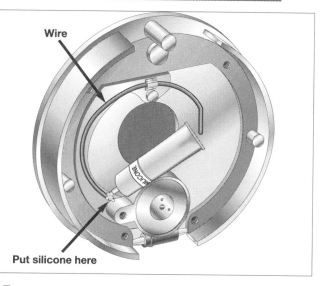

Wire

Put silicone here

As my travel trailer aged, the wires broke right at the brake magnets. When I installed the replacements, I decided to support the wires by putting a glob of silicone sealer on each magnet at the point where the electrical wires enter this component. To assure successful adhesion, the area must be clean. I have traveled for three years since performing this repair, and have suffered no more broken wires.
- *James M. Harmon, Notasulga, Alabama*

CLOSEUPS • CLOSEUPS • CLOSEUPS •

Strung Out

Have you ever wondered what the axle ratio is in your motorhome and tow vehicle? Here's a quick way to find out without getting dirty, or having to consult a dealer or a manual.

1. Place a strip of masking tape at the 6 o'clock position on the rear tire.

2. Attach a piece of string to the drive shaft with masking tape. Lay it out so that the shaft will roll it up as it turns.

3. Drive the vehicle forward one tire revolution, making sure the tape on the tire stops exactly at the 6 o'clock position once again.

4. Cut the string on the drive shaft where it meets the shaft.

5. Measure the length of the string, and divide it by the circumference (not the diameter) of the drive shaft. The circumference is exactly one turn of string around the shaft. The figure arrived at using this method equals your rig's axle ratio.
- *Harold Yetley, Marshalltown, Iowa*

HANGING AROUND

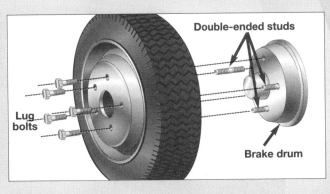

Double-ended studs

Lug bolts

Brake drum

Hanging a trailer tire presents a problem because many use threaded lug bolts rather than automotive-style studs and nuts. This makes it difficult to lift the heavy tire into position and hold it there while trying to line up the bolt holes. If these holes are not perfectly aligned, it is almost impossible to catch the threaded holes in the brake drum. I solved this problem by purchasing three double-ended studs with threads matching those in my trailer's wheel hubs. Whenever I have a flat, or I simply wish to rotate the tires, I remove a wheel and temporarily install the three threaded studs in the brake drum. This allows me to hang the replacement wheel in place while I install two lug bolts in the remaining holes. (My trailer uses five bolts per wheel.) When this has been accomplished, I remove the threaded studs one by one and replace them with the factory bolts. The cost of the double-ended studs was approximately $2 each—an investment that I think is well worthwhile in terms of reduced aggravation and backaches.
- *John M. Birmingham, New Port Richey, Florida*

CLOSEUPS ◆ CLOSEUPS ◆ CLOSEUPS

BRILLIANT THOUGHT

It has been my experience that the taillights of older RVs become dim and hard to see in daylight. Here's an inexpensive trick I have used that works well in solving this problem. I remove the red lenses and clean all debris and accumulated grime from inside the taillight housing. With this completed, I apply strips of aluminized duct tape to the old reflective surfaces of the light housing, and carefully burnish it into place. This creates a much better reflective surface than the original plated plastic. The job takes only a few minutes and, I think, is worth the effort. It may well prevent an accident due to dim lighting.
- *Mike Robinson, Powder Springs, Georgia*

CLOSEUPS ◆ CLOSEUPS ◆ CLOSEUPS

FANCY FAN

Engine drive fan

Radiator

Electric fans

If you're the owner of a tow vehicle, you are probably treated to high engine temperatures and more engine-fan noise than you'd like whenever the going gets tough. This is usually the result of the thermostatically controlled engine-fan clutch engaging whenever it senses increased cooling needs. In hot climates, the roar may never subside—making it a constant irritation to vehicle occupants.

Fortunately, there is a solution. You need only equip your tow vehicle with a couple of the new-generation, high-volume, electric radiator fans. These are easily attached to a vehicle's radiator core, and are readily available from most automotive outlets and many performance-oriented mail-order houses. However, make certain that you purchase only high-capacity electric fans designed for applications of this type.

Once installed, the fans can be wired to operate manually through a dash-mounted switch, or to activate automatically through a temperature sensor, or both. I suggest the latter, since it gives the driver greater control over engine cooling, especially in traffic.

The fans can also be set so that one comes on at a lower temperature than the other. Whenever a slow-up occurs, the fans can be turned on in anticipation of an engine temperature rise. A thermostat in the circuit is advantageous because cooling will start when needed, even if the driver forgets to flip the switch.

Additionally, the extra drag produced by a continuously engaged, high-capacity, steel fan will noticeably reduce overall fuel economy. And, because conventional fans and thermostatic hubs are bolted to the water-pump shaft, the supporting bearing often gets quite a workout. This can result in premature failure, particularly if the fan itself is even slightly out of balance. With this change, the original engine-driven fan can sometimes be removed altogether, since it may no longer be needed in the presence of two high-output electric models. This will give the water-pump bearing a break, and allow the engine to produce more power with greater efficiency.
- *Richard Mater, Santa Maria, California*

TOO MUCH OF A GOOD THING

The large cockpit windows of a Class A motorhome certainly give a great view of surroundings en route, especially on perfect-weather days. But, when bright sunshine comes streaming in at certain times, these panoramic lenses to the world can become very uncomfortable for front-seat occupants. Moreover, such intense sunlight can be a driving hazard.

I solved this problem for less than $5 by making temporary translucent shades. These are easily installed when needed, and are simple to store when they aren't.

I purchased some off-white plastic shade material from a local fabric store (¾ of a yard was enough for my application). I then cut this material to fit the upper-cockpit window frames of my motorhome, using some solar shades al-

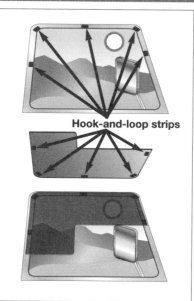

Hook-and-loop strips

ready in use for a pattern. (Paper patterns can be made and substituted if solar shades are not already installed.)

Then, I cut the forward lower edge of each shade to allow the driver a clear line of sight to each rearview mirror. I trimmed the rear portion of the shade slightly lower to provide increased protection without hindering vision. Next, I attached hook-and-loop tabs to the new shades at the same points used by my solar shades. On rigs not already so equipped, tab placement is optional. However, they should be in about the same positions as those shown in the illustration.

(Editor's note: Check state laws regarding window tinting and obstruction to vision before installing shades.)

- Thurman C. Burns, Athens, Alabama

ARRESTING THOUGHT

On my last RV trip, I stopped at a rest stop for a break. As I was getting ready to leave near dusk, I decided to do a quick underhood fluid check. As luck would have it, I dropped the oil-filler opening cap. After spending about 20 minutes looking for it in the approaching darkness, I decided to make sure that this event did not happen again.

I stopped at a hardware store in the next town and bought a 24-inch length of small-loop chain. Then, with a small washer and a

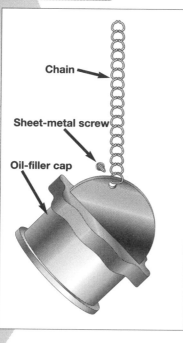

Chain

Sheet-metal screw

Oil-filler cap

sheet-metal screw, I attached the chain to the top of the cap (a rubber push-in type). I used a plastic wire bundle tie to secure the other end of the chain to a group of wires near the top of the firewall, leaving a little slack to allow for engine movement. No more lost oil caps for me.

- Jack Ewald, West Union, Ohio

SHAKY POINT OF VIEW

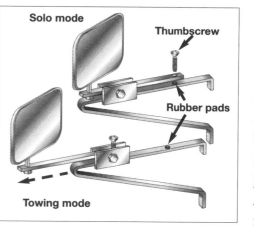

Solo mode

Thumbscrew

Rubber pads

Towing mode

I have adjustable slide extensions on my truck mirrors, which use a single setscrew to hold the mirrors in position. This works well for maintaining the extension adjustment, but does nothing to assure a jitter-free view to the rear. There is a distinct up-and-down motion imparted to the mirrors by road vibration and wind.

However, I was able to stabilize my view to the rear by picking a point about 1 inch from the inside end of the sliding adjustment bracket, then drilling and tapping it (¼-20 threads), as illustrated. When completed, I installed a ¼ × 1½-inch thumbscrew, along with a rubber "scuff" pad at both the solo and towing mirror positions.

Once the mirror is adjusted in or out as necessary, a quick turn of the thumbscrew ensures that everything remains rock solid.

- Ron Loen, Fresno, California

SPURT STOPPER

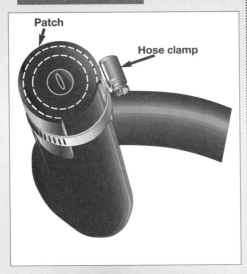

Pinhole oil or water leaks in delivery lines can be stopped by applying virtually any kind of rubber over the hole, and then installing a screw-type hose clamp. An old hose, cut in half, works well.

This fix will usually last for 50 to 100 miles, which should be enough to get you to a service station.

- BARRY MOFFATT, COSTA MESA, CALIFORNIA

ANOTHER WAY

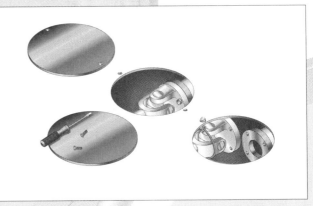

If you tow a rear-wheel-drive car and regularly unhook the driveshaft before getting underway, you might want to try installing an access hole about one foot across in the floor (as indicated in the sketch). Simply unbolt the driveshaft and tie it securely aside. This requires the backseat to be removed each time, but it saves jacking the car up and crawling underneath in all types of weather.

- THEODORE I. BAUER, TOLEDO, OHIO

CHANGING THE BED

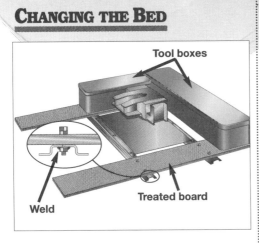

Because I lease my pickup truck, I must minimize the number of holes drilled in the bed. Attaching my toolboxes with such a limitation was a real problem until I devised a simple wood framework. To each end of the fifth-wheel hitch-mounting flanges, I welded a stainless-steel nut. These nuts are held in place during welding with the use of a matching bolt and nut. With the nuts affixed, I bolted two 2×6-inch Wolmanized, or treated, boards to the hitch flanges. Then I attached all my storage units to these boards with metal angle brackets and straps. Since the boards must be elevated slightly to clear the hitch, I secured wood spacers to the underside of each runner. This provides equal height support along the runners' entire length.

I have used this method in three different trucks, and it works great. The storage units and boards can be removed in minutes for installation in another vehicle.

- FRED A. HIGGINS, ROYAL OAK, MICHIGAN

R E S T R A I N I N G   O R D E R

*T*he one thing I always felt was missing in the back of a pickup truck is adequate tie-down spots. There's always something that has to be secured during travel. I solved this recently while I had the fiberglass shell off the truck. I positioned ⅜-inch eyebolts in the bottom of each of the stake slots. By facing the eyebolts downward toward the bed floor, they are always available, but out of the way when not in use. (Of course, if you have a shell, it must first be removed, so you can install lockwashers and nuts on the eyebolt threads.) I replaced the original hold-down bolts with eyebolts when I reinstalled the shell. This is an easy task, especially suited for those not wanting to remove the shell from their truck in order to install eyebolts in the stake pockets. Now, to make use of all these new tie-downs, I always keep a supply of bungee cords in the truck, so I can conveniently secure nearly any type of cargo that I carry.

- DENNIS E. RAY, ST. LOUIS, MISSOURI

Editor's note: Bungee cords can be hazardous when under tension.

CHIMING IN

Have you ever noticed how many vehicles travel along the highway with their turn signals blinking, mile after mile? It's obvious that the drivers are not aware that their signals did not turn off. To correct this problem on my rig, I connected an audible chime to the turn-signal circuit.

Using Radio Shack part no. 273-071 ($8.99) or its equivalent, connect the electrical leads directly to the prongs of a heavy-duty turn-signal flasher (red and white to one prong, black to the other with the Radio Shack part). Twist the exposed wires around the prongs, and solder in place. Do this quickly in order to prevent the soldering heat from damaging the flasher. Also, make your connections close to the base of the prongs, so you can reinsert the flasher into its socket.

No special mounting of the chime is necessary, as it can be tied to existing wires with a wire tie. It can also be mounted with two self-tapping screws to any flat surface.

- Vayne R. Davis, Tucson, Arizona

MUD-BOGGING DEFINED

While I was returning from a drive on mountainous backroads in Idaho, the front end of my 1990 F-250 4x4 truck began to shake. After I got back to the main highway, I racked my brain trying to figure out what the problem was. After all, the truck had been performing well when I went into the backcountry.

In desperation, I finally removed the wheel covers to check for loose lug nuts. Finding them all tight and feeling a bit lazy, I tossed the hubcaps in the back of the truck and drove on. To my surprise, and relief, the truck performed normally. Not knowing the cause, I expected the vibration to return at any time.

Many wary miles later, it dawned on me. The wheel covers had loaded up with mud when I drove through a very muddy section of the backroad. The uneven distribution of mud in the caps caused the vibration.

Now, whenever I expect to encounter muddy backroads, the hubcaps come off.

- Ben Lewis, Independence, Missouri

THE EASY WAY

When greasing the wheel bearings of my trailer, I used to have considerable trouble seating the grease seal in the hub. It was difficult to get it started straight.

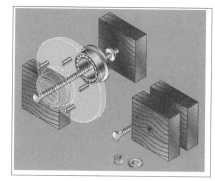

I solved my dilemma by making a tool from two wood blocks. Each is large enough to cover the hub opening. I also bought a carriage bolt long enough to span the distance through the hub, the grease seal, and the two wood blocks.

The blocks can be made of several thicknesses of plywood, glued together. The hole drilled through the center of these pieces should be absolutely straight and just large enough for the bolt to pass through. I use a washer between the block and the nut to protect the wood.

To use this tool, I put one block in place over the outside of the hub, and then install the carriage bolt through it and the hub. The seal goes in place next on the inside of the hub, followed by the other wood block.

I finish by installing the nut and slowly tightening it until the seal is forced into place. During this process, it sometimes helps to use a small hammer to tap the block adjoining the seal. The result is a grease seal that is accurately placed every time.

- Marvin Bryant, Littleton, Colorado

SOCKET TO IT

During our summer vacation this year, the heater hose in my 24-foot mini-motorhome had a hole rubbed in it after the hose somehow fell against the alternator pulley. This occurred miles from any repair station, and I was not carrying any spare parts.

After thinking the situation over for a few minutes, I came up with the idea of cutting the damaged heater hose in two, inserting a ½-inch deep-drive socket into the hose and rejoining the pieces. Not having any hose clamps, I wrapped the repair securely with duct tape, and my rig made it to my intended destination without further incident. A permanent repair should be made as soon as possible.

- Junius M. Miller, Calico Rock, Arkansas

POLE-VAULTING VEHICLE

I've noticed that owners of all sorts of towed motor vehicles tend to leave the tow bars in place during stopovers with their RVs. So long as it doesn't block visibility, this method works just fine. The problem is that many of the retracted tow bars I see are held in place by bungee cords or ropes.

This practice is extremely dangerous. Such restraints could either fail or break through the plastic grille to which they are often attached. The resulting incident may be costly in terms of mechanical damage or injury, should the tow bar drop and cause the vehicle to flip over.

The proper method of securing a tow bar is with a safety pin and clip installed by a certified welder. Anything less is taking chances.

Also, check for high-tensile-strength mounting bolts. These are critical links in the towing system, and should not be mere hardware-grade bolts. Use at least SAE grade 5 fasteners at all stress points. These are medium-carbon, heat-treated steel, having a tensile strength of 120,000 pounds per square inch (psi). They can be identified by the three hash marks on the head. Weaker, low-carbon steel bolts have a 74,000-psi rating, and no marks on the head.
- EUGENE STAGNER, ANAHEIM, CALIFORNIA

CLOSEUPS • CLOSEUPS • CLOSEUPS

THE SQUEAKY WHEEL

I have a Class C motorhome on a Ford E-350 chassis. It has standard-type wheel covers. When the RV was less than a year old, I began hearing an annoying squeak while driving under 35 mph. It seemed to come from the front end half the time and the rear end the rest of the time.

The frequency of this squeaking increased to such a point that I began to worry it had something to do with the powertrain, the wheel bearings, or the brakes. I knew any of these would be expensive to repair, so I decided to try and track down the problem myself.

I removed the wheel covers and looked for loose parts, but I saw nothing out of the ordinary. So, I took the rig out for a spin for another listen without the wheel covers. I heard nothing.

After some serious thinking, I concluded that the wheels were flexing just enough to make the prongs on the wheel covers squeak. I wrapped a continuous piece of electrical tape around the outside of these prongs, figuring it would prevent the metal-to-metal contact needed to produce a squeak.

I was right. This approach solved the noise problem completely, and has left me with a lot more money in my pocket than I might have had after replacing parts needlessly.

I replace the tape whenever I remove the wheel covers.
- ROBERT C. WHITNER, PENACOOK, NEW HAMPSHIRE

CLOSEUPS • CLOSEUPS • CLOSEUPS

BRIGHT IDEA

We recently noticed that our taillights were rather dull, even after cleaning the contacts in the connection between the truck and trailer. I removed the lenses and noted that they were dirty, and also that the reflective area of the light housing was not bright any longer. To make them brighter, I simply cut a piece of aluminum foil to fit behind the bulb. Crumple the foil slightly and flatten it out before gluing it behind the bulb. A 3-inch-square piece of foil worked well for my light fixtures.
- CARL NEMECHEK, SALINA, KANSAS

CLOSEUPS • CLOSEUPS • CLOSEUPS

WATCH THE SEALS

If you change your own oil and filter, make certain that the old gasket is still attached to the filter when you remove it. Should it stick to the engine block and you spin on a new filter without noticing, your driveway will end up looking like the Alaska oil spill. Once you start the engine, its oil pressure will quickly displace the two rubber seals.

BETTER BOLTS

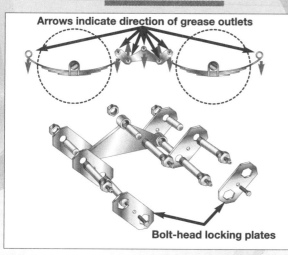

Arrows indicate direction of grease outlets

Bolt-head locking plates

The shackle bolts and bushings on my 29-foot trailer needed to be replaced, but I thought that greasable "wet" bolts might be a better choice than those used for original equipment. Pressurized grease follows the path of least resistance, so I reasoned that placing the outlet holes parallel to the frame would only force lubricant into the unworn area of the shackle bushing. Using seven wet bolts per wheel, I placed the grease outlets as indicated in the illustration to assure proper lubrication.

Before applying grease, I jack up the trailer to unload the primary wear area between the bolt and the shackle bushing. This allows fresh grease to squeeze into where it's needed most. Because positioning of the wet bolts is critical, I did not trust the spline ridges to hold them permanently in the needed configuration. So, I made separate bolt-head locking devices from steel place and secured them in place with the addition of a ¼-inch bolt, which required drilling and tapping each shackle.
- VIRGIL A. KROEGER, TEMPLE CITY, CALIFORNIA

CRANKY CRUISE CONTROL

When the cruise control on my 1979 Pace Arrow decided to retire, I spent considerable time trying to find repair parts. I needed a replacement for the throttle actuating vacuum servo.

In desperation, I took my rig to a General Motors dealer, as it has a Chevy chassis with a 454 engine. I found out that the cruise control was not GM, but a brand called ARA.

The parts man said he had never seen a unit like that on a GM vehicle.

I next visited a shop specializing in cruise controls. Imagine my surprise when the technician sent me to a Chrysler dealer. Even more amazing was the fact the stock replacement part they offered me was identical to the unit removed from my Chevrolet chassis.

The ARA system was apparently cloned from the Chrysler cruise control, and many ended up on motorhomes such as my Pace Arrow. ARA is no longer in business, however, so parts for their products are no longer available.

Fortunately, the entire episode came to a happy ending. The Chrysler servo bolted right into the Chevy mount. Even the cable connections were identical.

So, if your Chevy parts man shakes his head at your cruise control problem, slip over to Chrysler. It's a lot cheaper and easier than replacing all the existing cruise control cables and circuits with a complete, new GM system.
- JIM PRENTICE, BRANDON, MANITOBA, CANADA

JUNIOR'S WINDSHIELD WIPERS

While traveling with our fifth-wheel one night, bugs seemed to start raining on our windshield. The windshield wipers and spray only smeared them. We finally cut through the oily mess with a couple of our trusty baby wipes, and turned on the regular wipers. Our clean, clear windshield enabled us to continue our journey without further mishap, thanks to our pack of trusty baby wipes.
- ALBERT LILLIE, WICHITA FALLS, TEXAS

A LITTLE EDGY

In time, windshield wiper blades lose their efficiency, and vision through the windshield can become distorted during rainstorms. Fortunately, they can be restored to near-new operation by using a small piece of 270- to 320-grit sandpaper. Just slide the sandpaper against the rubber edge of blade that contacts the glass. Run the sandpaper the length of the rubber four or five times. This removes the hardened wiping edge and exposes fresh, soft rubber. The wiper will now be like new again.

TREADFUL ADVICE

Several years ago, the driver of an 18-wheeler gave me some advice on the importance of checking tandem trailer wheels—and gave me some how-to's. This information has been helpful to me on more than one occasion and may serve others, as well.

When stopping to refuel or rest, take a few minutes to check your trailer or motorhome wheels. In addition to a visual once-over, be sure to perform a tactile inspection. A tire that is hotter than the rest is probably under-inflated and may, in fact, be punctured.

Touch the hubs, also. A higher temperature than the other hubs is indicative of a bearing or brake problem (lack of lubrication/failure to fully release). A hub that is considerably cooler than the others may indicate that the brake on that wheel isn't working properly.

Of course, during this type of a check, take into consideration that tires and hubs facing the sun will normally be somewhat warmer than those on the shady side.
- J.J. BROWN, YARDLY, PENNSYLVANIA

DOUBLE DUTY

While at my local RV dealer's parts department recently, I found an AC 2-quart oil filter for my Chevrolet 454 engine. This filter (AC part no. PF 932) replaces the standard 1-quart AC PF 35 filter whenever space permits a longer filter case to be used.

The larger filter increases the engine's oil capacity by 1 additional quart. It has the advantage of circulating the oil through a larger filtering surface, and it also seems to allow for a bit more cooling of the lubricant.

Although this particular filter is not stocked by any of the local auto-parts stores in my immediate area, I have found that it's available through Chevrolet dealers and some of the larger RV dealers.
- BOB ZIMMER, SCHAUMBURG, ILLINOIS

MEMORY MINDER

If you are one of those people who changes the engine oil in your motorhome or tow vehicle, chances are you have one or more other vehicles that you take care of, as well. It has been my experience that none of these vehicles ever has the same size filter or oil-pan drain plug. I usually can't remember these numbers between changes.

To make this task quick and simple, I used an indelible-ink pen to write the socket size and oil capacity needed on a handy, smooth surface under the hood of each of my vehicles. In addition, I wrote down the corresponding filter part numbers in the same location. Now, I can tell at a glance what I need to perform an oil change on a given vehicle. And, if I'm on the road, I have alternative filter numbers handy in case I can't find my regular brand; there's no need to fumble through conversion books, which some stores may not even have available.
- TERRY CHASE, SALISBURY, MARYLAND

HELPFUL HOSEDOWN

Over the years, I have found that many windshield-washer nozzles miss their intended mark. Rather than helping clean dirt from the windshield, the poorly aimed devices merely assist in creating streaks. This irritation can be solved with a simple modification.

On vehicles that have fixed windshield washer nozzles (many now have nozzles built into the wiper arm), merely disconnect the washer hose from the nozzle and insert a small plastic sleeve (hollow coupler). Attach an additional length of matching-diameter hose, and route the open end to the center of each respective wiper arm, aimed at the glass. With this done, use a few small nylon-wire ties to hold the hoses in place. Make sure the ties are not too tight, or water flow will be impeded.

The next time your windshield is dirty, just activate the washer system in the normal fashion. You'll have greatly improved delivery of washer fluid. I have used this for years.
- CHARLES F. GEYER, PUNTA GORDA, FLORIDA

THE POINT IS...

As the years go by, our eyes have more trouble adjusting to things up close. And in my case, this is a daily chore when I view the dash as I drive. When I drive my Jeep, I know what the gauges are telling me 'cause I'm used to the layout. Then, I drive my wife's Cherokee and I have to regroup for those gauges. The wide, factory "normal" area for water temperature can cover quite a range! Then, there are the motorhome and the Geo we tow behind it, and those gauges that I have to get used to. Luckily, I found a very simple solution. I mark each gauge at the "normal" spot for the pointer, so at a glance one can tell all is well. All you have to do is mark the face of the gauge with a wick pen or grease pencil, or stick a small arrow cutout of adhesive-backed paper to the glass of the gauge. Now, I can tell at a glance if anything is a little off.
- LYLE A. ALLEN, NEWPORT, OREGON

SWITCHING OCTANE

We all know the hazards of engine pinging (detonation). This condition can be especially troublesome when towing a heavy trailer.

My new Ford van has two gasoline tanks. I bought the extra capacity primarily for extended range; however, I soon found another advantage.

The van runs fine on regular unleaded fuel most of the time. But occasionally, when climbing steeper grades and negotiating long pulls, I hear the engine ping.

Now, with two tanks, I have the best of both worlds. I put premium unleaded in the smaller tank and regular unleaded in the other. Most of the time I just run off the regular tank, switching to the higher-grade gas whenever the situation warrants.
- WAYNE GUYMON, FULLERTON, CALIFORNIA

CHARGE

Keeping RV engine and house batteries fully charged can be difficult if the rig is used infrequently. You can solve this problem by using a household timer to operate the RV's built-in converter/battery charger or an independent charger.

Make sure that no other appliances are turned on, because most timers are not rated for high-current loads. Some converter/chargers can require considerable current, but not while maintaining a battery that is already charged.

Set the timer to go on for an hour or so each day, plug the charger into it, and—bingo!—automatic battery maintenance. Unless the battery you're charging is the "maintenance-free" variety, check the electrolyte level periodically.

TORQUED OFF

I got tired of searching through the owner's manual of my ¾-ton pickup for the proper lug-nut torque every time I rotated tires. My frustration was alleviated, however, when I struck upon the idea of writing this figure inside each hubcap with a waterproof marker. I did the same for my trailer wheels.

I carry a torque wrench in my toolbox, so I never have to guess about torque values. Proper tightness keeps from warping wheels and the pickup's expensive front disc-brake rotors.
- LEON WINTER, SHERIDAN, WYOMING

IN CAMP

TIRE COVER SAVER

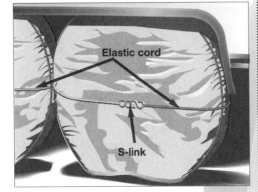

Elastic cord

S-link

To protect our RV tires from weathering and sun rot, I purchased vinyl tire covers. In the high winds of Texas and the coastal areas, the covers would blow off the wheels. As a solution to the problem, I purchased elastic cord and metal S-chain-end links from the hardware store. (Elastic cord can also be found at boat and canvas dealers.) I measured the diameter of the wheel, and doubled this figure for the cord length. I found that a 56-inch length was just right for our 15-inch tires. I tied an S-link onto each end of the cord, and slipped it over the rear of the tire and cover. The ends are brought around to the front and the elastic cord ends are hooked together. Now the tire covers stay put, even in strong winds.
- *CARL R. HARTUP, FORT WAYNE, INDIANA*

TIDY TRASH

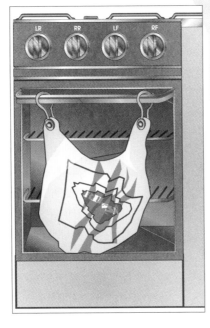

We have a micro-minimotorhome; therefore, we need to utilize every bit of unused space. Trash is one of those nuisances that everyone has to deal with. We came up with a method of attaching plastic shopping bags to the oven door handle using two "old-fashioned" shower curtain holders. We just slip the two holders over the oven door handle and attach the bag. This keeps the bag secure from spills, and provides a very easy method of removal.
- *J. F. MARTINA, OCEANSIDE, CALIFORNIA*

SATELLITE DISH BREAKDOWN

¼ x 3½-inch coupler retaining pins

Assembled dish

The 18-inch satellite dishes are becoming very popular in campgrounds, but there's one drawback for those of us who do not want to mount the dish on the roof: The awkward L-shape makes it difficult to store. Though most dishes can be disassembled using screws and bolts, I found an easier way to do it. I purchased two ¼ × 3½-inch coupler retaining pins (the ones with a loop on one end and tiny balls imbedded in the metal on the other), and drilled ¼-inch holes at the spot welds located at the junction of the arm and the dish. I then inserted the pins into the holes. All I do now is pull the pins and the satellite dish disassembles into two halves for flat storage. In place of the pins, you can also use wing-nuts and bolts.
- *JOE BARTA, BARBOURSVILLE, WEST VIRGINIA*

BASKET BASICS

We prefer to use the campground shower facilities whenever possible during our RV trips. However, these are often very wet places. Finding a dry spot on which to place clean towels, clothes, toilet articles, etc., can be a challenge.

To overcome this dilemma, I purchased a sturdy wicker basket with a high-top handle. It measures approximately 25 × 12 inches, though dimensions are certainly not critical. Just make sure it has a recessed bottom.

Everything the individuals in my family need for a trip to the shower house fits very nicely in the basket. Inside the stall, it can be set on a small bench or hung on a clothes hook. In the lavatory area, it can rest on the countertop or floor. Either way, the basket contents always stay high and dry.
- *BETTY R. STEWART, FAIRVIEW, TENNESSEE*

LEAVE A LIGHT BURNING

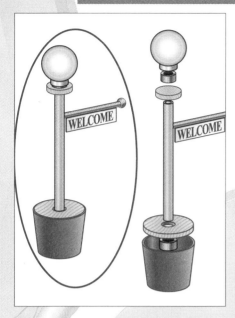

Here's a simple porchlight project for neighborly campers that costs around $35 and breaks down for transport. It's only plastic, but that's part of its beauty.

Start with a 1-foot-diameter plastic planter, and precut some plywood top and bottom center supports. The 2-inch white plastic PVC pipe, available at most hardware/gardening stores, and assorted plastic fittings can be painted if desired, but they look just fine in white.

Electrical power can be either 120 volts AC or 12 volts DC, depending on your taste. We chose the white plastic globe for soft light dispersion and resistance to breakage, but a number of different styles are adaptable. The addition of plastic flowers is totally up to the boss of the family!
- *RONALD PARSONS, KIRKSVILLE, MISSOURI*

SUN LIGHT

*I*n our camping family of two adults and five children, our youngest still prefer having a night light. However, we spend much of our time in primitive campgrounds and can't always hook up to electricity. We've found battery-operated lights rather expensive, and we don't like using lanterns because of the fumes they emit and their potential fire hazard.

With all this in mind, we purchased a Brinkman Solar Max tier-style garden light, on sale for $19.99. The device provides up to eight hours of low-intensity lighting after exposure to only four hours of sunlight. The illumination it offers is adequate for our needs, and recharging is easy. We just attach it to the side of our pop-up during the day to prepare it for another night's use.
- *JOANNE EARLE, NORTH CLARENDON, VERMONT*

EASY CHOCKS

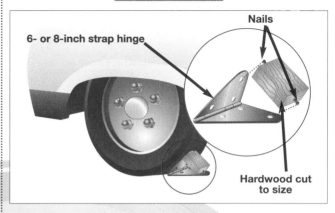

6- or 8-inch strap hinge

Nails

Hardwood cut to size

A 6- or 8-inch strap hinge and a small piece of hardwood are all that are needed to fabricate a collapsible wheel chock. A nail is driven partially into the ends of the hardwood that's cut to size. The protruding nails fit into the screw holes in the ends of the hinge, holding it in position. These homemade chocks fold flat for easy storage.
- *ROBERT J. SMITH, ANTIGO, WISCONSIN*

BUGS NO MORE

Bugs are a fact of life in many camping environments. Still, we were not willing to give up the pleasures of sitting out under the awning in the evening. The obvious solution was to enclose the sides of the awning with screens. Tent camping had taught us that zipper entrances are a nuisance, especially when your hands are full.

We solved this problem by purchasing two mosquito-net screen panels that together were 2 feet longer than the three sides of the awning. This 2-foot overlap became the doorway. The inner screen is pegged to the ground; the outer screen lays against it and closes the opening. A few fishing sinkers sewn into the bottom hem of the outer screen keep it in place. Hook-and-loop fasteners attach the screens to the RV, and a muslin panel closes off the space between the RV and the ground.
- *HERBERT SUTTON, TREASURE ISLAND, FLORIDA*

LIGHT AND AIRY

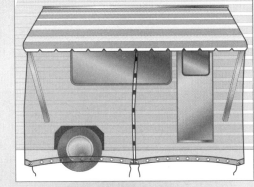

Seems like it always rains when we camp. Sound familiar?

To help keep dry without a closed-in feeling, take two crystal-clear shower curtains, and fold and sew the bottom edges while snugly encasing an appropriate-size rope. This will allow the curtains to slide into the accessory track of your awning roller bar.

Once the curtains are installed, you can connect the center edges together by using self-adhesive hook-and-loop fasteners. The lower edges (formerly the top of the curtains) can hang freely, or they may be anchored by the shower-hook holes.

Though this method will not completely seal your rig's under-awning area, it will keep it reasonably dry while affording a full view and plenty of light.

Each standard shower panel measures 6 × 6 feet, and may be washed in a machine or with a bath towel. The curtains fold and store easily, and they cost very little (about $5 each).
- *JAN AND JOHN SERWINSKI, TAYLOR, PENNSYLVANIA*

A HOUSE WITHIN A HOUSE

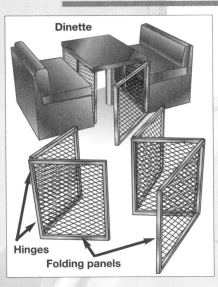

Dinette

Hinges
Folding panels

Many people who travel with pets find occasions when the animals need to be temporarily confined. However, pet carriers or other containers can be unwieldy and bulky, even in a large RV. I solved this problem by building a removable, fold-flat cage for use under my rig's dinette table. I built it in two parts. One has three hinged panels, including the door; the other has just two. I made a frame from mitered 1 × 1-inch wood trim that I glued and corner-joined together. Using a staple gun, I attached ½-inch wire mesh (from the fencing department of my local hardware store) to the frame. I finished the project by installing hinges, hooks, eyelet screws, and metal-clasp shower-curtain rings.

To use the cage, I just slide the pieces into place under the dinette, and hook the respective shower curtain rings onto eyelet screws installed in the horizontal table support. Alternatively, you can install eyelet screws into the RV's interior wall just under the dinette to accomplish firm retention of the cage components. When it's time to eat, reverse the process and stow the folded lightweight cage anywhere that is convenient.

I have found this system very handy for traveling with three little dogs. I have never seen anything like it, though I have known people who went to the trouble of choosing an RV with suitable sleeping quarters for their dogs!
- *JANE E. ARONOFF, BLOOMINGTON, INDIANA*

QUICK COIL

*A*bout five years ago, my wife and I purchased our first fifth-wheel trailer. As with large purchases of any kind, there was a period of learning. One of the first problems I had was trying to store the electric shore-power cord after a weekend of camping. It seemed nearly impossible to get it back in the same space that it came out of just a couple of days before. I tried several methods of stuffing and coiling—all to no avail.

Finally, after breaking camp during a rain and getting the cord dirty, I decided to clean it with spray-on vinyl protectant upon our return home. What a difference this made. Five years later, it is still easy to replace the cord in its storage area. The protectant seemed to lubricate the vinyl covering, as well as make it easier to bend.
- *DANA HASSLER, ANTIOCH, TENNESSEE*

QUICK TIP TO TRICK ANTS

A sure way to keep ants from crawling on your outdoor picnic table is to clean out four cans of tuna fish, cat food, etc., and fill them halfway with water. Place a can under each leg of the table. No more ants.
- *MARY ANN NUNES, BARRINGTON, NEW JERSEY*

CUTTING TECHNOLOGY

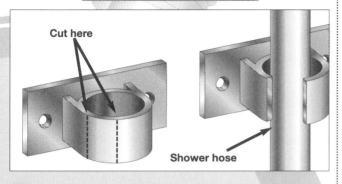

Cut here

Shower hose

The shower hose in many RVs is held in place by plastic guides through which the hose is threaded from the tub faucet to the spray head. Using the shower head to rinse out the tub requires disconnecting the hose and removing it from the guide loops. Once cleaning is complete, the process must be reversed to return everything to its original configuration.

However, by cutting a small slot in each guide ring, the shower head and hose can be easily removed and replaced. Cut the slot with a fine-toothed saw, and finish with a file. Make the opening slightly smaller than the hose diameter, so it will only slide through with some effort. Also, make the guide ring cut on the side opposite from where the hose usually rests.
- *WALTER SAN FANANDRE, NORTH BELLMORE, NEW YORK*

FIELD INGENUITY

On a recent trip I purchased some unique awning lights and wanted to display them immediately. However, I had no store-bought awning hooks available, and there was no RV-supply dealer nearby. In order to hang the lights, I purchased a package of ⅛-inch-diameter nylon cord for $1.19. I also bought six small S-hooks from a local hardware store.

Next, I cut six identical lengths of cord (each approximately 6 inches long) and tied a double knot in each end. This allowed me to insert the knots into the awning groove to hide them from sight. The only visible portion of these "hooks" are the neat and uniform nylon hoops. The S-hooks are installed over the hooks and used to cradle the wiring of the awning lights. If you take the time to melt the knot ends with a match (do this in a well-ventilated area, as smoke may be toxic), you can be assured that they will never unravel. They will also hold as much weight as your awning decorations may demand.
- *W. KEITH BROWNING, JACKSONVILLE, FLORIDA*

MOBILE CATHOUSE

Storage compartment door

Pet door

Oak strips

Plywood

Hardware cloth

Because we travel with three cats, I have made a screened box that is attached to the outside of our trailer when we set up. Many people have commented on our "cathouse." The box itself is made of ¾-inch oak strips covered with 12-inch hardware cloth. It fits into the opening of one of the outside storage compartments. The compartment door forms the top. The back of the box has a homemade pet door that allows the cats to come in under the bed. Another pet door lets them enter the trailer.

The cathouse has been used on two different trailers with just a little modification. On one trailer, the box could set on the rear bumper. Our current trailer requires mounting the box on the side.

The box is very carefully designed to fit snugly into the opening (even compressing the weather-stripping).

A notch was cut to allow for the lower aluminum frame; the box extends to the lower edge of the trailer. A bungee cord is stretched across the top that holds the compartment door (roof) firmly in place. We remove the box when underway or in camp if there are wild animals in the area.
- *FLOYD L. FARRIER, BEND, OREGON*

LIGHT POLE, OR LIGHTPOLE?

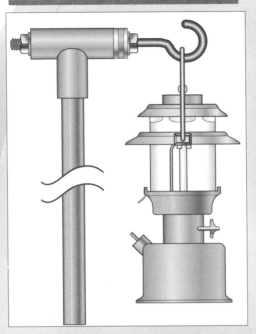

Three weeks before our annual desert camping trip, my wife informed me that this time we should take along our outdoor gas lantern.

However, a quandary developed as we tried to imagine where we would hang the lantern. We travel very lightly and without any type of portable table. Seldom do we find benches, tables, or other structures in the boondock areas we frequent.

We racked our brains to come up with a design for a lantern hanger small enough to be effortlessly packed away when not needed, and yet sturdy enough to support the weight of the lantern. It wasn't as easy as we had expected.

We rejected many designs that turned out to be too clumsy, including those based on tripod-type stands. I was about ready to give up when my wife suggested a design, which we finally adopted. She said, "Why don't you just pound a rod into the ground and slip a tube over it?"

The idea not only sounded good, but it was easy to build and met all of our requirements.

Our hanger design evolved into a simple hook on which to hang the lantern, and a vertical PVC pipe to elevate it a few feet above the ground. The plastic pipe slips over a metal rod that is driven into the ground like a tent stake.

We found that we could purchase all but one of the neces-

sary pieces at our local hardware shop. The ground stake was the exception, but we located what we needed at a steel supply house.

Construction: The basic elements of our lantern hanger can be seen in the accompanying illustration. The device is made up mostly of standard PVC parts used in plumbing, sprinkler systems, etc. Blank PVC plugs are cemented into the opposing open ends of a ¾-inch tee, and then drilled to accept a threaded metal utility hook. The hook itself is retained by two flat washers (on either end), a lock washer, and a nut. The hanger is completed by gluing the finished tee section to a length of Schedule 40 PVC pipe (length is your option). We used a 24-inch length of ¾-inch-diameter steel rod, sharpened at one end, for our ground stake.

Setup: To set up the lantern hanger, all we do is pound the metal stake into the ground (leaving about a foot protruding). Slip the PVC pipe onto the stake, and hang the light source.

Though Schedule 40 pipe is pretty stiff, the vertical pole still leans off-vertical under the weight of a lantern. This isn't a problem, and in fact, is an advantage when the wind blows. Because the pole bends slightly during these times, it absorbs some of the energy of the wind and reduces the side load on the ground stake.

- BETTY AND PHIL McGOWEN, REDWOOD CITY, CALIFORNIA

BURNER BUGS

It seems as though spiders love to build their webs inside the LP-gas burner tubes of RV refrigerators and water heaters. To discourage their efforts, take a small plastic medicine bottle and punch several holes in the cap. Add mothballs and set the bottle near the burner apparatus tubes of your LP-gas appliances. The spiders dislike the smell and therefore tend to stay away.

While on the subject of LP-gas, propane is both colorless and odorless in its natural state. Refineries add a sulfur-containing chemical called Mercaptin to produce the strong odor necessary for leak detection.

When a propane tank is nearly empty, you may sometimes smell this substance inside your RV, making you think there is a leak when none exists. If you detect this strong smell, and checking shows no leaks, the problem is probably a low propane tank.

- JAMES BENSON, CINCINNATI, OHIO

Twistin' and a-Turnin'

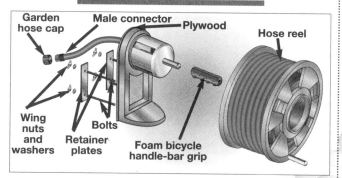

Garden hose cap
Male connector
Plywood
Hose reel
Wing nuts and washers
Bolts
Retainer plates
Foam bicycle handle-bar grip

Most of my RVing is in national forests, where campsites far outnumber water faucets. This made hose handling a regular activity. However, I greatly reduced the amount of time spent winding and unwinding hoses when I purchased and modified a standard hose reel. The cost for the Suncast model I selected was about $16. I followed all assembly instructions, except I substituted a 12-inch hose with a male output for the leader hose. I mounted the entire package on an 8 × 17 × ½-inch piece of plywood, and then bolted it to my trailer's bumper with 5/16 × 6-inch bolts, retainer plates, washers, and wing nuts. To get the female threads on the leader end of the main hose for attachment to water faucets, I wound two lengths of hose onto the reel. The outer hose was reversed, and then I connected male thread to male thread through a hose coupler. When in camp, I lock the reel onto its bumper-mounted hub, and add an extension hose from the output to my rig's water-fill hatch. In addition to the advantages of easier handling and an expected longer hose life, I have a simple way of draining the hose when breaking camp. Once the full length of hose is re-wound, I tuck the loose end under an outer coil of hose and rotate the reel on its mount until the water stops draining. I then remove the reel and pack it for travel. For dust protection on the road, I slide a shortened foam-rubber bicycle grip over the mounting hub's inner O-ring, and screw a garden-hose cap onto the output-hose coupling. During the off-season, I unbolt the hub assembly from the rear bumper and store it indoors.

- E. D. "Bud" Bluecher, Sacramento, California

Cool, Clean Water

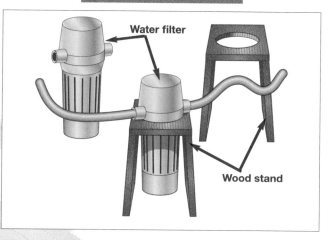

Water filter
Wood stand

When connecting to a water source at a campsite, there is no way to know the condition or quality of the water entering the RV. In some cases, water is from a local well and is not treated. Contaminants, such as rust, sludge, sand, and scale may flow into your vehicle's water system.

Water filters are a good protection against such problems, and are readily available for RV use. However, many RVers connect a filter to the hose and let the assembly just lay on the ground; this is a tacky-looking solution.

I made a stand for my water filter, to hold it in an upright position. I used 1 × 8-inch pine, though a waterproof grade of plywood will also work. Dimensions are not critical, as the hole for the filter need only be made sufficiently large to accept the unit. The stand can then be painted to match the color of the RV. Adapters must be installed to match both the male and female ends of the water hose.

A good grade carbon-impregnated filter will remove solid particles, as well as chlorine taste and odors. However, few will make water microbiologically safe without adequate disinfection, either before or after the filter.

Parts for the entire setup, including the stand, should cost about $30 at most well-equipped hardware stores.

- Glen Diebert, Fayetteville, North Carolina

Flying Old Glory

We always fly Old Glory when camping, but we are constantly having to unwrap the flag from around the pole due to the wind. To solve the problem, we purchased a piece of plastic pipe about 3 inches longer than the flag's width and big enough to fit loosely over the pole. We drilled two 3/16-inch holes at each end of the pipe, at 90-degree angles, at the location of the flag grommets. Tie wraps were then threaded through the holes, securing the grommets. After sliding the pipe over the pole to the tip ornament, we put a round-head wood screw in the pole 3/8-inch from the end of the pipe. The screw sticks out ½ inch, keeping the pipe in place. Now, we display our flag proudly.

- Gary and Deborah Crawford, Palatine, Illinois

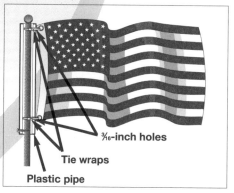

3/16-inch holes
Tie wraps
Plastic pipe

NO MORE SURPRISES

Have you ever camped at a site with a wooden table and benches that had rough seats and splinters? To combat this situation, I cut some indoor/outdoor carpeting into 10-inch × 8-foot strips. (Low-pile carpeting would also work.) I lay these strips on the benches and secure them in place with short bungee cords or small pieces of heavy string. When not using them on campsite benches, I use the carpet strips to cushion folding chairs, tools, and all those other necessary camping items that I carry in the back of my truck. This helps protect everything and cuts down on annoying rattles. Upon returning home, I just roll up the carpet strips and secure with bungees to store them.

- BUD VOGEL, ONTARIO, CALIFORNIA

ANTENNA ALTERNATIVE

For someone who needs a sturdy TV-antenna mount for his travel trailer, but doesn't want to invest in a permanent roof or side mount, here's an inexpensive solution. Buy a standard TV-mast section from either a hardware or an electronics store, and attach it to the trailer tongue jack post with nylon or poly-propylene straps.

My mast came from a True Value hardware store and cost $10. I found the poly straps in a discount store's sporting goods department for just $1 each. I selected a 10-foot mast for my needs, but purchasing 5-foot sections would provide easier storage and more installation flexibility. Three 5-foot sections would be ideal, and is probably about as high as the antenna should be without using guy wires.

- GEORGE B. CASE, COOS BAY, OREGON

TV mast

Nylon straps

BOONDOCK CONVENIENCE

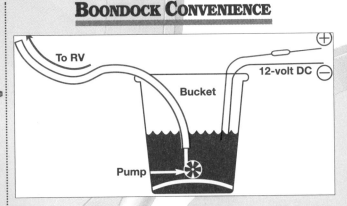

To RV

Bucket

12-volt DC

Pump

I camp mostly in unimproved national forest campgrounds where it is often necessary to replenish the RV's freshwater holding tank with a funnel and a bucket. However, some years ago, a fellow camper suggested an easier way to complete this task. His method consisted of a pail, a 12-volt DC bilge pump, and a length of plastic tubing. He carried the pail from the water source to his RV, submerged the pump in the bucket, and then hooked it up to the trailer battery for electrical power. When the pump emptied the container, he started over.

Being half-lazy, I decided to mount my pump permanently in the bottom of a bucket. Then, I purchased a folding grocery cart and two 3-gallon water jugs. I start the refill process by filling the jugs at the campground water source, and pulling them back to my rig on the cart. Once there, I empty the jugs into my waiting transfer pail, put the pump output hose into the freshwater filler port, hook up the pump to RV battery power, and wait. The process is fairly quick. My whole setup—pail, cart, pump, tubing, battery clamps, and wiring—came to less than $25. I can attest to the fact that this equipment eases the process of refilling the rig with fresh water when camping in the boondocks.

- ROBERT WISWELL, SHELBY, MICHIGAN

LIGHT WAND

In many years of traveling—beginning with a tent, and now a travel trailer—I still have not found a better solution than this for hanging the outdoor gas lantern.

I carry a folding ironing caddy for this purpose. It fits under the picnic table, and allows the lantern to be hung directly above. This makes it ideal for eating or playing cards and board games. Easy reading is possible by just standing the caddy next to your chair. Of course, it also may be used to hold clothes, as I iron during my trailer travels.

My combination ironing caddy and lantern holder takes up very little space, is simple to use and inexpensive, and can also be used at home. Products like this may be purchased at most department or hardware stores.

- ESTELLEN TALBOTT, RIALTO, CALIFORNIA

PATRIOTS, ARISE!

Looking for a convenient way to display the flag from your fifth-wheel trailer? I started with the purchase of a ½-inch pipe flange, a 12 × ½-inch threaded steel pipe, and a flag kit. Also needed are four sheet-

Threaded steel pipe

½-inch flange

metal screws. Assemble the flag kit first. Then, screw the 12-inch pipe into the flag and insert the flat pole into the pipe. As a clearance test, hold the flange flat against the forward surface of the fifth-wheel pin box. Select a mounting location free of interference with the fifth-wheel's overhang. With the position of the flag holder identified, center the flange on the pin box and mark the hole locations. Drill to match the screw size you've chosen, and after painting both the flange and pipe to match your rig, permanently install the flange.

When you want to fly the flag, just screw the 12-inch pipe into place and slide the flat pole in place. This whole project, including the flag kit, should cost less than $15.

- PAUL SHANNON, EUGENE, OREGON

FOR PRIVACY'S SAKE

On occasion, we have a guest spend the night with us in our fifth-wheel trailer. We put the visitor up on a sofa that's housed in the slide-out.

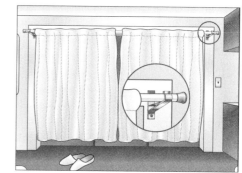

Since I like to rise early and make coffee, I am always concerned about disturbing our guest.

To isolate the sleeping area, I installed permanent brackets for a curtain valance rod over the slide-out opening. My wife fashioned a partition from lightweight drapery material, which we place on an adjustable, long-reach curtain rod.

Now, it's a simple matter to install the curtain on its brackets for the comfort and privacy of a guest.

- ROY CRAWFORD, LAKE DALLAS, TEXAS

Ring Sling

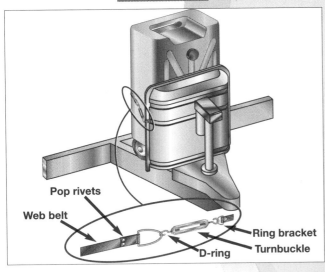

Pop rivets

Web belt

Ring bracket

D-ring

Turnbuckle

Here's a neat way to tote a portable gray-water tank. Soon after I noticed how well the tank fit behind the propane bottles on the A-frame of my trailer, I devised a method for attachment. I drilled two holes in each side of the decorative propane-tank covers to match those already in the store-bought "ring brackets." I mounted these to the cover with bolts and nuts. Next, over each ring bracket, I squeezed shut one end of a 3-inch turnbuckle, so they remain permanently attached to the tank cover. Using pop rivets, I then attached a D-ring (with the flat side facing the gray-water tank position) on one end of the web belt. To finish my tank-storage device, I hooked the web belt on one turnbuckle and brought it around the gray-water tank to determine the correct strap length. Then, I pop-riveted a ring on the other end of the strap.

Now, all I have to do is place my portable gray-water tank in position, hook the stray D-rings over the turnbuckles, and tighten. The tank rides securely; no longer do I have to store it inside my rig where it could cause a mess. It took me approximately 30 minutes to mount the components listed here—all of which can be purchased at a hardware store.

- George Swigert, Maineville, Ohio

Double-Duty Chairs

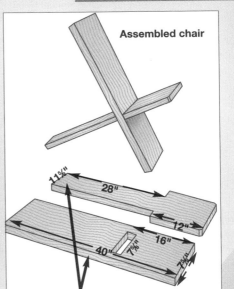

Assembled chair

11⅝"

28"

12"

16"

40"

7⅞"

7⅞"

1" x 12" lumber

How many times have campsite companions dropped by for a cup of java and conversation? What, there are no more chairs available? Likewise, think of those times when you've needed large, flat boards for leveling or jack support, and none was available.

As you can see in the illustration, all you need to address both these issues is the "Quick Connect Camping Convenience." To make one of these utilitarian chairs, you'll need two pieces of $2 \times 12 \times$ 40-inch planking.

Cut a rectangular hole in one piece, and as shown, shave the two sides down on the other pieces. Slip one through the other, and you have a very comfortable camp chair. If you pull the pieces apart again, you have an extra leveling block. As a jack support, the broad boards work well even in sand.

After you've made the first chair, you'll notice that other models can be customized. Lower or raise the center hole to accommodate folks of varying height; carve rounded depressions in the seat portion to fit a specific person a little better; or round off the tail portion to settle into the ground better. You can paint them to match or contrast, varnish or leave unfinished. They're now yours to play with.

Jim Brightly, Moorpark, California

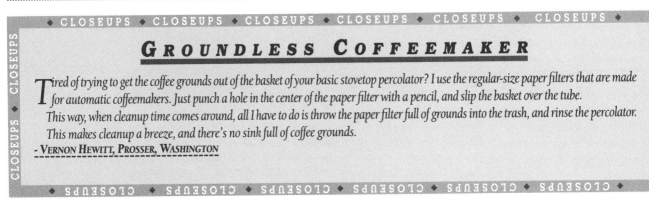

◆ CLOSEUPS ◆ CLOSEUPS ◆ CLOSEUPS ◆ CLOSEUPS ◆ CLOSEUPS ◆ CLOSEUPS ◆

GROUNDLESS COFFEEMAKER

Tired of trying to get the coffee grounds out of the basket of your basic stovetop percolator? I use the regular-size paper filters that are made for automatic coffeemakers. Just punch a hole in the center of the paper filter with a pencil, and slip the basket over the tube.

This way, when cleanup time comes around, all I have to do is throw the paper filter full of grounds into the trash, and rinse the percolator. This makes cleanup a breeze, and there's no sink full of coffee grounds.

- Vernon Hewitt, Prosser, Washington

TELL ME 'Y'

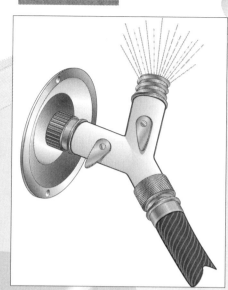

I use a garden hose Y-adapter with two shut-offs in my rig's water delivery hose to help prevent getting air in the plumbing after hooking up at a campground. You can use a quick-disconnect to reduce setup time.

After everything is connected, make sure that both shut-offs on the Y are closed. Turn on the water at its source, then slowly open the Y-valve on the side not connected to the rig to bleed off any air in the hose. When water flows, close that valve and open the one to the RV. Now you won't have air and water spurting out at the sinks, shower, and toilet after every campground hookup.

I also use the Y-adapter when I'm ready to disconnect. Turning off the water at the source, I open the unconnected valve to relieve the pressure before attempting to remove the delivery hose for storage. This saves me from getting sprayed during the process.
- *Norbert E. Fox, North Olmsted, Ohio*

SOLAR CLOTHES DRYER

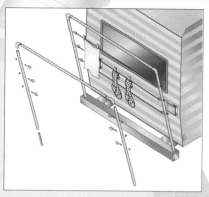

We like to camp in the Arizona desert off by ourselves. With no trees to which we can tie our clothesline, I came up with the idea for this portable setup.

First, remove the sewer hose from the rig's square rear bumper. Next, drill an angled, ½-inch hole all the way through each end of the bumper (as shown).

You'll need to make a stop at a hardware store for two pieces of 60-inch-long steel electrical conduit and one 83-inch length, a couple of 90-degree elbows and a half-dozen threaded eyebolts. Have a welding shop weld a 6-inch piece of solid-steel rod in one end of both 60-inch conduits to reinforce this section of the tube.

Drill corresponding holes in the two 60-inch tubes to accept the eyebolts. Use two per line, and secure in place. Finish by inserting the assembly into the holes previously drilled in the bumper, and then threading the clothesline into position.
- *Robert H. Burke, Niles, Michigan*

MIDLIFE REGRESSION

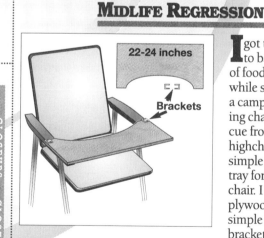

22-24 inches

Brackets

I got tired of trying to balance a tray of food on my lap while sitting around a campsite in a folding chair. Taking a cue from a children's highchair, I made a simple slide-over tray for my folding chair. I used ⅜-inch plywood and two simple U-shaped brackets made from 1 × ¹⁄₁₆-inch steel strap.

Bracket length is determined by the type of folding chair used and the thickness of the arms. These should accommodate the combined thickness of the plywood and the chair arm, plus allow for each slide-on, slide-off action during use. The fabricated brackets are attached to the wood tray by a single screw. Tray width probably will be between 22 and 24 inches, again determined by chair width.
- *Calvin B. Pendley, Tucson, Arizona*

STOVE-TOP TABLE TOP

When my wife and I bought our RV two years ago, we wanted to add a personal touch by installing a stove-top cover that would not only add function and dress up our rig, but would also support the weight of a portable television when needed.

We looked for a couple of weeks in various local RV stores for stove-top covers. Most carried metal versions that would keep the stove clean, but were not strong enough for our purpose.

During this process, we were also searching for a portable outside table, since we enjoy sitting outdoors under the awning once we're set up in a campground. But, in addition to being rather expensive, most collapsible tables we found were just too bulky for our rig.

Being unsuccessful in our search, we struck upon an idea that would solve both problems at once: We would build our own stove-top cover that could also be converted into a portable table. We made ours to fit the Magic Chef range in our rig, but it should be easy to adjust the dimensions to match other brands.

Start by measuring the inside perimeter of the stove top. The height should be adjusted to clear the top surface of the burner grates. Some stoves will require a slightly taller front molding.

A good material for the edges of the cover is pine. The horizontal surface, however, can be made from ½-inch particle board

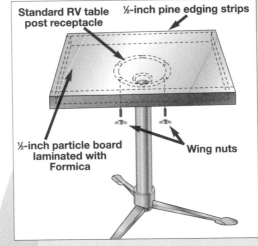

Standard RV table post receptacle

½-inch pine edging strips

½-inch particle board laminated with Formica

Wing nuts

measured to the full outside perimeter dimensions of the stove.

The next step is to install Formica on the cover's outer surfaces. Use a good contact cement designed for this purpose. Be sure to follow directions closely, which usually call for coating both sides and letting the glue dry until tacky.

Glue the side strips in place first, followed by the front and back. The rough edges can be smoothed with a file or router. Next, put the top layer in place and carefully smooth edges with a file.

To make the completed stove-top cover work as a portable table, it is next necessary to install recessed threads. On the underside of the cover, draw a diagonal line from each corner. Place a standard RV table-post receptacle in the center, and mark through its mounting holes as they correspond to the diagonal pencil lines. Drill the appropriate-size holes for the recessed thread assemblies, and hammer into place.

To use your new stove cover as a table, secure the post folder with wing-nut bolts, insert the post, and add a pair of portable aluminum table legs (available at most RV stores). Reverse the procedure to return your table to a stove-top cover. The approximate cost for everything described here is about $60.

- Roger Brittan, Huntington Beach, California

TIRED OF TRIPPING

My fifth-wheel trailer draws electrical energy continuously to operate its on-board battery charger, clocks, etc. Therefore, I keep the rig plugged into an outside electrical outlet whenever it is stored next to my home.

This plan worked fine during clear weather. But, when it rained, water would seep into the exposed outlet and trip the ground fault circuit interrupter (GFCI). I had to remember to unplug the extension cord whenever rain was in the forecast. On those occasions when I forgot, I would know right away, since the GFCI circuit breaker also powers my automatic garage door. Naturally, the ritual became a pain.

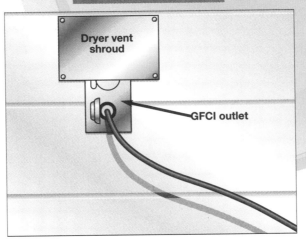

Dryer vent shroud

GFCI outlet

To alleviate my frustration, I procured an exterior-style clothes-dryer exhaust vent and duct extension. After removing the sheet-metal tube and round flapper valve from the assembly, I trimmed the shroud to fit over the troublesome electrical outlet. This addition effectively shields the outlet from rain, while still allowing full access to the receptacle. Four nails, a little caulking, and 30 minutes of work completed the job. As luck would have it, shortly after I installed this cover, a 2-hour rainstorm arrived to test my fix. The GFCI remained untripped.

- Frank P. D'Ascensio, Bridgewater, New Jersey

PRIVATE LINE

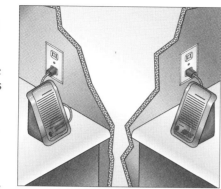

From time to time, we travel with family or friends. Occasionally, we are not able to obtain campsites adjacent to each other. In that regard, communicating can be a hassle.

Running between our friends' trailers in a pouring rain just to ask them something is not my idea of fun. And then there are the times when we may not be dressed or ready to face the world, but need to talk with our companions about plans for the day.

To overcome these shortcomings, we take along our General Electric home-intercom remotes. These operate on 120-volt AC power and transmit through standard electrical wiring.

Most parks offering electrical hookups operate through one power transformer. This allows the intercoms to operate. Another plus of these devices is that they have several channels to pick from should there be any interference with other campers.

Once plugged in, all that is required to talk to another RV is the push of a button. When not needed, they cannot be used to monitor the occupant in the other RV unless activated at both locations. This keeps private conversations private.

I find that this approach to campground communication is even better than using a CB radio. General Electric remotes are available at most department stores. Wal-Mart, for example, sells them for $19.95 apiece.
- LARRY P. GONNELLO SR., RAYTOWN, MISSOURI

CLASSY CABLE JACK

*M*any commercial campgrounds now offer cable television, or a connection to a centralized TV antenna. When visiting other people in their RVs, I've seen coax cable coming in through open windows, lying across the floor, taped under cabinets, and even running up through the rooftop refrigerator vent—all in the name of obtaining better TV reception and more channels.

I didn't want to duplicate such temporary installations, so I purchased a male-to-male coax connector, four female slip-on coax fittings, and 60 feet of coax cable. I drilled a ¼-inch hole next to my rig's left front parking light, and installed the threaded male connector using the accompanying nut and washer.

Because our television has to sit on the engine cover of our Class A motorhome, I routed coax cable from the fender-mounted connector to the engine cover. I cut it 3 feet longer than I needed, and attached the female connectors to each end for attachment to the outside jack and our television. When not in use, the excess coax is wound up and stored under the dash.

The extra two female connectors were used on the remaining length of coax cable (about 52 feet). So far, this has given me more than enough coax to connect to campground cable systems.

To keep the exposed connector on the fender clean and dry, be sure to install a protective rubber or plastic cap when it is not being used.
- JOHN MCLAUCHLIN, SEQUIM, WASHINGTON

DIVERSIONARY TACTIC

While I was trying to adjust the temperature of the water flowing from the RV shower head, the volume would change just enough to allow the diverter valve to revert back to the bathtub mode. This was both annoying and wasteful of the on-board water supply (my family and I like to go places without hookups).

The problem went away after I modified a ¼-inch-thick piece of rubber into a simple collar affair that slides under the diverter knob. This holds the valve firmly in the up position. The collar remains in place until someone who wants to use the bathtub needs to return the diverter to its normal position. The device is easily removed on those occasions.
- BERNARD ALEXANDER, CLARK, NEW JERSEY

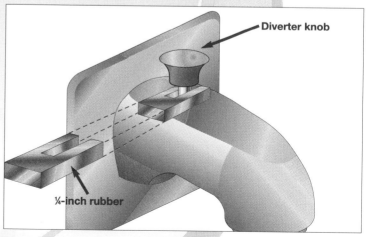

Diverter knob

¼-inch rubber

HANG NAIL

Insert staple here

RV side wall

Door holder

RV door

When it's nice and warm during the summer months, I like to leave the door to my fifth-wheel open with only the screen between my family and the outside. Unfortunately, where we are located, we often experience very strong winds—so strong that the wind will slam the main door closed before we can catch it.

As with many RVs, the door holder consists of a metal side-wall-mounted bracket with a small knob on the end. This engages a plastic receptacle on the entry door. Under normal conditions this works just fine, but not when our local wind blows. I came up with the idea of sliding a 1½-inch fence staple over the metal bracket and into the plastic fitting on the door. This simple arrangement solved the slamming-door problem.

- GORD FIELD, SUDBURY, ONTARIO, CANADA

BACK TO BASICS

Last fall, we wanted to make a big kettle of chili for a cool fall campout. We decided we needed to come up with a kettle support system that was heavy duty and easy to store. We did this by using square steel stock having 1-inch and 1¼-inch dimensions.

This project requires:
- Five pieces of 1¼-inch square stock (each 2 feet long)
- Four pieces of 1-inch square stock (each 2 feet long)
- Two pieces of 1-inch square stock (each 6 inches long)
- Four bolts with matching nuts
- Access to welding equipment

With these materials and a little time in the shop, you can fabricate a fire-ring holder similar to ours. The two A-frames with sliding legs allow for height and level adjustment (see illustration).

The entire assembly comes apart easily and fits nicely into an RV storage compartment. This kettle holder is ideal for large group cookouts.

- CHUCK DENSMORE, RAVENNA, OREGON

CLOSEUPS • CLOSEUPS • CLOSEUPS

HITCH AND LOCK

I've seen many owners who have slammed the front of their fifth-wheel onto the truck bed rails by driving away while thinking that the hitch was latched securely. Although you can make a visual check to verify that the latching mechanism is closed, I have come up with a simple procedure that provides additional peace of mind. After hooking up, raise the front jacks approximately 2 inches (lowering the fifth-wheel). Manually lock your trailer brakes by actuating the brake controller, and drive forward slowly. If the hitch is locked properly, the trailer will move with the truck. If it's not, and the truck and fifth-wheel separate, at least it won't fall onto the bed rails.

- JERRY ROBINSON, WHITTIER, CALIFORNIA

CLOSEUPS • CLOSEUPS • CLOSEUPS

DRIP DETERRENT

Every time I try to hook up a campground water supply to my trailer, it is a hassle to get a tight, leakproof connection between the hose and the inlet fitting. It seems that the inlet fittings are usually too small to get a good grip.

To solve this problem, I went to a garden supply store and purchased a quick-disconnect hose-coupling assembly (about $5). I attached one end to the trailer inlet and the other end to the hose, where they remain permanently. I can now be hooked up to city water in a matter of seconds.

To protect the coupling on the trailer from gathering grime on the road, I use a plastic cap that I bummed from a hydraulic hose supplier. It fits perfectly. Then, I seal the hose opening with a small cork.

A final tip: Fill the hose with water before hooking it to the RV. This will prevent air from entering the plumbing system.

- B. C. McCREA, PORT ANGELES, WASHINGTON

DAMP DERRIERE

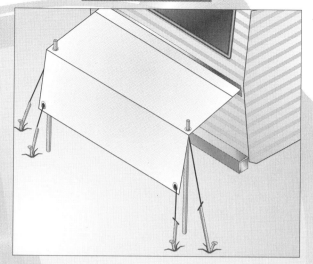

The morning sun shines golden across the eastern sky. It invites the early riser to mount his or her trusty bicycle for a tour of the area. For other RVers, the brisk morning air calls for a hot cup of coffee while reclining outdoors in their favorite lawn chairs.

Both types face a problem, though, if a heavy dew has covered the bikes and chairs. Either be prepared to mop up the moisture, or suffer the indignation of a moist backside.

The common solution used by most folks is to hide these items under the RV. But, with the combination of insects, mud, wheel supports, and leveling jacks found in the same area, this approach isn't always suitable.

My method is to add a cover-all to the back of the RV. It's not expensive, and doesn't take up a lot of storage space when stored.

Start by purchasing a length of awning rail to match the width of your rig. About 7½ feet should do it. You can get this at an RV service and parts store. It may even have a short remnant to give you.

I prefer to install the awning rail across the back of the RV. This way, I can cable and lock my bikes and chairs to the rear bumper when I'm away.

You'll need a tarpaulin about 6 × 8 feet with a rope sewn down one side. It will slide into the slot of the awning rail.

A couple of grommets (one on each side) will be needed to index the wood or metal support poles. Depending on your installation, supports should measure 3½ to 4 feet long.

Army/Navy surplus stores have a good variety of tarpaulins, tent poles, and ropes with which to finish and secure the cover-all. Use tent stakes and rope to hold the tarp supports upright and rigid, so the rain can run off and the wind will not disturb the setup.

- DORANCE GALLOWAY, DAVISON, MICHIGAN

TO THE CORE OF THE MATTER

I read in "10-Minute Tech" once about an outdoor carpet storage tube that could be made from PVC drainpipe and mounted on the rear bumper of an RV. I liked the suggestion, and found that it worked well. However, the problem was rolling the carpet tightly enough to get it into the storage tube.

After some experimentation, I found the task much easier when the carpet was attached to a solid core. My final solution uses a length of wooden closet rod cut slightly shorter than the storage tube, and some hook-and-loop fasteners with special glue designed for attaching this material to rough surfaces.

I glued small tabs of the fuzzy side to the carpet at 12- to 18-inch intervals. To allow the glue to adhere better, I first used a razor blade to carefully "shave" the grass carpet at each attachment location.

Larger tabs of the hook side of the fastener were glued at the same spacing along the length of the wooden rod. The larger tabs eliminate the need for perfect alignment between the carpet and rod. Once the glue is dry, the carpet is ready to be rolled up. Because this system allows a much tighter roll, I could fit the same-size carpet in my storage tube as I did before attaching the rod.

- STEVEN BAKER, SNOHOMISH, WASHINGTON

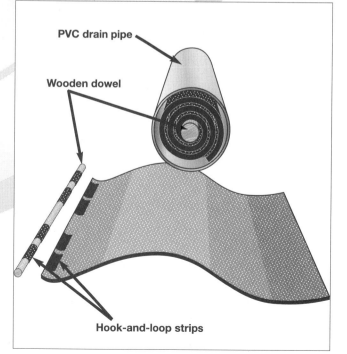

PVC drain pipe

Wooden dowel

Hook-and-loop strips

CLANDESTINE CLOTHES

The concept of storing a bag full of dirty clothes in the same closet as clean clothes never appealed to us. Then, we tried storing the bag in the bathtub, but we got tired of having to remove it each time the

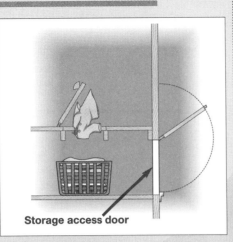

Storage access door

tub was used. Finally, I asked my husband what was directly under the closet floor. "A storage compartment," he said. The next question that came to mind was whether the storage area was big enough to hold a clothes basket. When he said it was, I immediately envisioned adding a laundry chute to our rig.

The door for the chute was cut between the floor braces, and then hinged. A handle was added for convenience. Now, all we have to do to keep soiled clothes separate from the fresh is pull open the chute door and drop the apparel into the basket below. When the basket fills up, there is sufficient room in the underfloor storage area to move it to one side and insert another basket. This allows us to go several days between visits to the laundromat. Although not all RVs are configured with access to the area beneath the clothes closet, a large number are. Therefore, this modification should work for a fair number of our fellow RVers.
-DAVE AND PAT TOHR, CHULA VISTA, CALIFORNIA

NO TIME FOR COFFEE

Do you use your favorite old coffeemaker in the rig, but wish it had a timer so the coffee would be ready when you get up each morning? I have a solution for you.

Go to your favorite discount store with about $6 and buy a timer that is designed to turn house lights on and off while you're not home. The timer can be plugged into an outlet in the rig, then the prepared coffeemaker plugged into the timer. Set the timer to the time at which you want to smell coffee as you awaken the next morning.
- GEORGE TAYLOR, MUSCLE SHOALS, ALABAMA

FABULOUS FIREBALLS

Many of us enjoy the special touch that a campfire adds to our "night life." Unfortunately, we sometimes find that dry wood is nowhere to be found when we need it. To combat this hurdle, I use a trick that the Air Force taught me at a survival school—petroleum jelly and cotton balls.

To make them, just dip a cotton ball into a jar of petroleum jelly, and voila! you have one of the best ways ever devised to light a campfire. These "grease balls" burn for quite a while, and are hot enough to ignite just about any type of wood.

In addition to being reliable, they are very inexpensive to make, take up little storage space, and can be conveniently stored in zipper-type plastic bags. You can even make them up as you need them.
- MARK MASON, ALTUS, OKLAHOMA

BOONDOCK RESOURCEFULNESS

Ever since my RV refrigerator went out, I have made sure to take a cooler with me on all trips. I recently decided to upgrade to a larger ice chest. While looking for a newer model, I had the bright idea of locating one with a screw-in drain plug. Finding this on a 48-quart Igloo unit, I proceeded to modify it by installing a short, ¾-inch pipe nipple, sealing washers, and a water faucet. I reused the jam nut from the original drain to secure everything into place. I now have not only a standby cooler in case my refrigerator fails again, but a practical way of transferring water into my fifth-wheel trailer while boondock camping. It's a simple matter to put the cooler on top of my tow vehicle's tool box, and head for the nearest water outlet. After filling the ice chest, I drive back to my trailer, attach a hose to my add-on faucet, and drain 12 gallons of fresh water into my rig's holding tank. One more trip, and my RV's water tank is nearly filled.

This common camping accessory is a must for people who hate to make trips to the water source at primitive campgrounds as much as I do.
- R. H. BOULEWARE, ROCK HILL, SOUTH CAROLINA

TAPPING WATER

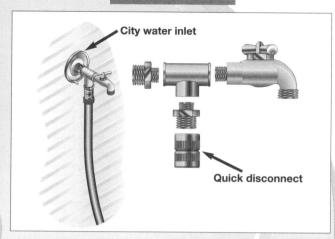

City water inlet

Quick disconnect

Using parts commonly available through most hardware or plumbing stores, you can make a convenient and removable outside faucet for your RV. Another advantage to this setup is that it orients the water supply hose vertically to prevent strain on the line and its connection.
- *RON TRAVERSE, CHINO VALLEY, ARIZONA*

COINLESS LAUNDRY

*R*ecently, I discovered a great technique to save money and avoid long waits at coin-operated laundries. When I break camp, I empty the water heater into a large beverage cooler and add dirty clothes, biodegradable soap, and a tennis shoe to act as the agitator. The cooler gets strapped on the rear bumper of my motorhome or set in the rear of the dingy vehicle. A few hours of driving scrubs the dirt right out. I rinse anywhere I can find fresh water and a drain. The soapy water is dumped, fresh water added, and then I drive down the road for a few more miles. Once I get set up in camp, a reel-type clothesline goes up, so sunlight can do the drying.

I use a different technique when boondocking in one place for an extended period. The washing machine of choice is a 5-gallon plastic bucket with a hole cut in the center of the lid. I fashioned a churn handle from a broomstick, and then attached a wide, cross-shaped dasher to the business end with stainless-steel screws. Granted, the neighbors look at me a bit oddly as I sit under the awning, churning away, but this method sure gets clothes clean.
- *JAY WALLEY, SPARKS, NEVADA*

DUMBBELL TO THE RESCUE

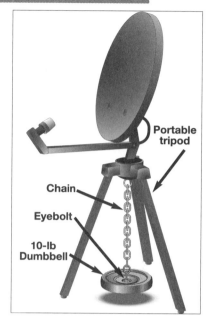

Portable tripod

Chain

Eyebolt

10-lb Dumbbell

A large number of RVers are using portable tripods to mount their satellite dishes while in camp. Securing the tripod while in use can be difficult when used on concrete, asphalt, gravel, or even super-hard ground. Some commercial tripods come with a corkscrew device that "digs" into the ground, providing a connection point for the other end of a shock cord, which provides stability in winds, etc. But it is difficult to use unless the ground is soft. A 10-pound dumbbell weight with an eyebolt attached through the center hole works great. Attach one S-hook to each end of a small chain strong enough to support in excess of 10 pounds. For best support, the dumbbell weight should hang approximately 2 inches above the surface the tripod will rest on. This gives the tripod a low center of gravity.
- *JOHN C. LEHR, LAKEWOOD, COLORADO*

PORTA-PORCH

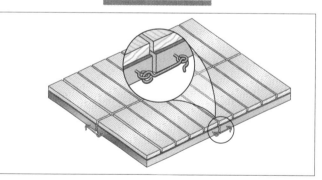

Using 2 × 2-inch lumber, I made four frames measuring 18 × 24 inches. I decked these with 1 × 4-inch boards, then I placed a locking-gate hook and eyes on opposite corners of each frame.

The four frames hook together to form a portable porch, which we placed just outside the door of our RV. The pieces are easy to handle and store, and they hose off nicely if painted.
- *JACK AND T.C. BROOKS, BLOOMINGDALE, OHIO*

IMAGINATION-OF-THE-MONTH AWARD

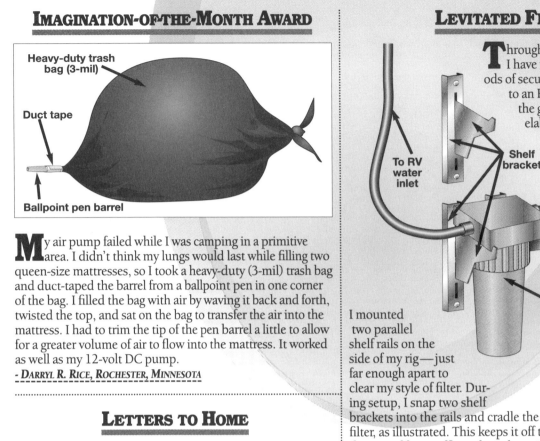

Heavy-duty trash bag (3-mil)

Duct tape

Ballpoint pen barrel

My air pump failed while I was camping in a primitive area. I didn't think my lungs would last while filling two queen-size mattresses, so I took a heavy-duty (3-mil) trash bag and duct-taped the barrel from a ballpoint pen in one corner of the bag. I filled the bag with air by waving it back and forth, twisted the top, and sat on the bag to transfer the air into the mattress. I had to trim the tip of the pen barrel a little to allow for a greater volume of air to flow into the mattress. It worked as well as my 12-volt DC pump.
- *DARRYL R. RICE, ROCHESTER, MINNESOTA*

LETTERS TO HOME

My wife has always liked to write letters, but wasn't very com-

4"

26"

16"

fortable accomplishing the task in our RV. She asked me to make a lap board that would fit the dimensions of her favorite chair in the rig.

The illustration shows what I designed, constructed from a piece of ⅜-inch plywood. It is a project that should be easy for others to duplicate. To make it an attractive table for writing, card playing, or crafts, I rounded the corners and applied a varnish finish.
- *D. R. HANEY, YUMA, ARIZONA*

LEVITATED FILTER

Throughout my trailering years, I have noted numerous methods of securing in-line water filters to an RV. Some are just laid on the ground, while others are elaborate wood stands, which occasionally convince local Fidos that the devices are a stump. To avoid such peril,

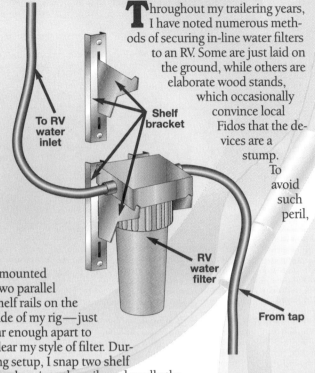

To RV water inlet

Shelf bracket

RV water filter

From tap

I mounted two parallel shelf rails on the side of my rig—just far enough apart to clear my style of filter. During setup, I snap two shelf brackets into the rails and cradle the filter, as illustrated. This keeps it off the ground and out of the way of foot traffic and overly curious dogs. It also allows me to use a unit that functions nicely on low-cost, disposable charcoal filters.

The only other item required to complete this project is a short length of water hose between the filter housing and the RV inlet. I elected to make mine of clear vinyl tubing, so I can examine the water quality after filtration.

The length of the shelf rails, brackets, and overall spacing of components is, of course, dictated by the model of water filter being supported. These dimensions must be determined on an individual basis.
- *H. P. SURCON, EDMONTON, ALBERTA, CANADA*

♦ CLOSEUPS ♦ CLOSEUPS ♦ CLOSEUPS ♦

MEMORY TRICK

*E*ver forget to put your television antenna down before getting on the road? Well, we have, but not anymore. We now hang our ignition keys on the handle that raises and lowers the antenna. We immediately retract the antenna after removing the keys from the handle.
- *JIM AND NANCY TAYLOR, TUCSON, ARIZONA*

♦ CLOSEUPS ♦ CLOSEUPS ♦ CLOSEUPS ♦

NEW VERSION, OLD IDEA

I improved my tandem-axle wheel stabilizers by adding a chain tightener that's used around farms. After building the appropriate top and bottom blocks that can be wedged nicely between the tires, I countersunk a ⅞-inch-diameter hole 1 inch deep on the long side of each cut block. A ⁵⁄₁₆-inch hole was drilled through the remaining thickness of block. A 6 × ¼-inch eyebolt was attached to each block using a nut and a ¼-inch-wide flat washer. The chain tightener's end hooks were closed around the eyebolts when the fit was accomplished. The chain tightener is made by Dixie Industries, part no. 48949, and sells for around $9. To use, I simply position the blocks with the chain tightener open, and then close the lever.

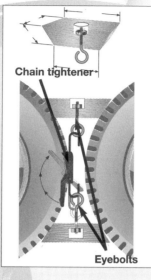

Chain tightener

Eyebolts

- RICHARD A. MCKENNEY, SPOKANE, WASHINGTON

STABILITY DEFINED

Forget hauling around those loose stabilizer support blocks. I decided to forego this hassle by permanently attaching pieces of used 4 × 4 × 7-inch redwood blocks to my RV's stabilizer jacks. First, I installed two ¼-inch eyebolts per jack pad. The threaded screw eyes were turned into the wood to a depth

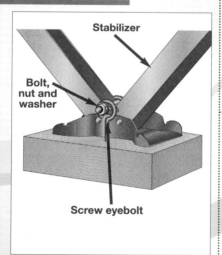

Stabilizer

Bolt, nut and washer

Screw eyebolt

that allows a clearance between the stabilizer jack arm and the 4 × 4-inch pad (pilot holes were drilled first to help prevent splitting). The final step calls for bolting the pads into place using washers to keep the bolt head and nut from sliding through the eyebolt openings. With the jack pads in place, my rig's stabilizing jacks now provide an excellent footing, even on soft ground.

- ROD FRASER, CAMPBELL, CALIFORNIA

PINNING CEREMONY

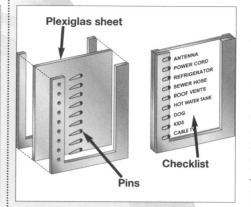

Plexiglas sheet

ANTENNA
POWER CORD
REFRIGERATOR
SEWER HOSE
ROOF VENTS
HOT WATER TANK
DOG
KIDS
CABLE TV

Checklist

Pins

Having worked with the airlines all my life, and given the many tasks required to ready an RV for travel or habitation, I naturally rely on a checklist. Just as cockpit crews do, I have checklists for setting up, as well as preparing for departure. After many attempts, I think I've finally found the best configuration.

I constructed a three-sided frame with a Plexiglas window for protection of the list. The top side of this frame is open so the checklist can be inserted. On the left side of the frame, I drilled holes appropriately angled downward to receive and hold wooden pins in line with each item on the list. The angle prevents the inadvertent loss of pins while traveling. Each pin is painted red on one end.

As I set up the RV for our campground stay, I insert each pin so the red end is visible for each item already accomplished. I know at a glance when everything is properly set. At departure, I insert the pin with the neutral end out as I begin securing items for travel. When none of the red pins are visible, I know the vehicle is ready for departure.

The size of the checklist will depend on the chosen mounting location. Mine is just inside the entry door, and is approximately 4¼ × 4¼ inches. The 1-inch pins are made from ⅛-inch-diameter dowel stock.

- J.F. MARTINA, OCEANSIDE, CALIFORNIA

◆ CLOSEUPS ◆ CLOSEUPS ◆ CLOSEUPS ◆

CAMPING ACCORD

When backing your trailer into a parking spot, have you ever succeeded in getting it parallel to the patio? I must rely on the right-side mirrors, which allow limited visibility. One day, I struck upon the idea of laying out a piece of cord in the campsite, parallel to, and about 10 feet from, the patio edge. Now, I can back my rig into place just by watching out the driver's door window. I line up the side of the trailer slightly inside the cord, and lo and behold, the rig ends up exactly where I want it on the first try.

- JAMES T. DAVIS, ANACORTES, WASHINGTON

◆ CLOSEUPS ◆ CLOSEUPS ◆ CLOSEUPS ◆

WHAT A PAD

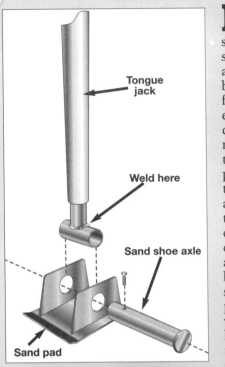

Tongue jack

Weld here

Sand shoe axle

Sand pad

I used a commercially available sand pad from a semi trailer to achieve a more stable tongue-jack footing on my travel trailer. This required only a minor modification to the jack post. A short section of pipe with an inside diameter that matches the outside diameter of the sand shoe axle was cut to fit between the sand shoe ears. This piece was then welded horizontally to the base of the trailer-jack post to allow removal of the sand shoe during travel. (In my case, that was a desirable feature because the large foot pad hung too low for safe ground clearance when the jack was retracted.) Semi trailer sand shoes come in 10 × 10-inch and 12 × 12-inch surface-area sizes. Because of the pivoting axle, they readily adjust to the ground contour while keeping the jack post plumb. The approximate cost of parts is $20 for a new shoe and axle, or you can pick up a used version at a truck salvage yard.
- *John A. Schena, Galway, New York*

ROCK-AND-ROLL BLUES

For as long as we've owned our fifth-wheel trailer, my wife and I have been troubled by its tendency to rock back and forth whenever we walked around inside. In spite of jacks, stabilizers, and wheel chocks placed on both sides of each tire, the wheels would still roll slightly whenever weight was shifted inside.

We had seen commercially manufactured wheel chocks wedged between the tires of other rigs, and thought this might be a solution to our problem. However, the combination of not knowing for sure how well they worked, and the price of nearly $100 per pair, kept us from buying a set for ourselves.

I felt that I could build an equivalent product for a few dollars and a little time. The accompanying illustration shows how to fabricate a set of homemade chocks. They should work on any tandem-axle RV.

The few materials needed are:

1.) Four pieces of 4 × 4-inch scrap lumber measuring 8 to 10 inches long.

2.) Two 18-inch lengths of threaded rod. (As a minimum, I suggest using ⅜-inch-diameter rod. Larger diameters should also work well.)

3.) Four hex nuts and two wing nuts matched to the threaded rod.

4.) Six flat and six lock washers.

As a sidelight, I was given the 4 × 4-inch scraps needed for this project by my local lumberyard. These were pressure-treated fence-post trimmings. I purchased all other parts at a hardware store for less than $5.

After you've assembled your new chocks, install as illustrated. However, do so only after you've parked and leveled your rig. We learned this lesson the hard way. Jacking the trailer from the front with the chocks tightened in place will bend the rods.

What a difference these chocks have made for us. The "rock and roll" is gone, and we saved a bundle of money in the process. I made these almost three years ago, and with the help of a wood preservative I applied, the chocks have held up just fine.
- *Jeff Barnum, Rockville, Maryland*

PARTY SNARLS

I grew tired of always having to untangle my RV party lights every time I wanted to use them. The problem was easily solved when I devised a holder out of scrap wood. Notched appropriately, this simple project now keeps my rig's string of lights in place during travel. It also works well for securing electrical cords, as shown here.

- CHARLES FINN,
BELLE, MISSOURI

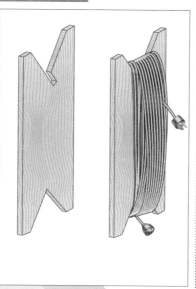

QUICK AND SIMPLE LEVELING

I am enclosing a sketch of a device that we have used with our motorhome during the last three years. It has proved very efficient when leveling the rig.

We had 7-inch-long, 2-inch-square tubes welded to the four corners of the motorhome chassis. Next, we bought two manual trailer A-frame jacks from Camping World. It's important to get the side-crank style instead of those that crank from the top. Our local machine shop did the rest.

The shop's mechanics welded 1¼-inch-diameter tubing to each jack post. They also ground off the attachment plate that would normally be used for a trailer installation, as it wasn't needed for the project.

During use, the jacks are inserted into the square chassis tubes on the low side of the motorhome. A few cranks level the rig. Dimensions vary because each installation will depend upon chassis height, etc.

- TOM CLEMENCE, PENTICTON, BRITISH COLUMBIA, CANADA

Chassis end frame

Welded square steel tubing

Trailer A-frame jack

NAILING IT DOWN

M any of us use indoor/outdoor carpeting at the entrance to our RVs, particularly when parked on grass or dirt. However, the wind often blows the carpet away from the door.

To stop this problem, I use four to six 35mm film-container caps and the same number of 20-penny nails. Pierce (drill or punch) the

center of each cap, and then hammer the nails into the ground through each corner of the carpet. You may want to install additional hold-downs around the edges.

- NORMAN LATTER, HEMET, CALIFORNIA

CLOSEUPS • CLOSEUPS • CLOSEUPS

MAGNETIC MEMORY JOGGERS

Save those thin square or rectangular magnets that some companies pass out with their advertising on the front. (I was lucky enough to con my insurance agent out of a handful.) Next, attach a blank, self-stick note pad to the non-magnetic side. Voila! You now have an instant memo holder that you can attach to any convenient ferrous surface inside your RV. I personally like the metal range hood.

Here are a few ways I put the note pads to use:

1. A checklist for setup upon arrival at a destination.

2. A shut-down checklist for use when preparing to depart.

3. A record of propane refills.

4. A list of places to visit around the campground.

5. A running "things-we-forgot-to-bring" list.

Another suggestion is to cover the checklists with transparent tape. This will allow you to use a washable marker to line-through each item as it is completed. When finished, just wash away the marker and save the list for the next trip.

- DICK SPOULA, CHICAGO, ILLINOIS

SOLID FOUNDATION

As illustrated, I assembled a couple of inexpensive hydraulic stabilizing jacks for my motorhome using readily available parts. These jacks effectively eliminate vehicle sway and rocking motions when in use. They also work great during periods of high wind. For convenient storage, they stack together compactly.

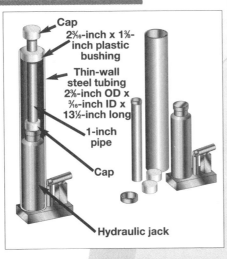

Cap
2¾6-inch x 1⅝-inch plastic bushing

Thin-wall steel tubing 2⅜-inch OD x ⅞6-inch ID x 13½-inch long

1-inch pipe

Cap

Hydraulic jack

Each stabilizer costs approximately $15 to construct and can be built in just a few hours. Although the illustration shows an 18-inch vertical dimension, this could vary from rig to rig. Therefore, I would suggest measuring the distance between the bottom of the rear bumper on your loaded RV and the ground to determine this specification. Subtract about an inch to provide sufficient clearance for installation.

- DICK CRISWELL, LEXINGTON, KENTUCKY

HOOKUP WITH A LINE AND SINKER

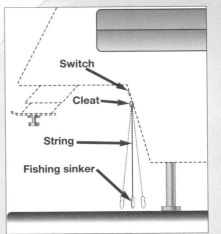

Switch

Cleat

String

Fishing sinker

While full-time RVing, I have observed numerous fifth-wheel owners going through fits in the process of hooking up. After backing up the truck to line up the kingpin, most drivers get out once or twice to raise or lower the fifth-wheel.

To eliminate this, I attach a cleat to the front end of the trailer next to the electric jack switches. After the front jacks have lifted the trailer to the release position, I fasten a string (that's permanently attached to a fishing sinker) to the cleat, so the sinker is just touching the ground.

This serves as measure of the exact height of the fifth-wheel before unhitching. After the truck is moved, the fifth-wheel is then raised or lowered to level, as usual.

While in the campground, I leave the sinker dangling. Then, for a flawless kingpin alignment, I raise or lower the front jacks until the sinker is again just touching the ground. The string and weight are then removed from the cleat until the next setup.

- GEORGE MILLS, BURBANK, CALIFORNIA

PRACTICAL POCKETS

*I*t is easy to leave things such as pliers on a campground table, or a water-pressure regulator near the water source, and not remember where you put them until 50 miles down the road. To eliminate such forgetfulness, I purchased a carpenter's apron for less than $1.50. In it, I now carry pliers, screwdriver, water regulator, water-heater lighter, keys for outside storage compartments, polarity tester, electric adapter, hose washers, and a few paper towels.

When setting up and breaking camp, I lay nothing down. All the items required to complete my appointed rounds are in the apron pockets, where they stay until needed. My small investment has paid big dividends; I haven't lost anything since I bought it.

As a memory jogger, I wrote the words "Put The Step Up" across the front of the apron in permanent marker.
- HARTLEY STEEVES, PORT CHARLOTTE, FLORIDA

SLIPPERY CIRCUMSTANCES

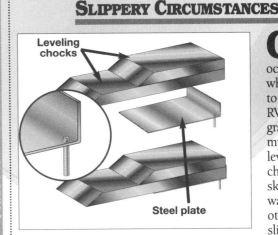

Leveling chocks

Steel plate

On more than one occasion, when trying to level my RV on wet grass, I had my tapered leveling chocks go skidding one way or the other on the slippery surface. To solve this problem, I got a steel plate with a 1¼-inch flange and a 2 × ⅛-inch-diameter steel pin for each chock. The pins are welded to the flange as shown, and act as cleats. This has made my "grass chocks" absolutely stable during the leveling process on unimproved surfaces.
- OWEN C. SMITH JR., BALTIMORE, MARYLAND

QUICK SHADE

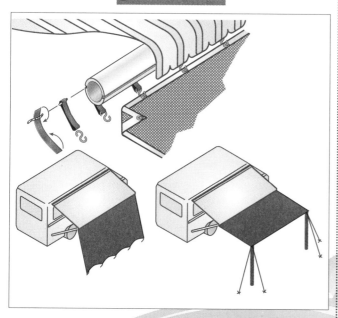

Have you ever needed additional sun- or weather-protected space under your RV awning? Perhaps you have wanted to shade a large group of friends during hot summer days, or have had to cancel an outside meal because of bad weather. Maybe you'd just like to have more shade outside your rig. If so, all of these problems can be solved for about $25 worth of materials, and a little effort.

Start by purchasing a polyethylene tarp (usually blue in color) with a length dimension shorter than your RV's awning tube. Using fabric strapping material, make up four to seven short straps, as shown in the illustration. Sew in a 3/16-inch rope across one end of the straps, and either install a metal grommet on the other end, or loop the strap back on itself and stitch in place. The number of straps you need will depend upon the number of grommet holes existing in the tarp.

Insert the rope end of the straps into the extra slot on the awning tube. These will be left in position when you retract the awning for travel. If end caps prevent installation of the straps as suggested, drill a 1/4-inch hole into the tube slot, to allow the straps to be maneuvered into place.

Purchase sufficient small S-hooks to correspond with the number of grommet holes in the tarp. Using a pair of pliers, crimp the hooks in place in the tarp, as shown. These hooks can now be attached to the straps.

They will support one side of the tarp, so the other end can be held in place by poles and rope, tied off to trees, or taken out far enough to be staked to the ground. The possibilities are limited only by your imagination.

Because this extension is installed on an inside slot of the awning tube, the valance of the RV awning will automatically ensure proper drainage away from your rig.
- *KEN KIRRY, NORTHBORO, MASSACHUSETTS*

A NEW ANGLE

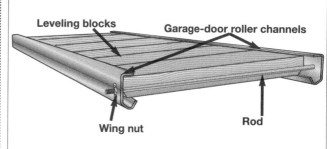

Igot tired of trying to store and secure all the leveling blocks that I take along in my RV. To overcome this frustration, I acquired two 7-foot lengths of overhead garage-door roller channel, and bolted them to the underside of my trailer's frame. As installed, the channels will accept 2 × 10 × 16-inch wood blocks. The blocks are beveled to allow them to easily slide into and out of the storage channel, and two metal rods on each end prevent the cargo from falling out. Wing nuts secure the metal rods.

The beveled ends also come into play during use. By orienting the blocks face up and face down, I can make the bevels fit together to create an extended plank. The angle cuts also make it easier for the trailer tires to ride up and over them during setup. When it comes to leveling blocks, any kind of wood can be used. However, I selected the type that is weather-treated for extended life.

To make retrieval easy, I drilled one block and attached rope through it. This is the first to go in the storage channel. Next, I inserted the remaining blocks, making sure that the rope remained on top so it couldn't get tangled on road hazards during travel. Now, when I need blocking, all I have to do is remove one metal rod and pull on the rope.
- *DONALD W. COBB, GREENE, NEW YORK*

SURPRISE!

My wife and I recently purchased a fifth-wheel trailer that we think is great. However, we did run into a problem shortly after the purchase.

In the process of getting ready to hook up, I raised the front electric jacks too far and snapped the weld on the left leg. It dropped to the ground. I wired it up until I could get it welded again.

To prevent this serious problem from happening again, I wired in a limit switch to cut off the power when the jacks reach the properly retracted height. The switch can be purchased at Radio Shack, or a similar electronics parts store. However, make sure you select a weatherproof switch, rated to carry heavy-duty doses of 12-volt DC current.

Now, when the jack leg comes into contact with the limit switch, the contacts open and the jack motor stops. Hope this helps someone else avoid the same problem that we had.

- HARRY B. ROBINSON, LIVINGSTON, TEXAS

GETTING TO THE POINT

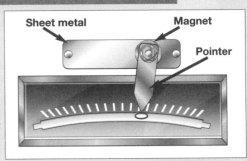

Sheet metal · Magnet · Pointer

Being a member of what some refer to as "gravel-pit campers," I use Bureau of Land Management campsites and remote U.S. Forest Service campgrounds a great deal. Most of the sites in these types of facilities are not the level pads one expects to find in developed RV parks.

One of the problems I used to run into several days after unhooking was that I couldn't remember the bubble level's position prior to setup. This translated into considerable trial and error as I tried to reconnect to the tow vehicle.

I was able to eliminate this frustration by installing a piece of sheet metal just above my bubble leveling device, and then making a metal pointer to which I attached a small, pot-holder-type magnet.

At unhitching time, I position the magnetic pointer on the sheet-metal strip—directly above the bubble—where it remains throughout my stay. The pointer reminds me, at a glance, just how much I need to elevate the trailer gooseneck before attempting to back my tow vehicle under it. Hooking up is now a one-shot affair.

- ALLEN BENCH, KENNEWICK, WASHINGTON

STRAIN SAVER

Here is how I made a hitch-jack block that saves considerable time and strain when hitching and leveling a travel trailer. Folks with manually cranked jacks will really appreciate the work it saves.

Using 2 × 5-inch boards and nails or screws, assemble a stair-stepped platform (see diagram).

After the trailer is parked, determine how much front-to-rear leveling will be needed. If the hitch must be raised considerably, place the jack post on the highest step of the block. Conversely, if the tongue must be lowered significantly, select the lowest step on the block.

After using this device a few times, you will be able to quickly judge which step to use to minimize the work at hand.

- CHARLES McAFEE, HALEYVILLE, ALABAMA

GOOSENECK GADGET

Hitch-slip pin · Hose clamp · Piece of rubber hose

For owners of fifth-wheel trailers, storing the 12-volt DC umbilical cord in an orderly manner presents a problem. Normally, the cable is wrapped around the hitch-pin housing, or just left dangling to the ground where it can drop in dirt or water.

I decided to overcome this problem by attaching a 3-inch hitch-slip pin to the electrical cable. I use an adjustable hose clamp to hold the slip pin in place, but only after installing a short length of rubber hose over the cable to prevent chafing by the clamp. With this in place, I can coil the umbilical and secure it out of the sun and weather.

- JIM L. HAMMOND, PIERRE, SOUTH DAKOTA

SOLO SOLUTIONS

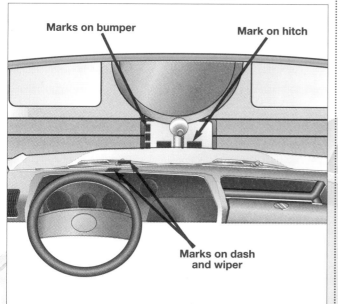

Marks on bumper

Mark on hitch

Marks on dash and wiper

More often than not, I travel alone whenever I use my Tioga motorhome. It used to be that whenever I wanted to take my tag-along car on a trip with me, I had to deal with the frustration of hitching up unassisted. That's why I developed the following system.

At home, on my driveway, I hooked up the tag-along's tow bar to the motorhome. Next, I assumed a convenient position in the driver's seat of the car. From there, I sighted a line across the dashboard, over the top of the windshield wiper, to the rear bumper of the motorhome. I then marked these spots.

Using electrical tape as vertical reference, I again sighted across the two points on the dashboard and wiper. Then, I readjusted the tape on the bumper until I had a straight visual line between all three markings. With care, I could achieve a dead-center line-up between the tow bar and the hitch ball on the motorhome.

My next problem was to gauge the distance between the tag-along and the motorhome's bumper. With the car hooked up on a dead-center line, I raised the hitch and secured it in its vertical storage position.

After this was done, I visually noted and marked a prominent point on the tow bar that corresponded to a specific area on the motorhome bumper. Using electrical tape again, I laid out a horizontal line on the bumper. I moved this experimentally up and down until a line-of-sight match was perfected with the mark on the tow bar.

Using all these reference points, I now can accurately position the tag-along behind the motorhome within ½ inch of where it needs to be for a perfect hookup on the first try.

I finished the job by painting all alignment points. This gave me a permanent hookup grid-sighting system.
- John Finck, San Bernardino, California

LEVEL IDEA

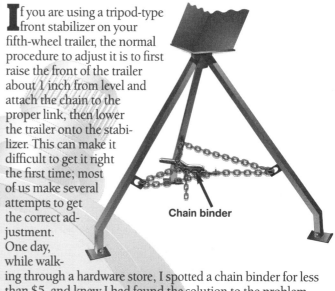

Chain binder

If you are using a tripod-type front stabilizer on your fifth-wheel trailer, the normal procedure to adjust it is to first raise the front of the trailer about 1 inch from level and attach the chain to the proper link, then lower the trailer onto the stabilizer. This can make it difficult to get it right the first time; most of us make several attempts to get the correct adjustment. One day, while walking through a hardware store, I spotted a chain binder for less than $5, and knew I had found the solution to the problem. Now, all I do is raise or lower the fifth-wheel to the level position, put the tripod under the kingpin, set the chain to the nearest link, and apply the chain binder to tension it properly. Set-up and take-down times are only around 3 minutes each.
- Mike Steffen, Livingston, Texas

REFLECTIVE GUIDANCE

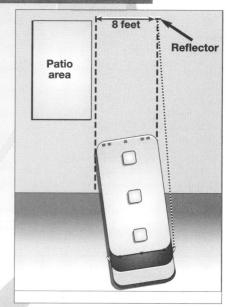

8 feet

Reflector

Patio area

To help me when I'm backing my RV into a campsite, I first step off 8 feet from the patio area and place a reflector where I want the rig's left-rear wheel. Day or night, I can see the exact spot where I need to stop backing. Nearly any reflector will do the job, and many are available. However, I was lucky. I found some temporary reflectors, used by blacktop crews, that had been scraped off by a snow plow.
- Owens Kollar, Queen City, Missouri

TAKE A LOAD OFF

My wife and I noticed our fifth-wheel kingpin was dangerously exposed to children playing around our trailer whenever the rig was unhitched from the truck. Not wanting to look for a hospital during a camping trip, I decided to prevent an accident before it happened.

In shopping for a kingpin stabilizer jack, I noticed that one coast nearly $100. This prompted me to make my own, a move that turned out to be much cheaper and handier. I bought a basement beam jack for $20 at a lumberyard, and cut ½ of the pipe to a dimension of 54 inches. To this pipe, I spot-welded the jack's accompanying base plate, and then threaded the plug into the opposite end.

I then welded the top plate to a piece of 3-inch inside-diameter steel pipe, which I cut to a length of 2 inches.

Finally, I welded this entire assembly to the threaded rod that came with the jack, and screwed it into place in the modified post. I spray-painted the finished unit to match our trailer. For less than $25, I now have a hand stabilizer and head saver.

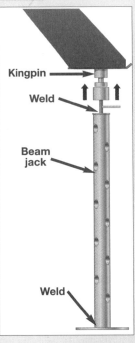

Kingpin

Weld

Beam jack

Weld

CHANNELING JACKS

When placing stabilizing jacks under my trailer, it always took two hands to hold the jack steady while taking the last few turns on the jack screw. This is a frustrating job, done on hands and knees, when the jack twists out from under the trailer frame just as it's starting to take the weight of the trailer. I solved the problem by welding a 3-inch-wide piece of U-shaped steel channel to the top of each jack screw.

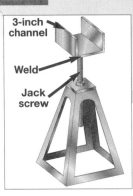

3-inch channel

Weld

Jack screw

Now, the last couple of inches of travel on the jack screw find the jack held captive by the channel as it slips around the trailer frame member. Make sure the channel stock you select is slightly wider than the trailer frame member. Any welding shop will do the job in a short time, at little cost.

- R.D. McGar, Wimberley, Texas

OH, WHAT A RELIEF IT IS

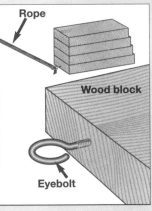

Rope

Wood block

Eyebolt

Getting down on your knees to remove wood blocks from under the stabilizers can be quite painful—especially if you suffer from bad joints. An easy solution takes only a few minutes to create and costs virtually nothing.

Simply screw an eyebolt into the end of your base block, and thread a 12-inch-long piece of rope through the eye. Knot each end of the rope. Now, pile on as many leveling blocks as you need.

When you're ready to break camp, raise your rig's stabilizers, and grab the base block rope at each location. Just give it an easy pull, and all your wood blocks will slide out together. This won't cure bad knees, but it sure makes this task easier.

- Bill and Carrol Wright, Santa Rosa, California

FORGET ME NOT

*H*ere is an idea for those who, on occasion, leave things undone when getting the RV ready to move to another destination. Who hasn't forgotten from time to time chores such as retracting the TV antenna, rolling up the awning, and removing the leveling jacks and tire sunshades? Having fretted over these items too many times, I looked for a solution.

I found it in the form of 1 × 6-inch ribbons, to which I attached hook-and-loop fasteners on each end. These allowed the ribbons to be made into loops. Then, with a felt-tip marking pen, I wrote important tasks on individual ribbons.

Now, I attach these ribbons to my rig's steering wheel as I accomplish each set-up task. They remain on the steering wheel until it's time to move on. During camp breakdown, the ribbons are removed and stored in a convenient location until needed again.

The ribbons really work, and I can now get under way without the gnawing, did-I-do-everything anxiety that I used to experience. When the wheel is empty, I know that everything has been stowed away properly.

- Lila Nuttall, Penticton, British Columbia, Canada

WORKING AT THE END OF YOUR ROPE

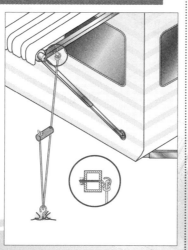

Even though keeping an extended RV awning secured against severe winds can be a problem, a sturdy safety strap can be easily made from locally purchased materials. The only RV modifications needed are two ¼-inch clearance holes drilled in the upper rails of the awning support arms. Because you will be inserting an eyebolt into each of these holes, it's important to make sure these bolts will not interfere with the operation of the awning.

Install the eyebolt with the opening facing outward, and secure in place with a nut and washer. Now, fasten and secure the end of a sturdy ¼-inch nylon line to the eyebolt.

Pass the remainder of the rope through one side of a predrilled 1 × 7-inch wooden dowel (see illustration), then through the eye of a lawn screw that has been firmly implanted in the ground. Run the line back up to the other side of the dowel, and tie a large knot in the end. Take up the slack to tighten. Of course, one line and dowel are required for each side.

Before cutting off any excess line, be sure that there is sufficient length to allow adjustment in all awning positions. I have found that when the awning is fully extended in its normal position, the dowels fall midway between the lawn screw and the eyebolt.

Drill the holes in the dowel only slightly larger in diameter than the rope you've chosen. The line will slip if they're too big. Paint the dowels a bright color for visibility.
- JOHN C. DRECHSLER, HENDERSONVILLE, NORTH CAROLINA

CHOCK AND LOCK

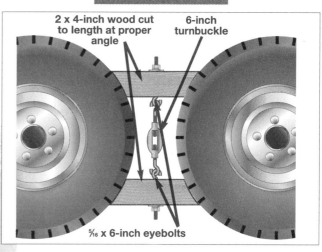

2 x 4-inch wood cut to length at proper angle

6-inch turnbuckle

⁵⁄₁₆ x 6-inch eyebolts

For around $40, you can buy a metal device designed to chock trailer tires on one side. We accomplished the same result for around $5, which went to the purchase of two ⁵⁄₁₆ × 6-inch eyebolts and a 6-inch turnbuckle. (Smaller eyebolts may work better for your particular situation.) Making the wood blocks required a bit of trial and error to get their lengths and angles just right to provide the proper spacing for the hardware and to grip the tires. We squared up some scrap pieces of 2 × 4-inch lumber, and cut two of them to length at the proper angles with our table saw. Then, we made two more pieces with their ends at the same angle, long enough to be glued together (carpenter's glue) to form 3-inch-thick blocks. We located the centers of the blocks and drilled ⅜-inch holes for the eyebolts. To finish the job and protect the wood from the weather, we coated the blocks with floor enamel, well-thinned to soak into the wood. We found that one set did a good job of immobilizing the trailer, and that these chocks store easier than the commercial versions.
- EDSON B. SNOW, POMPANO BEACH, FLORIDA

STACKING 'EM HIGH

Leveling the front of my fifth-wheel from side to side while unhitching has always been a little bit of a problem. I had to carry various-size blocks, since my electric landing jacks are not independent of each other. I was able to solve this problem by obtaining some scrap lumber and purchasing hinges at a hardware store. I used three boards for each leg; each board, cut in 1-, 2-, and 4-inch-thicknesses, is 6 × 8 inches. I used four 2½-inch utility hinges per side (two to a board), which cost around $8. The boards are stacked in order of thickness, with the thickest on the bottom. The hinges connect the top and bottom boards to the center piece, so now any combination of blocks can be used by simply flipping the sections.
- KENNETH C. RUHNAU, SUN CITY, CALIFORNIA

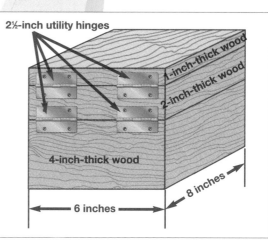

2½-inch utility hinges

1-inch-thick wood

2-inch-thick wood

4-inch-thick wood

6 inches

8 inches

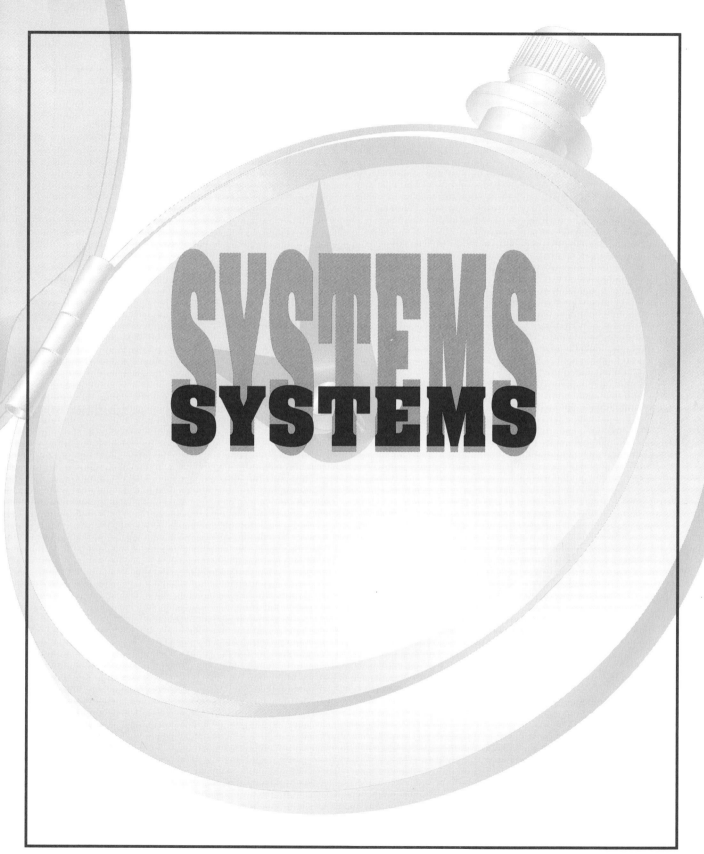

SYSTEMS

QUIESCENT PRESSURE

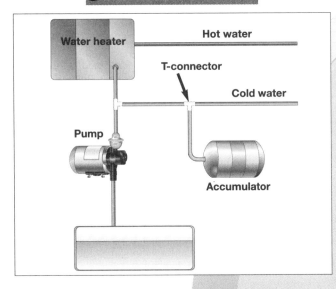

In my mind, the demand water system installed aboard most RVs leaves something to be desired—namely, the incessant water-pump operation that occurs when boondocking. As it happens, there is a relatively simple solution. A captive air tank with an internal rubber bladder is available from most plumbing-supply houses. These "accumulator" tanks are made for residential water systems that rely on well pumps for pressure. However, they can be readily adapted to RVs, and come in a variety of shapes and sizes to make the job easy. After some searching, I found one that fits perfectly under the bed of my rig. It is a 4.5-gallon model that holds about half this amount of water in actual use.

The accumulator cost me $55, but it is possible to find other sizes to fit individual needs and pocketbooks. Remember, however, purchasing a tank that's too small will not accomplish much, and getting one too large means weight, size, and cost limitation. The 4.5-gallon version works very well. A shower of impressive length can be taken without even operating the water pump.

Installation is very simple. Just cut a cold-water line anywhere in the high-pressure side of the RV's water system. (Be sure to drain this line first.) Install a T-connector, and the appropriate length of hose to reach the accumulator tank opening. Securely clamp all hose connections, charge the tank with the prescribed air pressure, and the job is done.

These devices function by storing water pressure against a preset air pressure (usually around 15 psi) on the opposite side of a rubber diaphragm. Incoming water displaces the diaphragm until the water pump's pressure switch activates. Pressure is maintained until a faucet is opened aboard the RV, and the water pump will remain silent until about 2 gallons of water have escaped from the system. At this point, the pump will start and run until the accumulator is refilled and repressurized.
- KEITH C. FRANCE, DOUGLAS, WYOMING

WOBBLE-PUMP WOES

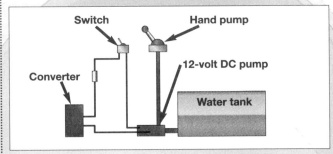

I purchased a new fold-out camper this year that came equipped only with a hand-operated water pump system. I quickly converted to an electric pump. The project was simple and had a total cost of $48.

Materials required:

One small 12-volt DC water pump rated at approximately 1.5 gallons per minute (gpm)

One 3-amp switch

One in-line fuse holder with fuse

Appropriate length of 12- to 14-gauge stranded automotive wire

Two appropriate-diameter hose clamps

Be sure that pump electrical demand doesn't exceed the capacity of the RV's converter (my pump draws only 1.6 amps).

To install, mount the water pump on the RV's floor near the water-tank outlet. Cut the water line, making sure to leave enough length attached to the tank to reach the pump inlet. Connect the outlet of the pump to the faucet hose. Secure both with hose clamps. Make electrical connections as in the diagram.

While a pump that delivers only 1.5 gpm may not sound like much, it's a lot more than can be pumped by hand during the same time.
- JIM SNODDY, GREENWOOD, SOUTH CAROLINA

MUFFLING THE WATER PUMP

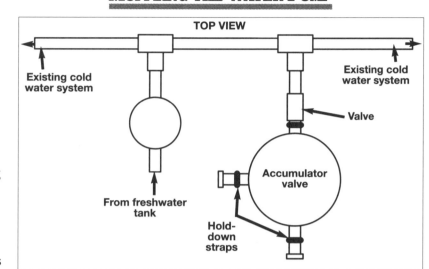

Most of our camping is without hookups in undeveloped areas. There is only one major irritation we have with being self-contained: the frequent and noisy operation of the fresh-water pump. Turning the water on really low to conserve the supply causes the pump to cycle on and off almost continuously. Not only is this bothersome, it wears out the pressure switch. Flushing the toilet at night wakes up everybody, including the dogs, and there is a major fluctuation in water pressure when the pump cycles on and off. While showering, pressure changes can cause water temperature to vary widely.

We had put up with these problems for a long time before finding a good solution—the accumulator tank. Essentially, this container stores a limited quantity of water under a head of air pressure until you open the tap. The air pressure provides water flow initially, and the pump then cycles on. Because of the tank, the pump takes considerably longer to start when the faucet is turned on. The flow is much more consistent, and gone is the staccato "rrrrrrp" of the cycling. When the pump comes on, it runs until pressure in the accumulator tank is restored.

We recently adapted a commercial accumulator tank sold in Sears' farm machinery catalog for approximately $25. It's designed to be used in certain applications of small water pumps drawing from underground wells. Accumulator tanks are also available in supply stores like Camping World.

Installation of this device was fairly easy, and all plumbing connections were easily obtained and adapted to the RV's water system. We placed the accumulator near the water pump outlet, a requirement that meant locating sufficient space to mount the tank vertically according to the instructions.

As a precaution against future tank leaks, we installed a shut-off valve between the water pump and the accumulator. If this valve is closed, the system will operate exactly the way it did before installation of the pressure reservoir.

Our installation works better than we had hoped. The problems have either disappeared or are greatly reduced.

Afterward, both pressure and volume remain high whenever a faucet is opened. The pump does not come on until about 3 cups of water have been drained.

With the pump switch turned off, water flow remains almost constant until the accumulator is empty (3 quarts). This is ideal for after-bedtime water needs.

- PHIL AND BETTY McGOWAN, REDWOOD CITY, CALIFORNIA

OIL CAN RESCUE

The potable-water storage tank inlet on our fifth-wheel trailer requires a 90-degree funnel when we periodically cleanse the tank with bleach and baking soda. I struck upon the idea of modifying a plastic quart-size oil container to simplify this process. I merely cut the narrow side of a well-washed and rinsed container to produce the perfect 90-degree funnel. This not only assures that the algae-killing bleach reaches the tank without spillage, it greatly eases the addition of powdery baking soda to the tank.

As luck would have it, a 1-quart container will accommodate the entire contents of a large box of baking soda. Once poured into the special funnel, the powder is easily slurried into the water storage tank, where it removes the disagreeable odor and taste caused by the disinfecting bleach treatment.

- VICTOR & MARCELLA SCHWEIKERT, NORTH FORK, CALIFORNIA

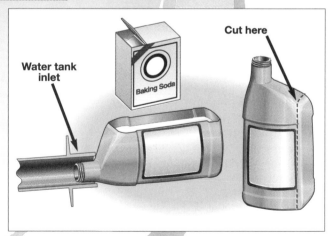

TOPPING OFF WITH EASE

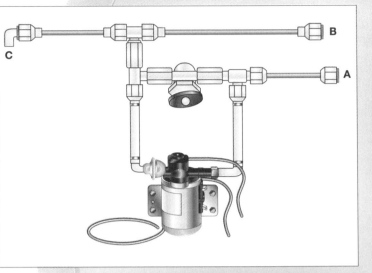

Being able to fill our freshwater tank while still attached to a city-water hookup is quick and, in bad weather, luxuriously convenient. No longer do you need to stand in the rain, rushing to fill the tank before departure. A shut-off valve installed across the RV water-pump plumbing connections is a relatively easy do-it-yourself project that generally helps make life on the road easier.

With the demand system in most modern RVs, the water pump has a check valve installed to prevent city water from backflowing through the pump and filling the storage tank. This can be bypassed with an open/close valve so it's only a matter of opening the valve (see diagram) to fill the tank.

When I performed this modification, I used a plastic open/close valve just so I could keep the same material throughout my rig's plumbing system. However, a brass valve could also be used. My RV's water lines have flared fittings. This made it necessary to adapt from flare to Qest connections, available at RV-supply stores, to accomplish the hookup shown. This is best achieved by fabricating pipes with a ½-inch flare on one end, and a ½-inch pipe fitting on the other.

The hoses between the pump and plumbing help dampen the pump's vibrations, which otherwise could cause fittings to loosen. The three open connections attach as follows: (A) line from freshwater holding tank, (B) cold-water inlet line to water heater, and (C) incoming city-water connection to cold-water faucets.

- Jerry Lyle, Orange, California

FLEXIBLE FLAP

The plastic LP-gas tank cover on my travel trailer is difficult to remove. This required much effort every time I wanted to turn the tank valves on or off, or simply see if it was time to switch tanks because one was empty. Deciding that there must be an easier way, here's how I solved this problem.

I noticed that the flexible plastic cover was molded from two separate halves. These were riveted together during production.

I carefully cut the front half of the cover from side to side with a sharp razor. This created a flexible flap that can be pulled up to access the tanks. After this, I applied strips of self-adhesive hook-and-loop tabs to hold the cover securely closed during travel. It's a quick modification, to be sure, but one that allows me to get to my rig's LP-gas tanks quickly, without having to remove the cover.

- Donald Howard, Street, Maryland

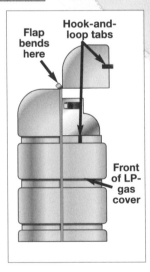

Flap bends here

Hook-and-loop tabs

Front of LP-gas cover

A MYSTERY SOLVED

Have you ever pulled into a campground, hooked up, and retired, knowing that the rig's freshwater tank was nearly empty? Upon awakening, were you greeted by the sound of water dripping from the freshwater fill spout because the tank was overflowing?

If so, the problem can be traced to the one-way check valve found inside the onboard water pump.

This valve is supposed to prevent city water from leaking into the storage tank—a job that most perform reliably for years. When this little-known component fails, a mysteriously filled freshwater tank results every time you hook up.

The fix is simple. Repair or replace the existing valve. Alternatively, if the pump is getting old and weak anyway, replacing it will simultaneously correct the leaky check-valve problem.

- Richard Mater, Santa Maria, California

AVOIDING SOGGY SLIPPERS

When the water heater in an RV springs a leak, the failure often goes unnoticed until well after the rig's subfloor and carpet are soaked.

For this reason, I suggest that owners fabricate a small catch basin from galvanized flashing material, and install it under the water heater. Of course, the most ideal time to accomplish this modification is at replacement time. However, since most RV water heaters are not difficult to remove and replace, this precaution may be viable even for units in good condition.

Start by cutting a piece of flashing material (available at hardware stores) to the proper length and width dimensions of your rig's water heater. Allow an additional margin so that ½-inch tabs can be

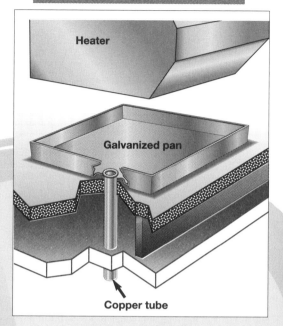

Heater

Galvanized pan

Copper tube

turned up to form the edges of the catch basin. Either solder or seal the corners to make them watertight.

Complete the pan by drilling a ¼-inch hole in its base. Solder a corresponding-size tube to the bottom, and drill a matching hole through the RV's floor. Set the assembly in place, making certain that the drain tube extends ½-inch below the floorline. Reinstall the water heater.

If the heater leaks now, it won't ruin the inside of your RV. And should a small leak occur while you're out boondocking, you may be able to postpone repair or replacement long enough to return to civilization.

- A.W. WAGNER, CLEVELAND, TEXAS

WINTERIZING TIP

As every RVer who lives in colder sections of the country knows, an RV's plumbing must be adequately protected against freezing. This can be done by blowing out the water lines with compressed air, or by filling them with nontoxic antifreeze.

I feel safer using antifreeze, and decided to find an easy way to inject this fluid into the plumbing system.

I obtained a used automotive windshield-washer reservoir and mounted it near, but above the level of the RV water pump. The washer outlet is connected to the RV water lines through a winterizing kit manifold that I originally installed to draw antifreeze from gallon jugs, but can be installed using a two-way water valve. The line

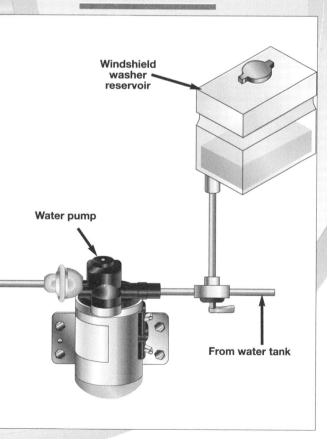

Windshield washer reservoir

Water pump

From water tank

from the washer container is connected to the inlet side of the pump.

Air formerly got into the system when I switched between jugs—a problem that is now eliminated with the washer reservoir. I simply pour nontoxic antifreeze into the container and allow the RV's water pump to push it through the plumbing system. Because the washer container is mounted higher than the pump, the lines are full, eliminating the need to prime the system.

Of course, once all the pipes are full, I allow some antifreeze to run into the sink and bathtub drain traps. I also open the toilet valve to make sure that antifreeze circulates through it, as well.

- KENNETH T. DESCHELER, ST. CHARLES, MISSOURI

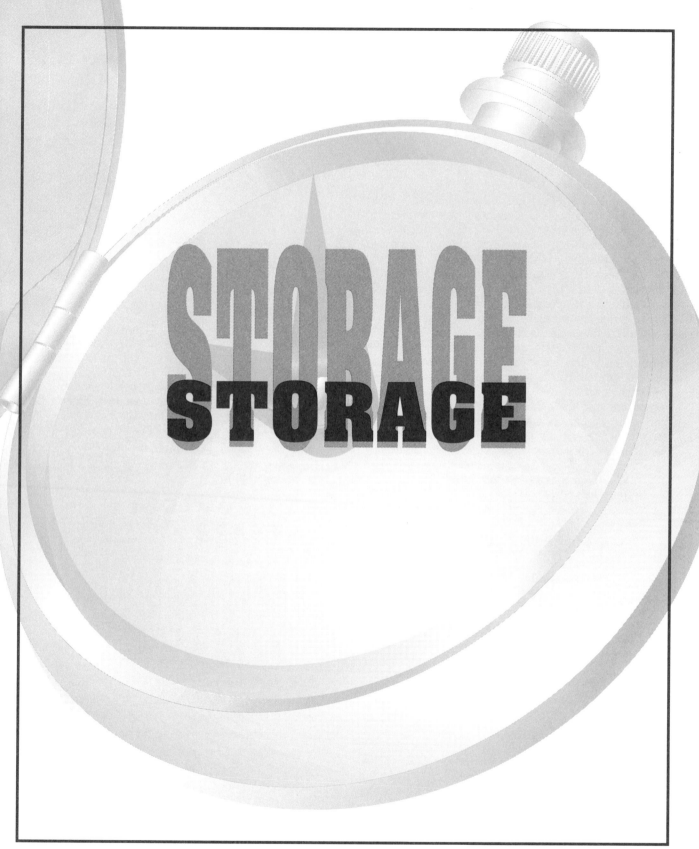

STORAGE

TRAILER CONDO

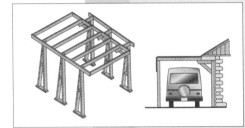

Parking our new trailer out of the hot sun, and protecting it from weather, were accomplished with the use of three sawhorses. Local set-back regulations prevented me from building a permanent shelter next to the fence along my property line (the only place feasible in my case), yet I wanted something more substantial than a bothersome tarp. A portable structure would be considered legal.

So, I proceeded to construct an inexpensive, easy-to-build cover using sawhorse brackets braced with 2 × 4- and 2 × 6-inch lumber. The finished shelter is not attached to either my garage or fence, and works well as a free-standing unit. It's also solid; it didn't sag during a 10-inch wet snow.

I used corrugated steel for the roof, except for one panel of translucent fiberglass, which I installed as a source of natural light. A roll-up blind on the front makes the finished unit almost like a garage.

Of course, modifications can be made to fit the situation. For instance, I had to go higher than the eves on my garage to keep from giving up width. I just stair-stepped the beams, as illustrated. Other folks may not require such a modification.

Moving our lightweight Casita travel trailer in and out is a snap with the use of the jackpost dolly wheel.

- Dan Richter, Lakewood, Colorado

POSITIVE PRESSURE

Holes
Bumper
Holes
Airflow
Airflow
Sewer hose
Cap

I recently modified the bumper of my RV to assure quick drying of the internally stored sewer hose while I'm traveling. I drilled two ½-inch street-side holes in the front of the bumper, and two more in the back of the bumper on the curb side. This combination produces a positive pressure, which forces air into the bumper, through the sewer hose, and out the rearmost exhaust holes. Not only does this eliminate odor buildup near the rear bumper, it also greatly reduces the tendency of this structure to rust internally as a result of exposure to constant moisture and humidity.

- Richard E. Barrett, Santa Ana, California

GOING UP

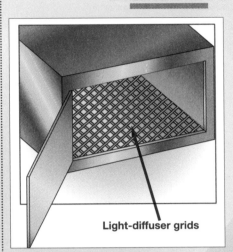

Light-diffuser grids

We once had a water leak in our travel trailer during a heavy rainstorm that soaked the clothing packed underneath the rig's bench seats. To prevent a reoccurrence once the leak was repaired, we bought several 2 × 4-foot light-diffuser grids at the hardware store. These were cut to fit under the bench and cabinet storage areas in the trailer.

The contents of these compartments are now protected from leaks and spills, because everything is ½ inch off the trailer's floor. The plastic grid is easily cut with diagonal cutters, inserted into each square, and odd-shaped storage areas are readily accommodated with a little careful planning. An added benefit to this project is that stored items slide on the grid, making them much easier to retrieve.

- Franz and Marcia Reisch, Las Cruces, New Mexico

◆ CLOSEUPS ◆ CLOSEUPS ◆ CLOSEUPS ◆

LOW-COST CLOSET CONTROL

*H*ere's another space saver that also helps to keep things in order while on the road.

The closet in the rear of my trailer runs parallel to the road, and when traveling, the hangers kept falling off or sliding into a wrinkled bunch. The solution was simple. I purchased a 4-foot-wide, plastic-covered wire rack designed for closet organization from our local Home Depot store for under $10. I then cut it to loosely fit over the top of the clothes rod with the bent lip facing up to act as a retaining barrier for stored items such as towels, toilet paper, and other light stuff. The rack is fastened to the back of the closet wall with the clips included, but is not attached to the closet rod. It just rests on it. This allows me to lift the rack slightly to remove the clothes hangers, yet has enough weight to hold the hangers in place while under way.

- Richard M. Clark, Long Beach, California

◆ CLOSEUPS ◆ CLOSEUPS ◆ CLOSEUPS ◆

SOGGY SPOUSE

I happen to be married to an avid fisherman. Now, this type of human will pursue his wily quarry through sunshine or rain. Unfortunately, the latter instance seems to occur more frequently.

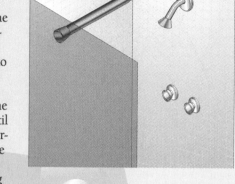

This caused me no problems until my favorite fisherman would come back to our motorhome soaking wet. Finding a place for his wet clothes inside the confines of our RV was never easy.

Finally, seeing the damp mass of clothes piled on the bathroom floor one too many times forced me to act. I insisted that this piscatorial practitioner rig up some kind of drying rack to hang them on.

He proved his resourcefulness by purchasing a spring-loaded, adjustable curtain rod. He had it set up in the shower stall of our RV within 5 minutes after bringing it home.

The curtain rod has rubber tips on each end, and is held firmly in place by spring tension. Consequently, there's no need for drilling or screws. Costing about $10 at a hardware store, these rods come in chrome and colors, and will span from 3 to 5 feet.
- *MILDRED WHITE, LA MESA, CALIFORNIA*

FRAMED FOR A COVER-UP

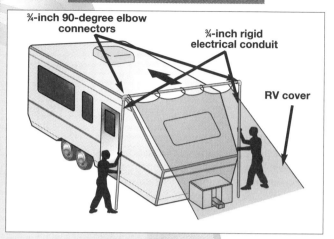

¾-inch 90-degree elbow connectors

⅝-inch rigid electrical conduit

RV cover

Using a cover to protect your RV while in storage goes a long way toward preserving its finish, but getting the material on and off can be quite frustrating. To make the task easy, I purchased three 10-foot sections of ⅝-inch rigid electrical conduit and two right-angle elbow connectors (90 degrees). Total cost was less than $5.

Place a connector at each end of the one conduit and attach the other lengths of conduit to each connector. You now have a U-shaped frame. Lay the cover out in front or back of the RV and attach the short end of the cover to the horizontal cross-member of the frame using string or wire.

With the help of another person, one on either side of the rig, lift each vertical pole and carry the cover over the top of the RV until it is completely covered. Do not use flexible conduit, because it is difficult to raise the cover over the RV.
- *ALLEN KUHN, LOS ANGELES, CALIFORNIA*

OVERLOOKED STORAGE

For additional storage, I boxed in the open, unused space between the structural beams of my fifth-wheel's gooseneck. These convenient containers store my rig's cumbersome water hose and fittings, as well as long lengths of cable TV wire. The extra-long storage area houses my fishing poles. This location keeps them very handy. The doors of the storage compartments are secured with standard hinges and hasps that are available at any hardware store. The door material can be made from almost any flat stock metal, wood or plastic.
- *RAY IVERSON, RAYMOND, CALIFORNIA*

CONCEPT CHANGE

Do you want more shelf space in your RV freezer? Buy a Rubbermaid Wrap Organizer, which is designed to hang inside a cupboard door to hold boxes of foil

Wrap organizer

and plastic wrap. Simply lay this item in the freezer compartment with the opening facing outward. Voila! You now have just under a square foot of extra shelf space with room underneath for the convenient storage of ice cube trays or small packages of food.
- *ROSEMARY BUTTERWORTH, SOQUEL, CALIFORNIA*

THE CUTTING EDGE

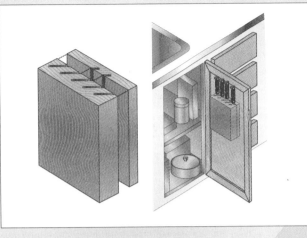

Treat yourself and your RV homemaker to the advantages of a multiple-knife scabbard. You will find it very easy to make, and install, a knife holder like the one depicted here. Once completed, you can expect to enjoy at least the following advantages:

- Knives are kept handy for easy selection and use.
- The danger of getting cut while sorting through drawers is eliminated.
- The keen edges of knives will last two to four times longer.
- No more will your cutlery counter block slide off onto the floor, scattering knives everywhere.
- You will have more counter and drawer space in the galley.
- Knives will be kept conveniently clean and out of sight.

I made my knife scabbard from pieces of ¼- and 1¼-inch mahogany. The slots were cut at a 45-degree angle to make knife selection easier. The angle also will accommodate wider-bladed knives without intruding excessively into the under-counter cabinet.

These openings can be varied in depth to suit a particular cutlery set, though if you do this, keep in mind that the scabbard may not accept replacement knives purchased later on. In any event, short-bladed paring knives should have narrower slots to keep their handles from moving about in transit.

After you have assembled the scabbard, insert the knives you have chosen to see how far down from the top of the cabinet door the holder should be mounted. The primary user should be present at this time to determine which undercounter cabinet door will be the most convenient for each access.

Check, too, to see whether part of an existing shelf will have to be removed or trimmed to allow for clearance of the scabbard and its cargo.

If you glue the finished project to the cabinet door, be sure to remove any existing finish that might hinder a good bond. I was able to use clamps to hold my knife scabbard in place while the glue set.

- RICHARD B. BUTLER, TRUTH OR CONSEQUENCES, NEW MEXICO

SHELVING IT

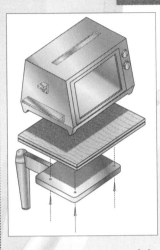

I installed a Braund TV shelf (available at Camping World) under the eye-level kitchen cabinet in my RV. But rather than holding a television, the shelf supports a toaster oven, instead. The entire assembly can swing out of the way when not needed. Of course, other appliances could be used, including a microwave, as long as the weight doesn't exceed 40 pounds.

These shelves also work well when added to the end of a countertop to expand the available working area. They come with a small metal plate that is predrilled for attaching a platform. You can add a plywood shelf of whatever size you may need.

Depending upon where you choose to mount the swing-out shelf bracket, you may need to add a decorative metal chain to its base to limit travel. We had to do this because of a nearby plastic splash shield that could be easily damaged if the toaster oven were to swing into it.

- GORDON MUNRO, VICTORIA, BRITISH COLUMBIA, CANADA

CLOSEUPS ◆ CLOSEUPS ◆ CLOSEUPS

SPRING STORAGE

I have a suggestion for securing small items inside an RV in motion. Some time ago, I began using spring-loaded drapery-style rods to prevent the contents of cupboards from spilling out when the doors are opened after travel.

However, I found that small items would still slip by these restraints and jump out at me at the first opportunity. As a remedy, I cut cardboard into pieces a couple inches high and placed them between the bar and the contents of the storage area.

This worked, but I did have some difficulty working around the cardboard when looking for something specific. I recently developed the ideal solution.

I still use the spring tension bars across my rig's cupboard openings, but have replaced the opaque cardboard with thin plexiglas strips cut 2 to 3 inches tall. I leave the plastic in place all the time. I don't have the problem of storing the cardboard sections anymore, and I can quickly see what has fallen over.

- VIRGINIA HAMMONS, LOVELAND, COLORADO

CLOSEUPS ◆ CLOSEUPS ◆ CLOSEUPS

PRACTICAL PIPE

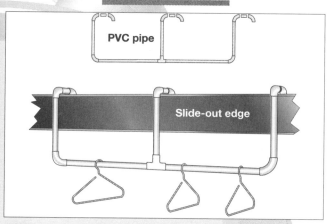

PVC pipe

Slide-out edge

We travel full-time in a fifth-wheel with a slide-out. As it was, when we did the ironing, there was nowhere to conveniently hang the finished garments. I had some scrap pieces of PVC pipe, from which I fashioned a clothes-hanging rack that hooks over the inside edge of the slide-out. The project was a success, and the setup has proved to be quite functional. It doesn't even have to be removed during travel.
- CLARENCE J. HALL, STEPHENS CITY, VIRGINIA

FISHERMAN'S DREAM

*F*ishing rods, particularly fly rods, can be a storage problem in a trailer. I used to weave the rods between overhead cabinets' door stiles. This was unsatisfactory, because the rods were always stored on the bottom of the cabinet. Everything had to come out of the cabinet in order to recover them.

When I acquired my fifth-wheel, I throught the problem was solved because it had basement storage. It didn't take long to discover that the problem was not solved, only relocated. When I wanted a rod, it was still on the bottom of the cabinet and in great danger of being damaged.

It wasn't until I installed new rain gutters on my house that I thought of the perfect solution. I cut a leftover aluminum downspout to a length sufficient to span the width of one of the RV's basement-storage compartments. Covering the sharp, exposed edges with duct tape, I mounted the downspout to the exposed trailer-frame members with nylon wire ties.

Now, I just put the rods in their fabric cases and slide them into this ideal storage space where they ride safely.
- RICHARD T. AMON, SEBRING, FLORIDA

DINETTE DILEMMA

RV dinettes that convert to beds are often optimistically called "two-sleepers." However, with a little effort, an extension can be added to achieve

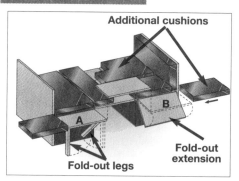

Additional cushions

A

B

Fold-out legs

Fold-out extension

something closer to two-sleeper reality.

I haven't provided construction dimensions, because they will vary from rig to rig. Material is 1×2-inch lumber for the legs and ½-inch plywood for the extension surfaces.

Sections A and B are hinged along the side of the dinette benches, where they remain folded until needed. When flipped up for use, the hinged legs fold downward to support the extension. A separately stored extension is then laid in place to bridge the gap between the two flip-up units. Plan the additional extension width so passage down the aisle is still possible. We store the extra custom-made cushions under the seats.
- BOB BLAZER, HUNTINGTON WOODS, MICHIGAN

PRACTICAL PLANK

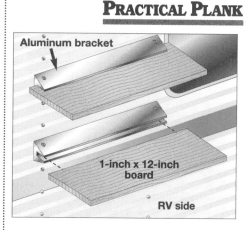

Aluminum bracket

1-inch x 12-inch board

RV side

We've installed a handy shelf bracket that can be screwed to the outside of an RV and permanently left in place. We mounted ours directly over an exterior electrical outlet, so that we can use a coffeepot, a frying pan, or other electrical appliance right on the shelf.

Most large hardware stores carry triangular-shaped shelf brackets that come in several colors and various lengths. Also available are many different sizes of prefinished book shelves.

Bracket installation is easy. Just locate the structural frame members in the area where you wish to install the shelf. Use caution when drilling holes to avoid electrical and plumbing lines. After the bracket is secured, simply insert the shelf—and enjoy.
- BILL AND CAROL WRIGHT, SANTA ROSA, CALIFORNIA

THE SPACE PROGRAM

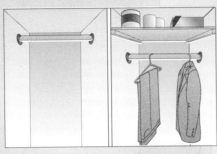

We own an 18-foot, older-model, self-contained travel trailer with all the usual amenities. However, even now, when we come back from a trip, I try to think of things that I could change or improve to make it more comfortable.

The one thing we can always use is more shelf space. After thinking about where I could add a shelf, I opened the wardrobe closet and realized that it was long enough to hang a formal gown (something we very seldom take with us).

Since the clothes bar was located at the top of the closet, all I needed to do was to remove the bar and brackets, put two shelf supports on either side of the walls, cut an appropriate-size piece of plywood, then rehang the brackets and the bar.

I chose to drop the bar 6 inches so we could store canned goods in this area. Our clothes are also easier to hang, and nothing touches the floor. We have a nice extra shelf that looks like it came from the factory.

- JACK EWALD, WEST UNION, OHIO

GETTING SPACEY

New shelves

Barrel bolts under table

When we were sitting at the dinette table in our motorhome at mealtime, there never seemed to be enough space for plates, bowls, cups, etc. The area between the bench seats and our table appeared to me to be an ideal place for an additional shelf.

I made two shelves that fold down along the side wall of the rig when not needed and up when more tabletop is desired. Piano hinges were used to mount the shelves to the wall, and barrel bolts installed under the existing table to hold the shelves in the extended position. This works great when just two people are aboard. However, if guests arrive and more dining or entertaining space is needed, it's a simple matter to fold the shelves flat against the wall.

- DAVID E. WATKINS, POMPANO BEACH, FLORIDA

SHELF HELP

Most motorhomes and travel trailers have adequate interior storage and shelves. However, my wife and I do a large amount of cooking and recreational living outside our trailer, and we found we needed exterior shelves for temporary use. We solved this problem with the simple addition of adjustable shelving attached to the exterior wall.

To make your own, purchase lengths of slotted wall-support standards and shelf brackets from your local hardware or builder's supply store. The support standards are available in 1-foot increments of 2 to 6 feet. Shelf brackets may be purchased in depths ranging from 6 to 14 inches (in 2-inch increments).

You can also buy precut and/or prefinished shelf boards to match your intended needs. I have found that anything longer than about 2 feet tends to collect so many items that teardown time increases. Two shorter shelves are usually more than enough for items such as cooking utensils, outdoor games, and so forth.

To affix the slotted support standards, first decide where the shelves will be positioned. Keep in mind that fastening screws should be driven into the RV's wall studs. Since most RVs have sheet-metal screws attaching the exterior skin to these studs, it's best if you use these holes to mount the support standards. This helps avoid the possibility of putting a stray screw into hidden wires and plumbing. Use stainless-steel screws for maximum durability.

- CARL P. HARTUP, FORT WAYNE, INDIANA

SLICK SLIDE-OUT

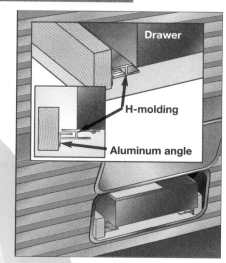

The storage area located beneath the floor of my RV's dinette is so deep that the back half was unreachable from outside. Considering this a waste of good storage space, I decided to build an extra-large drawer in which I could keep all stockpiled items within easy reach.

To assure that the drawer would remain level when extended, I mounted tracks of ¾-inch aluminum secured to two wood 2 × 4s attached to the floor of the RV. The drawer itself is fitted with two sections of aluminum H-molding that ride on the aluminum angle supports. This type molding is available at most lumberyards, because it is often used to construct a soffit under the eaves of a house.

- R. D. McGar, Wimberly, Texas

WOODWORKING WOMAN

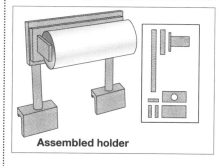

Assembled holder

A while back, my wife, Lois, took a woodworking class at our local high-school evening program. As others in the class were making wooden rabbits and animals to place on their front lawn, my practical wife devised a paper-towel holder for the cooking area of our pop-up camper. She designed it to be easily removed when the camper top is down.

To manufacture her functional invention, she used ¾-inch wood to form a 13½ × 5¼-inch rectangle, to which she attached a plastic, commercially made paper-towel holder. The tops of two 12¼-inch dowels were attached to the back of this rectangle. Dowel bottoms were secured to the depicted clip-on brackets. These brackets, made of six pieces of 5 × 2¼-inch wood, were dimensioned to slide easily over the RV's kitchen-sink backboard.

In addition to the paper-towel holder, my wife installed a holder for a butane lighter (used to start stovetop burners), which hangs on one side, with hooks on the opposite side to hold hot pads.

- William Rossnagel, Ironwood, Michigan

CLOSEUPS • CLOSEUPS • CLOSEUPS

BOXING MATCH

If your RV kitchen looks anything like ours, there is one cabinet that houses all those cooking fluids you just can't do without: sauces, oils, and what have you. At home, things stay put, but in an RV that's been on the road awhile, you don't know where you might find these items. Something may even leap out to unexpectedly greet you the first time you open the cabinet.

On one occasion, a bottle top leaked and made an unforgettable mess in our rig. A simple solution to this problem also accomplishes the good environmental deed of recycling. It is the use of empty quart and ½-gallon milk cartons to hold many potentially messy liquids. Cut the cartons off about 4 inches from the bottom, and pack them snugly in the cabinets where you store bottles. Milk cartons also work well under the sink for holding dishwashing detergent, cleansers, brushes, etc.

Use your imagination, and your spilling worries will become a thing of the past.

- Armand L. Thielker, Arroyo Grande, California

GRATE, JUST GRATE

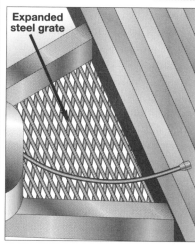

Expanded steel grate

I never seemed to have a place for our stabilizing jacks, leveling ramps, and wheel chocks inside my tow vehicle, especially when they were wet and dirty. So I decided to make a permanent place for these items by cutting a piece of expanded metal grate to match the underside of the trailer tongue and attaching it with self-tapping screws, as shown in the illustration.

Everything now rides nicely in this spot during travel. When I set up at a campground, I use the space to store hitch components.

- Mike Barondeau, Roscoe, South Dakota

ADDING COUNTER SPACE

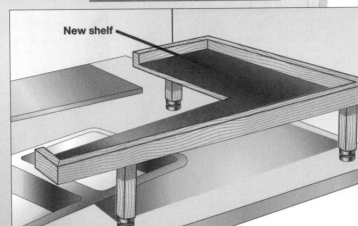

New shelf

Kitchen counter space is at a premium in any RV. If you find yourself short in this department, you may want to do what I did and build a sturdy shelf assembly that sits 6 inches above the area around the kitchen sink. Depending upon your needs, it can be made either portable or permanently attached.

The shelf is made of ½-inch plywood and is covered on all sides and edges with Formica that matches my existing countertop. The legs are 1-inch-square metal tubing, with flat plates welded to one end to allow attachment to the plywood. Wooden legs would also work well.

The feet are made from adjustable furniture glides, so the shelf can be individually leveled to your rig; 1-inch rubber crutch tips prevent movement during travel.

To figure the size and shape of your shelf, measure the open area around your sink, and then plot it on a cardboard template. You could also use graph paper to make a scale drawing of your countertop area, and then plot it on a template. Though I made my shelf 6 inches high, you could make any height desired. If even more space is required, don't overlook building a similar shelf for the dining table.

This was the first time that I had worked with Formica; I found it to be quite easy. However, make sure you use a sharp, fine-tooth blade when cutting the material, and use care when aligning it during final gluing to the plywood. Follow the cement-glue manufacturer's directions.

Material Required:
¾ × ¾-inch wood strip cut from scrap
½ × 27 × 32⅜-inch plywood
⅓ sheet Formica
Contact cement
Ten 1-inch drywall screws
Three 1-inch rubber crutch tips
Six ⅜-inch screws
Three 1×1×6-inch square metal or wood legs
Three ⅛ ×1×3-inch metal plates
Three adjustable furniture glides
Glue for crutch tips
Tools Required:
Table saw with fine-tooth blade
Electric drill with ¼-inch bit
Screwdriver
File
Arc welder (if using metal legs)

This shelf is not difficult to make (in about 4 hours), and I have found the extra 2½-square feet of counter space to be well worth the effort.
- JACK O'RAN, SANTA MARIA, CALIFORNIA

ON THE RACK

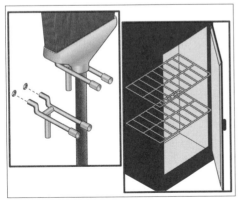

Trying to maximize storage in an RV is always a challenge. While at the local building supply, I came across two especially useful items to overcome this hindrance.

The first is ordinary pegboard hooks. These come in a wide variety of configurations with almost infinite uses. The hook I chose was intended for hanging a hammer, but it also works great for securing a small broom upside-down in a wardrobe closet.

Most RV walls are thin enough to allow these hooks to be mounted directly. Simply drill ³⁄₁₆-inch holes where required (make sure there are no wires or plumbing behind the panel to be drilled). Use the 1-inch pegboard grid as a template, but exercise caution.

Tall cabinets can be subdivided by using lightweight wire shelving that comes in two widths—12 and 16 inches. Lengths span up to 12 feet, but the store can cut them to any dimension you specify. If you are lucky, the depth of your RV's cabinet will match one of the two widths. If so, just install four screws on the inside walls and position the shelf on top of them. Other size cabinets may require the use of supporting brackets.
- TOM KIRKGAARD, PASADENA, CALIFORNIA

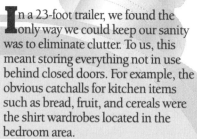

CLEARING CLUTTER

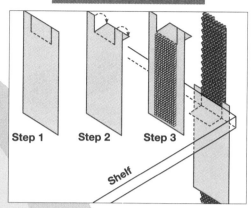

Step 1 Step 2 Step 3

Shelf

In a 23-foot trailer, we found the only way we could keep our sanity was to eliminate clutter. To us, this meant storing everything not in use behind closed doors. For example, the obvious catchalls for kitchen items such as bread, fruit, and cereals were the shirt wardrobes located in the bedroom area.

However, in gauging the size of the kitchen cupboards, we found sufficient additional volume with a noticeable lack of shelving. The question became how to install more shelf area. We felt the cupboard walls were too light and thin to allow the use of conventional fasteners like screws—even if we hadn't minded drilling holes that would end up being visible.

As an alternative, we applied adhesive-backed hook-and-loop material to the cupboard's interior walls in the same places we would have installed adjustable shelf brackets. We put the hook side of the material on small shelf supports cut from 20-gauge aluminum (four to each shelf).

Each of these homemade brackets has two ½-inch cuts made about ¼ inch from the outside edges. Once the center section is bent at a 90-degree angle, two vertical "ears" remain. These ears allow the ¼-inch plywood shelves (which we custom-fabricated for each cupboard) to hold the brackets in place against the hook-and-loop material. The overall weight addition to the trailer from this setup is negligible.

We also found hook-and-loop material equally useful for hanging pictures and for preventing items in the lower kitchen and bedroom cabinets from sliding around while the rig is on the road. This material leaves the walls unmarred, is unobtrusive, and has allowed us to change our minds at will on where to hang or locate something.

Finally, we attached the hook side of the material to several light, inexpensive plastic baskets, and the loop side to the floor or shelves of various cabinets and storage bins. We use the baskets to secure small, irregular items that might slide around enroute. They all stay in place nicely, regardless of how rough the ride.

- JUDITH B. GLAD, PORTLAND, OREGON

DESIGNER DRIP-DRYER

When we took delivery of our new 26-foot travel trailer last year, my wife found the kitchen counter just a little too small to hold a conventional dish drainboard. Using an idea we have seen in our recent travels through Italy, I purchased a 10 × 22-inch plastic-coated wire-shelf assembly from Wal-Mart, and hung it upside-down directly over the trailer's kitchen cabinet.

This was accomplished by first installing four eyebolts through the underside of the overhead cabinet. The bolt eyes had to be opened just slightly to act as hooks for the shelf legs. The threaded eyebolt shank was also adjusted to assure that the shelf would hang parallel to the counter surface.

Now, as the dishes are washed, they are placed on the metal shelf to drain directly into the sink. This frees up the kitchen counter space normally used for a drainboard. The modification does tend to block some of the illumination from the overhead sink light, but I think that is a small price to pay for the extra counter space.

- AL KUEHNAPFEL, LAKE ARIEL, PENNSYLVANIA

COUNTER MEASURES

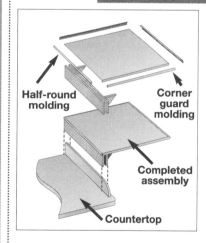

Half-round molding

Corner guard molding

Completed assembly

Countertop

My small RV has very limited counterspace, which is a problem when preparing meals or washing dishes. I eliminated this frustration by making a removable drainboard that slips onto the splashboard next to the sink. This provides a secure working surface that is easily removed when the extra space isn't needed. No special clamps or permanent fasteners are required to make a snug fit. (The size of the drainboard, of course, will have to be determined by the needs of each builder.)

The corner molding used around the edges prevents water from running over the sides, and I hid those ugly raw plywood edges by adding half-round strips. The project was finished with two coats of waterproof varnish. This practical project is easy and rewarding to make.

- WALTER C. SORENSEN JR., SALEM, OREGON

CABINET CHAOS

Going down the road may be one of the great joys of the RV lifestyle, but it can also produce some unwanted surprises. More than once we have opened the entry door of our trailer to find the contents of one or more cabinets dumped on the floor. Many RVers solve this problem by using spring-loaded curtain rods across each shelf. The two primary difficulties with this approach are that (1) these curtain rods may not fit all cabinets, especially those in the bathroom, and (2) such temporary restraints are generally not very attractive.

A more permanent, visually appealing, and adaptable solution is to mount wood dowel rods in vibration-sensitive cabinets.

To begin, cut a wood dowel (⅛-, ³⁄₁₆-, or ¼-inch diameter) to a length that is ½ inch wider than the shelf width. Next, drill into the vertical sides of the cabinet framework two ⅜-inch-deep holes of the same diameter as the rods selected. These holes should be drilled 2 to 4 inches above the shelf being guarded—high enough to hold contents upright, but low enough to allow their easy removal. Also, drill as close to the front of the shelf as possible.

Finish by staining the rods to the selected color, and then install them by flexing the rods slightly as you slip the ends into the appropriate retaining holes.

The rods look very professional, and they can be installed in virtually any size cabinet and stained to match the surrounding woodwork in your RV.

- Chester and Linda Wells, Cedar Park, Texas

Drill hole here

Wood dowels

RUB-A-DUB-DUB, STUFF IN THE TUB

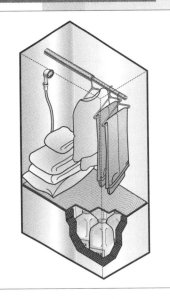

One step we've taken to expand storage in our travel trailer is to cut a piece of ½-inch plywood to fit over our bathtub. We didn't hinge it, nor did we take great pains to make it fit exactly.

With the plywood in place, the tub is used for storage of bottles of drinking water and a small laundry basket, which we use as a clothes hamper. We use the top to hold pillows, sheets, and blankets that are needed when our living-area sofa is used as an extra bed. About 3½ feet above the platform, we installed a spring-loaded expansion curtain rod. It holds a few items of clothing—a warm jacket for cold nights or dressier clothes for going to a restaurant.

Needless to say, we try to shower in campground facilities. However, we have found it takes less than five minutes to unload everything from the shower area if we have to use our own shower.

- F. G. Currie, North Attleboro, Massachusetts

PLUMBING PAL

Wood strip

False floor

Wood spacer strips

Water lines

The freshwater lines running to the kitchen of my 1992 travel trailer are routed through the middle of an outside storage cabinet. This made them vulnerable to damage from items loaded in that area. To protect these lines, I installed wood spacer strips on the compartment floor, and overlaid this foundation with ¼-inch plywood to form a false floor. The plywood clears the water lines, and provided them with protection from jacks, tools, supplies, etc.

I also placed a hardwood strip (about ¾ × ¾-inch) just inside the outside access door frame. Now, when I place heavy objects in the compartment, the wood protects the door frame from damage.

- B. J. Cargile, Dallas, Texas

STEPPING OUT

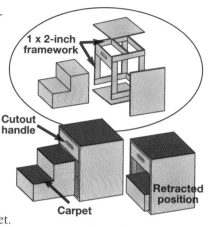

1 x 2-inch framework

Cutout handle

Carpet

Retracted position

My wife is handicapped, and though she is mobile with a cane, the standard two-step entry that came with our RV is very difficult for her to negotiate. I overcame this obstacle by building a set of telescoping stairs out of plywood, covering the tread area with carpet.

The dimensions of the stairs should be such that they can fit easily in the door of the RV for traveling. They should also be as light as possible, so it's easy to boost them from the ground to the floor level of the rig, but, at the same time, quite sturdy.

With these specifications in mind, I used prefinished ¼-inch plywood to make the sides of a shell, and then glued and nailed these to a 1 × 2-inch framework. Both the top and bottom sections are made from ⅜-inch plywood. The top is further reinforced by a 1 × 2-inch board attached across the center of its dimension. I discovered that cutting a handhold on both sides of this "porch" greatly helps its portability.

When positioned for use, the steps should point rearward so that users can grasp the factory handhold at the entry door. I added an extra handhold on the inside of the RV, so my wife can start off with a firm hold, then transfer to the other hand once outside, and vice versa.
- *ROBERT W. BATES, IDAHO FALLS, IDAHO*

GEOMETRY 101

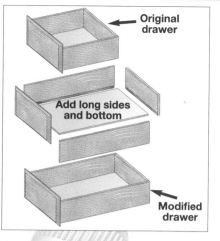

Original drawer

Add long sides and bottom

Modified drawer

Nearly all of us can use additional drawer space in our RVs. My husband and I expanded our rig's space by nearly 50 percent with very little effort and a few pieces of plywood and paneling.

When replacing a drawer we had removed for cleaning, we noticed the space from the front of the drawer cabinet to the wall of the trailer was nearly twice the length of the actual drawer. The drawer guide extended the entire distance.

Using ½-inch plywood, we cut longer sides for the drawers to make them fill the available cavity, less about 3 inches. New bottoms were cut from ⅛-inch paneling, and the original drawer faces were attached. By switching drawers from one location to another, we avoided the need to rebuild all of them. For instance, those in the kitchen, bathroom, and wardrobe were all the same width and depth; only their lengths varied.

We were innovative in the bathroom, and created an odd-shape drawer larger than the original that fits neatly around the plumbing.

Since accomplishing these modifications, we have made it a practice at RV shows to see if other trailers have been "short-drawered," as ours was. We have found many.
- *MARY PENNINGTON, LAKELAND, FLORIDA*

CLOSEUPS • CLOSEUPS • CLOSEUPS

A SOLUTION OF SQUIRT

*N*oticing that it takes an abundance of water to properly rinse the toilet clean after use, I tried lining the bottom of the bowls with single-ply toilet paper. This helped considerably, but was still not the full solution I desired. I then decided to use a spray bottle with a squirt-gun-like stream to wash away the residual deposits on the side of the bowl. While looking for a decent spray bottle, I came across a spray bottle that was not only a dollar well spent for the cleaning chore, but it also saves lots of water.

DONALD W. HELEN, MARTVILLE, NEW YORK

LOVE THOSE PIANO HINGES

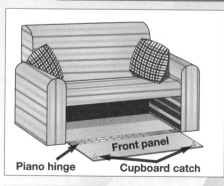

Piano hinge   Front panel   Cupboard catch

If you don't have the type of sofa bed that pulls out from the couch, you can improve access to the available storage space by altering the front panel. Install a piano hinge on the bottom of the access panel and corresponding frame section of the sofa. A cupboard latch mounted in a strategic location keeps the door in place.
- *U.M. AND ERIC MAYA, HUNTSVILLE, ONTARIO, CANADA*

CARDBOARD CAPER

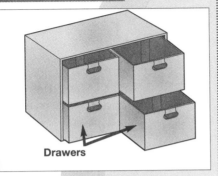

Drawers

I bought a 30-foot travel trailer because of its large closet across the rear wall. Our family includes six children, and storage has always been a big problem. With this rig, we have yet to fill up all the available space. In fact, we found that there was a little too much closet space.

I decided to customize this extra space to our specific needs by purchasing five fold-together cardboard chests of drawers. Each chest has four drawers. These units are very lightweight, relatively sturdy, and at $3 each, quite economical. The oversize closet now contains 20 drawers without affecting the area needed for hanging apparel.

A secondary benefit is realized when it's time to load or unload the trailer. Packing for a family our size has always been a chore. Now, all we do is take our lightweight chest of drawers into the house and place our clothes neatly inside. These are easily carried back to the rig, eliminating the need for suitcases and duffel bags. I expected this setup would work well all along. However, we were surprised when we noticed that fewer trips were being made to the laundry room while we were on the road. The reason is simple: Clothes remain neat and clean inside their respective drawers.
- *LAWRENCE P. GONNELO SR., RAYTOWN, MISSOURI*

MORE COUNTER SPACE

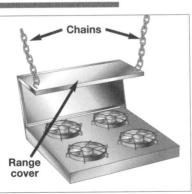

Chains

Range cover

There has never been enough counterspace in my RV. However, I have a folding cover over my range and have found an easy way to put it to work. I fold the range cover back as I normally would, then I fold the front half parallel above the range. To complete my temporary shelf project, I then take two lengths of chain and some hooks, and hang the front half of the cover from the range hood, over the range, giving me 3 square feet of extra counterspace.
- *JACK H. NEAL, YUCCA VALLEY, CALIFORNIA*

STORAGE IN CHECK

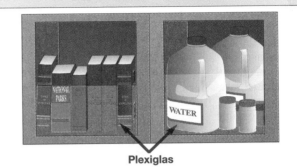

Plexiglas

To keep items in the cabinet from shifting and pushing open the doors (especially the overheads) and falling to the floor while on the road, I placed a section of Plexiglas inside each door. I purchased 5-inch-high Plexiglas in sizes that matched the widths of the doors, plus 4 inches. Each piece rests against the frame of the cabinet, and the items no longer fall out when the door is opened. For taller items, cut the Plexiglas higher. The pieces can be stored in the back of the cabinets while in camp.
- *WANDA OCHOCKI, MARSHALL, MINNESOTA*

BASKING BRIDEGROOM

Our Bounder motorhome has lots of storage and many cabinets. As full-timers, we need them all, especially the two large shelves under the kitchen sink. However, there was a small problem with the latter area: The bottom shelf was only 6 inches off the floor. This made the sizable area below the shelf difficult to use.

To save my 6-foot-tall wife from having to get on her hands and knees in order to utilize this 18 × 27-inch space, I came up with the simple idea of a slide-out shelf. Upon investigation, unfortunately, I found the cabinet door opening to this space was a few inches narrower than the side walls. This negated the possibility of side-mounted slides.

Commercially made, bottom-mounted drawer slides solved my dilemma. Using a 17½ × 26½-inch piece of ⅜-inch plywood (with corner strips added for neatness) and a set of bottom-mounted slides, I was able to recapture the function of this difficult-to-access undersink storage area.

I'm still basking in my wife's appreciation of this project.
- *BILL JUDEVINE, EUGENE, OREGON*

Into Storage for More Storage

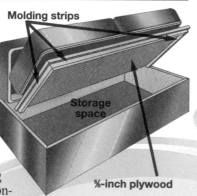

Molding strips

Storage space

⅝-inch plywood

Three years ago, I purchased a 24-foot travel trailer for weekend outings and annual vacations. Little did I know at the time that within two years my wife and I would be full-timers. Upon entering this realm, we soon confronted the common full-timer's dilemma—the need for additional storage space.

Where did we find it? As with many RVs, our rig had a fold-out sofa bed designed to sleep an occasional visitor. We realized that such a small bed would probably never be used and that removing the bed altogether would free up considerable amount of storage space.

We removed 20 or so wood screws to separate the bed from the base, and stored the entire unit so the next owner of the trailer would have it.

In place of the bed, which provided marginal seating support under the cushions, I installed a piece of ⅝-inch plywood, which I cut slightly larger than the existing opening. Molding strips were glued and nailed onto the underside of the plywood to keep it from sliding beyond the frame. The wood was painted to match the color of the upholstered base.

We were pleased to note that the rigid wood provided twice the seating support we used to have. More importantly, though, we now enjoy an extra 9.25 cubic feet of easily accessible storage space. In an RV, this is a huge increase.

Further modification, such as hinging of the cover, is possible, although I have not found this to be necessary. All we do to access the new storage area is remove the two couch pillows and lift the plywood. (Oh, by the way, we've never needed the bed.)
- *Dan Hill, Palatka, Florida*

Space Constraints

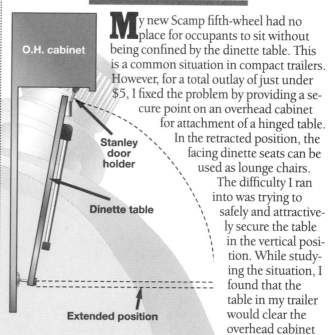

O.H. cabinet

Stanley door holder

Dinette table

Extended position

My new Scamp fifth-wheel had no place for occupants to sit without being confined by the dinette table. This is a common situation in compact trailers. However, for a total outlay of just under $5, I fixed the problem by providing a secure point on an overhead cabinet for attachment of a hinged table. In the retracted position, the facing dinette seats can be used as lounge chairs.

The difficulty I ran into was trying to safely and attractively secure the table in the vertical position. While studying the situation, I found that the table in my trailer would clear the overhead cabinet by about 2 inches. With this in mind, I bought a Stanley door holder (model 75-6360) and installed it on the outer bottom edge of the table, as illustrated. I removed the rubber foot from the door holder, drilled a hole in the rubber, and screwed the foot to the overhead cabinet. It is positioned so that the table must be firmly pushed upward to engage and disengage the door-holder leg from the rubber foot.

Now, when the table is up, the move-around space in my small trailer is nearly doubled. When down, the door holder rotates out of the way and is almost invisible.

For a longer dinette table that doesn't clear the overhead cabinet, a security chain such as those used on entry doors could be employed to hold the table to the face of the overhead. The chain should be removable, so it will store away neatly when not in use.
- *John W. Irwin, Austin, Texas*

Pooped Prop Rods

Sometimes the gas-charged lifting devices used on car hatchback lids, hoods, and trailer beds lose their power. When this happens, the lid drops onto your head.

Since it's often costly to replace these components, you can make a prop rod holder out of PVC tubing slightly larger in diameter than the offending cylinder. You can either disconnect the shaft from the pivot point, or split the PVC and install it by sliding the tubing over the shaft. Make sure the new support tubing is shorter than the large end of the lifting unit; otherwise the lid won't close properly.

To use, just raise the lid or bed and position the PVC between the prop rod's pivot point and the cylinder.
- *Robert Schrader, Lawndale, California*

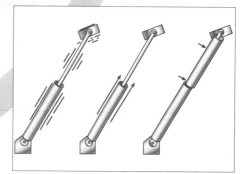

NEVER ENOUGH STORAGE

After my wife kept asking for more shelf-type storage space in our 1992 Starcraft tent trailer, I came up with a $20 solution: a storage shelf originally designed to go over a home toilet. This spring-loaded unit is very common; I got mine at Wal-

Mart. The shelf system comes with six poles and three shelves. You will have to decide which poles work best for your particular application. I used four of the poles with the springs that fell all the way into the bottom section so that the unit wasn't too tight on the ceiling. The shelf system is easy to break down when the tent trailer is folded for travel.
- *CARL GUADAGNI, YUBA CITY, CALIFORNIA*

KEEP 'EM HUNG HIGH

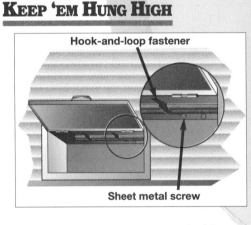

Hook-and-loop fastener

Sheet metal screw

Small things like fishing rods and tubular items, such as some folding chairs, can be hung from the roof of your storage bins. This protects them better, and keeps them out of the way of supplies that are moved in and out frequently. Use double-sided hook-and-loop fastener tape, a sheet-metal screw not shorter than ½-inch, but not longer than the roof structure is thick (usually the floor of your RV), and a fender washer. Precut the hook-and-loop material to about one full loop on each side, so that the ends almost meet each other after running around the object to be fastened. Fasten the screw through the washer and the middle of the hook-and-loop tape, and into the roof of the compartment. Now your goods can stay secure and out of the way.
- *DALE TAYLOR, PENSACOLA, FLORIDA*

FLOOR DRAWERS

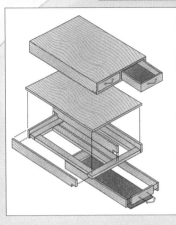

To save the floor of my Suburban for various utilitarian uses, I had to find a place for lawn chairs, tools, a portable barbecue, supplies, etc. To solve the dilemma, I built a 2 × 4-inch framework measuring 67 inches long and 48 inches wide. It fits just inside the wheel wells and right up to the middle seat.

I screwed 1 × 8-inch boards to the sides, back, and middle of the frame to support the ⅜-inch plywood top. I made drawers to fit inside this structure using 1 × 6-inch boards for a frame and ½-inch plywood for a bottom. A standard 10-foot section of conveyor rollers, cut in half, makes a perfect base for the drawers to glide on inside the 2 × 4-inch framework. (Many warehouses have old rollers around, which you may be able to purchase inexpensively, or you can buy new ones.)

The plywood top is covered with automotive carpet and trimmed in aluminum molding, which can be found at most hardware stores. I also added dividers to the drawers to make compartments for holding different size traveling paraphernalia.

The unit is built so the Suburban's middle seat can still be used, or if desired, folded down for more room.

Should it become necessary, the entire setup can be lifted out and transferred to another vehicle.

After using this drawer project for a while, I can't imagine not having it; storing and retrieving contents are so easy. The basic unit will also fit in vans and pickups to help keep these vehicles free from clutter. For security, the drawers can be locked.
- *DAN RICHTER, LAKEWOOD, COLORADO*

◆ CLOSEUPS ◆ CLOSEUPS ◆ CLOSEUPS ◆

CLOTHES HANGERS CONTINUED

*T*o keep clothes on hangers from sliding to one end of the closet rod, slide a piece of vacuum cleaner hose over the rod. The corrugations keep the hangers in place. To keep the hangers from jumping off the rod, bend a reverse curl on the end of the hook, and decrease the opening of the hook so it snaps slightly over the vacuum cleaner hoses.
- *B. D. SENSEL, ENGLEWOOD, COLORADO*

◆ CLOSEUPS ◆ CLOSEUPS ◆ CLOSEUPS ◆

WINDOW WAREHOUSE

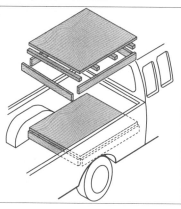

The problem for many travel-trailer owners is where to store the rig's storm windows when they're not needed. With our trailer, there isn't any on-board place where they can be conveniently kept. To solve the problem, I built a false floor in the front-half section of our pickup bed. I used 2 × 4-inch lumber for the framework, and added 1 × 2s on top of these, so I would have a full 3½ inches of vertical storage space for the windows. I then covered the entire structure with ⅜-inch plywood and made a 1 × 4-inch removable end panel for access to the area.

The length of the storage compartment is dependent upon the longest storm window to be housed. To protect the contents from travel damage, I pad below and between each one with heavy cardboard and old blankets.

- DON IVIE, MEDFORD, OREGON

BOOK BUNK

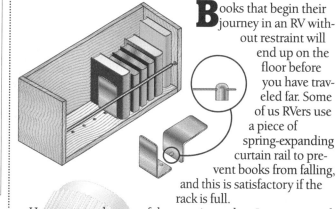

Books that begin their journey in an RV without restraint will end up on the floor before you have traveled far. Some of us RVers use a piece of spring-expanding curtain rail to prevent books from falling, and this is satisfactory if the rack is full.

However, to take care of the occasions when I want to travel with fewer books, I have made a stop that pegs into the shelf and fits under the last couple of books.

This is a piece of sheet aluminum, bent squarely and cut to lend both vertical and horizontal support. It extends about 3 inches under the books. The book stop has a ¼-inch peg riveted near its edge, which fits into holes drilled in the shelf at 2-inch intervals. This permits it to be positioned to steady any number of books.

When the shelf is filled, I store the stop against the end book.

- PERCY W. BLANDFORD, WARWICKSHIRE, ENGLAND

CONVERTING TO STORAGE

Everyone can use more storage space, and in most cases, RVers use every nook and cranny to house "stuff." If your rig is equipped with a sofa bed that is never used for sleeping, here's a convenient way to transform the available space. Remove the bed from the sofa; in my case, it left me with a 49 × 31 × 13-inch space. Construct a box to fit your available space, and mount it in the area previously occupied by the fold-out bed.

The box is made of ½-inch plywood, with the top made of ¾-inch plywood for extra strength. Use 2 × 2-inch wood at all joints to create a frame, and a 4-inch piano hinge to secure the lid. Use 2-inch drywall screws to assemble the box.

- ARTHUR E. ROBINSON, GLENDALE, ARIZONA

A SPARE MOMENT

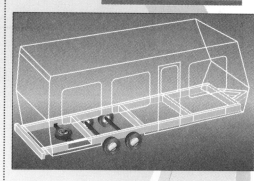

I decided to remove the factory-mounted spare tire from the trailer's rear bumper, so I could use the space for a bicycle rack. Looking for a place to reposition the spare, I struck upon the idea of using a pickup-truck carrier—the kind that mounts below the vehicle.

Purchasing just such a carrier from a local auto-wrecking yard, I installed it as illustrated. I think this is a more practical place to carry a trailer spare, and is safer because it deters theft.

To make pressure checking a bit easier, I added a Schrader valve-stem extension to the tire before stowing it away in the new holder.

This might work for others, too.

- O. E. BLINZLER, CAMARILLO, CALIFORNIA

STORAGE WINDFALL

Unused storage space   **New access door**

Every RV owner knows that, regardless of the length of the rig, there is no oversupply of storage space. Imagine my surprise at finding a large empty space just behind the AC generator cabinet while removing the rear bed in my 1989 Tioga D-23 motorhome. The area, which was inaccessible, consisted of at least 4 to 5 cubic feet of unusable space.

I obtained a Fleetwood-produced access door that matches my rig (like the one covering the shower plumbing opening on the driver's side), cut an appropriate hole in the rear wall of the motorhome, and installed the door. Next, I lined the forward end and top of this "new" compartment with insulating board. I am amazed at the amount of increased storage space I now have, and the num-

ber of RVing necessities that can be carried in this spot. I suspect this empty space exists in all D-23 model Tiogas and Jamborees that have a rear bed.

A word of caution, however. You must be careful of hidden wiring and structural framing when cutting the access hole. The fiberglass, Styrofoam, and lauan panel cuts easily with a saber saw. If cutting suddenly becomes difficult, you may have hit a frame member. Should this occur, simply adjust your dimensions in the opposite direction.

(Editor's note: Be certain that AC shore power is disconnected, and that the on-board generator is stopped during the sidewall cutting operation. Disconnecting the ground lead on all batteries is also advisable.)
- RALPH TAYLOR, ALBUQUERQUE, NEW MEXICO

LOAD UP THE AMMO BOXES

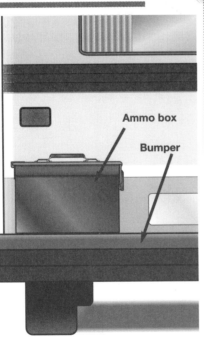

Ammo box

Bumper

RVers are always looking for extra storage space, and I found mine at a local Army-Navy surplus store. I purchased two old 20mm ammunition boxes to mount on the rear bumper of my trailer.

I used four 5/16-inch bolts to fasten each of the boxes to the bumper, and painted them with rustproof paint the same color as the bumper. Since they are pretty much waterproof, I use them to store things that are used outside the RV. I use one box for sewer connections and electrical needs, and the other box for leveling blocks, jack stands, and so forth. This helps keep the inside storage compartments clean, and everything is easy to access.
- GENE ALBERT, MATTAWAN, MINNESOTA

CONTROL THOSE CEREAL BOXES

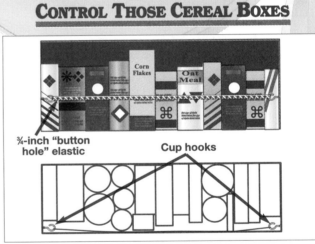

¾-inch "button hole" elastic   **Cup hooks**

While on the road, we have problems with various items such as cereal boxes, food containers, and video tapes shifting around in the cabinets. In many cases the doors are pushed open and the items end up on the floor. A simple solution can be made with cup hooks and ¾-inch "button-hole" elastic found in any fabric store. Simply screw in cup hooks on opposite cabinet walls at a height that is slightly above the center of the items you want to hold, and about midway from the front to back of the cabinet. Measure the width of the cabinet and cut a piece of the elastic ½ that measurement. Hook one "eye" on one cup hook and stretch elastic to the other cup hook. The new restraint system can be easily unhooked when in camp.
- EDMUND R. STRICKLER, LIVINGSTON, TEXAS

SIMPLE SEAT STORAGE

I own a 1993 Ford ¾-ton truck. It isn't a Super-Cab like my previous model, and I admit that I initially missed all the extra storage. However, upon investigation, I noted that there was an 8-inch space just behind the full bench seat that I thought would make ideal storage for travel books and maps.

Cut out and remove

This area can be accessed through the bench-seat armrest area simply by removing the cardboard from the back of the seat, and then cutting a rectangular hole in it to match the opening of the armrest. This modification opens up an otherwise difficult-to-use storage area to vehicle occupants, even while driving. Though it doesn't replace the extra space of a SuperCab, the area can at least be made functional with this simple alteration.

- RICHARD KOCH, NOKOMIS, FLORIDA

PARTITIONED PACKING

R ather than just throwing your cooking gear into the RV storage bin, why not customize the RV storage area to suit your needs? We arranged our cooking stove, propane tanks, and utensils into

Galvanized steel

Rolled edges

convenient groups, and measured the space needed for each of these elements. Next, we placed the groups so they formed a rectangular shape. I cut pieces of cardboard box and taped them together with duct tape to rough out the prototype design for my shelf unit. After making a few minor adjustments, I had exactly what I wanted. The cardboard and measurements were taken to the local sheet metal shop, where they duplicated my prototype out of the galvanized metal normally used for furnace duct work, and did so for a very reasonable charge. There is no front or back to the unit, so they "rolled" all outside edges to prevent any sharp edges. The unit is then placed into the regular storage locker built into the RV.

- JOSEPH W. BUSCH, ST. CLAIR SHORES, MICHIGAN

RECREATIONAL READER'S RACK

I have the habit of reading at night to get sleepy, but have no desire to get up and out of my bed to put my reading material and glasses on the countertop. I fastened a plexiglass wall rack (like the kind you find in offices to hold brochures and magazines) right next to my bed within easy reach. It's just right to hold my book and the case with my reading glasses. I also taped a couple of my favorite pictures on the back under the clear Plexiglas, so my "reader's rack" also acts as a double-duty picture frame.

- MARILYN WEAVER, OKLAHOMA CITY, OKLAHOMA

HANGING SHELF

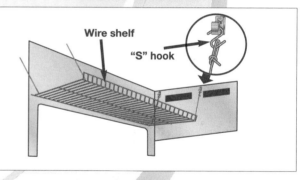

Wire shelf

"S" hook

F or you tent trailer fans who never have enough shelf space, here's a simple way to keep diapers, paper towels, paper plates, and other lightweight "soft goods" out of the way. We fabricated a hanging storage area using a precut, "ventilated," vinyl-coated, wire shelf available at most department stores. Our shelf is 6 feet long by 12 inches deep and has a 2-inch lip. The mounting system is comprised of four nylon cable clamps that are attached to the ceiling using ½-inch No. 8 pan-head wood screws. Make sure you attach these clamps to the portion of the ceiling that is backed by support structure, and that no hidden wiring is in the way. Using equal lengths of ⅛-inch nylon rope and S-hooks, the shelf is attached in minutes. We installed the shelf with the lip pointing up, which acts as an edge guard and prevents items from falling off. This shelf—or another size shelf—can be positioned virtually anywhere, and of course, can even be used in hardwall trailers and motorhomes. When traveling, the shelf rests out of the way on the bed.

- PAUL WOLF, STRATHAM, NEW HAMPSHIRE

DANCING CLOTHES HANGERS

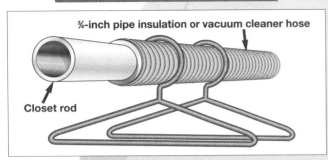

¾-inch pipe insulation or vacuum cleaner hose

Closet rod

After taking several trips on rough highways, during which we could not keep our clothes on the rack, my wife suggested we use Styrofoam pipe insulation (used to keep pipes from freezing in extremely cold weather). I cut a piece of ¾-inch insulation and slipped it over the length of the closet rod, securing it with small bungee cords. You can also use cable ties. The hangers now stay put.

- RAY AND JANICE RICHARD, BATON ROUGE, LOUISIANA

TEMPORARY STORAGE SHED

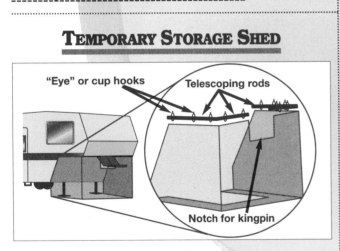

"Eye" or cup hooks

Telescoping rods

Notch for kingpin

To create a temporary storage shed, I utilized the space beneath the front overhang of my fifth-wheel trailer. I purchased the following items at my local discount store: 36 cup hooks with safety clips, enough ⅜-inch cafe rods to cover the three sides of the front portion of the fifth-wheel, 36 cafe curtain clips, and a section of fabric (you can use a nylon-reinforced tarp, vinyl, shower curtain, or tablecloth, to name a few). To install, mount the cup hooks under the front section of the fifth-wheel, space the curtain clips on the rods, and install the rods in the cup hooks. Separate the fabric into two pieces, each long enough to go from one side of the fifth-wheel to the center with at least 6 inches of overlap. Attach the fabric to the curtain clips. Use a rock or piece of wood to hold down excess fabric at ground level. Connect the seam at the hitch with extra curtain clips. This project cost $2-$3 per linear foot, and took about 15 minutes to install.

- WALT AND DORITA ESTES, SARASOTA, FLORIDA

HANGING AROUND

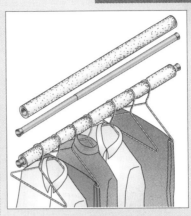

To expand our traveling wardrobe, we installed a closet bar in the tub area of our travel trailer. To keep the hangers from swinging widely and falling off en route, we covered the bar with a 4-foot section of foam pipe insulation.

With this addition, our hangers stay evenly spaced, and the clothing secure.

- JOHN AND JAN SERWINSKI, TAYLOR, PENNSYLVANIA

EXTENSION COURSE

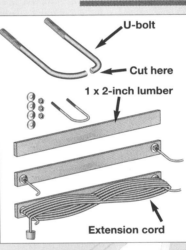

U-bolt

Cut here

1 x 2-inch lumber

Extension cord

A long extension cord is a needed item in any RV, but the longer it is, the more difficult it is to handle. I made a carrier for a 50-foot cord, which I have used with complete satisfaction for 10 years.

To make one of your own, you'll need a 2-foot piece of 1 × 2-inch lumber, one standard-size U-bolt measuring 2¾ inches across by 5 inches tall, two self-locking ¾-inch nuts, and four ⅜-inch flat washers. The U-bolt will probably come with two ¼-inch nuts in place, and a flat crossbar. Discard the crossbar. Assemble as illustrated. The entire project should take less than 10 minutes.

One critical pointer: Tighten the self-locking nuts until snug, but not overly so. The U-bolt half sections must be loose enough to be twisted by hand.

When complete, the rack will accommodate a 50-foot, three-wire, ribbon-type extension cord without twisting or tangling. (Be sure that the cord you use is rated for RV applications.) The secret is to wind the cord on the bolts in a figure-eight fashion. This is even faster than wrapping it around and around.

To use, just turn one of the bolts inward, and slide the cord off. Allow it to fall to the ground. Holding one end of the extension, walk to where you need it. The cord will quietly unwind itself, rather than follow you in a tangled bundle.

- H. A. STEEVES, PORT CHARLOTTE, FLORIDA

High-Flying Bikes

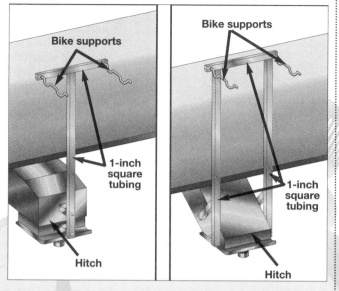

Bike supports

Bike supports

1-inch square tubing

1-inch square tubing

Hitch

Hitch

I don't know how unique my fifth-wheel's front-mounted bicycle rack is, but nearly everywhere I stop, other RVers take time to comment on it and ask how to build one for themselves.

My rack is constructed using 1-inch-square steel tubing (³⁄₃₂-inch wall thickness) to fabricate a single vertical support leg. This piece was welded to another of the same tubing, thereby creating a T-shape. The vertical leg measures 39 inches, the horizontal piece 18 inches. I purchased two bicycle supports from the local bike shop, and positioned them 16 inches apart. Using ⅔-inch steel pipe for spacers to prevent the bikes from rubbing the front of the fifth-wheel while under way, I drilled the hitch box, and bolted the carrier into place. Be sure to use care to avoid weakening any structural components.

Because of the hitch configuration on his fifth-wheel, my neighbor found it more convenient to build his bike rack using two vertical legs. Both styles are illustrated. Though I'm sure that many different variations are possible, these two work well. In addition to allowing easy observation of the two pedal-powered vehicles while traveling, the elevated rack design keeps the bikes relatively clean.

- Jim Davis, Anacortes, Washington

Space Recovery

Bolts onto trailer frame

Portable holding tank

Angle iron

My family and I spend three weeks at our special lakeside campground every year. However, the camp has no hookups, and we have to take along our 15-gallon portable holding tank so we can empty the waste tanks when they fill up. Once we set up our fifth-wheel, we don't move it until we're ready to head for home. Over the years, carrying this bulky tank became a problem as the number of things we hauled along increased.

Checking out the possibilities, I found that the tank fit perfectly into an unused area between the floor joists of our trailer. After the purchase of about $10 worth of materials, and a little welding, I made an under-trailer carrier that holds the tank securely in place. Because of the carrier's hinged design, access to the tank is quick and easy.

- John Velthoen, Modesto, California

TOWING

RV WEIGHT WATCHER

In the event that you have trouble locating a public scale, here is a relatively simple do-it-yourself method for determining trailer-tongue weight. All that is required is a 0- to 300-pound bathroom scale, two pieces of 1-inch pipe (approximately 8 inches long), one 4-foot section of 4 × 4-inch lumber, and a wood block that is the same height as the scale.

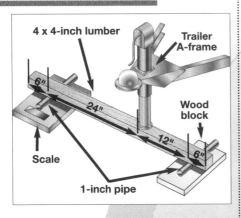

4 x 4-inch lumber
Trailer A-frame
6"
24"
Wood block
Scale
12"
6"
1-inch pipe

With these items placed in accordance with the diagram, the trailer's tongue weight can be calculated by multiplying the scale reading by three. (Example: a scale reading of 200 × 3 = 600 pounds hitch weight.) Note that the maximum weight measurable by this equipment is 900 pounds. To obtain an accurate reading, both the trailer and the 4 × 4 beam must be level.

- JAMES BROWN, YARDLEY, PENNSYLVANIA

$65 OR 65 CENTS

All of us like to know where the end of our trailer is when passing traffic on the road or backing into a campsite. Truckers put lighted markers on the bumpers of their rigs. I was eager to put these on my trailer until I found they cost around $65 per pair.

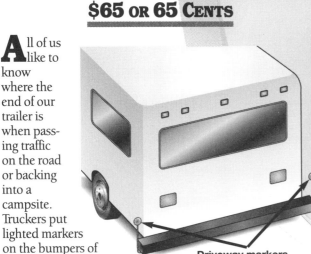

Driveway markers

At my local hardware store, I found reflective driveway markers selling for 65 cents a pair. I bent each to a 90-degree angle, and using a small U-bolt, I attached these to the rear bumper of my trailer. When the reflector markers are mounted to the bottom of the bumper, it looks very professional.

- RAY ALLEN, ROANOKE, VIRGINIA

SIMPLE SYSTEM

Wheel chock

In our world of high-tech gimmicks, it is easy to forget the simple basics. The proliferation of trailer/tow vehicle hookup products is an example. If you can line up the tow vehicle with the trailer or fifth-wheel, you can also position the hitch without assistance. All that is required to use my method is reasonably accurate initial vehicle alignment.

When backing into position, stop the tow vehicle as the hitch approaches a comfortable 12 to18 inches from the trailer coupler. This is easily estimated. Next, place a wheel chock behind one rear tire of the tow vehicle.

Then, measure the distance (with a small pocket tape measure) between the centers of the hitch and ball and the fifth-wheel kingpin. Using this dimension, move the wheel chock exactly the same distance toward the trailer. Make sure that the block remains in line with the projected path of the backing tow vehicle's rear tire.

Return to the driver's seat, and slowly back the tow vehicle until it stops against the repositioned chock. When this occurs, the ball or fifth-wheel hitch will be aligned with the trailer coupler.

- R.J. SLIGER, TUCSON, ARIZONA

◆ CLOSEUPS ◆ CLOSEUPS ◆ CLOSEUPS ◆

CANNY COLOR CODING

I pull a fifth-wheel trailer, and there have been times when I could not quite see if the hitch latch had closed properly behind the engaging hitch pin; everything is painted black.

To solve this problem, I masked off the hitch and painted the movable latch a bright color. Now, I can tell if everything is meshed properly before I pull away from each stop.
- BOB CHAPMAN, CORPUS CHRISTI, TEXAS

Editor's Note: *The driver should physically install a safety pin after the handle seats.*

A NUTTY IDEA

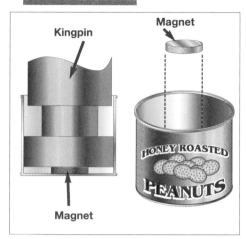

The dry lubricating pads that are used to eliminate the greasy mess on fifth-wheel hitches are a blessing. Still, one must be careful to avoid contact with the perpetually dirty kingpin when venturing under the overhang to access the trailer's front compartments. I have discovered a simple and inexpensive solution. First, enjoy the peanuts from a 3½-inch deep can. After washing thoroughly to remove the nut oils, cement a ceramic magnet to the inside bottom of the can, using any durable adhesive. Simply set the can in place on your fifth-wheel's kingpin each time you disconnect. Paint the can a contrasting color, or use bright tape to remind yourself to remove it. Also, save the original plastic lid to contain the mess that ends up inside the can.
- WILLIAM J. REINER, MECHANICSBURG, PENNSYLVANIA

QUICK HITCH CALCULATION

When it comes time to hitch up our fifth-wheel, it seems that we always have to guess the correct height of the front jacks for positioning the kingpin in the saddle. An easy way to eliminate this problem is to mark the front landing jacks for future reference. When the fifth-wheel is parked, raise the front jacks to their maximum height and mark the left-hand jack in 1-inch increments. Clean the surface as necessary, and use a permanent-marking pen of contrasting color. An etching tool will provide longer-lasting markings. Accuracy is not important.

When unhitching, record the height, on the scale when the fifth-wheel is clear of the hitch. Keep a pencil and pad of paper inside the switch compartment for convenience. An estimate of fractions is close enough. When hitching again, lift the front jacks to the previously recorded height and back the tow vehicle for easy hookup.
- ARTHUR F. JUNE, MONUMENT, COLORADO

HELPFUL HITCH

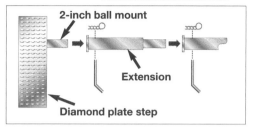

2-inch ball mount
Extension
Diamond plate step

After purchasing a new pickup truck and slide-in camper, I was a little dismayed to find that the rear entrance step was almost 3 feet off the ground. This makes it quite an effort to get into the camper. Of course, while parked at a campground, a set of folding steps provides an acceptable solution. But this is a little inconvenient when shorter stops are made at rest areas, eateries, or gas stations. To eliminate the need for me to jump up into the camper during these times, I had a step made that fits into the Class III trailer-hitch receiver on the truck.

First, it was necessary to extend the trailer hitch beyond the rear of the camper. This required a 12-inch extension. I had mine custom-made, but these are also available from most RV-parts stores. Next, I had a step made using part of a 2-inch utility ball mount and a ¼ × 6 × 18-inch piece of diamond plate. This was reinforced with a border of 1-inch steel stock. Because the entrance door to my camper is slightly off-center, I had the step plate welded similarly off-center to improve its function. The project was finished by covering the completed step with Astro Turf rug.

Of necessity, the step protrudes a few inches behind the camper, but not enough to make it a pedestrian hazard. I secured the strip in place with locking hitch-retainer pins to discourage it and the extension bar from getting "lost."
- THOMAS R. CLEM SR., SILVER SPRING, MARYLAND

• CLOSEUPS • CLOSEUPS • CLOSEUPS •

STABLE REFLECTIONS

We have clamp-on-style tow-mirror extensions on the doors of our GMC pickup, which we use when towing our trailer. These were easily attached and worked well. However, due to the jarring effect, the mirrors needed readjustment every time a door was closed.

To fix this, I purchased two 1-inch hose clamps, and installed them on the ball and socket just behind each mirror. I adjusted the mirrors one last time, and tightened the clamps firmly. Now, the mirrors stay right where I want them throughout my RV trips.
- HAROLD MILLER, LEROY, MICHIGAN

• CLOSEUPS • CLOSEUPS • CLOSEUPS •

A Strapping Idea

I used to worry about the trailer's electrical connector pulling loose from the receptacle on the tow vehicle. It happened several times, causing the trailer lights and electric brakes to fail.

The fix was simple; I just added a large radiator-hose clamp to the trailer electrical line. After inserting the plug, I positioned the clamp over the receptacle's hinged protective flap, and tightened it securely. No more surprise disconnects have occurred.

- Emil Haglan, Conway, Pennsylvania

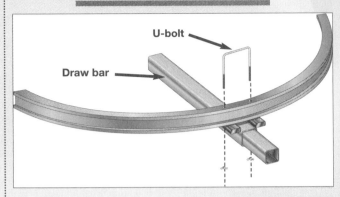

Labels: Tow-vehicle receptacle, Hose clamp, Trailer plug, Tow-vehicle receptacle

Ez Lubin'

The job I least enjoy during the hookup process with my travel trailer is greasing the spring bars and ball mount of my hitch. When I get out the grease can, I just know I'll end up with some of it on my clothes.

At home in the driveway, it's a lot easier to cope with, but on the road, when you're hooking and unhooking every day or so, it's a different story. What I did was drill two 7/32-inch holes through the top of my EazLift Ball mount, over the tops of the tubes that hold the spring bars, and used a 1/4 × 28-inch tap to cut some threads in the holes. Simply screw in the Zerk grease fittings, and you're ready to add a few pumps of grease the easy way. Finish hooking up the chains of the spring bars, and you're ready to hit the road.

- Howard Spindler, Camino, California

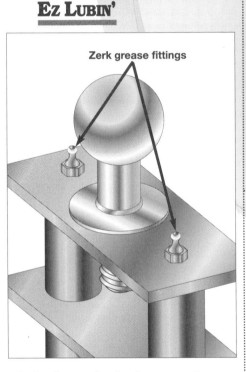

Label: Zerk grease fittings

Wrenching Experience

In 1992, I purchased a Pull-Rite hitch for my Ford van. This system allows me to tow my 32-foot travel trailer with ease. Not only is the hitch designed to swing through a large arc, it also can be set up as a conventional towing platform. This, however, requires that the draw bar be centered and bolted in position. No problem, except during Wisconsin winters. I quickly tired of crawling under the van to insert the two bolts that secure the hitch rigidly in place, and then trying to hold them with a wrench while turning the nuts from below. After some thought, I went to a spring company that bends shackle bolts for use in leaf-spring assemblies. I asked the company employee to bend a square-shaped U-bolt that would accomplish the same task as the two individual bolts I had been using. For less than $5, I came away with a U-bolt sized perfectly to fit over the hitch draw bar from the top.

Now, all I have to do to secure the hitch is drop this piece into place, and install and tighten the nuts.

- William F. Appleton, Kaukauna, Wisconsin

Labels: U-bolt, Draw bar

CLOSEUPS • CLOSEUPS • CLOSEUPS

PREVENTING TOIL OVER SOIL

Are you tired of getting all greased up when you remove your ball mount from its receiver? There's a simple solution.

Just pull a plastic grocery bag over the whole unit, and grab the ball mount wherever you want. The plastic will stick to the hitch ball, and the remainder of the bag can be draped around the oily parts.

Leave the bag in place until you hitch up again. This will protect you during the interim, should you brush up against the ball mount during your stay. When you are ready to hitch up the trailer, just peel the bag off and throw it away.

- H.A. Steeves, Port Charlotte, Florida

SPRING BAR STORAGE

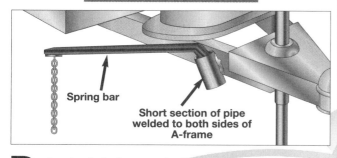

Spring bar

Short section of pipe welded to both sides of A-frame

During the shakedown cruise of my first travel trailer, I quickly realized that the load-equalizing-hitch spring bars were going to be a problem—a problem to store, a problem to keep clean, and a problem to work around without getting myself greasy. However, I overcame these concerns.

Two short sections of pipe, with an inside diameter slightly larger than the large end of my Eaz-Lift spring bars, were welded to the trailer tongue. Care was taken to clear the trailer body and propane bottles.

When I unhook now, I simply place the greasy end of the spring bars into their storage receptacles. Not only is this method convenient, but because I no longer have to lay the bars on the ground, daily cleaning and greasing are unnecessary.

- LESTER GROSS, LAKESIDE, CALIFORNIA

SPRING BAR TENT

After recently buying a larger trailer that requires an equalizing hitch, it didn't take me long to conclude that I didn't want the spring bars lying in the dirt.

I created a convenient storage place for these items by making a visit to a local electrical contractor. I asked for scrap pieces of 2½-inch electrical metal tubing (EMT). A couple of 2-foot-long sections proved to be perfect for what I had in mind.

I had both pieces of EMT welded to the bottom of the trailer tongue, and then painted them to match the

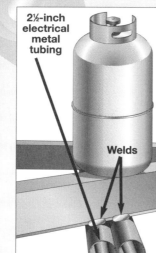

2½-inch electrical metal tubing

Welds

Spring bars

trailer tongue. The receptacles now house the hitch spring bars whenever my rig is unhitched. The 2-foot-long tubing allows enough chain to hang out so that the stored bars can be padlocked in place.

- DALE MAGGIO, SCOTTS VALLEY, CALIFORNIA

WHITE JAWS

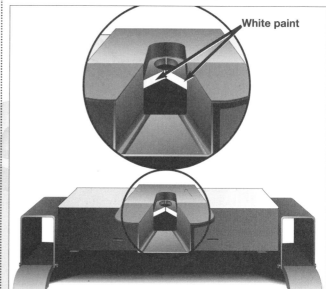

White paint

Ihave tried various ways to verify that the jaws in my fifth-wheel hitch are closed after connecting my trailer. To make the process easier and quicker, I painted the leading edges of the locking jaws white. When the fifth-wheel is hitched, this area is fairly dark and the white paint shows up very well. I know the jaws are closed properly when I see white all the way across the opening.

- RICHARD P. STALEY, FT THOMAS, KENTUCKY

SLICK, RICK

If you have a hand-cranked A-frame jack on your trailer, here's a quick way to line up your tow vehicle during hookup. First, crank up the trailer high enough to allow the hitch ball to clear the coupler, and then position the handle vertically, as illustrated. Aim the center of your tow vehicle at the handle as you slowly back up, and the ball will end up in just the right place. I hardly ever miss. This works for me even with my truck's tailgate up. However, if you need more height, use masking tape to attach a straight stick to the jack handle temporarily.

- HENRY J. CORMIER,
CLAREMONT, NEW HAMPSHIRE

'SPRING' TIME

The only problem I experienced with my PullRite Super 5th fifth-wheel hitch was when the truck was operating solo. The swivel hitch head would slam from side to side whenever the truck struck a bump or negotiated a hard turn. To control the loud noise this caused, I made a simple modification to the hitch; total approximate cost was $10. I used the following parts:

Four ¼ × 1-inch machine screws @ 25 cents each

Four 1½-inch automotive fender washers @ 10 cents each

Two 4-inch springs @ $3.98 each

To install these parts, I drilled and tapped four ¼-inch holes—two in the head assembly and two in the base. (If a tap set is unavailable, substituting self-tapping screws should also work.) Using the four machine screws and washer, I mounted the springs so that both were under slight tension. This stabilized the hitch head dramatically. While it still rocks under hard pressure, the head no longer swings under its own weight between the limits of its travel range. This modification reminded me that silence truly is golden.

I cannot take credit for this idea, as I saw it on a Texas-licensed pickup in Temecula, California, last year. After some considerable thought, I couldn't come up with a better plan. However, I did tell my wife that the modification would be a five-minute job. She always uses a times-10 multiplier on my estimates, and once again she was correct. It took me approximately an hour, with at least 10 trips to my workbench.

- STEVEN MAINS, RIVERSIDE, CALIFORNIA

4-inch spring

Machine screws

Fifth-wheel hitch

LABOR SAVER

String

PVC pipe

Cap

I tired of simply dropping my hitch's equalizer bars in the dirt and gravel when unhooking. This meant that I had to frequently clean and relubricate the ends—a messy job. To address this situation, I made inexpensive protectors from PVC pipe.

These are easy to make. The only items needed for construction are two 1½-inch PVC caps, 8 inches of 1½-inch diameter Schedule 40 PVC pipe, PVC glue, and retaining string.

I don't even have to store these covers when traveling. They are tied directly to the equalizer bars, as illustrated, ready to keep unwanted debris off the lubricated ends.

- WILLIAM M. CARVER, LAS CRUCES, NEW MEXICO

DOUBLE-DUTY HITCH

Fifth-wheel hitch

U-bolt welded on hitch

Two years ago, we planned an RV trip to Alaska with our 26-foot fifth-wheel trailer. We needed all the storage space that we could find, and even needed to make use of the area occupied by the rig's spare tire.

Because our trailer had no spare tire rack and we didn't want to put a bumper rack on it, we decided to locate the spare in the pickup bed. Our concern over security was alleviated by a local welding shop. We had a large U-bolt welded to the hitch side brace.

The cost was $5 for the welding work, and we already had the chain and padlock with which to secure the spare tire. This arrangement worked just great for us.

- JOE TURNER, BAKERSFIELD, CALIFORNIA

CONTROLLING THE SHAKES

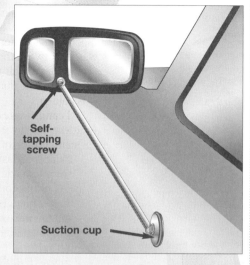

I've spent hours looking for a side-view mirror that was to my liking, but I soon found that there was too much vibration to allow clear vision. I didn't want to drill holes in the doors of my truck, so I fabricated a stabilizer from a discarded piece of TV antenna. After flattening the ends, I drilled each end and bent each to the proper angle. A self-tapping screw was used to hold one end to the mirror, and the other was fitted with a plastic suction cup. The suction cup holds nicely to the side of the door and lasts for a fairly long time. I only had to resecure the suction cup two to three times during a three-month trip.
- *WILLIAM DOERRER, PANAMA CITY, FLORIDA*

PROMINENT REMINDER

*T*o prevent movement during travel, Fleetwood models equipped with slide-out units are delivered with two rubber-tipped safety retaining bars. These are to be installed at each end of the slide-out when in the retracted position. However, on our first trip, we forgot to install these bars because they were out of sight and, therefore, out of mind. This allowed the slide-out to vibrate to a slightly extended position. My husband solved this problem on future trips with the purchase of two "gripper clips," like those used to hold brooms and garden tools against the wall at home. These were attached to the inside front trim at each end of the slide-out. The safety bars are now stored in these clips while we're camping. Because they are highly visible in this location, we are easily reminded to reinstall them upon retraction of the slide-out.
- *DOROTHY M. HANKE, VAN ALSTYNE, TEXAS*

HITCHING HEAVEN

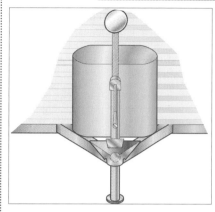

Having trouble hitching your trailer alone? Try these clever ideas from three of our readers.

1. Purchase a convex mirror (the larger the better) from an auto-parts supply. Install this on a small wooden post, which will be temporarily placed on the trailer-jack post. Adjust the mirror so you can see the hitch from the driver's seat of the tow vehicle. Its height should be about even with the center of the rear window.

When you back within a few feet of the trailer, you should be able to line up the coupler and the hitch ball without difficulty. Remove and store the mirror for traveling.
- *BOB COWAN, TAHOE PARADISE, CALIFORNIA*

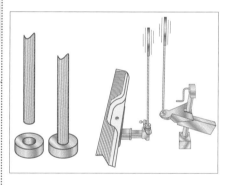

2. There's an inexpensive way to solve the problem of solo hitching that works every time. Buy two small circle magnets with holes in the center. Glue a couple of 36-inch-long wooden dowels into the magnets, and spray-paint the top 6 inches of each dowel.

When preparing to hitch up, set one of these assemblies on top of the hitch ball, and the other on the trailer coupler. Use the tow vehicle's rearview mirror to line up the rods while backing. Stop when the dowels are within a couple inches of one another. Remove the magnets, and finish backing. Both the magnets and dowels are available at hardware stores.
- *MARLIN W. ABBY, WEST SALEM, ILLINOIS*

3. Ever wonder during hookup if you've raised the tongue of your travel trailer enough to clear the tow-vehicle hitch ball? Here is a simple way to be sure:

Glue a magnet to a small bubble level and position it near the trailer tongue jack. When unhitching, and before lowering the tongue, adjust the level to center the bubble. Leave in place so that during hookup, you need only raise the tongue sufficiently to once again center the bubble. This will let you know the jack is high enough for hitching.
- *SUSAN SAND, AIKEN, SOUTH CAROLINA*

GAP DETECTION

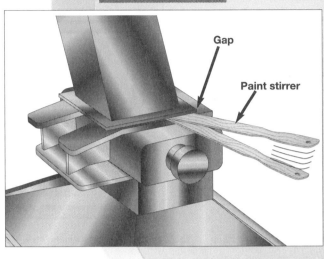

Gap

Paint stirrer

My fifth-wheel trailer, like many others, has a friction-reducing disk fitted around the hitch pin. However, shortly after installing this item, I realized that the gap between the hitch pin and the hitch had been reduced considerably. In normal operation this doesn't matter, but as the trailer's tongue weight is being transferred to the front support jacks during unhitching, the narrowed gap makes it difficult to determine just when all the weight is off the hitch. On many occasions I have found myself lifting the truck with the trailer jacks without realizing it. This meant that I had to lower the trailer and start all over again. Even watching carefully, I found it hard to tell for sure when to stop.

It was during one of these episodes that I blundered onto a very simple way of detecting hitch/hitch pin separation. Before cranking away on the trailer jacks, I insert a thin piece of wood (a paint-stirring stick is ideal) into the gap between the fifth-wheel hitch and the trailer tongue. I make sure that it's fully seated against the friction disk.

Now, when separation starts to occur, the opposite end of the stick will move downward. By a simple lever principle, the slight motion imparted to the stick at the gap opening is magnified at the opposite end. This has eliminated those frustrating up-and-down cycles that used to plague me.

- Frederick G. Young, P.E., Mishicot, Wisconsin

REVERSAL OF VISION

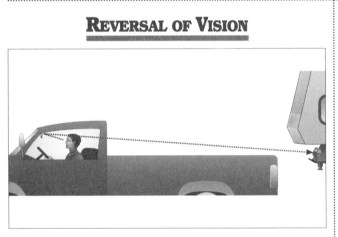

I use a 1985 Ford SuperCab pickup with a bed-mounted toolbox to tow my 25-foot fifth-wheel trailer. Because the truck is also equipped with high-back bucket seats, it is virtually impossible to see the hitch from the driver's position. This made hooking up quite difficult.

To solve the problem, I installed a 6-inch bird's-eye (convex) mirror on the kingpin box of the trailer. This gives me a full view of the pickup bed and hitch. Backing slowly, I can center the trailer and hitch every time.

And, by viewing the spot mirror through the truck's rearview mirror, the reverse image is corrected. This eliminates all confusion. If I need to go right to line up the hitch, I go right; no more having to calculate and reverse the needed steering inputs in my mind.

- Dave Woodwell, Las Cruces, New Mexico

HANG IT UP

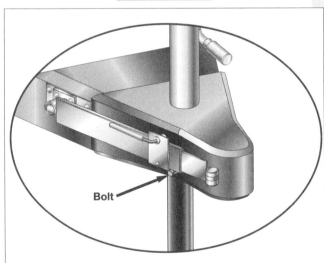

Bolt

Do you have problems with your friction sway control during hookup? Maybe you can't find a good place to store it while you're parked for a few days? If this is the case, weld a ¼× ½-inch-long bolt to the hitch coupler of your trailer. When you unhitch, just rest the sway control on the bolt to keep it conveniently stored up and out of the way. This also makes it a simple matter to drop the unit into place on the hitch head when you're ready to move.

- Francis Konda, Sioux Falls, South Dakota

HITCH-UP VISION

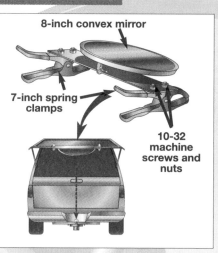

8-inch convex mirror

7-inch spring clamps

10-32 machine screws and nuts

The process of hitching up my trailer to the truck can sometimes be a real chore. Since I have a shell mounted on the pickup bed, my vision is somewhat limited, and placing the ball under the coupler in the exact location can lead to great frustration, especially when hitching up by myself. I solved the problem by building a simple clamp-on mirror.

I bought two 7-inch spring clamps and a 12-inch-long piece of flat steel, 2 inches wide and ⅛-inch thick. I attached the flat steel to the spring clamps using four No.10-32 machine screws and nuts. I then mounted an 8-inch convex mirror (obtained at a truck-supply parts house) to the flat steel. The device is clamped to the end of the lift gate on the shell, and adjusted so that I can see the ball mount. To improve visibility, I attach a piece of tissue to the greased ball. The new mirror has saved me a lot of time and yelling if I happen to find someone brave enough to guide me.
- *PHIL WINTER, OAK HARBOR, WASHINGTON*

LOST PINS REVISITED

Pop rivet or sheet metal screw

Plumber's chain

In more than 30 years of trailering, I have never lost a pin that is used to secure the spring bar brackets. I simply slip a 6-inch-long piece of plumber's chain on the pin, drill a hole in the bracket, and pop rivet or screw the chain to the bracket. The weight and restraint of the chain will keep the pin from rotating or moving. It can't be lost, and it will be right there to remind you to use it. All this for less than a dollar's worth of material.
- *EDSON B. SNOW, POMPANO BEACH, FLORIDA*

NO MORE LOST PINS

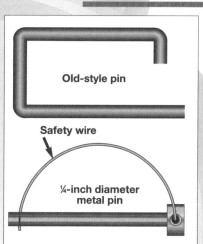

Old-style pin

Safety wire

¼-inch diameter metal pin

During an extended trip to Alaska, we experienced several rough sections of road. After a routine check while taking on fuel, we discovered that the pins holding the spring bar brackets in the up position had disappeared. This left us very concerned—we could lose our spring bars if the brackets were to release because the pins were gone. We immediately purchased two pins with safety wires for $3, and no longer worried about losing our spring bars. These pins are ¼-inch in diameter and available at hardware and RV-supply stores.
- *PAUL E. SMITH, NEW WINDSOR, MARYLAND*

HIDEAWAY HITCH

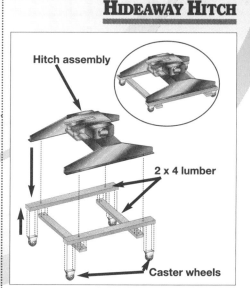

Hitch assembly

2 x 4 lumber

Caster wheels

If you remove the fifth-wheel hitch from your pickup between RV trips, and you're tired of wrestling this bulky mass into storage, here's a solution that worked for me. Just build a 2 × 4-inch wood framework to match the dimensions of your fiver hitch, and install small caster wheels on the bottom. Drill holes to line up with those in the hitch base.

When you unseat the hitch assembly, set it on the dolly and install the regular hitch pins to secure everything in place. I use a RBW fifth-wheel hitch, but this suggestion should work equally well with other brands. As constructed, I can store my hitch and its dolly out of the way under the rear of the trailer.
- *O.E. BLINZLER, CAMARILLO, CALIFORNIA*

HAPPY HOOKUP

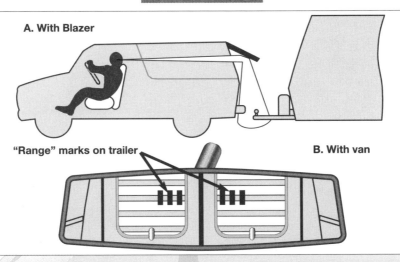

A. With Blazer

"Range" marks on trailer

B. With van

It seems everyone has a favorite method for hitching up a travel trailer. Here are a couple I've used successfully over the years. When I had an early-model Blazer for a tow vehicle, I learned that I could tip the top-hinged rear window up to a certain angle in order to see a reflection of the ball hitch and trailer tongue. Once I got the angle right, I cut a wooden dowel to support the rear hatch in the proper position to be used as a makeshift mirror.

This method will work on any towing vehicle that has a rear window that hinges at the top. Many pickup shells are so equipped. In some light conditions, it helps to lay a piece of cardboard on top of the glass to increase the mirror effect.

Later, when I sold my Blazer and purchased a van, I had to devise a new system for hooking up. I hooked up to the trail-er and parked on a straight and level lot. Using masking tape for a temporary marker, I placed a strip across the middle front of the trailer at a level I could see in my rearview mirror. Then, I inked marks on the tape at various intervals, and checked again in the rearview mirror to determine which of these marks fell closest to the center posts of the two rear windows.

Once this setup procedure was done, I put permanent marks on the front of my trailer. I added extra marks about an inch outside the first two. Now, when I back up to the hitch, the outside marks let me know when I'm getting close, and the inner ones let me know when to stop. A little adjustment is sometimes needed, but not often.

- RICHARD WARD

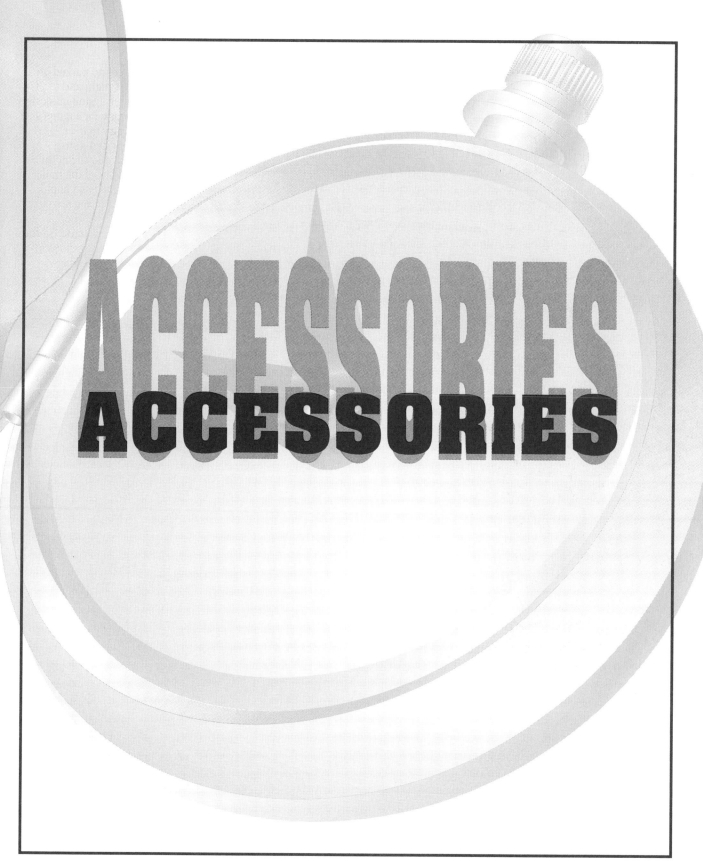

ACCESSORIES

JUST A REMINDER

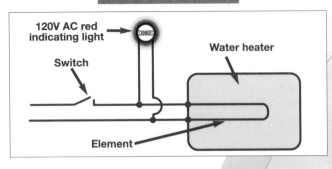

120V AC red indicating light

Switch

Water heater

Element

My new travel trailer has a gas/electric water heater, which is a great improvement over the gas-only heater in my old RV. However, there is a potential problem with this design that I have overcome at a cost of less than $5.

The 120-volt AC electrical switch for the heating element is located on the side of the water heater itself. This is out of sight, and sometimes out of mind. Should we return home from a trip and decide to drain the heater tank, an expensive repair might result if the rig is later plugged into shore power to keep the batteries charged. The heater element is not designed to operate without water in the tank, and given the above scenario, will burn out quickly.

I alleviated this concern by installing inside my trailer a 120-volt AC red indicating light (Radio Shack part no. 272-704), which glows whenever the heater element is on. I positioned the bulb in a very visible spot on the trailer's front interior storage cabinet, and wired it as illustrated. This helps me remember to turn off electrical power to the water heater before I disconnect from shore power.
- Cecil W. Wager, Smyrna, Georgia

(**Editor's Note:** Always follow approved wiring codes when modifying RV electrical circuits, especially those carrying high voltages.)

STOP AWNING FLOP

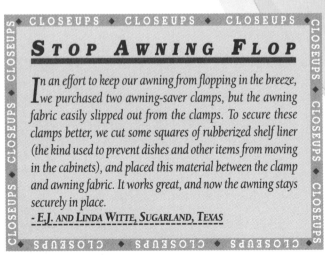

In an effort to keep our awning from flopping in the breeze, we purchased two awning-saver clamps, but the awning fabric easily slipped out from the clamps. To secure these clamps better, we cut some squares of rubberized shelf liner (the kind used to prevent dishes and other items from moving in the cabinets), and placed this material between the clamp and awning fabric. It works great, and now the awning stays securely in place.
- E.J. and Linda Witte, Sugarland, Texas

CUNNING COOKING

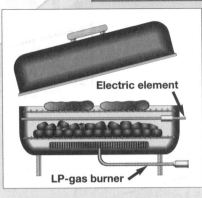

Electric element

LP-gas burner

I save valuable space in the family camper by carrying and using only one outside grill, rather than both a gas and an electric one. An LP-gas conversion kit was added to a 110-volt electric grill that I already owned. With hookups, I use shore power for cooking. Dry-camping meal preparation is done with LP-gas.

Because grills are usually messy after each use, I purchased a plastic tote box for convenient storage. Again, with space at a premium, even the tote box sees double duty. I set the grill on top of this box and use it for a cooking table, with a cookie sheet underneath the grill to catch any drippings.

Once everything has cooled, I place the cookie sheet on the bottom of the storage container and the grill on top of it. This setup eliminates the need to clean the grill after every use. All LP-gas conversion parts and the tote box were obtained from my local hardware store.
- Ken Bednarz, Ropesville, Texas

MINOR MYSTERY

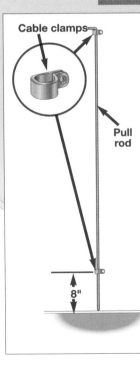

Cable clamps

Pull rod

8"

In the past, the pull rod for my 21-foot RV awning always got lost in my rig's storage compartment just when I needed it most. This frustration was eliminated for less than $1, with two self-tapping screws and two plastic cable clamps (.035-inch diameter). Metal eye screws could also be used. I mounted the first clamp about 8 inches above the floor in my RV's hall closet. Placing the rod inside this clamp, I installed the second clamp one inch below the hook end of this device. It's a simple fix, to be sure, but having a permanent place to store the pull rod has ended my perplexed scrounging once and for all.
- Jerry Peterson, Muskego, Wisconsin

RESTRAINER ORDER

Worried about losing your air-conditioner cover while traveling, risking damage to the unit itself, and then having to pay $125 for a new cover? Here's the solution I came up with to avoid such unnecessary heartache.

Wire ties

Thread heavy-duty electrical wire ties at equal distances through the top and bottom cover vent holes on both sides of the unit.

Pull them as tight as you can to assure they are securely fixed, and your worries are over.
- *CHUCK MILLER, FORT THOMAS, KENTUCKY*

HOME SWEET HOME

After storing my RV for a few weeks, I found that a robin had nested and set up home inside my RV's roof-mounted air conditioner. This forced me to cancel a couple of short

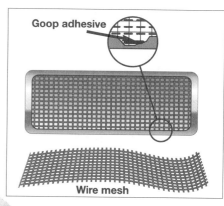

Goop adhesive

Wire mesh

trips, though I didn't mind watching the new family grow. However, now that the fledglings have moved to the raspberry vines in my backyard, I decided to avoid future trip cancellations.

Making a trip to the local hardware store, I purchased a small section of ⅜-inch square-wire mesh (hardware cloth). This was cut to fit inside the heat-exchanger opening of the air conditioner, and secured in eight places with Goop brand adhesive. Not only does this keep the birds out, it also helps prevent hail from damaging the unit's fragile condenser-core fins.
- *FRANCIS L. HOMLY, CRYSTAL, MINNESOTA*

PARTY LINE

How many times has this happened to you? A topic of conversation comes up between you and your spouse over a telephone call made to friends or relatives. The next thing you know, one of you is saying, "You didn't tell me about that!"

Telephone calls can be very frustrating when traveling because they must usually be made from a pay phone. Since there's obviously no extension, one person misses much of what is said. When the other takes a turn, many of the topics get repeated.

To overcome this problem, we use a little device called the Amplified Portable Telephone Listener. It's available from Radio Shack for $8.95.

The product is a small battery-powered amplifier/speaker unit, which has a wire lead and suction cup that attach to a telephone receiver. When connected, it amplifies the conversation so anyone nearby can hear what's being said on the other end. It even has a volume control.
- *LLOYD L. DARNALL, BROOKINGS, SOUTH DAKOTA*

CAMPER QUICK STEP

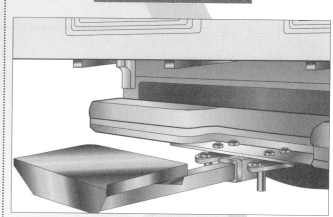

To make the loading of bulky supplies into my 9½-foot camper easier, I had a simple step made that fits into the 2-inch hitch receiver on my truck.

The actual step, which is elevated 4 inches above the support tube, measures 12 × 30 inches and is welded in place. I glued a nonskid surface onto the step for safety.

The step is easily removable, and its design eliminates the need to use a portable step stool for getting into the camper.
- *GEORGE PAUL JR., MINOT, NORTH DAKOTA*

THERE'S ALWAYS A CATCH

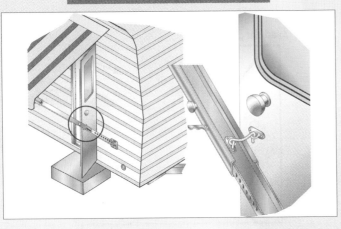

After my trailer awning was installed, I found that the forward arm was very close to the door catch on the side of the rig. The position of the awning arm, despite being the best possible of the various mounting locations available, made the door catch useless whenever the awning was extended. This is apparently a common problem, especially on smaller RVs.

My solution was to make an extra-long hook that is fastened to the forward awning arm and stays in place even when the awning is rolled up. I used stainless-steel parts purchased from a marine store: a 1-foot length of ³⁄₁₆-inch rod, and two ½-inch "pad eyes" (also called "flange eyes" and "eye straps"). The total cost for these materials, including screw fasteners, was less than $10.

Awning arms are fabricated of aluminum extrusions that are designed to slide inside one another. This requires careful selection and placement of the pad eye in order to prevent interference later on.

While the awning is in the open position, locate an area on the arm where a pad eye can be mounted near the outside edge of the open door. Mark this area with a pencil. Consider screw-head clearance on the inside of this portion of the arm, as you may have to use flathead screws to assure enough clearance between the sliding sections.

With the awning still open, mark a corresponding location for the second pad eye on the RV door frame (the only place where screws will hold securely). Make certain that the eye is properly positioned to accept the hook that will be attached to the awning arm.

Bend the ³⁄₁₆-inch rod into the shape of a latch hook. I used a small vice, a hammer, and vice grips. Size the length of the hook so the door will be positioned where you want it, once it's latched in place. Consider potential wind forces on the open door, and shape the hook accordingly. After fabrication, I polished this piece with a file and sandpaper to make it smooth.

Drill the necessary holes, then attach the pad eyes. To prevent water from leaking into the door, I ran a bead of sealer around the base of this eye. Finish the project by permanently installing the hook on the awning-arm pad eye. The hook length needed for my particular installation was 7 inches. This dimension, as well as the finished shape of the hook, will vary from rig to rig.

- JOHN COONS, FORT LAUDERDALE, FLORIDA

THRIFTY ENTERTAINMENT CENTER

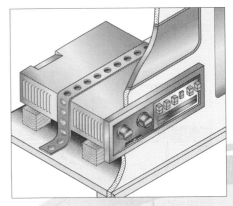

My 1990 Lynx Prowler trailer came from the factory wired for stereo, but it lacked a radio. I had previously removed a radio from one of my cars, and because it produced sound quality I particularly enjoyed, I installed it in the space provided in the trailer. An RV owner who doesn't have the budget for a new aftermarket sound system can find some good bargains in wrecking yards.

To begin with, I temporarily connected the radio outside the trailer's speaker wiring. It worked perfectly, and allowed individual control of all four speakers.

I decided to proceed with the installation, carefully planning each step before making any cuts in the wood paneling. I found the existing opening to be too small, so I had to enlarge it to fit the Cordoba radio. In this particular case, I also had to cut an access opening in order to get the radio into the blind cabinet area for the final installation.

Once the radio was inserted behind the bulkhead, I placed wood blocks underneath to raise it to the needed height. I used plumbing strap to hold it in position. Clamps or wire could also be used, as long as there is plenty of air space around the radio to allow for proper heat dissipation.

After connecting the power and speaker wires, I closed up the access opening. This was easily done by attaching two small wood pieces across the back of the cut-out panel. It is held in place by screws that run through the bordering panel into the added crosspieces.

Since every installation will differ, it's impossible to give exact directions for every circumstance. In most instances, the general procedures that I followed should work. An experienced woodworker should find the project rewarding.

A few notes of caution:

1. Do not cut into or remove any essential structural supports.

2. Avoid driving screws or nails beyond wall panels, where you might damage hidden electrical or plumbing circuits.

3. Make sure the radio is securely held in place.

4. Check with a qualified radio technician if you are unsure about the radio's wiring color code.

5. Do not connect the radio's dial light, as this will eventually drain the trailer battery.

- KENNY JOHNSON, CLARINDA, IOWA

THE GREAT COVER-UP

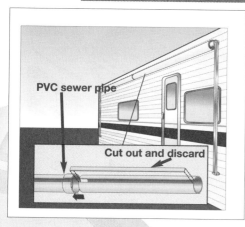

PVC sewer pipe

Cut out and discard

When my travel trailer used to sit under its storage shelter for long periods, the awning roller would collect a great amount of dust, pollen, bird droppings, and other airborne debris. Then, the next time I'd roll out the awning, the first 12 to 18 inches would look terrible.

To remedy this problem, I purchased two 10-foot lengths of standard PVC sewer pipe. Using a sabre saw, I cut a 1¾-inch strip out of each length of pipe, so it could be opened enough to slide over the rolled-up awning. This setup solved my dirty awning problem once and for all.

Depending upon your rig's awning length, the second piece of pipe may overlap the first. Cut it as necessary to obtain a length appropriate to your RV.

- WENDELL QUAKENBUSH, ALBANY, GEORGIA

PORTABLE GRASS

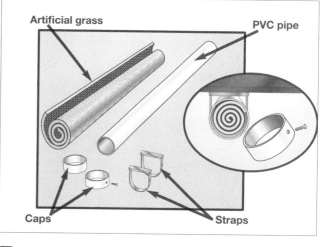

Artificial grass

PVC pipe

Caps

Straps

I finally tired of trying to roll up or fold the artificial grass that I place outside my RV's door whenever I set up camp. The material is unwieldy, and after several days' use, is often quite dirty.

To overcome this dilemma, I purchased a piece of 6-inch-diameter PVC pipe, tow end caps, and metal strapping from my local hardware store. A 6½-foot length of pipe is big enough to house about 14 linear feet of the plastic turf.

I glued one of the end caps in place on the pipe, and then drilled a hole through both the pipe and the end cap on the opposite side. With this done, I used the metal strapping to suspend the entire assembly from the frame members of my trailer. It can be located either in front of or behind the wheels, depending on one's preference.

Once the grass is rolled up and inserted into the pipe, I install the removable end cap, align the pre-drilled holes, and insert a bolt to secure it in place during travel.

- DEAN GROMETER, SAN JOSE, CALIFORNIA

KEEPING THE LID ON

Several years and a couple of RVs ago, I nearly lost the cover to my rig's roof-mounted air conditioner. As luck would have it, I happened to look down on the roof of my RV from a two-story building and notice cracks. I repaired the cover before catastrophe had a chance to strike.

Several major cracks had developed around the cover hold-down bolts. I decided to try my hand at making a set of reinforcement channels. I found it easy, and I am sure that most anyone could do the same.

Tools and equipment required for the task are minimal. Metal shears, a ruler or yardstick, pliers, hammer, drill motor, bit, pencil, and paint are all that are needed.

The sheet metal I purchased was galvanized house flashing, available at many building-supply outlets. It's light-gauge and easy to cut with hand shears; however, use extreme care while cutting the metal, since the edges are sharp as razors.

I bought a 6-inch × 10-foot precut roll of the material because I needed four strips measuring 4½ × 30 inches (two per air conditioner). You may be able to get by with less if you only have one air conditioner on your rig.

To protect yourself from cuts during construction, installation, and afterwards, I recommend folding the long edges over about ⅛ of an inch. If you don't have access to a professional metal brake, fold the edges over in a series of 90-degree bends with a pair of pliers, and finish by hammering the edge flat.

The next step is to again fold each long edge to 90 degrees at a height of ⅜ of an inch to form the channel. This can also be done

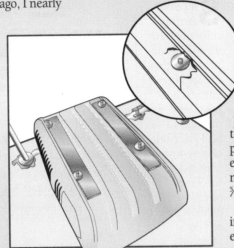

with pliers, or over the corner of a board of adequate length. Do away with the sharp right-angle corners at each end of the channels by folding them toward the inside at a 45-degree angle. Hammer flat to finish.

Next, determine the location for the mounting holes. It isn't necessary to remove the air-conditioner cover to accomplish this, only the nuts and washers that hold it in place. Hold the channel in position over the exposed bolts and lightly tap it to mark the metal. Center punch each location and drill a ⁵⁄₁₆-inch hole.

Some air-conditioner covers have ribs molded into the plastic structure. This is no problem, except that the holes you drill in your reinforcement channel will be slightly off centerline.

You should paint the finished channels to protect them from the elements. While the sheet metal is galvanized, the freshly cut edges won't be. Give the metal a coat of primer intended for use with a galvanized finish, and then paint the channels with a color coat of your choice.

Mount the channels on the air-conditioner cover using the existing nuts and washers. You may prefer to get some ⁵⁄₁₆-inch automotive fender washers at your local hardware store to provide a larger hold-down surface area than the original washers. If the holes you drilled are off center, you will have to trim one side of the fender washers to realize a proper fit.

After the installation of your reinforcement channels, you'll be able to head down the road with confidence that your air-conditioner covers won't end up as splintered debris on the byways, or worse, come off and smack some unsuspecting tailgater in the windshield.
- BILLY M. WEISZBROD, GREENVILLE, TEXAS

WINTER CAP

One of the annoying problems of storing my trailer for the winter has been the mold and slime that form on the rolled-up awning. This is caused by rain and snow, forced into the roll during storms; the awning doesn't have a chance to dry out properly until spring. I have tried several methods to alleviate this problem, but to no avail.

This year, I capped the ends of the awning roll with the bottom portion of a 2-liter plastic bottle (cut as shown). The awning material slips into a slit I made in each cap; the awning shaft fits into a hole drilled in the bottom. This method seems to work well.
- LESLIE SCHWIEZER, ANNAPOLIS, MARYLAND

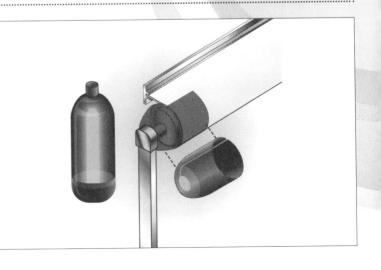

AWNING PROTECTOR

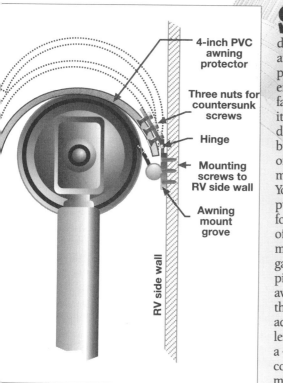

4-inch PVC awning protector

Three nuts for countersunk screws

Hinge

Mounting screws to RV side wall

Awning mount grove

RV side wall

Since our awning does not have an aluminum protector that encases the fabric when it's closed, we decided to build one out of easy-to-find material. You'll need to purchase a 10-foot long piece of 4-inch medium-gauge PVC pipe (if your awning is less than 20 feet, adjust pipe length to suit), a 4-inch PVC connector, cement, six ¼ × ¾-inch countersink stainless-steel bolts and nuts, and five 3-inch stainless-steel hinges and countersink bolts and nuts.

Split the pipe and coupling in half, and cut it lengthwise on a table saw, using the fence to guide it straight (have a helper hold the pipe while sawing). File the rough edges round and sand smooth. Lay both pieces flat, and drill three holes through each piece and the coupler to join the two sections lengthwise; countersink from inside the pipe. Glue and bolt together, then let set until solid.

Measure awning fabric (add 1 inch extra to measurement for slight overhang at each end). Cut off each end equally to match the measured length. Sand smooth and round the square corners, if desired.

Position the five hinges equally along the length of the cut pipe. Place a hinge pin against the outside edge of the PVC, and drill mounting holes from the outside; countersink from inside of the PVC. Mount hinges to PVC cover. Determine where the opposite end of the hinge will mount on the RV side wall. Loosen the awning rail attached to the side wall of the rig and have a helper lay the awning cover alongside. Position the hinges behind the awning rail and secure with all the screws; tighten the awning rail. When the screws are secure, lay the awning cover over the rolled-up awning. The hinges will allow the newly made cover to move as needed when rolled down or up.

- KEN AND FLO PRATER, GALLOWAY, OHIO

PINNED DOWN

We were forever breaking or losing the little plastic cotter pins that lock the lifting handles on our Carefree awning. After searching for new pins (at least twice per season), we stumbled across a great replacement. A metal shower-curtain hook in each awning arm did the trick, and they are actually much easier to use. The metal hooks are sturdier and offer more security, as well. The old plastic versions were easily pulled out by anyone who thought it funny to see our awning fly in a gust of wind.

- DICK AND NORMA WILSON, LETHBRIDGE, ALBERTA, CANADA

ROOF RASH

TV antennas similar to Winegard's bat-wing style should be checked periodically to make sure the various elements are not chafing the roof when the antenna is retracted. This is particularly important on a rubberized, or even aluminum, roof that offers little wear resistance to such localized friction. If chafing is evident upon inspection, the antenna wings should be gently bent up until they clear the roof surface.

- WALTER F. RONFELDT, SCARBOROUGH, MAINE

AWNING FACE-LIFT

Years of exposure to sun, rain, snow, wind, and travel can take their toll on an RV awning. This is especially so when it comes to the protective, neutral-colored wrap material.

To repair my aging awning, I purchased two tubes of yellow PlastiDip. After applying only two coats to the uncolored awning wrap, I found that the material sealed the awning perfectly. By being elastic, this product provides a leak-proof coating that also resists sun damage.

I did this work two summers ago, and the repair has held up well despite our hot Florida sun. PlastiDip is manufactured by DPI Incorporated, P.O. Box 130, Circle Pines, Minnesota 55014.

- A.L. FULLER, HUDSON, FLORIDA

VEXATIOUS CACOPHONY

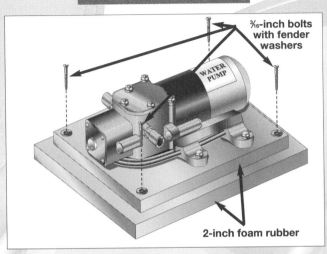

⅜-inch bolts with fender washers

WATER PUMP

2-inch foam rubber

I decided to stop using my RV's floor as a sounding board for the freshwater pump. Hearing the staccato "brrrrrap, brrrrrap" every time a faucet was opened soon became more than I could stand. The irritation was eliminated by fastening the pump to a piece of 2-inch foam rubber. I used ⅜-inch bolts with fender washers and self-locking nuts for the attachment hardware. Next, I set this unit on another piece of foam rubber, and attached the entire assembly to the floor with wood screws and fender washers. The operating racket of the pump is now almost inaudible.
- *FRED WOBSER, SANDUSKY, OHIO*

FADED MEMORIES

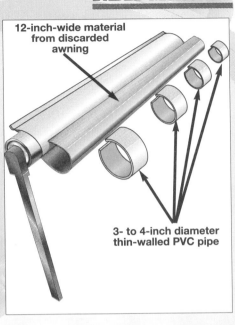

12-inch-wide material from discarded awning

3- to 4-inch diameter thin-walled PVC pipe

Many RVers leave their rigs in places like Florida and Texas for the summer, only to find upon their return that the intense sunlight has bleached a strip along the top of the unit's awning. To help eliminate this, I cut a 12-inch-wide piece of material from an old discarded awning. I matched this to the length of my own awning, and laid it across the top of the roll. Next, I cut 4-inch rings from a 3- to 4-inch-diameter thin-walled PVC pipe. These were then slit so they could be snapped onto the awning roll and around the protective material layer to hold it in place. Fading has been greatly minimized.
- *CLYDE V. MACMASTER, RICHMOND, MAINE*

WEATHER-WISE RVING

Have you ever been on the road or out camping when the weather turned threatening? If so, you should consider purchasing an inexpensive weather radio to keep you informed.

The U.S. Weather Service has transmitters that cover most of the country and broadcast local and regional atmospheric information.

There are two types of weather radio receivers available. One must be turned on and off manually. The other can be operated similarly, or can be set to automatically alert you in response to an emergency signal generated by the Weather Service during periods of hazardous weather.

Weather radios are available at most consumer electronics stores. Prices start at approximately $25.
- *GEORGE TAYLOR, MUSCLE SHOALS, ALABAMA*

JUGS ON THE JOB

Here's a good way to protect your RV awning from wet weather and recycle used plastic at the same time. My awning is exposed, with no end caps. After extended periods of storage or heavy rain, I always find water in the center of the rolled-up awning. The water seems to enter the awning through the grooves on the canopy roller, eventually settling in the center portion.

My solution was to cut the top and one side off a plastic antifreeze jug (I thoroughly cleaned it first), then cut two slots: one in the side so the canopy would slip between it, the other cut in the end so it would slip over the end of the roller. I made some holes in the end that hung down under the roller so it could be tied, and now I have a snug-fitting end cap for winter storage.
- *IAN MORRISON, TORONTO, ONTARIO, CANADA*

SANITATION

YOUR WORST NIGHTMARE

Sometimes the waste tank's valve handle pulls right out by the roots without releasing the contents of the holding tank. There you are, stuck with no way to open the valve. Attempting to replace a valve under these circumstances might be quite an undesirable job. I have found that the best way to pull the slider under these conditions is to cut the plastic valve body, as illustrated. Next, reach in with a pair of long-nose pliers and gently pull it out. Care is a requisite to avoid a catastrophe. This done, you may then rinse out the tank and proceed with the replacement of the valve. A second method is to braze a self-tapping screw to the end of the severed T-handle shaft. If you turn this tool cautiously into the broken slider, the threads will often engage sufficiently to allow you to pull the valve open one last time before replacement.
- *JOHN W. CAREY, LOS ANGELES, CALIFORNIA*

HIDING THE HOSE

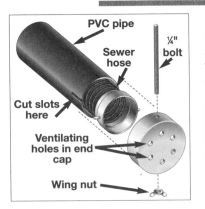

I devised a non-standard sewer hose storage setup that has worked well for us. It is simple and inexpensive, and cuts down on road wear. Our sewer hoses travel in an 8-foot length of 4-inch PVC pipe suspended from our trailer frame. The smooth interior of the PVC pipe is friendly to sewer hoses and doesn't scrub holes in them like the inside of a rusty bumper often does. To accommodate the attachment projections on the sewer hose fitting, I hack-sawed slots ⁵⁄₁₆-inch-wide × 2 inches long in both ends of the storage pipe. Thus, I can store a sewer hose on each side of the trailer. Wing nuts and ¼-inch bolts secure the plastic end caps in place. The optional ¼-inch ventilation holes in the end caps allow the hoses to air out and dry, while a few holes drilled into the bottom of the PVC pipe also help drainage.
- *JAMES F. DEPAUW, NORTH OLMSTED, OHIO*

LUBE THAT VALVE

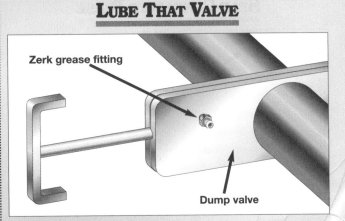

Having a problem with stiff, sticky dump valves that refuse to slide smoothly? I found an easy way to keep my dump valves in perfect operating condition, thanks to the installation of a simple Zerk grease fitting. Drill into the side of your dump valve as shown, and install the grease fitting. Then simply give it a couple of squirts with your grease gun every six months, and your sticky valve woes will be a thing of the past.
- *STAFFORD BROCHU, COLORADO SPRINGS, COLORADO*

HOLD THAT HOSE DOWN!

I have seen many a pile of rocks next to the sewer drain inlet at many dump stations. As most people know, these are for piling on top of your drain hose to keep it from popping out while dumping. Although the odds of such a calamity are low, it pays to be cautious, as a spill of this nature goes beyond just creating a mess; it's usually a very unhealthy mess that isn't very easy to clean up properly. But I've come up with an RV sewer hold-down that is designed like an old-fashioned bean bag, except that it is larger and filled with sand, not beans.

Use a strong, light- to medium-weight material with a tight weave, such as canvas or denim. The bag itself can be made to whatever dimension you choose. Mine has a cut dimension of 16 inches wide by 25 inches long. When folded in half lengthwise and sewn together, the finished dimension is 15×24 inches. (This is the perfect use for an old pair of jeans; one sewn-up leg should do the trick!-Editor) Fill the bag about 60 percent full (approximately 14 pounds) with sand, but don't overfill; you want it to be flexible and form-fitting.

Next time you make a "dump stop," just lay your new hose holder over the top of your dump hose and relax.
- *LEON R. MILLER, RENTON, WASHINGTON*

SELF-CONTAINED RINSE

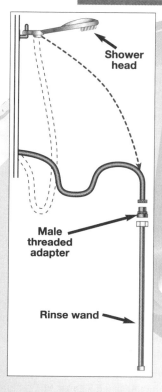

Shower head

Male threaded adapter

Rinse wand

Not many of us like to clean the toilet and black-water tank after a stay at our favorite campground. Obviously, this is the job nobody wants, so dad usually gets to do it.

For a really thorough cleaning and draining, you want to get rid of every last bit of waste. This requires the use of a pressurized-water rinse system, such as the one illustrated here.

First, there are a few equipment requirements that must be met: The shower/tub enclosure must have a detachable shower head. The hose should be long enough to reach the toilet (however, if it's not, a longer hose can easily be added).

Detach the hose from the shower head, and screw in a ½ × ¾-inch male threaded adapter (Ace Hardware part no. 70538, cost $2.19). Then, screw on a Rinse Wand (Camping World part no. 4678, cost $5.98).

Now, with the shower hose attached to the adapter and the Rinse Wand, you can insert the wand into the toilet. Turn on the water from the shower, and proceed to clean your toilet and black-water tank the easy way. The jet spray should dislodge even the most stubborn tissue.

The nice thing is that everything is done inside. When finished, simply disconnect the adapter and reattach the shower head to the hose. This method also eliminates the need to string a long hose through a window or a doorway to accomplish the cleaning.
- *W. J. Laborde, Pride, Louisiana*

CONVOLUTED PROJECT

Ineeded a way to keep an unruly sewer hose under control when it was stored in my RV's holding-tank compartment. I accomplished this with a piece of 2 × 2-inch wood, cut to match the approximate collapsed length of sewer hose I use. I drilled a ⅛-inch hole ½ inch from both ends of this piece, and firmly inserted a 5-inch length of wooden dowel pin to form a hose stop.

When I'm ready to break camp, I wash out the sewer hose, install it over the wood holder and compress it to the

Dowel

Sewer hose

2 x 2-inch lumber

Dowel

minimum length. This done, I insert another wooden dowel at the previously unpinned end to hold the hose in place. Because this last pin must be removed and replaced by hand, the fit should be a bit looser than the one on the opposite end. This holder works perfectly. It keeps the hose neat and in a fixed place inside its storage area.
- *Byron Krieber, Anchorage, Alaska*

STUFF FETCHER

Basement storage areas are nice, but sometimes reaching items in the far end of the compartments can be downright frustrating. A simple solution can be found at almost any hardware store: an extendible pole used to replace light bulbs in high ceilings. You don't need the light bulb changing adapter, just the pole. Drill a suitable size hole in the plastic end of the extendible pole, and screw in a hook used to hang planters. Now, you can reach into the far corners of the compartment, and collapse the pole for each storage when not in use.
- *William H. Jones, Irvine, California*

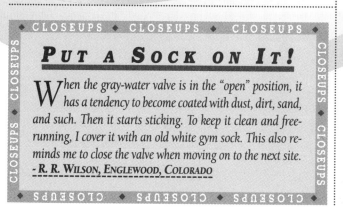

SERIOUS ABOUT SODA

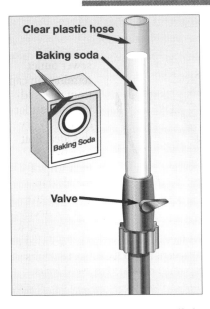

Clear plastic hose

Baking soda

Baking Soda

Valve

After flushing out all of the winterizing RV antifreeze from my rig's freshwater tank and plumbing each spring, I like to fill up the freshwater tank, add a little baking soda, and let the mixture sit for a few hours to sweeten the tank. Having experimented over the years, I finally found a quick and simple method of accomplishing this task.

I have one of these screw-on-type water-hose filler extensions with a small shut-off valve attached. I just fill the plastic extension with baking soda, place it into the filler opening, and turn on the water. This sure beats trying to poke the soda into the filler with my fingers.
- *NORMAN HEWITT, KLAMATH FALLS, OREGON*

CLOSEUPS • CLOSEUPS • CLOSEUPS

TWO TO ONE

A number of RVs are designed with a rear kitchen. This may place the gray-water tank, as well as its termination outlet, some distance from the black-water tank and valve. The drain hose must be switched between locations to empty the two tanks. Here's how I handled the problem on my rig.

I installed a terminator cap with a garden-hose connector on the rear gray-water drain. During campground setup or dumping procedure, I connect the dump hose directly to the forward-mounted tank, and a garden hose (cut to the correct length to reach the drain receptacle) to the rear gray-water outlet. I then insert both hoses into the sewer opening of the campground or dump station, where they drain independently of one another.

A good way to store the dedicated gray-water-drain garden hose is inside a 1½-inch-diameter PVC pipe clamped lengthwise to the RV's frame. Standard matching PVC end caps secure the hose in place for travel.
- *DWIGHT BEACHLER, MEDINA, OHIO*

WHERE THERE'S A WILL, THERE'S A WAY

Searching for an easy way to flush out the black-water tank of my RV, I considered several options. The hole in the bathroom wall for a garden hose seemed too messy. Anyway, our bathroom is on the curbside and would have required a long hose to reach around the unit at the dump station.

A kit is available that places a fitting near the bottom of an RV with a hose installed into the side of the holding tank. However, most dump-station water hoses don't have garden hose-type couplings. My homemade solution turned out to be simple and economical.

I noticed that a roof vent was located on the streetside of our rig just above the black-water tank drain valve. Checking inside, I found an extra-thick closet wall near the same location. Carefully loosening the paneling, I discovered the ideal solution. The vent pipe was con-

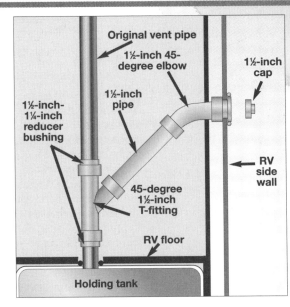

Original vent pipe

1½-inch 45-degree elbow

1½-inch cap

1½-inch pipe

1½-inch-1¼-inch reducer bushing

RV side wall

45-degree 1½-inch T-fitting

RV floor

Holding tank

nected to the top of the black-water tank, and there was adequate clearance for me to run a branch pipe out to the side wall of the rig.

I couldn't find a 45-degree T-fitting to fit the 1¼-inch vent pipe, so I used a 1½-inch T, bushed down at top and bottom. The branch line is a full 1½ inches and uses a 45-degree L at the top where it passes through the wall of the RV. (Be careful when cutting through the wall and blind bulkheads. There may be electric wires or water lines in these areas.)

Since installing this pipe as illustrated, I am now able to quickly flush the black-water tank of my RV with minimal effort. While this method might not be feasible on all RVs, and though it will require some planning and handyman skills, it's still worth checking out.
- *ROY ELLINGBOE, FRANKLIN, TENNESSEE*

GUTTER TALK

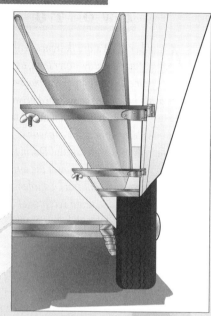

Using plastic rain gutters for a sewer-hose support works well until it's time to store them for travel. I found some open space between the frame and the skin of my trailer, so I decided to put it to use.

Two aluminum brackets hold the rain-gutter supports in place. I pop-riveted these to a couple of small hinges. Then, aligning the supports with bolts protruding downward from the trailer frame, I riveted the hinges to the rig's exterior skin. (Editor's note: Not all trailers will have bolts in this exact location.) A wing nut over the bolts makes for quick and easy removal.

This method allows clean, noninterfering storage of rain gutter-style supports. Several sections can be nested together. The dimension of each, of course, depends on the length of opening under your RV.

- RICHARD M. CLARK, LONG BEACH, CALIFORNIA

LEVERAGING

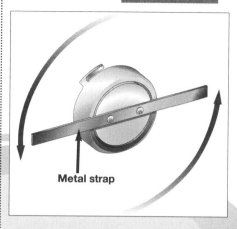

Metal strap

If you have difficulty wrestling the sewer-outlet termination cap from the holding-tank outlet of your RV, try this idea. Bolt on a 6- to 8-inch strip of metal strap. This will give you the necessary leverage to rotate the cap even under difficult circumstances. I decided to use aluminum in order to prevent rust. Of course, the bolts that extend through the cap must be sealed to avoid leaks. This modification makes future holding-tank service a breeze, and is cheaper than the $14 commercial version.

- ROBERT W. BATES, IDAHO FALLS, IDAHO

STICK SHIFT

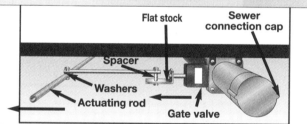

Flat stock • Sewer connection cap • Spacer • Washers • Actuating rod • Gate valve

Many RVs are equipped with sewer valves that, because of the mounting angle and lack of leverage, are very difficult to operate. My rig is one such vehicle. To simplify holding-tank service, I devised a lever/linkage arrangement that can be made from easily obtainable aluminum.

Incorporating washers to allow pivoting, I bolted a 24 × ¾-inch actuating rod to the bottom of my RV's frame. To this I fastened a ¼-inch rod, which connects to a flat-stock aluminum handle that I manufactured to replace the normal dump-valve T-handle. A ¼-inch piece of tubing acts as a spacer to prevent interference between the new dump-valve handle and the actuating rod. The new mechanism greatly reduces the effort previously required to empty the holding tank.

When traveling, I hook a short length of bungee cord to an eye-bolt at the end of the 24-inch handle, and attach the other end to a convenient bracket near the dump valve. This minimizes the chance that the valve will accidentally open while under way.

- KEN HAMPTON, EATONTOWN, NEW JERSEY

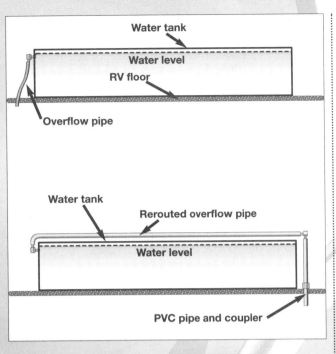

Water tank
Water level
RV floor
Overflow pipe

Water tank
Rerouted overflow pipe
Water level
PVC pipe and coupler

DISAPPEARING ACT

After filling the freshwater tank of my new bus-type motorhome, I noticed that the reservoir was a translucent plastic, which allowed me to see the water level. In checking further, I saw that the tank was equipped with an overflow pipe that was installed on the side about 1¼ inches down from the top. The water tank is a 65-gallon size, but is only 8 inches deep. I reasoned that the position of the overflow would only allow it to be filled to about 55 gallons.

Later, I drove to a dump station about 5 miles away. On arrival, I noticed that fresh water was draining from the rig. The water in the tank was now 3 inches below the top while the motorhome was on level ground. In other words, I was down to about 40 gallons after not using any on board and driving a mere 10 miles.

The fix was as simple as turning the right-angle overflow connector so that it faced up instead of down. I then rerouted the drain hose across the top of the tank to the opposite side of the rig. Keeping the outlet end as high as possible, I terminated it into a 1-inch PVC pipe, which I installed through the motorhome's main floor to the underside of the vehicle. This pipe not only diverts overflow water outside, but also acts as a siphon breaker. I used a 1-inch PVC coupler to prevent the pipe from falling through the hole in the floor.

I have had several RVs over the years that seemed to lose too much water. I just never investigated to see how much. I always assumed that the family was simply using too much water while camping. I have concluded that the problem may apply to many types of RVs. For this reason, I submit my fix for others to use.

- *MILTON SCOTT, PRINCETON, TEXAS*

AIR POWER RESCUE

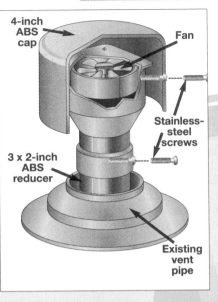

4-inch ABS cap
Fan
Stainless-steel screws
3 x 2-inch ABS reducer
Existing vent pipe

An odoriferous holding tank doesn't have to make it unpleasant for RV occupants. Using readily available parts, I came up with a power venting system that really does the job.

I started by removing the existing cover from the black-water tank vent located on the RV roof-top. This was replaced by a modified vent stack fabricated from a 3 × 2-inch ABS reducer, which also contains a 12-volt DC fan (Radio Shack part no. 273-243-B). Stainless-steel screws were used to fasten the fan assembly into the 3-inch end of the ABS reducer, and also to secure the 2-inch end of the reducer to the existing vent pipe. I then covered the fan mechanism with a 4-inch PVC cap, which was fastened in place by using stainless-steel hardware once again.

Providing power to the fan was easy. I ran two No. 18 wires down the vent pipe to a location near the toilet. Then, I drilled a hole large enough to allow the wires to feed out to a switch, a pilot light, a 12-volt DC power source, and a good electrical ground. The hole and emanating wires were sealed with epoxy.

After some experimentation, I found that there is enough clearance between the ABS reducer and the PVC cap to allow plenty of airflow. Now that the project is complete, whenever the rig is occupied, I turn the fan on periodically to keep the interior smelling fresh.

- *JOHN SAUNDERS, FALLBROOK, CALIFORNIA*

TOILET-SEAL TOOL

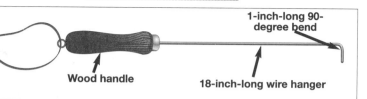

Wood handle

1-inch-long 90-degree bend

18-inch-long wire hanger

When toilet paper becomes trapped in the sealing groove of the toilet, the gate valve will not seal properly, allowing water to leak into the holding tank. Since the water that remains in the bowl after flushing helps prevent vapors from escaping from the holding tank, this groove must be cleaned; however, it's a messy job. To clear this groove, I cut a wire hanger 18 inches long, and made a 90-degree bend approximately 1 inch long in one end. I then bent a 1-inch section 180 degrees and doubled it back to provide a tight fit in the hole of an old wooden file handle. After driving the coat-hanger wire into the file handle, I drilled a hole into the top of the handle and installed a screw eye. To this, I then attached a rawhide shoestring and tied the ends together. To use, place the rawhide thong around your wrist, and twist the tool until the thong is tight. While the slide valve is open, run the bent end of the coat hanger around the groove of the seal, removing all foreign material. Make sure the end of the coat hanger is filed smooth, and do not place excess pressure on the seal. The rawhide strap prevents the tool from falling into the holding tank should the tool slip out of your hand.
- Ronald S. Hallowell Jr., Latrobe, Pennsylvania

FROZEN FITTINGS

If you've ever had problems putting new sewer hoses and fittings together, this tip is for you. I've found that if I put the plastic fittings in the freezer for about five minutes, they will shrink enough for the sewer hose to slide over them with no effort at all. Then, I just put the hose clamps on and go about my business.
- Jerry C. Davis, Lugoff, South Carolina

SEWER SUPPORT

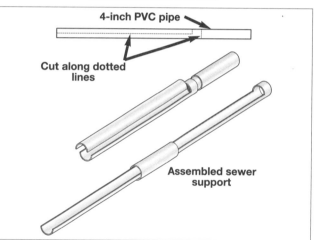

4-inch PVC pipe

Cut along dotted lines

Assembled sewer support

Having a drain-hose support that doesn't hold the hose properly is very frustrating. Here is a support that works well for me.

From a 10-foot piece of 4-inch PVC pipe (about $8), cut off an 18-inch piece. Next, cut off a 54-inch piece, mark 4 inches back from one end, and split the piece in half lengthwise, except for this 4-inch section. You now have two 50-inch pieces of half-pipe, one of which still has a 4-inch-round section at its end, to lay the sewer line in.

Slide both ends of the split section into the 18-inch uncut pipe, so a well-supported joint is formed. Run the sewer line through the uncut 4-inch end, and attach it to the motorhome. Slide the support up over the sewer connector (this will hold the support in place). Run the line through the 18-inch joint, and connect it to the site's drain. You can adjust the support to a length within the 18-inch limitation.
- W. A. Quakenbush, Albany, Georgia

TERMINATION TRAUMA

What do you do when you notice a leaky sewer termination valve aboard your RV, but aren't sure which gate valve is the culprit? Simple. Just add a small bottle of red or blue food coloring to the kitchen-sink drain, and mix with about 3 gallons of water.

Keep an eye on the sewer termination fitting outside the rig for a few minutes. If the dye shows up, the gray-water valve is to blame. No food coloring indicates the black-water valve is due for overhaul or replacement.
- Eugene Stagner, Anaheim, California

SEWER ADAPTER STORAGE

Not being smart enough to get the sewer adapter, with its 5-inch flange, into the 4½-inch bumper where the hose is stored, I devised a holder for it outside the bumper. Using an 18-inch length of ¼-inch threaded rod, I formed a U-bolt to fit around the rear bumper of the trailer. I then attached a 2 × 11-inch length of PVC pipe vertically to the bumper. The sewer adapter slips over the pipe, and is held in place with a clothespin. The new holder is mounted behind the spare tire, out of sight, but ready for use at the flip of a clothespin.

- MILTON F. WATTS, LINEVILLE, ALABAMA

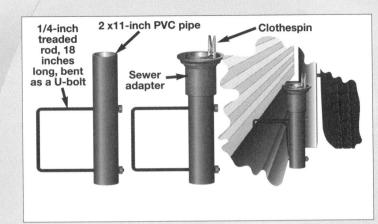

OVERFLOW WOES

As described in the following steps, I designed an overflow indicator for my tote-type holding tank by using a Camco water-filler fitting. I removed the short, clear, plastic hose that comes with the Camco fitting and replaced it with a 10-foot piece of clear, low-pressure water hose. This was secured with a worm-gear hose clamp.

Next, I attached the Camco fitting to the hose on the tote tank, and secured the other end of the clear plastic water hose to a female hose fitting having a Camco blow-out plug that was already installed. Removal of the plug's valve stem allows it to act as a vent when the cap is removed.

When I drain the holding tank on my trailer, I open the Camco valve and remove the valve-stem cap from the blow-out plug to create a vent. This allows me to view the waste-water level, and be ready to close the holding-tank slide valve when the tote tank fills to capacity. I close the Camco valve and replace the blow-out plug cap before traveling to the dump station with a portable tank. I reverse this procedure to empty the tote tank.

The whole dumping process is completed by removing the blow-out plug from the 10-foot plastic line, and then attaching a water hose to flush the tube.

- JACKIE KEW, GRAND ISLAND, NEW YORK

SOAP SNAG

We've traveled full-time for four years using our travel trailer as a home base and our motorhome/tow vehicle for touring outlying areas. This gives us a chance to really get to know an area.

However, we encountered a problem leaving the gray-water valve in the open position while the trailer was hooked up for an extended period of time. It seems that this procedure allowed a buildup of soap scum in the tank, clogging the outlet. Despite all attempts, we couldn't clear the blockage. All a local plumber could tell us was to put the drain line under pressure. We were skeptical of this approach.

Finally, we found an RV specialist who told us the following procedure:

Close the drain valve and fill the tank to the brim. Thoroughly rinse out the waste hose, then hold it at shoulder level while backfilling it with water. With this done, open the gray-water slide valve, and while still holding the waste hose well above the tank level, rapidly raise and lower it to create a "wave" action with the system.

After a few such cycles, we would quickly drop the hose into the sewer outlet and drain the tank. The weight of the water helped loosen the stubborn blockage. To clear out the soap buildup entirely, we had to repeat this process several times.

Now, when we leave the trailer to go on one of our two-week jaunts, we close the drain valve and fill up the tank. We also pour in some RV Trine to help dissolve any buildup while we're gone.

This really works well; try it!

- ERIN SETZER, ST. LOUIS, MISSOURI

SEWER HOSE PROTECTION

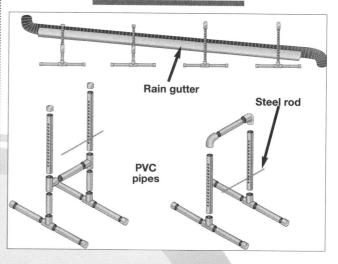

1-inch bands of rubber

Sewer hose

As full-timers, we constantly make and break camp. The wear and tear from taking the sewer hose out of the bumper storage container takes its toll. The rough finish and corrosion in the storage compartment built into the bumper scrapes on the sewer hose every time it's removed and put away. We extend the life of our hoses by placing 1-inch-wide bands of rubber from bicycle inner tubes in a number of locations; this protects the surface. Now our sewer hoses last twice as long.

- DAWN SANABIA, PAHRUMP, NEVADA

QUICK RINSE

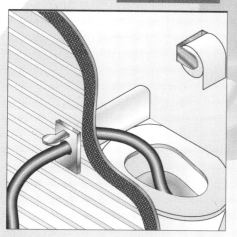

I used to get tired of dragging a garden hose through the front door, across the carpet and into the bathroom of my RV every time I wanted to flush the black-water tank.

To overcome this irritation, I bought two weatherproof outdoor electric receptacle covers—the kind used for a single outlet, with a hinged cover.

Next, I drilled a 1½-inch hole through the inside bathroom wall just above the toilet, making sure the RV was not connected to electrical power at the time, on the remote chance that I would find a 120-volt AC electrical wire inside the wall at that point. It's best to drill carefully, removing the interior paneling and the insulation to check for wiring before drilling through the RV's outside covering. The receptacle covers were installed on each side of the access hole, using the gasket provided. I ran a bead of silicone sealant around the outside cover for extra protection against wet-weather leaks.

Now, when it's time to rinse the toilet holding tank, I just feed the hose through both hinged covers and connect it to the rinsing wand.

- TOM TEST, FALLING WATERS, WEST VIRGINIA

SUPPORT NETWORK

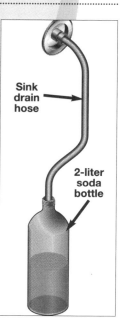

Rain gutter

Steel rod

PVC pipes

As all RVers know, wastewater drains better when there is a gradual, continuous drop from the RV to the sewer opening. This requires some type of sewer-hose support.

I cut rain gutters into 5-foot lengths to hold the hose on my rig. Wherever there is a joint, I install my homemade hose stands for support. Each stand is adjustable to accommodate various levels of terrain. I made a total of four to handle the longest run I might ever encounter.

Two of my stands have cross arms at the top of the assembly, with the holes drilled below, as illustrated. These allow the rain gutters and hose to be placed closer to the ground. The other two stands have the cross arm in the middle.

All are made from ½-inch PVC pipe, which is available at hardware and plumbing stores. I purchased a 3-foot steel rod, and cut it into four lengths of 9 inches each. The total cost for the entire project was only $14–much less than commercially made stands.

- DON BULLER, JEFFERSON, OREGON

POLLUTION SOLUTION

Sink drain hose

2-liter soda bottle

In an effort not to pollute the site that we camp on, I hook up an empty 2-liter bottle to my tent-trailer's sink drain hose by using an old washing machine water supply line. The hose is left a little loose on the camper side to vent the air out, but does not leak. When the bottle fills up, I dump it into a suitable drain or dump station, and reuse or recycle the bottle.

- BILL ARCHER, WINTER PARK, FLORIDA

REFILL DILEMMA

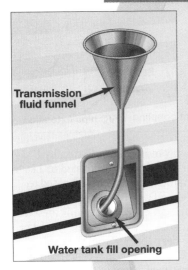

Transmission fluid funnel

Water tank fill opening

The water-tank fill opening on many RVs requires that a long, narrow filler tube be attached to the water hose in order to top off the tank. This works as long as there is city water available.

However, what would you do if you needed to add water to the tank from emergency-supply jugs? Or perhaps you just want to pour in a small dose of bleach to keep the tank bacteria-free.

I have found that a funnel designed for transmission fluid is ideal for these tasks. Its wide opening and long, narrow tube make it perfect for servicing the freshwater tank. The funnels are also cheap; auto-parts stores sell them for just a few dollars. Of course, never use this funnel for anything else!

- WARREN ROBB, TEMPE, ARIZONA

WRESTLING RUST

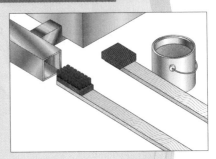

Rust formation inside the rear bumper of my RV would often cut and abrade my rig's sewer hose as it was inserted or removed. To solve this problem, I decided to scrape the internal surfaces clean, and then repaint them to prevent a reoccurrence.

I drilled two ⅛-inch holes in the wooden handle of a 2½-inch wire brush. Using large screws, I attached the brush to a 2½ × 60-inch board. This setup makes it easy to clean the rusty internal surfaces of the bumper. When finished, I washed out all loose debris with a garden hose.

Next, I stapled a 1 × 3 × 4-inch piece of sponge to a 2½ × 60-inch board, and applied several coats of exterior latex paint to finish the job. Now, the sewer hose glides in and out without the annoying damage I used to experience.

- MELVIN C. GARLAND, OWASSO, OKLAHOMA

STRINGS ATTACHED

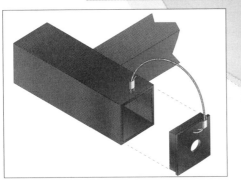

I used to drive up to a dump station with my RV, remove the square, rubber bumper plug to get out the sewer hose, and proceed to forget to put it back in place when I was finished. This happened several times, and I lost several plugs.

I solved the problem by making several lanyards to connect both endcaps to my RV's bumper. I did the same with some of the other losable caps found aboard my rig. Eighteen-inch lengths of monofilament grass-trimmer line (.088-inch) did the trick.

I drilled ³⁄₁₆-inch holes in the bumper and endcaps. I then looped the nylon line through the holes and crimped a ½-inch length of soft copper tubing to secure everything in place. The lanyards are short enough to prevent the caps from touching the ground, so now if I forget to reinstall them, they just hang there until I remember.

- THOMAS SEXTON, ASHFORD, ALABAMA

COMPRESSED HOSE

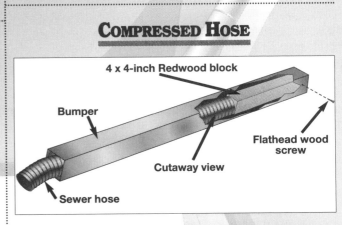

4 x 4-inch Redwood block

Bumper

Cutaway view

Flathead wood screw

Sewer hose

How often have you started to set up camp, and reached into the RV's rear bumper to pull out the sewer hose, only to find that it has worked its way into the center of the bumper, just out of arm's reach? Or worse yet, discovered that the hose has been sliding back and forth inside the bumper so long it now has tiny holes worn into it. To solve this problem, slide a block of 4 × 4 × 4-inch redwood or cedar into the bumper about 30 to 40 inches (for a 10-foot hose with fittings), then secure the wood block in place inside the bumper with ¼-inch flat-head wood screws run through the side of the bumper as shown. The block of wood keeps the hose from sliding deeper inside the bumper, and also compresses the hose enough to keep it from sliding around and developing holes in it.

- BOB GRIMES, REDDING, CALIFORNIA

GUARD DUTY

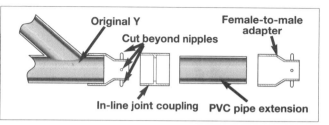

Aluminum strap · Vent · Wood fairings

The small holding-tank roof vent on my new fifth-wheel is on the right side of the coach and at the highest point on the trailer's roof. Here, it is most exposed to overhanging tree branches. After replacing the cover three times, I decided it needed some additional protection. To achieve this, I mounted two wood fairings fore and aft of the vent, and bridged across these with an aluminum bar, as illustrated. I used screws to attach the aluminum bar, so it can be removed for maintenance.

The fairings were cut from 2-inch stock, then set in a mastic compound that I verified was compatible with the rubber roofing on my fiver. Next, using an electronic stud finder to locate the roof framing (rapping with one's knuckles would also work), I screwed through the fairings and the rubber and aluminum roof skins, and into the trailer structure.

The length of the fairing should be adjusted to ensure at least two screws find a firm anchorage. The guard bar was made from 1½ × ⅛-inch aluminum strap, drilled and countersunk for flat-head screws.

I believe that it is important to protect the vent cover from both front and rear. My worst damage occurred late at night while backing into a space beneath the overhanging branches of a tree. Try that sometime with your wife shaking a flashlight and shouting unintelligible directions. This modification just might save a marriage!
- *DON LANDBERG, BEND, OREGON*

THE TERMINATOR

Original Y · Cut beyond nipples · Female-to-male adapter · In-line joint coupling · PVC pipe extension

The sewer termination on my motorhome, like many I have seen, was routed in an awkward location, 8 to 12 inches under the side of the vehicle. Every time I decided to do something about it, I backed off because the bayonet connection for the sewer hose was part of a more complicated tee. The job looked as though a major plumbing change would be required. Nothing could have been further from the truth.

The modification is one of the simplest do-it-yourself projects that one could undertake. Here's how:

First, procure a female-to-male termination adapter from an RV-accessory store, such as Camping World. Then make a trip to a home-supply store or a plumbing shop to obtain a piece of 3-inch diameter PVC or ABS pipe of the required length, a matching in-line joint coupling, one small can of appropriate cleaning solvent, and a can of pipe cement.

With a hacksaw, or even a sharp knife, cut off the four bayonet nipples on the existing sewer termination. Next, slip the joint coupling over the modified outlet, and determine the length of pipe needed to extend the new bayonet adapter to the desired location. Test the fit of the assembly without glue to assure correctness. When satisfied, apply cleaner and cement according to the directions on the cans, and assemble the pieces. If necessary, use steel plumber's tape to strap the extension in place.
- *GEORGE J. LAURER, WENDELL, NORTH CAROLINA*

DREADS SEEING RED

Recently, I failed to remember to shut the dump valve on my sewage tank after dumping. The next time that I dumped, I removed the cap on the end of the pipe to hook up the hose, and was surprised with the biggest instant mess you ever saw! To help ensure that I would never experience that situation again, I painted the outer end of the valve rod a bright red, all the way up the rod support. Now, when I glance at the valve, if I see any of the unpainted surface showing on the rod outboard of the rod support, I know the valve is not closed all the way.
- *WILLIAM L. COOK, LEO, INDIANA*

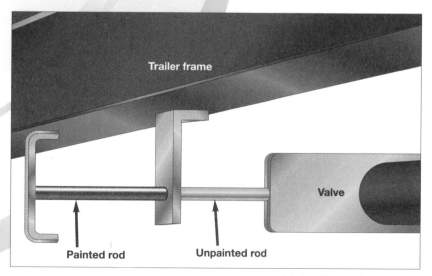

Trailer frame · Valve · Painted rod · Unpainted rod

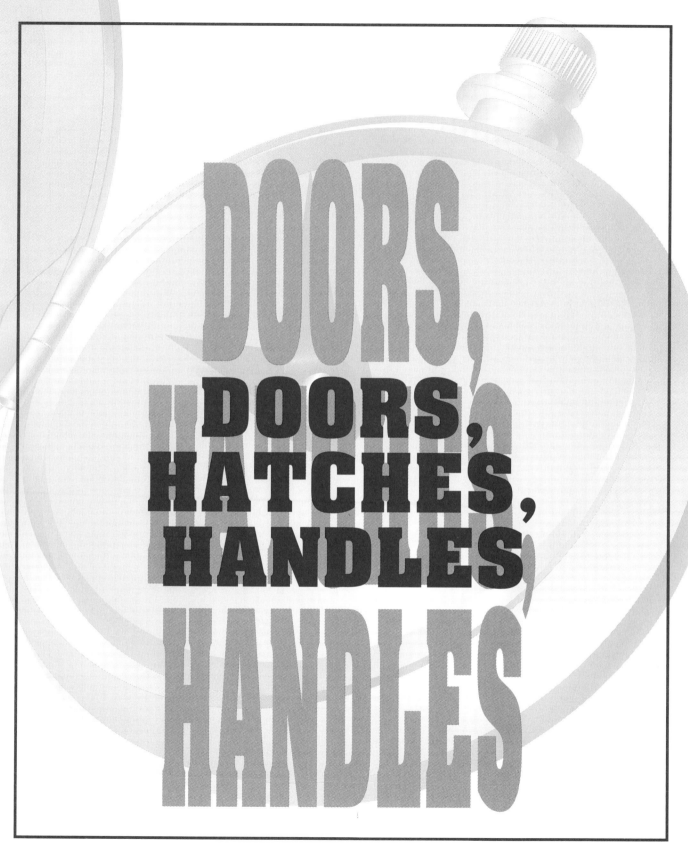

DOORS, HATCHES, HANDLES

STOWAWAY STOPPER

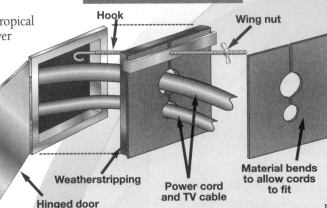

Hook

Wing nut

Weatherstripping

Hinged door

Power cord and TV cable

Material bends to allow cords to fit

When camping in the semitropical South, you quickly discover the abundance of insect life that surrounds you. Many of the critters want to explore your RV, and some would like to set up housekeeping.

In an effort to ensure the desired separation between us, I began searching for potential entry locations. I found that the AC power cord entrance was an open door to our unwanted visitors, and as this hatch opens to the space under our bed, I decided that a secondary cover was necessary to prevent insect intrusion. The flexible plastic material that I used is what makes it work.

I used ³⁄₃₂-inch-thick plastic from a discarded real estate sign. I suppose that plastic up to ⅛-inch-thick would also work, but it must be reasonably bendable without breaking or tearing, and must return to a flat condition when released.

To make a cover to fit your RV, first measure the power-cord hatch opening. Then, cut the plastic material you've chosen slightly bigger in all dimensions, so contact will be made around the outside perimeter.

Next, measure the power cord's diameter, and drill a hole in the new plastic cover to match. When this is complete, cut a slit as indicated, so you can slip it around the power cord. If you would like, you can also run your cable-TV wire through the insect stopper by adding an appropriate-size hole.

To secure the new cover over the utility opening, I made a hook from a standard coarse-thread bolt. A threaded J-hook and wing nut would also work. Drill a hole to accept the diameter of this bolt, and as you do so, place it in a position so the hook will draw the cover against the side of the RV when tightened. Finish the project by adding foam weatherstripping around the inside edges of the plastic cover.

- JOHN COONS, FORT LAUDERDALE, FLORIDA

POP TOPS

The two roof vent pipes on my 32-foot fifth-wheel are covered with snap-on rain caps. These caps stay on fine, as long as they aren't brushed by low-hanging branches.

However, we visit one particular campground that has a long, tree-lined entrance where the branches often drag over the top of our rig. After losing one cap, and having to search the driveway for another, I decided that I had to find a better way. Gluing them in place didn't appear to be the solution because keeping them rigidly in position might subject them to breakage.

I drilled a small hole in the edge of the vent caps and another in the top edge of the pipe. Using a short length of light-duty chain, I secured the caps in place. The chain doesn't show, and it successfully keeps the vent caps restrained whenever they get knocked loose.

- PAUL WEBSTER, LYONS, MICHIGAN

ALL LOCKED UP

The five original-equipment storage compartment locks on my trailer were very poor quality plastic devices. Wanting better security than these provided, I decided to search for good quality metal locks.

For simplicity, I wanted to have all five locks keyed alike. But when I expressed this desire to my RV-supply store, a salesman pointed out that purchasing five locks keyed the same might be expensive. However, he told me that the parts department purchased metal storage compartment locks in rather sizable quantities, and in only a few key codes. Because of this, he suggested I look through the parts bin to locate five locks with the same number.

It took me only a few minutes to find five matching locks with the same key number. The cost to replace my junk plastic fasteners with cut-key metal versions was only $2.95 each. I believe that the security of my outside compartment access doors is now much improved.

- WAYNE GUYMON, FULLERTON, CALIFORNIA

SPRING SOLUTION

On my last two travel trailers, I had a problem accessing the storage area under the dinette seats. The seats were hinged at the table's side, and there wasn't sufficient clearance to swing the seats up far enough to stay raised on their own. I had to use one hand to hold the seat, and the other to search for what I wanted.

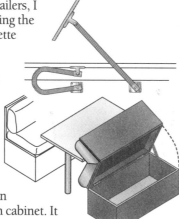

I had a similar problem in the over-the-sink bathroom cabinet. It was hinged at the top, and was too heavy for a normal cabinet spring to hold open.

I solved both dilemmas by using "hatch holders" obtained from a local marine-supply store. These were easy to install and operate. They hold the dinette seats and bathroom cabinet door open with no problem.

I can now search through the storage compartment with both hands if necessary.

- PAUL B. BECKER, LILLIAN, ALABAMA

LET IT RAIN

We have outside access doors on our travel trailer with piano-type hinges at the top. In the past, whenever it rained, the water used to run into our trailer through the hinges. We found an inexpensive solution to this problem.

After removing the top set of screws from the trailer's storage compartment doorframes, we cut weatherstripping to match the length dimension of each hinge assembly. The next step was to drill holes in the weatherstripping's mounting flange to match those already in the trailer.

We then fastened these strips to the doorframe with the same screws we had previously removed. A liquid sealing compound was also used for additional leak protection. Now, there are no more leaks!

- LARRY WIEBE, WHITEWATER, KANSAS

SAGGING SOLUTION

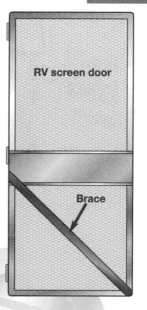

RV screen door

Brace

Few RV screen doors have any diagonal bracing, so most of them sag and bind even when new. As they age, these doors frequently become so badly distorted from dragging on the sill that they need replacement long before their time. It is so simple to correct this condition that I do not know why the manufacturers don't make the doors correctly in the first place.

The problem can be remedied by purchasing a strip of $\frac{1}{32} \times 36$-inch aluminum from a local hardware store. Aluminum this thin can be easily cut and trimmed with woodworking tools; even heavy-duty scissors will do the job.

Using blocks and a carpenter's square, raise the outer edge of the door until it is slightly above square.

Next, clamp the aluminum strip in place diagonally across the bottom section of the door, making sure the high end mates to the hinge side, as shown in the illustration.

Mark and drill the diagonal brace and door. Cut the aluminum strip to length, and angle its ends to match the door-frame. File all cut edges to remove burrs, and finish by pop-riveting the strip into place.

- SCOTT STEWART, HAMILTON, MONTANA

DON'T BUG ME

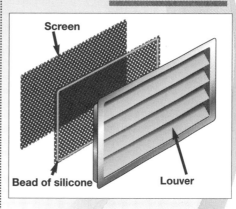

Screen

Bead of silicone

Louver

I used to have a problem with flies and mosquitoes getting into my trailer. They were getting in through the range vent hood. To stop it, I took the outside louver off, and cut a piece of window screen that would fit tightly inside the louver. Then I put a bead of silicone around the edges of the screen to hold it in. Be sure to caulk around the louver again before reinstalling it.

- TODD REVILL, DEXTER, MICHIGAN

AYE, MATEY

The manufacturer of my travel trailer used a "universal" power-cord hatch, which was not ideal. It required a great deal of effort to push the 30-amp power cord through a hole designed for a 15-amp cord. It also meant that I had a wet, muddy cord lying in a relatively inaccessible interior storage compartment whenever I broke camp in the rain.

I fixed the problem by purchasing a 30-amp, twist-lock, through-the-hull-style shore-power fitting from my local marine-supply dealer. I also bought the corresponding female power plug to install on my RV's electrical cord. (These specialized electrical components are also available in 15- and 50-amp versions, and all come with detailed installation instructions.)

During this modification, I disconnected the hard-wired RV power cord from the circuit-breaker box and laid it aside. Then, I removed the factory power-cord hatch cover, and to my delight, discovered the holes in the marine twist-lock fitting matched the existing holes. (Of course, this may not always be the case, so some additional modification may be needed on other RVs.)

I made an escutcheon plate from 22-gauge stainless steel, although aluminum, brass, or acrylic plastic would also work. If your RV does not have the traditional ribbed siding, you can skip this step altogether, and mount the marine power fitting directly through the wall of the RV. (Use caution when drilling

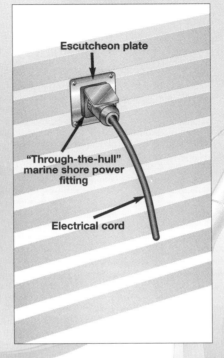

Escutcheon plate

"Through-the-hull" marine shore power fitting

Electrical cord

the wall, which may contain hidden plumbing and electrical lines.) Before final installation, I applied silicone sealer under the escutcheon plate to assure that it would remain weathertight.

Next, I ran stranded, color-coded, insulated, 10-gauge copper wiring through an insulating sleeve, and connected the new marine-power socket to the RV's circuit-breaker pane. I then installed the new cord socket on the existing RV power cord, along with a boot-and-screw coupling to waterproof the assembly.

This modification provides me nearly two extra feet of power cord, allows me to quickly remove and store my RV's electrical line in an outside cabinet, and has eliminated an entry point for insects and pests. When I did the project a few years back, it cost me $60 and two hours of my time.

If you decide to undertake this project, make sure that you understand the task at hand, use the proper size approved wiring for your application, and always observe correct wiring techniques and polarity. These considerations are critical to your safety! Also, be certain that your work conforms to the National Electric Code and Recreation Vehicle Industry Association standards, or your insurance coverage may be void. If you are unsure how to proceed, consult a qualified electrician.
- *I.J. KREGERS, WILMINGTON, DELAWARE*

GRAB THIS

I had bought a trailer, but never felt quite safe stepping out the door onto the metal step. I was always trying to get a left-hand hold.

So, one day I went to Wal-Mart and bought a $2.47 door pull. I attached it to the interior wall, just to the left of the door, at the right height for me. Now, by taking hold of the pull, I feel balanced and secure when stepping down on the metal step.
- *I.A. CROWELL, SPRINGFIELD, MISSOURI*

HEADS UP!

Original door

Cut here

Hinges

Overhead cabinet

I had a wide microwave compartment door in my new fifth-wheel trailer, which when open was impossible to get past without bumping my head. The problem was solved, however, when I cut the door in half and installed a full-length piano hinge. The door now folds in the middle, out of the way of foot-traffic when in use.
- *WILLIAM G. WOLTJEN, MURRELLS INLET, SOUTH CAROLINA*

SNAPPY APPROACH

You can make your own insulated vent covers from 2-inch-thick foam rubber purchased from a fabric shop. For a press fit, cut it slightly oversize with a sharp knife, and round the corners a little.

These foam covers will stop condensation from forming. They also will prevent unnecessary loss of heat, and will deaden rain noise that might prevent you from sleeping soundly. During the daytime, though, light can still filter through. The covers are easy to make and store. These covers can be made for about $3 each, but you will have to apply snaps if you intend to leave them in place for an extended period.
- *MARILYN E. FOX, NORTH OLMSTED, OHIO*

LATCH IT UP

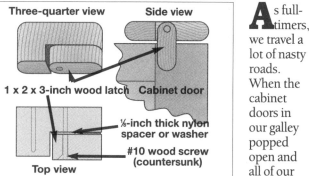

Three-quarter view   Side view

1 x 2 x 3-inch wood latch   Cabinet door

⅛-inch thick nylon spacer or washer

#10 wood screw (countersunk)

Top view

As full-timers, we travel a lot of nasty roads. When the cabinet doors in our galley popped open and all of our dishes ended up on the floor, we decided to build a few latches. We built our latches by using a piece of 1 × 2-inch oak (or other matching wood) and cutting it into 3-inch sections. The movable portion is cut (as shown) from these 3-inch lengths of wood. The ends of each latch were rounded using a belt sander, rasp, and hand file. Holes are drilled and countersunk so that the mounting screws do not protrude beyond the surface of the latch. The pieces are then sanded and stained to match the cabinets.

To install, locate the latch above the cabinet door and mark the location of the two mounting holes. Remove the latch and drill through the cabinet as marked, then screw it in place. Put a ⅛-inch-thick nylon spacer or washer under the moving piece, and install it with a No. 10 screw. A ¾-inch cork or felt disk on the back side of the moving piece keeps it from marring the cabinet surface.
- *BRENT VANFOSSEN, TULSA, OKLAHOMA*

RAIN CAP

*A*lthough the shore-power cord storage-compartment door of most RVs has a small sliding panel to protect the interior from rain, it must be closed to be effective. This is a difficult trick when the power cord is in use, and leaks often result. Since the compartment floor is almost always the trailer's floor as well, over time this condition will cause wood rot. To stop the entry of rainwater, I attached a Perko clamshell ventilator to the exterior of the door. This item is available at most boat dealerships. Though it does require some grinding to reshape the outline of the cover around the door lock, as well as the relocation of one mounting hole, the part fits the cord openings common to most trailers.

I attached this item using the smallest stainless-steel bolts and lock nuts commonly available, and had to file a small notch in the panel for it to close correctly. Silicone sealant was applied to the mating surface during installation of the cover. In addition, a large dot of silicone was positioned so that it slightly binds and holds the original sliding panel open when in use.

I also fabricated a hook inside the compartment to smoothly guide the power cord through the door and opening at the proper angle. This, however, may not be necessary on all installations. The entire job costs less than $5, and it will help preserve my trailer for many years of enjoyable travel.
- *FRED A. HIGGINS, ROYAL OAK, MICHIGAN*

DRAWER SLICK TRICK

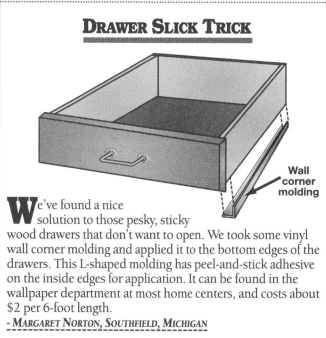

Wall corner molding

We've found a nice solution to those pesky, sticky wood drawers that don't want to open. We took some vinyl wall corner molding and applied it to the bottom edges of the drawers. This L-shaped molding has peel-and-stick adhesive on the inside edges for application. It can be found in the wallpaper department at most home centers, and costs about $2 per 6-foot length.
- *MARGARET NORTON, SOUTHFIELD, MICHIGAN*

TALES OF THE SILVER SCREEN

Keeping wasps from building their nest in the rear bumper's sewer-hose storage area was a problem on my fifth-wheel. However, I found a quick fix. I simply glued pieces of household window screen to the inside of the rubber bumper caps. This keeps out the wasps, but still allows air to circulate inside the bumper.

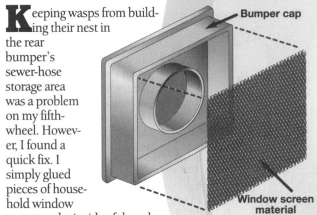

Bumper cap

Window screen material

- DON ROWE, ALBURNETT, IOWA

CATCHY HATCHES

The outside storage hatches on my trailer are equipped with only a key latch, which when left unlocked allows the doors to hang open an inch or so. Unless I latched them every time, I found that rain, rodents, wind, and bugs would find their way inside the rig. To solve this dilemma, I installed magnetic catches on the doors. I selected the type often used on residential kitchen cabinets. These are generally available at any hardware store for less than a dollar each.

I mounted one of these on each access door—near the lower corner, so they wouldn't get in the way as items are removed or stored. On my particular installation, I had to first attach the magnetic catches to a small block of wood in order to raise them up enough to clear the lip of the catch opening.

Depending upon how good a grip you can get on the door, once the magnets are in place, it may be necessary to either put a small knob on the door, or reduce the holding power of the magnet by putting a piece of tape over the opposing metal plate.

With this modification complete, I now unlock the outside access doors when I set up, and lock them when I pack up and leave. Since they appear closed, I don't worry about really locking them when I'm away from the trailer. Of course, I don't keep anything very valuable in there, either.

- STEVEN BAKER, SNOHOMISH, WASHINGTON

SCREEN TEST

Mirror retainer

Window screen

Removing RV window screens for cleaning has always been a hassle for me. Usually, either the plastic retainers broke, or I bent the screen frame trying to maneuver it in and out, or both. It didn't take long before I began to search for a better way.

The solution I came up with is simple, and costs only about 25 cents per window. I bought a supply of plastic mirror retainers used in residential bathrooms, and installed them in place of the unreliable window-screen holders that had been giving me fits.

On my particular RV, there is a bottom channel into which the screen indexes during installation. The rest of the screen perimeter, however, used to fit unrestrained into a recessed opening (once the old brackets failed).

It was near the top of this latter area that I drilled holes for self-tapping sheet-metal screws, which I used to secure my new screen retaining brackets. This done, I found that screen removal and installation could be accomplished with minimal effort and no damage. All I do is rotate the mirror grippers a half turn, and out pop the screens.

- B.R. WITT, ARLINGTON, TEXAS

BREATHING EASIER

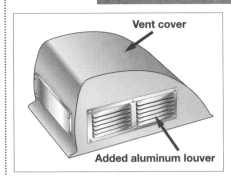

Vent cover

Added aluminum louver

To increase the ventilation of my RV's weather-resistant vent covers, I added a residential-style aluminum vent, available at most hardware stores. I had to cut the new louver down to size before laying it in place on the vent cover and then tracing around it. With this done, I drew another line ½-inch inside the first, drilled ¼-inch holes in each corner of this line, and used my saber saw to make the cutout in the plastic vent cover.

Next, I drilled ⅛-inch holes where needed in the louver and vent cover. Before pop-riveting the louver in place, I ran a bead of sealer around both sides and top. I left the bottom unsealed. This modification more than doubled the available ventilation.

- ROBERT TRUMBAUER, ALLENTOWN, PENNSYLVANIA

HINGE HELP

After a few years of use, the entry and screen doors on my RV may start to sag. This is often caused by wear on the unlubricated aluminum hinges. Of course, applying extra weight by applying pressure on these doors when entering or exiting accelerates such wear. When this happens, not only will closing effort increase, but the gap

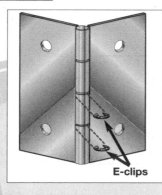

E-clips

at the top of the doors will increase to a point that the weatherstrip may no longer keep insects out of your rig.

I removed the excessive play at the hinges of my RV door by raising the door and then installing a ⁵⁄₁₆-inch E-clip in the resulting gap between the hinge members. These clips are available at many hardware or automotive stores. As I experimented, I found that either ¼- or ⁵⁄₁₆-inch E-clips would work, but I chose the latter because of the increased bearing surface. The size depends upon the diameter of the hinge shaft, but I suspect that most RVs are pretty much standardized in this respect. You can gauge the shaft diameter by holding a ruler next to the hinge and viewing through to the shaft.

For less than $1 worth of E-clips, I was able to fix my rig's sagging entry door. The only alternative I came up with was to replace the worn hinges at a much greater cost. Of course, the best remedy is to occasionally lubricate the hinges with light oil, and avoid putting excessive weight on the doors in the first place. The latter is difficult, however, with grandchildren aboard.

- HARLEY E. MAY, CINCINNATI, OHIO

MEASURE UP

After pulling our trailer over rough or winding roads, we used to find one or more of the kitchen drawers had rolled open. This creates an extremely heavy load on the drawer glide support, which will break it in a very short time.

We solved the problem by simply sliding a wood yardstick vertically through the drawer handles prior to pulling away (on particularly rough roads, add a bungee cord). The drawers stay closed because the ones that hold well keep the others in place. Plus, we've found it very handy having a measuring stick readily available.

- J. SANDSMARK, SEATTLE, WASHINGTON

"GLASS" DOOR SCREEN DOOR

¼-inch Plexiglas

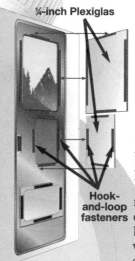

Hook-and-loop fasteners

I came up with an easy way to turn my screen door into a glass door, letting in light and giving great visibility to the outside, while keeping in cool or heated air. Each section of our screen door (ours had three) was measured so that we could have our local lumberyard cut exact-fitting pieces of ¼-inch Plexiglas.

Hook-and-loop fastener material was used around the edges of the door and the Plexiglas. The center section was installed on the outside of the door, to accommodate the sliding door that provides access to the door latch. The panels install in minutes, and can be easily removed for storage under a mattress or an outside compartment.

- EDITH EARNHEART, DALLAS, TEXAS

BATTLE OF THE BULGE

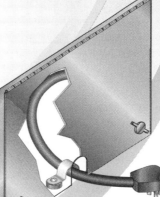

I had a problem with my RV electrical cord pressing against the plastic storage-compartment door when the line was extended for use. This warped the door, allowing water to enter. It also left a permanent bulge, which prevented a tight seal even after the electrical cord was stowed inside.

I decided on a fix that would support the cord where it exits the opening in the access door. To do this, I installed a ¹⁄₂₀-inch EMT electrical clamp to grip the heavy electrical line. To match the opening in the door frame, however, it was necessary to elevate the clamp slightly with a spacer. A ½-inch bushing worked nicely.

The clamp was secured to the RV floor with a sheet-metal screw, but not fully tightened. This allows me to easily remove the electrical cord and coil it for storage. When in place, the clamp keeps the cord securely centered at the door opening and prevents it from damaging the door.

- HOWARD R. EDWARDS, RUFFSDALE, PENNSYLVANIA

ELECTRICAL CORD ARMOR

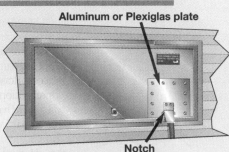

Aluminum or Plexiglas plate

Notch

The opening in the compartment door that allows the power cord to be used while the door is closed is usually provided with a plastic section that swings away. This access plate can break easily. And even when it does work, it makes cord-handling awkward and time-consuming, especially when it comes time to adjust the cord length or when opening the compartment door to access other items. I improved my system by cutting a notch in the lower part of the door and installing aluminum plates (you can also make them with Plexiglas), cut by hand, on each side of the door. They can also be painted to match the RV. A small latch removed from an old toolbox was then attached.

- BUDDY HINCKE, NORTH BEND, OREGON

FREE-FLOWING AND FILTERED

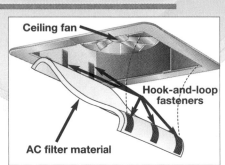

Ceiling fan

Hook-and-loop fasteners

AC filter material

Even the best-insulated coach or trailer can feel like an oven after baking in the strong sun. These super-high temperatures create a number of problems, drying out the wood and deteriorating plastics. It often becomes necessary to leave the roof vents open. It's also advisable to open a small non-access window to create some airflow through the interior. Trouble is, blowing dust and dirt also flows through the interior, leaving an unwelcome film of dust on everything. My solution was to get some air-conditioner filter material and cut it to the size of the vent trim. Since the average vent opening is about 14 inches, the material should be trimmed at least an inch wider. Next, cut some hook-and-loop tape into squares. Since the filter material doesn't have much surface for the adhesive to cling to, I cut some small cardboard squares and stapled one to each corner of the filter, with the cardboard acting as a minibacking. Line up the new filter with the vent and press each square to the trim so the backing sticks to the vent trim. Now, the heat can escape, but the dust and dirt will be filtered out. The small window can be treated in the same manner.

- PHIL WILLEN, WOODLAND HILLS, CALIFORNIA

CLAUSTROPHOBIC CLEVERNESS

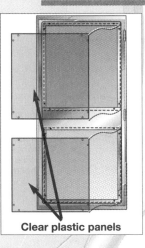

Clear plastic panels

Since most of our RVing is done in the summer and fall, the roof-mounted air conditioner gets used almost daily. This used to mean leaving the entry door closed—a condition that can turn almost anyone claustrophobic on bright, sunny days.

To remedy this, I have added clear plastic panels to the screen door. This allows the outside door to remain open, while still keeping conditioned air inside. This same modification works equally well in cooler weather when heat is necessary. The increased brightness affords a feeling of openness, and generally makes the trailer a lot cheerier. After converting my own family trailer, as well as three others, I have found that ³⁄₁₆-inch clear acrylic or Lexan works the best. The plastic is easy to work with, and cuts nicely on a table saw equipped with a plywood-cutting blade. For ease of installation, be sure to allow a ⅛-inch clearance on all sides when measuring screen openings to determine panel dimensions. After drilling slightly oversize mounting holes, I retain the plastic panels with 6 × ½-inch sheet-metal screws (approximately eight screws per panel).

Although this mounting method allows for removal and easy cleaning, in my case, I eliminated the screen material altogether and opted to leave the finished panels permanently in place.

- PETE MANAUT, RIDGEFIELD PARK, NEW JERSEY

AIRING IT OUT

Hook-and-eye latch

Bathroom door

Even when my RV is closed up for storage, I want to let air flow through without restriction—this prevents condensation, and of course, defeats mildew. When I left the doors to the bathroom open, I always returned to find them closed. I tried a variety of ways to hold them open, but the methods either didn't work or were too much trouble. The answer was to add an inexpensive hook-and-eye latch to each door, with the hook on the inside of the door and the eye on the outside frame. This holds the door open a few inches. To keep the hook from rattling when not in use, I added another eye on the inside of the door, to secure the hook.

- CHRIS CASWELL, LOS ALAMITOS, CALIFORNIA

MIFFED MOUSE

An RV with its power-supply cord dangling to the ground from the open slot in the utility-access door is mouse heaven. Stuffing the hold with cloth or hanging a plastic or metal can lid over the wire doesn't seem to do much good. After recently playing host to an unwanted mouse aboard my new RV, I decided to find a way to stop the little devils.

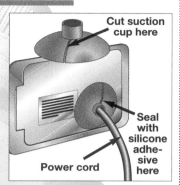

Cut suction cup here

Seal with silicone adhesive here

Power cord

I purchased an outboard motor flushing attachment from Wal-Mart (also available at Kmart and elsewhere). This is a wishbone-shaped gadget equipped with a garden hose inlet and two large suction-cup-like attachments.

I pulled off one of the cups and reamed the existing hole just enough so it would fit snugly around my rig's power cord. The next step was to cut through the cup from the outer rim to the center hole, so it could be installed over the cord. I sealed the cut in the cup with RTV silicone adhesive. During this phase, I was careful to avoid getting any adhesive on the cord. Once the sealant has set, the cut can be moved up and down the cord to the desired place and pushed snugly against the access door. This will completely cover the cord opening, frustrating the furry little freeloaders. The cup is small, effective, and unobtrusive, and stays on the cord ready for use.

One outboard motor flushing attachment has two cups, enough for two power-cord guards. This means you can share your creation with a friend.

- JoAnne Scarpellini, High Ridge, Missouri

FROSTY PANES

I had to do a little problem solving in the decorating department in our 1984 Pinnacle 27-foot motorhome a while ago. I never liked the curtain on the door to our unit, and when the material became faded and worn, I was only too glad to toss it...curtain rods and all. But then there was the matter of privacy. I finally thought of using some frosted-privacy-screen contact paper. You just cut it to fit, and press it right onto the inside of the window glass. It is a translucent, but not transparent plastic. Most larger hardware stores and assorted specialty outlets sell this product. Some mail-order catalogs also feature similar materials.

- Paula Hassler, Phoenix, Arizona

NO MORE MICE

Mice in RVs are no small problem. I think the easiest rodent entry is the electrical cord through the electric access door. My method of prevention was to make a 3 × 3-inch card of $\frac{1}{16}$-inch fiberboard with a hole in the center the size of the power cord. Here's how to do it:

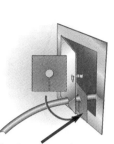

Fiberboard card

Cut one side to the center, so it slides over the cord. After sliding the card onto the cord, push the card inside the electric access door with part of the card pinched in the bottom of the door to hold it in place, and lock the door. If the TV cord goes into the same compartment, a second hole can be cut in the card the same size as the TV cord.

We have used this method for over 15 years, and it seems to work.

- John Brannen, Boise, Idaho

BLIND FRUSTRATION

Hook-and-loop strips

One of the little annoying problems in RVing today is having to regularly replace the small plastic miniblind brackets that snap into metal hold-down clips. Sooner or later, these brackets always seem to get broken, sometimes resulting in minor personal injury to the operator.

My solution was to use self-adhesive hook-and-loop fastener tape. I wrapped a length of the hook side abound the bottom blind bar, about 2 inches from each end, as indicated (don't affix to the slat). Next, I lowered the blind and stuck about 2 inches of the loop side to the wall, so it corresponds to the piece on the blind. When the blind is lowered during use, I gently push the bottom bar against the wall, so the hook-and-loop material mates. This holds the blinds securely over the roughest roads. Self-adhesive hook-and-loop tape comes in various colors, and can be purchased from a fabric or hardware store to match, or complement, any decor. The tape should never need replacement, and it won't snag surrounding curtains. Before installing the hook-and-loop tape, clean the mounting areas thoroughly with rubbing alcohol and a clean, lint-free cloth to remove traces of wax, oil, etc.

- Norm Westfall, Rosedale, British Columbia, Canada & Don LeBlanc, Mississauga, Ontario, Canada

COMPLEX ACCESS

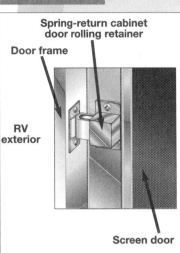

Spring-return cabinet
door rolling retainer

Door frame

RV
exterior

Screen door

My wife and I quickly became annoyed by the steps required to open and close the screen door on our travel trailer. First, the cover plate had to be slid away from the screen-door latch, the latch pulled, and then the cover pushed back into place. Explaining this procedure to our guests was even more annoying. I was able to dispatch our frustrations for only $1.59 and 10 minutes of my time.

I purchased a spring-return cabinet-door rolling retainer at my local hardware store and installed it on our trailer's screen door. I had to move the screen latch outward approximately ¼ inch to accommodate this modification, in order to prevent the latch from catching and holding the screen door shut. The only tools required for the task are a screwdriver and a small drill.

Now, when we enter or exit the rig, we need only give the screen door a slight push to latch it securely. The system works so naturally, guests don't even ask how to open the door anymore.

- R. D. Parpart II, Hobart, Indiana

MULTIFUNCTION STORAGE DOOR

Hinged doors are satisfactory in many situations, but if you want to arrange items stored under a seat, for instance, it may be easier to lift the door completely away, so you can reach inside without obstruction. You might even use the removed door as a tray or working surface.

In some cases, the cabinet surface and door might be constructed of solid wood or thick plywood. My under-bunk panels were thin plywood on strip framing. Therefore, I made a heavier door with similar-grain plywood, and installed a thickening strip along the bottom edge. There could have been a handle made near the top edge, but I preferred no projection, so instead I provided a gap for a finger hold.

The bottom edge of the new door is indexed and held in place by two metal dowels. These were made by driving screws (8-gauge is suitable), and cutting off the heads. The top of the door closes against pieces put across the inside corners of the storage opening.

Instead of using a metal or plastic fastener to hold the door in place, I made a gravity latch of hardwood, which swings easily on a screw and hangs down automatically in the closed position when left alone.

- Percy W. Blandford, Warwickshire, England

WARM AND COZY

*D*on't let the winter chill come through your RV windows. A shrink storm-window film may be the inexpensive solution to your problem.

Look for the product in display boxes at your hardware or building-supply store. The film is sold in kit form, each containing one 44 x 66-inch piece with 225 inches of double-stick tape. We purchased four kits to cover the windows in our 30-foot rig. With this amount, we were able to cover two large picture windows, in addition to six smaller windows. Extra tape is available, so you can reuse the shrink film next winter.

The first step to installing the film is to remove protruding window cranks. Don't worry if the remaining stem isn't flush with the frame.

The film is tough and will mold around these without breaking.

When you spread out the window film, be generous and allow at least a 2-inch border. It's easier to remove the top section of tape-backing paper first, adjust the shrink film, and then do the bottom section while pulling it taut. Next, adjust the side.

Using a hair dryer on its hottest setting, heat the middle of each window film and work out the wrinkles toward the top, bottom, and sides.

Trim away any excess film around the window's edge.

You will be amazed at how much warmer your RV can be in the wintertime with these clear, lightweight storm windows installed.

- Raye Swanson, Clarkston, Washington

FIX THAT FLAPPIN' DOOR

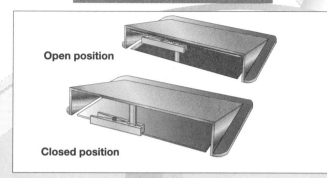

Open position

Closed position

How many times have you been awakened by the annoying noise created by the outside stove-exhaust-vent door flapping in the breeze? Well, I finally got tired of listening to that squeaky slapping and came up with a surprisingly easy fix. To hold the "flapper door" in the open position, simply open the door manually and place a clothespin on the metal support bar in front of the vent. Slide it up firmly against the door, and it will be held open without the annoying noise. To close the vent door for travel, reverse the procedure. Close the vent door and place the clothespin firmly against the door at the base of the vent.
- *JIM AND IVY SANDSMARK, NEWCASTLE, WASHINGTON*

MORE MOUSY MADNESS

*H*ere's another method we've found useful for keeping little rodents out of your coach. After being parked for an extended period of time, we discovered droppings everywhere, although we had closed off everything possible. It seems the critters had climbed up the electrical cord, and had chewed through the small spot where the cord entered to get into our trailer. After exterminating them (no small matter), we decided to prevent it from happening again.

We purchased a large, plastic funnel, cut off the narrow portion, and ran the electrical cord through it, including the plug, in the inverted position. Then, we reattached the narrow end by using hook-and-loop fasteners along the portion joining the funnel, and along the slit made to squeeze in around the cord.

Now, we can take the funnel barrier apart each time we move and use it again and again. It seems to be working; no unwanted guests have left any personal belongings. The cost is just a couple dollars, but it works like a million!
- *DICK KNOTH, WHITEHALL, MICHIGAN*

DIFFICULT DAMPER

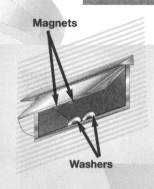

Magnets

Washers

Many RV range vent-hood outlets use external damper controls, which are very inconvenient. I solved the problem by using two small ⅔-inch flat washers, two 12-inch square magnets, and epoxy glue. These items can be purchased at any hardware store. In fact, "forget-me-not" refrigerator door magnets may suffice.

Using the epoxy, attach the washers to the inside center of the vent-hood outlet frame. Be sure the top half of the washers extend above the edge of the vent frame, so the magnets can make contact. Next, glue the magnets to the inside of the vent hood, opposite the washers.

The strength of the magnet is critical. It should be strong enough to prevent gusty winds from opening the damper. On the other hand, the magnetic field must be weak enough to allow the vent-hood motor to open up the damper on high speed. Start the fan on high; after the vent opens, any speed will hold it open.

Selection of the right magnet is the secret to success of this little enhancement. Depending on the velocity of your vent-hood blower, it may be necessary to experiment with various sizes of magnets to achieve the proper results.
- *ALTON OFFILL, MILES, TEXAS*

DOUBLE JOINTED

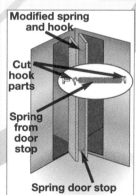

Modified spring and hook

Cut hook parts

Spring from door stop

Spring door stop

My wife and I own a 1993 27-foot trailer that has a bedroom door and bathroom door arranged as illustrated. After some thought, we decided that rather than having to open one door, close it, and then open and close the other door, we would hook them both together.

What we forgot was the different swing radius on each door—an oversight that resulted in pulling the threads of the hook out of one door the first time it was tried. After additional thought, we came up with an idea that has worked well for us.

We purchased a couple of regular spring-type door stops and modified one as shown. Both doors can now swing freely, because of the flexing action provided by the spring hook. This simple fix has cured a small, but annoying problem.
- *RAY AND MARY FREEL, ASTORIA, OREGON*

THE OPEN-AIR LOOK

We enjoy camping, and like to have the windows and doors of our RV wide open, so we can appreciate the experience. In some regions, however, this is not always comfortable because of high humidity.

For this reason, we took the screen door of our trailer to a local glass company, and had three ⅛-inch Plexiglas panels cut to fit it. These pieces were then installed in the door indentation behind the screen (some RVs have this inset in front of the screen). We used ½-inch foam-insulation tape to seal around the edges of the Plexiglas, and to act as a spacer between it and the screen.

To attach these pieces to the door, metal picture hangers (with the hook flattened) work very well. Be sure, though, to use metal screws to attach these homemade retainers to the metal frame of the screen door. Loosening these slightly allows the Plexiglas to be removed and cleaned.

This project is easy, and makes an inexpensive storm door that does not add a lot of undue weight to the screen door. The best part is you can leave the main door open with either the air conditioner or furnace running, so you can enjoy the outdoors.
- *BRUCE AND DOLORES GRADY, BRENHAM, TEXAS*

POWER WINDOW WINDERS

Our 1989 Holiday Rambler trailer has 10 windows that must be hand-cranked open. All the windows have blinds that are fastened down, and we found it hard to reach through the blinds to open and close the windows. To get around this, I removed the 8-32 × 1-inch slotted-head screws that hold the window handles in place, and replaced them with like-size Allen-head cap screws. I then modified a proper-size ball-socket Allen wrench by removing the "L" end so it would fit in the chuck of my electric screwdriver, and we now have power windows! We keep the screwdriver on a charger at all times, and have had some fun telling fellow campers our trailer is equipped with "power windows."
- *KEN AND SANDY CHRISTIE, UNION, MISSOURI*

CLEANING, PROTECTING

HANG THOSE TOWELS AND CLOTHES

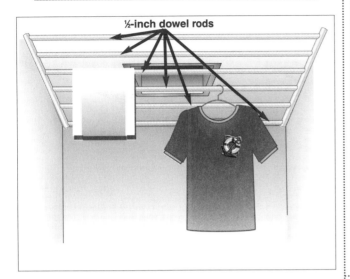

½-inch dowel rods

There are never enough towel racks in an RV, especially when on an extended trip. I made a frame the size of the top of my shower stall out of wood trim scraps, measuring ¾ × ½-inch. I screwed in four ½-inch dowel rods, which extended across the frame, and mounted it using hooks, just below the ceiling in the shower. My rack can be readily taken down since it is not secured permanently. The hang-up area is very useful for swimsuits and the extra towels used when we have guests.
- JIMMIE B. BUTLER, OOLOGAH, OKLAHOMA

MESSY MISTAKE

All of us who do our own vehicle maintenance have, at one time or another, run into the problem of inadvertent oil spills onto an otherwise clean concrete driveway. This happened to me recently with some hydraulic fluid. The liquid soaked in quickly, leaving an ugly stain.

I tried every chemical I had around the home. In desperation, I went into the laundry room and borrowed my wife's Spray 'n Wash stain remover. I sprayed the foamlike substance directly onto the concrete stain, covering it well. After waiting about half an hour, I rinsed the spot with a garden hose and a high-pressure nozzle, making sure I gave it a good wash-down. Once the concrete had dried, it looked like new. I now keep my own can of Spray 'n Wash in the garage for future inevitable emergencies.
- ERIC GREENE, DURANGO, COLORADO

FLEABAG HOTEL

Troubled with fleas in your RV that have attached themselves to your four-footed little friend? If so, here's an inexpensive, but safe, simple, and effective way of removing them from your carpet.

Using a shaker with large holes, just sprinkle some diatomaceous earth on the carpet and rub it in by hand, or with a broom. It won't show, but makes quick work of the flea problem; it also prevents flea eggs from hatching. I normally leave the earth in the carpet for about two weeks before vacuuming. Diatomaceous earth can be found wherever garden or swimming-pool supplies are sold; it's used in swimming-pool filters.
- JESSIE SEAVEY, TUOLUMNE, CALIFORNIA

NO MORE FRIDGE ODOR

When you return from an outing, defrost your refrigerator and wipe it dry. Place a section of newspaper on each shelf, including the freezer. Close the doors until your next trip. Remove the newspaper before cooling the refrigerator down. No more odor!
- DALE CARSON, BAKERSFIELD, CALIFORNIA

PROTECTING THAT PIGTAIL

Most travel trailers have a stone shield covering the front window. In order to reduce weather-related problems on the electrical connections in the pigtail connector between the trailer and the tow vehicle, I unhook one side of the stone shield, opening a space at the bottom just large enough to allow the insertion of the pigtail connector between the window and the stone shield, then rehook the shield. This keeps the plug out of the weather, involves no wrapping of the pigtail for storage, and can be done in about 30 seconds or less.
- L. N. PURCELL, PROSPECT HEIGHTS, ILLINOIS

CLOSEUPS • CLOSEUPS • CLOSEUPS

SEE-THROUGH SUGGESTION

With all the high-tech, innovative ideas, there still isn't a frost-free gas/electric RV refrigerator. Defrosting is still a periodic maintenance chore, but I have found a way to make it a lot faster and easier.

After cleaning the freezer section, I spray Pam (or any other cooking spray) through the freezer unit. Next, I line the walls with a suitable plastic wrap that's used for food storage.

When the ice and frost build up again, I turn the refrigerator off and wait 30 to 60 minutes before removing the food from the freezer compartment. This done, it's a simple job to peel away the plastic wrap, along with the unwanted ice.

- DESIREE PRITCHETT, SWEET WATER, ALABAMA

OAK TOP PROTECTORS

Try protecting your great-looking oak tables with Plexiglas. Using a piece of cardboard, outline the size of your table. Go to a glass store, and have them cut a piece of ¼-inch-thick Plexiglas to size. Attach clear plastic pads at each corner and in the center for additional support. These pads allow the wood to breathe, and are available at Camping World or hardware stores.

- DIANE SEARS, LIVINGSTON, TEXAS

YOUTHFUL APPEARANCES

To remove the dulling film from kitchen and bathroom sinks that seems to defy all other means, just rub fixtures with a baby-oil-soaked wad of cotton. The fixtures instantly become bright and shiny.

To make stainless-steel sinks look like new again, simply apply the oil in the same direction as the grain in the metal.

- DOLORES PHILIPP, LA PINE, OREGON

DRIP TIP

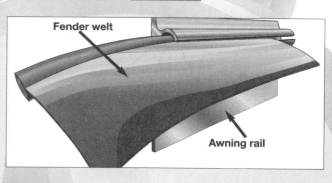

Fender welt

Awning rail

Two years ago, I bought a new travel trailer. For the 1½ years of ownership, exterior-staining black streaks caused by normal rain runoff was a terrible problem. The only place that did not streak badly was just below where the awning mounts to the trailer. Here the awning-attachment rail channeled the water to each end of the rig.

After months of trying to think of something that would act as a rain gutter on the streetside of my trailer, I struck upon an idea that makes good use of the existing awning rail. I found that automotive fender welt worked for me, so I ordered a batch from the J. C. Whitney catalog, part no. 13-3219y; (312) 431-6102. This material comes in 25-foot rolls ($6.99 per roll) and 10 different colors. I decided upon basic black.

All that is required for installation is to slice the fender welt into the awning rail, and then cut to length. I used a few drops of RTV silicone adhesive to hold it securely in place.

Now when it rains, the water cascading off the roof of the trailer drips over the fender welt—away from the side of the rig. I still get a few black streaks on occasion, but not nearly as many as before. The ones that do appear are not as severe and are much easier to remove.

- DONALD NEVENGLOSKY, TAMAQUA, PENNSYLVANIA

TACKY RVING

I found a unique way to keep the many trinkets in place that my wife puts on the shelves and counters of our RV. My method eliminates the need to remove and store these various items every time we relocate.

I use a claylike substance called Fun Tack. It's made by DAP, and is available at hobby shops. The material sticks to almost everything, but pulls off without leaving any residue. I use Fun Tak to hold our digital alarm in place, as well as a calendar, small pictures, and other decorative items, when on the road.

- CARL W. NEMECHEK, SALINA, KANSAS

BABY BASICS

Coffee spills occur frequently in our RV. Often, by the time I had a chance to clean up these accidents, the coffee would stain either plastic or wood areas. Upon my return home, I would work—with much elbow grease—at removing these stains.

On my latest trip, my wife included an old container of Baby Wipes. After the first inevitable disaster, I put one of the wipes to the test. Not only did it clean up the spill, it also removed other dried stains.

The Baby Wipes worked so well that I soon found myself cleaning other parts of the RV with them—areas where both automotive and household cleaners had failed.

- MYRON TANNENBAUM, MAMARONECK, NEW YORK

SPARKLING CLEAN

Whenever we've looked at used motorhomes, we've always been turned off by the dull and scratched fiberglass showers, toilets, and plastic sinks. Determined to keep our new home in the best possible condition, we found a way to keep this from happening to our bathroom fixtures.

Monthly, we wax all the surfaces with carnauba automotive wax, which dries very hard. This has not only kept everything new and shiny, it also helps keep the surfaces clean, since the water runs off very quickly. Even though our fiberglass shower is not any more slippery that it was before we began using the wax, we recommend that caution be used whenever you shower after waxing the first time. (Editor's note: The use of a non-slippery shower mat should always be used for additional safety.)

- LEONARD J. LeBLANC, LEWISBURG, TENNESSEE

BUG PROOFING

My wife and I are full-timers in a fifth-wheel trailer. We love the rig, but its expansive frontal area collects bugs at an unbelievable rate. Until recently, one of our setup rituals included washing off the insects after each day on the road. Now, thanks to a bright idea that recently popped into our heads, we are finally free of this chore.

Using a spray bottle, we apply a light coat of baby oil to the front of our RV. This we wipe with a clean cloth to assure complete coverage, taking care to avoid getting the view-obscuring oil on the front window.

After a few days of travel and bug-building, a quick rinse with a hose is all it takes to remove the grime; no more hard rubbing. Of course, the washing process also removes most of the baby oil. Though this requires reapplication, a couple of minutes for this purpose is a relative snap compared to the old way.

(Use caution around striping that is frayed or peeling, as lotion can dissolve any adhesive exposed to the baby oil.)

- LORIE AND JOE DiNICOLA, NORTH FORT MYERS, FLORIDA

A CLOSE SHAVE ABOVE

Our RV has the same fabric ceiling used in many RVs, and we have noticed that lint and fuzz tend to collect on it, especially in the kitchen and bathroom areas. While it can be cleaned, usually all that is needed to make the ceiling look fresh and new is to remove the "fuzzies." A cordless, hand-held fabric groomer removes surface fuzz and lint. Designed originally to remove "pills" (small balls of fuzz) from sweaters and other garments, these battery-operated clothes shavers usually can be purchased for $10 or less at drug, discount, and variety stores, or through catalogs. Best of all, they take very little storage space.

- KAY KENNEDY, PAHRUMP, NEVADA

A CHALLENGE DEFINED

*M*y husband and I bought an old travel trailer that had been sitting in a field for 15 years. It was indescribably soiled, stained, dusty, and dirty. It needed a cleaning from top to bottom, so I decided to mix up a solution passed down to me by my mother; I've never found another solution that works as well. Our RV shines like it was brand-new.

Here's my recipe: Mix 1 gallon of warm water with 1 cup of ammonia; add ½ cup of white vinegar and ¼ cup of baking soda. Stir well to dissolve the soda. The vinegar helps weaken the eye-watering effect of the ammonia. Of course, customary precautions should be taken when using any solution containing ammonia (adequate ventilation, gloves, etc.).

Although I have always found ammonia good for cleaning windows, nothing is quite as effective for shining windows and mirrors as rubbing alcohol. It is inexpensive and a real wonder when it comes to keeping polished steel faucets and other shiny objects spotless. I keep a spray bottle of alcohol in my bathrooms, my home kitchen, and my travel trailer.

-BONNIE BLUNK, GRAND JUNCTION, COLORADO

TOOLS

TOOLS

NOZZLE OF MANY USES

You can eliminate many water-hose connecting, disconnecting, and storage messes by using a threaded-nose, hand-held water gun. These common spray nozzles can be found in almost any hardware store or garden center. The benefits include:

- An easy way to control water flow after the faucet is opened.
- Allows easy temporary use of hose and nozzle for other purposes.
- Angle of gun prevents kinks in water hose and limits pressure on city water inlet. Note: It will limit flow volume, but not ultimate pressure when water is not flowing.
- Before hooking up, connect hose to faucet, install nozzle permanently on other end of hose. Turn water on and flush hose by aiming at bushes or grass, etc. It can even be used at this time to clean your windshield.
- Screw nozzle onto RV city water inlet, squeeze handle and release hasp, release handle and unscrew handle from connection.
- When leaving camp, disconnect nozzle, turn off faucet, squeeze handle and lock nozzle open with hasp to relieve water pressure, disconnect hose from faucet and drain it while coiling for storage. Release hasp and connect other end of hose to the nozzle to prevent any water from leaking into the storage compartment.
- Robert Wilbur, Westport, Massachusetts -

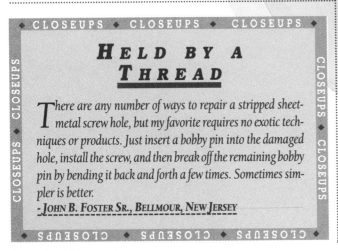

TACKLING DISORGANIZATION

On the very first RV outing with my family, I noticed that we needed a good tool kit and spare-parts supply. At the same time, I reasoned that a good way to keep all such items organized would be a fishing-tackle box. The model that I selected has four partitioned shelves for holding all types of small items, such as light bulbs, fuses, electrical connectors, hose washers, extra screws, etc. Other larger partitions work perfectly for storing pliers, wire cutters, screwdrivers, and so on. The big bottom compartment holds a hammer, a saw, and a socket set. It sure is convenient to grab one toolbox and know that everything needed for an RV trip is close at hand. Because tackle boxes come in a myriad of sizes and shapes, it should be easy for other RVers to find one that suits their specific needs.
- Jerome T. Gajdosik, St. Louis, Missouri

ELECTRICAL TEST BUZZER

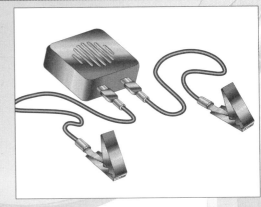

Here's a little tip I would like to share with our readers. Checking wiring (such as a brakelight terminal in a trailer connector) with a conventional test light often requires a second person. Faced with inoperative lights and no helper, I rigged a 12-volt DC buzzer with short wires and alligator clips. These parts are readily available at electronics stores such as Radio Shack. With this tester connected, you can tell if a circuit is "live" as soon as the power is turned on, without running back and forth from the cab or stacking bricks on the brake pedal.
- Ken Freund, Technical Editor

SCISSOR ACTION

To save money, I went to an automotive junkyard and purchased four scissor jacks for a total of $40. I welded these in place at each corner on my trailer frame. Next, I went to a pawn shop and bought a ¾-inch socket and speed handle for $3.

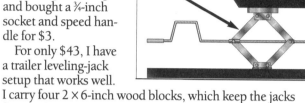

Automotive scissor jack

For only $43, I have a trailer leveling-jack setup that works well. I carry four 2 × 6-inch wood blocks, which keep the jacks from sinking into soft or wet ground.

- *RAYMOND AGOSTINETTI, SUGARLAND, TEXAS*

FANCY FUNNEL

Those of us who change our own oil know the frustration of putting a funnel into the valve-cover opening, only to have it tip when it is full of oil because it can't drain as fast as we're pouring.

I have found the remedy to this by cutting the top off a plastic motor-oil container and using it as my funnel. The spout is wide enough that you can pour as fast as you like, and is short enough that it doesn't come to rest on anything inside the engine, which could tip it over. The shoulder of the plastic container is wide, adding stability when the spout is inserted into the engine valve-cover opening or the oil-inlet spout. Best of all, the funnel doesn't cost a cent.

- *A. W. WAGNER, CLEVELAND, TEXAS*

A KEY TO THE MATTER

Bend here

Valve key

As I get older, opening the valve on the sewage holding tank of my trailer becomes more and more of a chore. This is mainly because the slide valve handle pulls parallel to the trailer and toward the rear. I'm not able to reach it from the rear of the rig in order to get a straight pull, and I cannot get much leverage on it from the side.

I looked into the leverage approach suggested in "10-Minute Tech" some months back, but wasn't able to use it because of the tank configuration in my trailer. Then, I stumbled onto a solution hanging on the wall of my garage. Many years ago when I first started RVing, I replaced the manual sprinkler valves in my yard with electric models and a timer to handle the watering. One of the items I abandoned was the 30-inch valve key that I used to turn the old-style valves on and off. Now, after 20 years, I could see a way to make it useful again.

Finding the metal very malleable, I placed the key in a vise and bent the key end 90 degrees to the handle. I can now reach the sewage slide-valve handle from the rear of the trailer and give it a good, straight pull. It works perfectly.

If you don't happen to have a two-decades-old sprinkler valve key lying around, they are still readily available at the local hardware store for a couple of bucks.

- *C. HAROLD MATHEWS JR., HIGHLAND, CALIFORNIA*

SHADE-TREE SECRET

When either lack of room or engine heat makes it hard to thread a spark plug into place, try putting a piece of rubber (or vinyl) hose on the end of the plug. When the plug tightens up, the hose slips and then can be easily removed. Finish tightening the spark plug as usual.
- *LARRY TUDOR, NORWALK, CALIFORNIA*

UNIVERSAL CURE

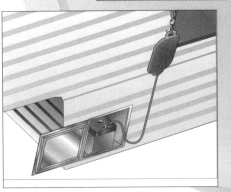

Adding distilled water to the batteries in my fifth-wheel trailer is difficult because they aren't on a slide-out rack. After trying several other methods and spilling water all over the batteries in the process, I finally came up with a convenient solution. I use a hot-water bottle that came with a shut-off clip and nozzle assortment. Using a small mirror in my left hand, I'm able to direct distilled water into each battery cell with precision. The flow is controlled with the shut-off, which I hold in my right hand.

This allows me to service the trailer batteries in just a few minutes. It works for me, and it probably gives the neighbors a good chuckle at the same time.
- *HOWARD HOLLAND, BISHOP, CALIFORNIA*

IMPROVISING

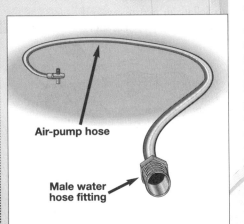

Air-pump hose

Male water hose fitting

Lots of RVers don't have either the luxury or the time to be snowbirds—able to go where a mild climate takes away the worry of RV freeze-ups. For many, the need to winterize is an annual affair.

Using compressed air to blow the on-board water lines clear is one of the tasks involved. But what do you do when compressed air isn't readily available? A suggestion from my son that I use the spare tire from my motorhome to provide the needed pressure answered this question.

To make an adapter, I removed the hose from an old air pump (one from a defunct 12-volt DC air pump would also work), and attached a male water-hose fitting to the end opposite the tire-valve fitting. Such fittings can be obtained at a hardware store, or you could just remove the end from a discarded garden hose.

When using this setup, I first drain the water heater completely. Then, making sure the water-heater drain valve is closed, I attach the air hose to the city-water inlet of my rig. The spare tire is removed from its mounting location and rolled near enough to allow the air hose to be connected.

When this is done, I go inside the motorhome and turn on a faucet. I leave it open until only air flows. I repeat this action at the other faucets aboard the rig.

Editor's note: During the winterizing process, don't forget to clear the on-board water pump and associated lines, the toilet, and shower valves, as well as the water tank and drain traps.
- *TONY BEQUETTE, VANCOUVER, WASHINGTON*

◆ CLOSEUPS ◆ CLOSEUPS ◆ CLOSEUPS ◆ CLOSEUPS ◆ CLOSEUPS ◆ CLOSEUPS ◆

CLEAN COILS

*A*fter reading an article about cleaning refrigerator cooling coils with compressed air, I gave it a try. But, due to the fact that the coils were far up in the cooling chimney of my RV, my air compressor didn't seem to do a very good job. Holding a mirror in the opening, I could see more dirt on the coils.

Deducing the need for more air volume, I pointed the nozzle of my electric leaf-blower up the chimney and turned on the switch. That blast of air cleaned all the debris away from the refrigerator coils almost instantly. Gas-powered leaf-blowers should work just as well.
- *JAMES F. SOUTHWICK, LEMON GROVE, CALIFORNIA*

How Deflating!

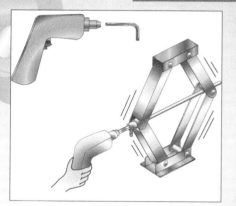

I have a quick way to deflate air mattresses and inner tubes that have conventional Schrader valves. Just cut the hose and adapter off a used aerosol can of tire sealant/inflator, and adapt it to your vacuum-cleaner nozzle.

After installing the adapter on anything with a Schrader valve, turn on the vacuum and deflate the item. It flattens them like a pancake.
- *ROBERT SCHRADER, LAWNDALE, CALIFORNIA*

Simple Solutions

In the January 1992 issue, "10-Minute Tech" featured an item on using an electric drill and modified crank adaptor for raising and lowering a rig's stabilizing jacks. I believe that my method is easier, because there is no need to change either the jacks or the crank.

I just insert a large Allen wrench in the check of my rechargeable drill. The angled part of the wrench will fit into the hole intended for the manual crank. Then, I run the jacks up and down with the drill as necessary.
- *LYNN O. ROBINSON, GRANTS PASS, OREGON*

SPRING TIME

Cleaning the burner tube of an RV water heater is easy with the use of a tightly wound 9 × ¼-inch spring. Just attach a piece of 2 × ½-inch-thick cotton to one end of the spring. It can be either tied or clamped between the coils to hold it in place.

Passing this device through the burner tube of an RV water heater often improves performance, and at the same time, gets rid of unwanted debris, spider webs, etc.
- *B. H. BLACK, MARTINEZ, CALIFORNIA*

A Pointed Reaction

At the end of the camping season last year, the threaded plastic plug in my rig's water heater broke off flush at the tank when I attempted to drain its contents for the winter. The plug was hollow, and broke in a manner that left practically no material on which I could get a grip. Of course, it didn't help matters that the plug was already difficult to access.

After three unsuccessful attempts to remove it, I came up with an idea that may help others in the same predicament. I purchased a piece of ⅛ × ¾-inch steel strap at the hardware store. Then, I ground a shallow taper on one end, so the tip would fit just inside the remains of the drain plug. In my situation, an approximately ¹⁄₃₂ × 6-inch taper was needed.

With this light machining accomplished, I heated the end of the makeshift tool with a propane torch until I could just push the pointed metal into the plastic. I left it there a few minutes to cool.

With this done, the damaged plug was easily unscrewed by using a crescent wrench on the exposed end of the embedded steel strap. The tank threads remained undamaged. This allowed the immediate installation of a new drain plug, one with a solid body and nonstick threads.

Here are a couple of additional hints for other people interested in using this fix. Keep the tool taper as long as possible, and heat the end only until it will barely push into the body of the broken plastic plug. Be careful; it doesn't take much heat. Practice the procedure with the outer end of the broken plug, assuming it was kept. Finally, do not push so hard on the tool that it cuts through the plastic plug and damages the aluminum tank threads.
- *TONY HOWARD, MONROE, WASHINGTON*

A Gripping Alternative

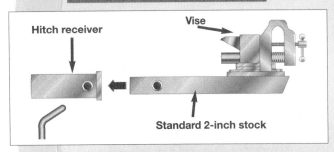

Hitch receiver

Vise

Standard 2-inch stock

Because of the many mechanical tasks I encounter while RVing, I have found it useful to have a heavy-duty vise with me on the road. The problem was how to secure it in the absence of a regular workbench. I solved this dilemma by bolting the vise to a piece of square hitch stock. All I have to do is plug the assembly into the hitch receiver of my tow vehicle. I've used this setup successfully for years.
- *Rees Bryn, Boardman, Ohio*

Getting a Handle on Handles

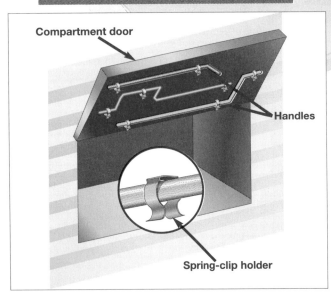

Compartment door

Handles

Spring-clip holder

I have several handles and cranks that are necessary in the setting up of my fifth-wheel trailer. It seems that these handles are always under something or falling on the ground whenever the storage door is open. To solve the problem, I purchased several broom and mop spring-clip holders. I attached them to the inside of my storage compartment door in the configuration of each of the handles. I arranged them so that the weight of the handles is in the down position when the doors are closed. That way, gravity won't pull the handles away from the spring-clip holders.
- *Ron Loen, Livingston, Texas*

Handle the Problem

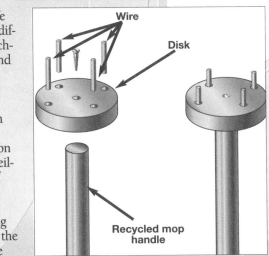

Wire

Disk

Recycled mop handle

My wife had difficulty reaching the hand crank that opens and closes the electric fan roof vent mounted on the high ceiling area of our fifth-wheel. Scrounging around in the garage one day, I came up with some scrap items that I used to construct a "hand-extension" device. She can now operate the vent herself and no longer needs to ask for assistance.

The handle of my little invention was taken from a discarded mop and a 1¾-inch round wood disk, cut from a piece of scrap 1 × 4-inch board. Four holes drilled part-way through the disk serve as receptacles for short lengths of stiff insulated wire, which I appropriated from some large-stemmed artificial flowers we had around the house.

I started by drawing an outline of the hand knob on the wood disk. This helped me determine exactly where to place the holes, so that the wire pieces, when installed, would grip the knob securely. After I drilled the disk and handle, as illustrated, the parts were both glued and screwed together. Now, it's a simple matter for my wife to use her hand-extension to raise and lower the roof vent at will.
- *John F. Koepke, Corpus Christi, Texas*

Clean Sweep

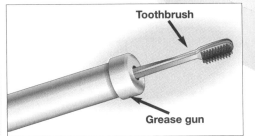

Toothbrush

Grease gun

To avoid the chance of forcing road grime into the great fittings of my truck, I cut down an old toothbrush and wired it firmly to the tip of my grease gun. It only takes a couple seconds to wipe the dirt from each fitting before positioning the gun.
- *George T. Balfe, Tucson, Arizona*

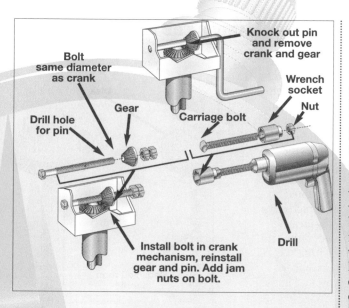

Knock out pin and remove crank and gear

Bolt same diameter as crank

Gear

Drill hole for pin

Carriage bolt

Wrench socket

Nut

Drill

Install bolt in crank mechanism, reinstall gear and pin. Add jam nuts on bolt.

POWER PLAY

Maybe you would like the convenience of a power trailer-tongue jack, but don't want to spend the money for a conversion unit. All you have to do is invest in a ½-inch high-torque electric drill and enough extension cord to reach a 120-volt AC electrical outlet. You'll have to modify the manual crank handle as shown, as well as construct a drill motor adapter, which will be used to engage the tongue jack mechanism.

My trailer has a hitch weight of 900 pounds, and this setup works very well. An additional advantage is that the drill motor can also be used on other projects.
- GEORGE WEIR, AMBOY, ILLINOIS

REALLY WIRED

There are many sheet-metal screws on an RV. However, as a result of the occasional retightening of items secured by these screws (such as the screen door), screw holes can become enlarged.

Sometimes, larger screws won't work because the heads are too large. You can save the day by using a piece of very fine wire, such as that used in metal window screens. Tie an overhand knot in the center of the wire, and place it over the end of the screw. Next, wrap the two wire ends into the grooves of the screw from head to tip. This will provide the needed surface area for the screw to grip when reinstalled.
- M. PELLETIER, SHINGLE SPRINGS, CALIFORNIA

NO MORE WIRE WORRIES

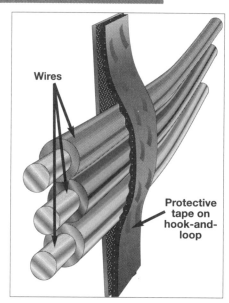

Wires

Protective tape on hook-and-loop

Since purchasing my motorhome, I have added five 12-volt DC light fixtures in various areas to increase my comfort. In areas where the new wiring was visible, I used decorative plastic wire molding. However, inside cabinets and other out-of-the-way places, I discovered another use for that wonderful stick-on hook-and-loop tape. At even intervals, I affixed one side of this material along my new wiring route. Sandwiching the wires together, I have pressed the opposing piece of hook-and-loop tape into place—leaving the protective paper layer where it was.

This method works very well on ceilings, interior cabinet walls, and anywhere else you don't want loose wires floating about.
- ROBERT G. THOMPSON, NEW ROCHELLE, NEW YORK

CRANKY CRANKS

Weld

I used to become very frustrated when trying to open my RV's crank-out windows through permanently installed miniblinds. Tiring of this battle, I finally made a tool especially for this task from a worn-out Phillips screwdriver.

So, I welded together a crossbar assembly having two ½-inch-long lugs, spaced 1½ inches apart (inside measurement). Of course, this dimension may vary with other window types. With this fabrication complete, I welded the crossbar onto the tip of the old screwdriver.

Now, whenever I want to open or close a window, I place the gripper through the miniblinds, onto the crank, and turn as required. This keeps my hands out of the blinds, and minimizes damage to the blinds' fragile slats.
- GERALD MCKENZIE, SEBRING, FLORIDA

CHANGING OIL

In the past,
when I
changed the oil in
my vehicles, I always made
a mess while draining the old oil filter. Finally, I solved the problem by punching holes in an old coffee can and placing it upside down in the drain pan. The can holds the used filter above the waste oil in the pan and allows it to drain thoroughly.

- KEN FREUND, TECHNICAL EDITOR

DRIVING FORCE

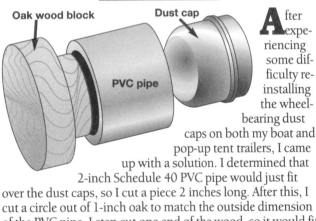

Oak wood block

Dust cap

PVC pipe

After experiencing some difficulty reinstalling the wheel-bearing dust caps on both my boat and pop-up tent trailers, I came up with a solution. I determined that 2-inch Schedule 40 PVC pipe would just fit over the dust caps, so I cut a piece 2 inches long. After this, I cut a circle out of 1-inch oak to match the outside dimension of the PVC pipe. I step cut one end of the wood, so it would fit inside the pipe. Now, by placing the PVC pipe over the dust cap and then fitting the step-cut oak block into the pipe, I am able to drive the cap into place easily. Another advantage is that the large end of the oak circle is perfect for driving home the wheel-bearing grease seals on the opposite side of the brake drums. This homemade tool works so well that three friends with trailers have asked me to make sets for them. All have found this to be a very satisfactory solution to an annoying problem.

Editor's note: Pieces of wood can get into bearings if soft wood is used.

- M. J. WALLIS, KENOSHA, WISCONSIN

FORMIDABLE FAILURE

Hex-head screw nut

Coupling nut

Some time ago, I installed a water-heater bypass kit in my travel trailer to facilitate winterizing. Everything worked fine the first year, but by the time the second season rolled around, I found that the lower water valve would not turn with simple finger pressure.

Unwisely applying pliers to the valve handle, I proceeded to immediately break off the thumb wing. Complicating matters was the remaining tapered valve stem; it was nearly impossible to grip and turn with pliers.

To solve this dilemma, I bought a ⅜-inch coupling nut, drilled and tapped a ¼-inch hole near its end, as illustrated, and inserted a matching ¼-inch hex-head set screw. I slipped the coupling nut over the valve shaft and tightened the set screw securely.

Now, all I have to do to open or close this valve is apply the appropriate wrench or socket. With this fix, others should be able to turn even the most petulant valve. Incidentally, an empty plastic film container is the perfect place to store the adapter until the next time it's needed.

- FRED L. TIMM, MILWAUKEE, WISCONSIN

FLASHLIGHT FRIEND

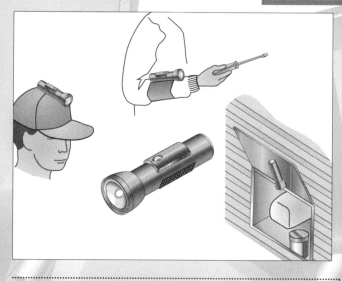

I have found that placing pieces of hook-and-loop fastener on a couple of small flashlights makes them infinitely more usable. The loop portion should be attached to the side of the light, and pieces of the hook portion placed at various convenient sites around the RV.

Choice places inside the RV include the sleeping area, close to the electrical service panel, and immediately inside the entry door where it may be easily reached from the outside.

On the exterior of the rig, place the hook material near the trailer hitch, gas valves, sewer and water hookups, power cord, and wheel wells, inside the bin where the leveling blocks are stored, and in any other location where you might need a light.

From my personal experience, two other valuable sites for the light are on the top of an old baseball cap, and on an elastic elbow supporter. When worn on the forearm, the light will point directly toward your working hands.

- SCOTT STEWART, HAMILTON, MONTANA

FRUSTRATION FIGHTER

When you buy that can of WD-40 or carburetor cleaner, the small plastic tube that is taped to the side always gets lost. To prevent this, drill a small hole through both sides of the cap, and slip the tube through it for storage.

- DON WEGENER, BACKUS, MINNESOTA

◆ CLOSEUPS ◆ CLOSEUPS ◆ CLOSEUPS ◆

ON YOUR KNEES

When it's raining and the area around the RV is muddy, it's difficult to connect the drain hoses, drain the tanks, disconnect them, etc., without getting wet and getting your clothes soiled. One way to solve this problem, somewhat, is to carry garden kneeling pads in the RV. These gardener's pads work well, but be sure to get them in yellow or bright orange so you won't leave them behind after the job is done.

- RALPH T. WELCH, ROSEBURG, OREGON

SOGGY SHIRT SLEEVES

When washing down an RV with a long-handled brush, water runs down the pole, past your hands, and ultimately drips from your elbows. To prevent this uncomfortable circumstance, cut the bottom off a plastic bottle (I used a 1-quart oil container), slip it over the handle about a foot away from the brush, and fasten the neck opening to the handle with electrician's tape. This makes a watertight seal.

Now when I wash my rig, the excess drains back into this container. Each time I dip the brush in the bucket, the accumulation is returned to the wash solution. This little modification has kept my arm dry on many long-handled wash operations.

- STANLEY E. FURMAN, PORT LUDLOW, WASHINGTON

IS YOUR JACK JUST A JOKER?

Hidden away in a dark corner of your RV may be a problem waiting to strike when you least expect it—your rig's chassis jack. The jack supplied with most vehicles is rarely used, but when you need it, it's because other alternatives are not available. Whether you have a flat tire or are mired in mud, the importance of a good jack quickly becomes obvious to the afflicted.

On a recent trip, I stopped to assist a fellow traveler who had experienced a flat tire on his folding camping trailer. He told me that he had bought the rig used, and it had never occurred to him to look for a chassis jack. It didn't have one.

"No problem," I said, as I walked to my RV to get my new hydraulic bottle jack. I had owned it for years, but this was my first opportunity to use it.

After positioning my jack under the wounded camping trailer, I was surprised to find that I could only get about one inch of travel from it. Investigation revealed a leaky seal through which all the oil had escaped.

We managed to change the trailer tire by first unhooking it, and then using wooden blocks under the rear leveling jack while raising the hitch with the tongue-mounted jack. This was a tedious operation, with real possibilities for an accident.

I later refilled my jack with hydraulic oil and tried it out on my 25-foot Pace Arrow. The front wheel lifted with a bit of effort, but despite the 3-ton rating of the jack, it would not raise the dual rear wheels.

This jack was not original equipment. I purchased it when I discovered my rig did not have a jack when I took delivery. I have since acquired a good quality 5-ton hydraulic jack that does the job. The morals to this story are: (1) Make sure you have proper jacks and lug nut wrenches for your vehicle; (2) Check them occasionally to confirm they are serviceable.

- J. C. PRENTICE, BRANDON, MANITOBA, CANADA

THE BLIND TRUTH

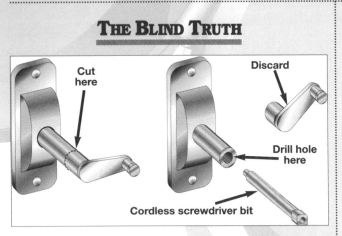

Cut here

Discard

Drill hole here

Cordless screwdriver bit

SECURE FUTURE

RTV silicone sealant

Opening the crank-out windows on RVs that are equipped with window miniblinds is one of those things that will drive a person nutty. The blinds are always in jeopardy of being permanently deformed from this frequent exercise. I decided that a slight modification was in order.

I began by cutting off the window crank handles. Then, I purchased some power screwdriver bits, which I installed in the remaining section of crank at each window. A little bit of glue secures these permanently in place, allowing me to use my rechargeable screwdriver at each modified crank to open and close my rig's windows. No more damaged blinds.

- JOE CHIPLEY, TULLYTOWN, PENNSYLVANIA

It's easy to turn regular nuts and bolts into reliable self-locking versions. Simply put a squirt of RTV silicone sealant around the bolt at the base of the nut. Often, the opening of the tube can be shoved over the bolt and lightly squeezed to produce a professional looking "dab." This will hold until the Big RV Roundup in the Sky.

A major plus to this method is that it prevents the rust and corrosion that often occur when traditional lock washers scratch protective coatings. I've applied RTV silicone to more than 20 nuts and bolts on one job, and it took only about a minute to do them all.

- BILL JOHNSTON, CARY, NORTH CAROLINA

RAT-A-TAT-TAT

Shortly after purchasing my first motorhome, I asked myself how I would change a flat tire if it became necessary. Of course, the coach came with a lug wrench, but it was obvious to me that even with an extension on this tool, I would be hard-pressed to loosen the large, and very often tight, lug nuts.

I considered the various gear-driven wrenches that, according to the advertising, would give me a mechanical advantage. However, about this time, I remembered the electrical power available to me from the on-board generator.

I then looked at industrial-quality electric impact wrenches. Coupled with the proper sockets and a proper-size extension cord, my new toolbox addition proved more than adequate to meet the challenge.

For RV owners who do not have a generator, most inverters should provide sufficient electrical power to run the impact wrench.

- DAVID C. SHEPARDSON, TULSA, OKLAHOMA

FREE LUBE AND OIL

Every time the cabinet door hinges squeaked in our RV, or any of a myriad of mechanical items needed a drop of oil, I always found that I had left my oil can at home. Or, if I hadn't forgotten it, it was lost somewhere in the truck's toolbox. By chance, I discovered the best oiler I've ever had—and it didn't cost me a penny. I simply recycle an empty 1½-fluid-ounce nasal spray bottle. The nozzle is easily removed with a slight sideways push. After a thorough rinsing, I dry it and then refill with my favorite lube (usually engine oil left in the container after I added a quart to my rig's engine). For anything that requires a drop of oil, these bottles work great. I keep several of them handy in the RV, truck, house, boat, and garage. I have also found these spray bottles useful for applying a soapy-water solution to propane joints when checking for leaks. Best of all, they are free (if you have almost-empty nasal-spray bottles stored in your medicine cabinet). Plus, by using them in this manner, you keep yet another piece of plastic out of the landfills for a while.

- FRED HUSON, BAYVIEW, IDAHO

BUNGEE CORDS 'LIGHTEN' THE WORK

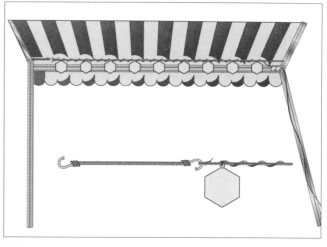

The outdoor string of lights that adds both decorative and useful night illumination can be a real nuisance to put up. Also, the quick removal sometimes necessitated by a sudden windstorm can present a problem. Here is a simple solution using the common bungee cord.

Set up your awning in the usual manner. String the lights across the front of the awning with attention to desired spacing. Temporarily use clothespins to secure the lights to the awning.

Obtain a piece of clothesline long enough to reach from one awning arm to the other. Tie one end of this line to the S-hook of a short bungee cord. Attach the opposite end of the bungee to the existing slot of the awning arm. With your awning extended, this slot faces the ground, and allows the support arm to slide in and out.

Take a second bungee cord of the same length and attach it to the awning arm slot on the opposite side. Pull on the clothesline and the second bungee until both cords are stretched to about half their maximum length. Mark the clothesline, and tie it to the second bungee S-hook. You now have a stretched line that will remain taut between the awning supports.

Leaving the line in place, transfer the lights from the face of the awning to the clothesline. Use electrical tape to hold the light string in place; be sure to tape only to the clothesline, not the bungees. Excess wire can be easily wound around the line and taped in place.

Using this setup couldn't be simpler. Just attach or remove the bungee cord ends from the awning support slots as the situation dictates.

We added one extra convenience by laying an extension cord in the awning arm and securing it so it could be plugged into the outside electrical receptacle of our RV. We wired this outlet to a switch beside our bed, thus allowing us to operate the patio lights from inside.

- TROY HUFFMAN, SHARPSVILLE, PENNSYLVANIA

BOUNTIFUL BUNGEES

Ihave found a very inexpensive and easy way to keep coiled water hoses, tarps, sewer hoses, or whatever under control. I call them mini-bungees. They are lightweight and can be made out of inexpensive, readily available

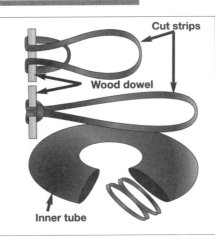

Cut strips

Wood dowel

Inner tube

material. Even better, they require only minimal tools and skill.

First, obtain one car or light-truck inner tube. The size determines the final length of the bungee, so if you need very long samples, you might pick up a semi-truck tire tube.

Cut the inner tube into strips ½- to 1-inch wide.

You'll have to experiment with what works for your needs. When you are finished, you will have what appears to be wide rubber bands.

Next, purchase a ⅜ × 36-inch wood dowel rod from a lumber-supply house. Cut the dowel into 18 2-inch pieces. Attach these to the mini-bungees as illustrated. To use, just wrap the rubber strap around whatever it is you're trying to secure, and loop the open end over the wood piece.

- WAYNE DEVOS, CINCINNATI, OHIO

INTO THE UNKNOWN

*A*bout to embark on a complex RV project requiring much disassembly? Concerned about how to get everything back together again? If so, consider using a video camcorder to photograph things as they were before you started.

You'll not only end up with an instantly available visual record, but as you shoot, you can verbally describe important points such as critical connections, components, and attachments. Replay the tape before you set to work. This way, you'll be assured of getting things correctly back together.

OLD LIGHTERS NEVER DIE

*D*on't throw away that empty disposable butane lighter (such as the Olympian Disposable Gas Match 5) just because it's out of fuel. The electronic spark lighters on these extended-tip gas "matches" will last for many more operations and are ideal for lighting the propane-stove burners aboard most RVs. Keep one handy in the cutlery drawer next to the stove. To distinguish this lighter from others that still have fuel, simply wrap a band of electrical tape around its base.

- KEITH BERTRAM, ESSEX, ONTARIO, CANADA

A LIGHT GRIP

*T*he other day, my husband and I were trying to replace one of the tiny light bulbs in our RV. We tried and tried, but because of the small access opening common to RV light fixtures, we just couldn't get enough of a finger-hold on the bulb to turn it.

Sometimes, the sockets and the bases become corroded, and forcing them will break the glass and cut your fingers. We decided that we needed something to grab the tiny bulb, so I bought a package of suction-cup window hooks—the type used to display small window decorations. I stuck the suction cup to the bulb, turned it, and out it came! Installation of the replacement bulb was just as easy.

- LOUISE MATHER, SOUTH WINDSOR, CONNECTICUT

HAIR-DRYER HOORAY

*C*arrying a hair dryer on our RV trips has saved my wife and me both time and money. Among other applications, we have used it to thaw out our freshwater hose when it had frozen solid one night, as well as to dry out rain-soaked items. A high-output hair dryer is a good piece of equipment to carry on any RV trip.

Editor's note: Be certain the hair dryer is plugged into an outlet protected by a ground fault circuit interrupter (GFCI).

- WADE BARBER, ANDALUSIA, ALABAMA

JUNK-BOX RESCUE

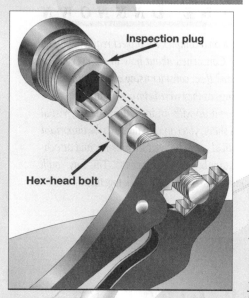

Inspection plug

Hex-head bolt

I do all my own oil changing and greasing on my 1990 GMC pickup with a standard transmission. The first time I tried to check the transmission-oil level, I discovered that I needed a large Allen wrench, which I did not have. I checked my junk box and found a 7/16-inch hex-head bolt that fit the plug perfectly.

Inserting the bolt head into the inspection plug, I used a pipe wrench to grip the bolt and remove the plug. Vice grips should also work.

This tip can save the day during a roadside breakdown. Of course, it will work with Allen plugs of other sizes too.
- *ORVILLE R. PALLETTE, SACRAMENTO, CALIFORNIA*

GASKET GIMMICK

I'm tired of water leaks. Before placing two surfaces together that require a sealing bead—for example, a rooftop vent, or an exterior door frame—you may want to try the following:

1. Place a ribbon of sealer around the opening.

2. Press in a 1/8-inch-diameter sash cord close to where the mounting screws will be installed.

3. Form the sealer around the cord until it is completely covered.

4. Join the surfaces, tightening the mounting screws around the flange with an even pressure.

The cord will keep the two surfaces apart sufficiently to assure a constant gasket thickness, and it will prevent breaking or distorting of the mounting flange.

A fishing line can be used in place of the sash cord for some applications. The heavier the line, the thicker the gasket.
- *BARRY MOFFATT, COSTA MESA, CALIFORNIA*

A 'SHORT' STORY

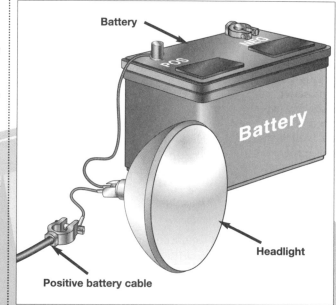

Battery

POS

NEG

Battery

Headlight

Positive battery cable

If you've ever installed a 12-volt DC accessory in your RV or automobile, you've also experienced momentary anxiety when you reconnected the battery terminals. Was everything wired correctly? Are there any unseen electrical shorts? Likewise, if your work was diagnostic and required leaving the circuit hot, you've probably seen the results of unintentional grounding—sparks everywhere, or so it seemed at that moment.

But there's a simple way to eliminate such worries in the future. Just connect a sealed beam headlight (rated for 12 volts DC) in-line between the positive battery post and the temporarily removed positive battery cable. Polarity isn't important, because the bulb will work regardless of hookup method.

This procedure will keep the 12-volt DC circuits active, so that accessory installation and testing can proceed. However, a more important benefit is that massive surges of current will be prevented, should you accidentally create a dead short in the system.

Instead of dangerously overheated or burned wiring, or perhaps injury to yourself, the only result of your indiscretion will be a glowing headlight. With the headlight in place, the bulb filament serves to protect the electrical system through its inherent resistance. This gives you an opportunity to realize that a wiring error has occurred, and a chance to locate and correct it before reconnecting the positive battery cable to its terminal.

Some people might suggest that, given the above scenario, an inexplicable electrical horror will occur during a dead short. Most disbelievers submit that the headlight will explode. However, I remind these folks that one can wire a 12-volt DC headlight directly across the terminal of a 12-volt battery and see only one result—a glowing headlight.
- *RICHARD MATER, SANTA MARIA, CALIFORNIA*

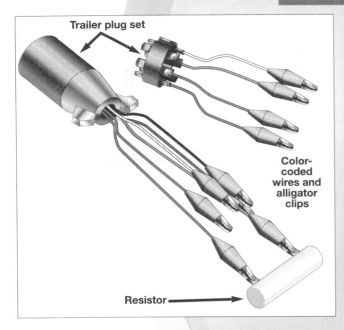

Trailer plug set

Color-coded wires and alligator clips

Resistor →

Ihave found this simple idea to be a great time-saver. My circuit checker makes it easy to check out the electrical system of both the trailer and the tow vehicle prior to hookup.

Start by obtaining a complete trailer electrical plug (male and female ends) to match the type on your trailer. Attach flexible wire leads and small alligator clips to each functional circuit pin (i.e., brakes, turn signals, stop lights, clearance lights, etc.). I used different color leads to help avoid confusion.

Install a bare terminal end on the hot battery terminal. This will be used to supply power to the individual circuits during testing. You needn't connect a lead to the ground pin, as this will remain unused during testing.

To make identification of each circuit easy, I applied labels adjacent to each terminal and painted the indexing keyway to ensure proper connector line-up.

During use, connect the leads from the various circuits, one at a time, to the power plug. Leave the alligator clip in place, and walk around the rig to verify that all lights are working.

To test the trailer brakes, I suggest making an "extension cord" with 18-gauge lamp wiring, two alligator clips, and a momentary-on switch at one end. This wiring should be long enough to reach to each trailer wheel. Connect the clips to the power lug and the brake circuit at the connector plug. Jack up each wheel one at a time, spin the tire, and push the switch. Braking action should be instantaneous.

The success of this assembly prompted me to construct a similar unit that plugs into the two-vehicle electrical receptacle. I used longer leads to allow easy connection to a voltmeter. This identifies circuits with incorrect values, i.e., high resistance. The tow vehicle brake circuit can be checked under load with the use of a wire-wound resistor (6 ohms at 25-watt capacity) connected to the brake lead and the vehicle's ground lead.

This inexpensive test has saved me much annoyance when something in the electrical realm goes haywire just before a big RV outing.
- *William F. Alexander, Newtown, Pennsylvania*

CLOSEUPS • CLOSEUPS • CLOSEUPS

DOWN TO THE NITTY GRITTY

*I*am sure that nearly everyone who has used a screwdriver has, at one time or another, experienced the sinking feeling that occurs when the tool turns, but the screw in question does not. Phillips head screws seem to be the worst culprits.

One way to increase your odds of success—by as much as 50 percent—is to first dip the screwdriver tip in valve-grinding compound. The grit in the compound will help the screwdriver bite into the screw head, aiding immensely in the removal of a stubborn fastener.

Valve-grinding compound is readily available at most automotive-supply stores. A 1½-ounce tube will likely cost you less than $1, and for this type of application, will probably last a lifetime.
- *R. Blattenberger, Mount Holly, New Jersey*

CLOSEUPS • CLOSEUPS • CLOSEUPS

RECYCLED HANDBAGS

*H*aving downsized to a van-type motorhome, I was amazed at the available storage space the manufacturers are providing. However, my big "fat" toolbox would not fit anywhere inside our new rig. While visiting garage sales, I spotted some large, ladies' handbags made of tough leather with very strong zippers. I bought three of them, ripped out the linings and deposited my tools inside these bags: Socket wrenches in one bag, end wrenches in another, and various items in the third. These bags can fit in just about anywhere; one place is in the coil of the water hose.
- *H. A. Steeves, Port Charlotte, Florida*

WATER WITHOUT THE BACKACHE

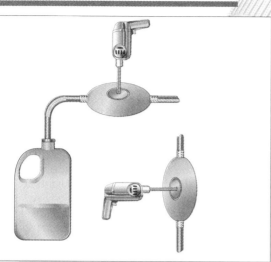

Having camped for many years in out-of-the-way places, we are always running short of fresh water. Nearly all the places we stay have water faucets, but we still have to lug the water to the trailer using 5-gallon containers, and then break our backs pouring in the water. I bought a small drill-motor pump that fits in the palm of my hand, and is rated at 200 gallons per hour or 3½ gallons per minute. I attached two pieces of water hose and called an old drill motor into service. I now fill the 5-gallon container at the water faucet and pump the water into the trailer. Electricity to run the drill motor comes from the small AC generator we carry at all times. Total cost for this back-easing project: less than $10.
- NORMAN HEWITT, KLAMATH FALLS, OREGON

CUSHION FOR THE HANDS

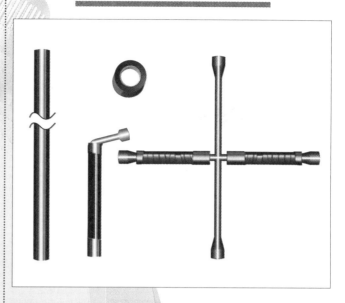

For those of us who find ourselves using brooms, lug-nut wrenches, or any other tool with a long handle, I have a solution for sore or even blistered hands. Take a ½-inch section of foam-rubber pipe insulation (tubular and split down the middle) and attach it to the tool handle. Wrap black-vinyl electrical tape around the insulation. Now, tender hands can be protected. Pipe insulation usually comes in 5-foot-long section in various diameters. I got mine for only $1.50 at Home Depot. A side benefit: The foam keeps your hands from slipping.
- J. G. WEIPERT, SCOTTSDALE, ARIZONA

HOMEMADE AIR

I have a need to winterize my camper, since we leave it parked in a campsite during the cold weather; having readily-available compressed air was important to me. There are a number of other uses for air, but unless you want to lug around a heavy, 120-volt AC compressor, you're stuck with a small 12-volt DC unit that's slow to use, but will get you by in a pinch. I also did not want to invest big bucks in an air compressor that I would not use very often, so I combined my cheap ($15) 12-volt DC air compressor with a portable air tank available from Wal-Mart for $20.

I rigged up my system for winterizing using a couple sections of air hose, a regulator (available from Sears), and an RV blow-out plug (with the Shrader valve attached). If you connect a quick connector at the end of the hose, the air tank now becomes accessible for filling tires and operating air tools, etc.
- BRENT HOLLAND, JOPLIN, MISSOURI

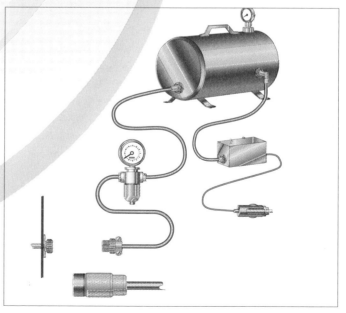